THE Do it yourself BOOK OF
DIY AND HOME MAINTENANCE

THE Do it yourself BOOK OF
DIY AND
HOME MAINTENANCE

John McGowan and Roger DuBern

Macdonald

A Macdonald Book

First published in Great Britain in 1985
by Macdonald & Co (Publishers) Ltd
London & Sydney

A member of BPCC plc

The "Do-it-yourself" Book of DIY
and Home Maintenance
was conceived, edited and designed
by Dorling Kindersley Limited,
9 Henrietta Street,
London WC2E 8PS

Project Editor
Rosanne Hooper
Editor
Phil Wilkinson
Project Art Editor
Neville Graham
Art Editor
Derek Coombes
Designer
Roger Priddy
Managing Editor
Alan Buckingham

British Library Cataloguing in Publication Data

McGowan, John
    The do-it-yourself book of DIY and home
    maintenance
    1. Dwelling—Maintenance and repair—
    Amateurs' manuals
    I. Title   II. DuBern, Roger
    643′.7   TH4817.3

    ISBN 0-356-10504-0

Filmsetting by
Chambers Wallace Limited, London
Reproduction by
Reprocolor Llovet, Barcelona
Printed and bound in Germany by
Mohndruck Graphische Betriebe GmbH,
Gütersloh

Macdonald & Co (Publishers) Ltd
Maxwell House
74 Worship Street
London EC2A 2EN

Contents

Introduction
Pages 6-10

Home decorating

Painting
Pages 12-27
Jobs 1-13

Wallpapering
Pages 28-43
Jobs 14-31

Tiling
Pages 44-55
Jobs 32-52

Carpeting
Pages 56-65
Jobs 53-67

Wooden flooring
Pages 66-77
Jobs 68-85

Sheet vinyl
Pages 78-81
Jobs 86-90

Panelling
Pages 82-87
Jobs 91-99

Plastering
Pages 88-93
Jobs 100-106

Windows
Pages 94-101
Jobs 107-116

Curtains, blinds and shutters
Pages 102-108
Jobs 117-119

Doors
Pages 109-112
Jobs 120-126

Choosing materials

Paints, stains and varnishes
Pages 114-117

Wall coverings
Pages 118-121

Tiles
Pages 122-125

Wooden surfaces
Pages 126-129

Floor coverings
Pages 130-133

Furnishing fabrics
Pages 134-136

Door furniture
Pages 137-139

Room-by-room guide
Page 140

Home contents

Cleaning, care and repair
Pages 142-147
Jobs 127-128

Renovating wooden furniture
Pages 148-155
Jobs 129-148

Renewing upholstery
Pages 156-159
Jobs 149-153

Lighting
Pages 160-163

Pictures and mirrors
Pages 164-167
Jobs 154-156

Storage and shelving
Pages 168-173
Jobs 157-159

Appliance fault-finding
Pages 174-176

Home maintenance

Electricity
Pages 178-183
Jobs 160-167

Plumbing
Pages 184-189
Jobs 168-176

Heating
Pages 190-193
Jobs 177-182

Insulation
Pages 194-197
Jobs 183-188

Roofs and gutters
Pages 198-201
Jobs 189-194

External walls
Pages 202-203
Jobs 195-197

Damp-proofing
Pages 204-207
Jobs 198-199

Rot and woodworm
Pages 208-209
Job 200

Household safety
Pages 210-211

Home security
Pages 212-216
Job 201

The home tool kit

Workshop equipment Measuring and marking tools
Pages 218-219

Saws and other cutting tools
Pages 220-221

Hammers Nails, tacks and pins
Pages 222-223

Screwdrivers Screws and wallplugs
Pages 224-225

Drills Chisels and planes
Pages 226-227

Scrapers and sanders Filling and plastering tools
Pages 228-229

Brushes Rollers and paint pads
Pages 230-231

Pliers and pincers Spanners and wrenches
Pages 232-233

Index
Pages 234-239

Acknowledgments
Page 240

Introduction

Your house is more than a home – it is likely to represent your largest investment and the basis of your financial security. If that investment is to remain sound, the house has to be protected by regular maintenance – inside and out. Anticipating problems and defects before they arise and redecorating before rot and rust set in, are the best policies.

What causes the problems?
Human beings impose the stresses of normal wear, tear, use and abuse on a home. But most problems are caused by nature, in the form of the elements, parasites and natural decay. Moisture rising from below ground and rain, snow and sleet attacking from above lead to damp and rust. The wind penetrates gaps in windows and door frames, disperses dirt and dust, may dislodge slates on roofs, and encourages movement in the structure of the house. Even the sun can be harmful: cracking and blistering paintwork, and discolouring curtains, wallpaper and paint.

Beetles in woodwork, birds nesting under the eaves and rodents in the cellar or attic cause problems if left for long. Small shifts or subsidence in the underlying land can result in movement and cracking in the structure of a house.

What are the solutions?
Most situations take years to develop into a major problem, but the sooner you take action, the easier and cheaper the work. There are two possible solutions: either call in a professional or undertake to do the work yourself.

The rewards of doing it yourself
The most obvious advantage of undertaking your own home care, maintenance and decoration is the saving in cost. The amount saved on professional fees will pay for further home improvements. These in turn help to make your home more comfortable, more attractive and more saleable. There is also the convenience of being able to do the work at a time to suit yourself and any other inhabitants. You can plan to vacate areas of the house to suit your lifestyle and do not need to supervise the progress of the work. But perhaps the greatest advantage is the satisfaction of seeing the results of your own work, and the knowledge that you can make your home as you want it, without relying on

outside help. The more you do yourself, the more skilful you become, and so the greater your satisfaction with the results.

It is important, however, to know when to call in the professional. By following the advice in this book, you will soon gain the confidence to cope with anything from putting up a shelf to dealing with a burst pipe. The more experienced you become, the less daunting you will find apparently complex, but in fact quite simple, jobs. In an emergency or if you are in any doubt about the safety of a particular job, it is often worth calling in expert help. Likewise, heavy structural work, such as building an extension, knocking through a wall or re-tiling a roof might be best left to a professional builder.

How this book can help

This book is for anyone with a home to maintain and the desire to improve it. It offers clear, easy to follow instructions for the willing, but inexperienced handy person. The book is divided into five self-contained parts – three main practical sections on "Home decorating", "Home maintenance" and "Home contents" – and two photographic reference sections: "Choosing materials" and "The home tool kit". Each section is identified by its individual coloured thumb tag and symbol. The sections are divided into individual subject areas, such as Painting; Electricity; Storage and shelving; Choosing furnishing fabrics; Measuring and marking tools. In the three practical sections these chapters are further organized into numbered jobs, which consist of illustrated step-by-step instructions on how to tackle the work.

Each chapter is introduced with an invaluable guide to the amount of time, the quantities of materials and the specific tools you will need before you start work, together with a list of jobs contained within the chapter. Where one basic technique is relevant to a variety of jobs you will find a self-contained "Basic technique" box, which serves the entire chapter. Many jobs involve similar steps, so cross-references to specific job and page numbers are to be found in bold type for quick, easy reference. You will also find references to specific pages in the "Choosing materials" and "The home tool kit" sections. The "Home decorating" and "Home contents" sections also include advice on colour and design and suggest

List of household terms

The following selected definitions are an introductory guide to commonly-used terms, to denote the parts of a house, decorating jobs and essential fittings. Other specific words relating to DIY are explained in the main body of the book.

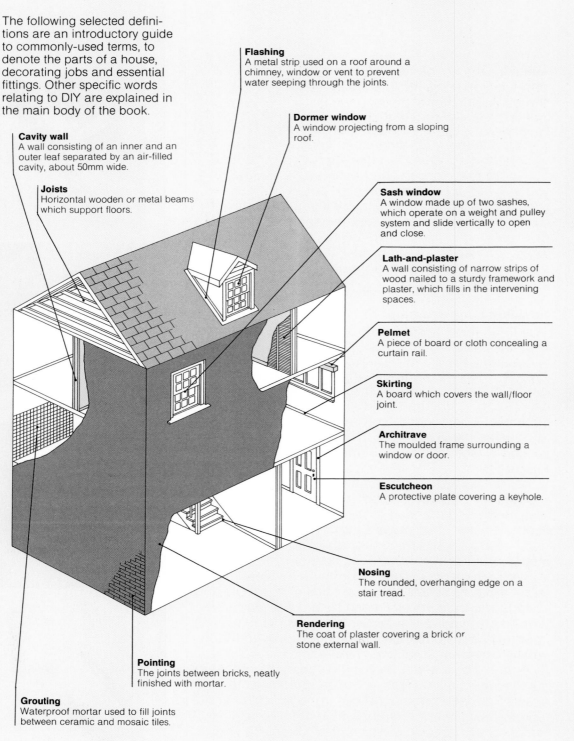

Flashing
A metal strip used on a roof around a chimney, window or vent to prevent water seeping through the joints.

Dormer window
A window projecting from a sloping roof.

Cavity wall
A wall consisting of an inner and an outer leaf separated by an air-filled cavity, about 50mm wide.

Joists
Horizontal wooden or metal beams which support floors.

Sash window
A window made up of two sashes, which operate on a weight and pulley system and slide vertically to open and close.

Lath-and-plaster
A wall consisting of narrow strips of wood nailed to a sturdy framework and plaster, which fills in the intervening spaces.

Pelmet
A piece of board or cloth concealing a curtain rail.

Skirting
A board which covers the wall/floor joint.

Architrave
The moulded frame surrounding a window or door.

Escutcheon
A protective plate covering a keyhole.

Nosing
The rounded, overhanging edge on a stair tread.

Rendering
The coat of plaster covering a brick or stone external wall.

Pointing
The joints between bricks, neatly finished with mortar.

Grouting
Waterproof mortar used to fill joints between ceramic and mosaic tiles.

B

Beading
A narrow, decorative edging strip.
Bevel
A slanting edge, such as the shape of a chisel blade.
Butt joint
Where two edges touch without overlapping.

C

Cantilever
A rigid structure fixed at one end and overhanging its support at the other.
Chalkline
A piece of string coated with chalk, which is snapped on a surface to leave a precise guide line.
Chamfer
A sharp corner or edge, smoothed to a 45 degree angle.
Cornice
A decorative moulding covering the ceiling/wall join.
Coving
A concave moulding covering the ceiling/wall join.
Countersink
To widen the outer edge of a drilled hole into a cone-shape, until a screw-head can be sunk below the surface.

D

Dowel
A headless wooden peg used to join two pieces of wood together.

F

Flush
When two adjacent surfaces are perfectly level.

G

Galvanized
Metal coated with zinc to inhibit rusting.
Gauge (screw)
A number indicating the diameter thickness of a screw e.g. No. 8.
Gypsum
Calcium sulphate used to make plaster.
Glue size
Thinned adhesive used to seal walls and ceilings prior to wallpapering.

K

Key
To roughen a surface to improve adhesion before painting or plastering.

L

Lagging
Insulating material used to cover tanks and pipes and to prevent heat escaping.

M

Mitre
To trim the ends of two lengths of wood or plaster to a 45 degree angle, so that together they form a perfect right angle.
Mortar
A mixture of cement, lime putty and sand, used to bind bricks together in a masonry wall.

Mortise
A recess cut in the edge of a door to house the protruding tongue of a lock.
Moulding
A length of wood, shaped to form a decorative strip.

Plumb bob
A small, cone-shaped weight attached to a line, which when held against a wall gives a true vertical.
Primer
A paint used to seal and key a surface before undercoat is applied.

Screed
A layer of cement-based material, used to level a floor.
Screed bead
A straight or angled strip or wire mesh, used to reinforce corners before plastering or to cover holes in plaster walls.
Scriber
A tool used to trace off the edges and contours of an area on to decorating materials.
Scrim
Strong, woven material, such as hessian, used to cover joins between pieces of plasterboard.
Stud partition
A wall made out of a timber framework covered with plasterboard.

Template
A pattern cut to specific dimensions, used as an outline for cutting the same shape from another material.
Thread
The spiral grooves in a screw.
Tongue and groove
Wooden boards or blocks with a groove down one edge and a protruding tongue down the other. The tongue slots into the groove of an adjacent piece, for a secure fixing.
Toggle
A small metal screw with a hinge or wings which open when pushed through a hole in a partition wall and so secure the screw in place.

Underlay
A protective layer of strong material laid on a floor under a carpet.

Veneer
An outer layer of decorative timber applied to a core of stronger but less attractive wood.

Wallplug
An expandable plastic or fibre encasement for a screw, inserted into a hole drilled in a solid wall to provide a gripping surface for the screw. It can be cut to length.

ideas for the decorative effects you can achieve by carefully following the jobs in the book. Throughout the book, additional boxes on safety, cleaning tips, points to remember, and charts on quantities and qualities of materials offer immediate, easy to absorb information. Each job has been carefully selected to give you the information, know-how and confidence to become your own painter, decorator, electrician, plumber and interior designer – an all-round home maintenance person, capable of tackling essential jobs around the house.

Getting to know your home
A good understanding of the geography of your home, how the plumbing, electrical and heating systems work and how the fixtures and fittings are assembled is an essential starting point for DIY. Emergencies, such as flooding, blown fuses and burglaries always come at the most inconvenient moments, and it is only through a good knowledge of the systems in the house that you can take the right action to handle and prevent such crises. Within the section on "Home maintenance", you will find "maps" of all the basic systems and clear explanations of how they work, together with detailed advice on specific tasks. With this knowledge, home maintenance will become a simple, routine matter.

Investing in the right tools and materials
Your first priority is to choose a good tool kit. In "The home tool kit" at the back of the book you will find a complete, illustrated guide to the tools you are likely to need, with detailed information about how and when to use each item, the range of types and sizes within each group, and tips on care and safety. You may wish to begin with a skeleton tool kit and gradually add to it as you tackle more jobs. Large and expensive tools, which you may only need once, are often available for hire from tool suppliers.

A knowledge of the range of decorating materials is as important as a good set of tools. The central section of the book, "Choosing materials", is a visual catalogue of the materials available for decorating walls, floors, ceilings, and for furnishings. It is backed up with a thorough comparison of types: their individual qualities, their relative costs, their ease of handling and so on, together with an analysis of the

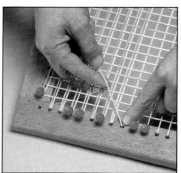

most suitable materials to choose for individual rooms and situations. It is worth buying the best quality you can afford; it will last longer and produce better results. Prices and qualities vary dramatically, so an exploration of your local DIY shops and supermarkets will probably reveal the best buys.

Planning and preparation

The main ingredients of successful DIY are time and patience. Since many jobs in the home are "one-offs", it is vital to take the time to work steadily towards perfect results. Laying a parquet floor, plastering a wall or panelling a ceiling, for example, may be jobs you only ever need to attempt once. Mistakes and materials are expensive, so serving your apprenticeship on the job leaves little or no margin for error. Your best insurance against mistakes is careful planning and preparation. Each section in the book and each job within it is presented in a clear, logical sequence, beginning with planning and preparation, followed by the detailed stages of the work to be done. The time you take in the early stages is always well rewarded in the final results.

Enjoying your home

Improving your home is an enjoyable experience if you know what to do. The more you do to encourage the services of the house to run smoothly, to improve the standard of the decoration and to make the furniture and furnishings as good as new, the more you will appreciate your home. And the more you practise, the better the results will be.

The future

Once you have successfully completed a few DIY jobs, you will find you develop the confidence and experience to undertake a wider range of jobs. Once learnt, these skills are never forgotten, but you may need reminders and new challenges. We hope this book will prove a continual source of help, ideas and reference both in the day-to-day running of your home, and when you decide to redecorate or move house.

Safety tips

◇ Use all power and cutting tools with great caution, keep flexes well clear and lock all tools away immediately after use.
◇ Avoid drilling into walls if you suspect pipes or electrical wires lie behind.
◇ If you smell gas, call the authorities immediately.
◇ Always install a fire extinguisher in a workshop and a kitchen.
◇ Repair cracked pipes immediately or call in an expert.
◇ Only use ladders that you know to be completely safe.
◇ Wear goggles to shield your eyes when stripping paint or wire brushing; gloves to protect your hands from chemicals; and a mask if there is a lot of dust.
◇ Pour any left-over chemicals back into the original container or into a clearly labelled jar.
◇ Keep chisels, saws and other cutting tools sharp. Blunt blades slip easily and can cause accidents.
◇ Whenever you hire equipment from a shop or from friends, make sure you know exactly how to use it.

Home decorating

Painting ◇ Wallpapering ◇ Tiling ◇ Carpeting
Wooden flooring ◇ Sheet vinyl ◇ Panelling
Plastering ◇ Windows ◇ Curtains, blinds and
shutters ◇ Doors

Decorating the interior of your home is rewarding only if the results are good. And to be sure of the best return on your investment of time, enthusiasm and materials, it is important to take each job stage by stage and to use the correct equipment. This section outlines the tools and materials you will need, explains how to estimate quantities of paint, wallpaper, tiles or timber, for your size of room and suggests how much time to put aside, *before* you begin work. It tells you how to plan out the job, how to prepare the surface, and how to undertake necessary repairs. It then moves on to detailed step-by-step coverage of specific jobs and basic techniques. Relevant advice on dealing with tricky areas, and diagnosing problems and faults are also included. And within each section you will find ideas on effects you can achieve through the imaginative use of colour, texture and individual design, in conjunction with the techniques covered in the section.

Painting

Estimating time and quantities ◇ Tools and equipment ◇ How to fill cracks and holes
Preparing bare wood ◇ Stripping old paint
How to apply paint ◇ Using ladders safely
Fault-finding ◇ Textures and finishes

Good paintwork is to a house what a good complexion is to a human face. It reflects the general condition and attitudes of the owner, it provides a background for more striking features and highlights, and lends an individual quality to the whole appearance.

Choice of paint is the first major decorating decision, and it is worth taking time to choose the most suitable colour. It is also important to select the right type of paint for each job to avoid repeating the work before you are ready for a change. Modern materials give better and faster results than ever before and a competent repainting will last for many years with new, hard-wearing paints. Although paints are now sold under various descriptions such as vinyl silk or satin finish, emulsion is still used for walls and ceilings and gloss for woodwork and metalwork. In spite of the slightly higher cost of these materials, it is still usually cheaper to paint than to paper.

Preparation of surfaces before painting is all-important, since untreated cracks and flaws will rapidly appear through new paintwork and may even be exaggerated. Any time "saved" in preparation is counter-productive, for you will treble your working time by soon having to strip off new paint to redecorate properly.

Points to remember

◇ Make sure you have enough paint before you start work.
◇ Prepare ceilings first, then walls, and finally, wood and metalwork. Repaint in the same order.
◇ Test paints on a small area of wall before buying the full quantity.
◇ Use the undercoat recommended for the colour you have chosen for the top coat of gloss.
◇ Fill cracks and remove dust before painting.

For more information on types of paint, see Choosing materials, pp. 114-5.

Planning

New decoration will only be as good as the planning and preparation of the work. The first step in any redecoration job is to decide on the extent of the initial structural and repair work required, before estimating time, costs and quantities of materials needed. This work will depend on the age of the house and its condition.

Modern houses

In a post-1950's house, the timber is unlikely to be well seasoned, so, when central heating is installed, the woodwork may split, shrink and warp away from the walls, causing cracks that need filling. Many modern homes however, do have the advantage of low-maintenance accessories, such as plastic gutters and downpipes, and anodized aluminium windows that do not need paint.

Older houses

Different problems arise in older houses. The walls, usually solid, encourage damp which must be cured before decorating can begin. The lath and plasterwork in ceilings and walls deteriorate over time, so cracked plasterwork will need to be repaired or replaced before painting or wallpapering.

On the woodwork a thick layer of paint is likely to have built up over the years. If the paintwork tends to chip badly, it is best to strip back to bare wood and start again.

Estimating time

Home decorating invariably takes longer than you think. The times (right) give an estimate of the number of hours needed to paint a 3m × 4m room in average condition. Convert this into your own room sizes and allow more time for any extra coats. Remember, however, that your skill and experience, the care you take in your workmanship, the speed at which you work and the number of hours a day you actually work, including meal breaks, will all influence the total time needed to complete the work. Try to arrange three to four uninterrupted hours for each session and, if possible, avoid changing from natural to artificial light. Remember to build in a little extra time for cleaning brushes and equipment at the end of each session. When totting up the total number of days needed to complete the whole room, allow for the time needed for the paint to dry between coats. As a rough guide, emulsion takes about four hours to dry, but gloss should be left overnight.

Ceilings

Washing and filling

(1)-(1½) hours

Applying stabilizing primer

(1)-(1½) hours

Applying emulsion

(¾)-(1) hour

Walls

Preparing and priming

(2)-(3) hours

Applying emulsion

(¾)-(1) hour

Doors, windows and skirtings

Sanding and filling (allow more time if stripping to bare wood)

(2)-(3) hours

Priming patches

(¼)-(½) hour

Applying undercoat

(3½)-(4) hours

Applying gloss

(3½)-(4) hours

Estimating quantities

To estimate the amount of paint you need, first calculate the area of each surface to be covered by multiplying the height or length by the width. Take all your measurements in metric units to avoid conversions, since paint is sold exclusively in litres and manufacturers quote coverage in square metres (m^2) per litre on their cans. Then total your surface areas. Some types of paint go further than others, so consult the table (right) for the area covered by specific paints. Brands may also differ so, if in doubt, refer to the covering rate specified on the label. To find the total number of litres of each type of paint needed, *per coat,* divide the area by the covering rate.

When measuring the area of walls, include windows and doors as part of the surface, unless they are significantly large. This will allow a little extra paint in case the walls prove highly absorbent. A wall measuring 1.8m high by 3.5m wide has a total area of $6.3m^2$. If it was to be painted in vinyl silk emulsion with a covering rate of $15m^2$ per litre, the area ($6.3m^2$) divided by the covering rate ($15m^2$) would give the number of litres required: 0.42 litres per coat. Windows are difficult to estimate, but as a guide, allow $2m^2$ for a small window, $4m^2$ for a medium-sized window, and $5m^2$ for a large one. Remember to allow for any extra space taken up with alcoves and chimneys.

Ceilings
Multiply the widths of two adjacent walls and allow for any alcoves.

Doors, windows and skirtings
An average window measures $4m^2$. Most doors measure $4m^2$ ($2m^2$ per side) including frame and trim. For the skirting area, multiply total length by height.

Walls
Measure the height and width of each wall, without deducting window and door areas, and add the multiples together for the total wall area.

Covering rates of paints

The covering power of paints varies with the type of paint, the porosity of the surface and the thickness of the coat applied. Non-drip gloss and jelly paints, for example, will not cover such a large area as liquid gloss or emulsion, but since the coating is thicker, fewer coats may be required. Most stains and varnishes will go further than paint while primers will not stretch so far. Bare plaster and textured surfaces absorb more liquid, so it is often more economic to add water to a first coat than to apply an extra top coat.

Paint type	Covering area (in m^2 per litre)
Universal primer	7-8 (wood)
	9-11 (metal)
	5-9 (plaster)
Aluminium primer-sealer	11-13
Acrylic primer/undercoat	15-16
Alkali-resistant primer	9-11
Primer/sealer	10
Stabilizing primer	6-12
Metal primer	9-11
Undercoat	15
Gloss (liquid)	17
Gloss (non-drip)	12
Silk finish (oil-based)	12
Eggshell finish	15
Emulsion, matt (non-drip solid)	14
Emulsion, vinyl silk	15
Aluminium paint	12-14

The number of coats
The type of paint, the colour and the surface determine the number of coats to be applied. You will need an extra coat, for example, when covering a dark colour with a lighter one, but not when using a dark final colour. When decorating previously unpainted wood, use primer and an undercoat before one or two coats of gloss. If painting over old gloss you may need to apply one or two coats of undercoat, to leave a good base for the gloss.

A third coat of emulsion is sometimes needed to obliterate a dark background. Glossy emulsions may also need an extra coat.

Tools and equipment

Cheap tools produce poor results. However tempting it is to save money, this is always a false economy, because good-quality equipment lasts longer, even improving with age; is more satisfying to use; and, most important, promotes a finer finish. Always choose brushes well packed with pure hog's bristle; use new pads and brushes for undercoats until they stop shedding hairs, and reserve cheap brushes for priming. Clean tools thoroughly and store them in a cool, dry, well-ventilated place. Before using any equipment, check that it is thoroughly dry. (*For more information, see The Home Tool Kit, pp. 230-1.*)

Strippers and scrapers
To soften old paint, you will need either an electric hot-air gun, a gas blowtorch or chemical stripper; and two scrapers to strip the paint off flat surfaces – one narrow, one broad. For clearing irregular areas, such as window frames and mouldings, choose a shavehook with a combination of straight, convex and concave sides, it will prove more versatile than the straight-sided, triangular type.

Large scraper

Small scraper

Shavehooks

Hot-air gun

Gas blowtorch

Chemical stripper

Cleaning and storage
Wash and dry scrapers and shave-hooks or scrub with wire wool, before wiping with a lightly oiled rag or petroleum jelly, and store in a dry place. If shavehook edges have become blunt, sharpen with a file or grindstone.

Clean shavehooks and scrapers with wire wool then wipe with petroleum jelly or a lightly oiled rag.

Sanders and fillers
To repair cracks and dents, a filling knife, filler and tray are all that is needed. Most surfaces need abrading before receiving paint. Glasspaper comes in grades from 00 (fine) to 3 (coarse) and the medium or fine grades are the most useful. A longer-lasting, though more expensive alternative is aluminium oxide paper. A range of medium-grade silicon carbide papers (240 and 180) will also help to provide a good key for new paint on smooth surfaces. It is tough, durable, creates less dust and produces a smoother finish than glasspaper. It can be used dry, but lasts longer when wet, since it will not clog. A cork, wooden or rubber block used as a "hand hold" for abrasive paper will ease the work on flat surfaces. For large areas, electric finishing sanders help to speed up the work. An orbital sander, which can be hired, provides the best finish, although a disc sander or mesh disc attached to a power tool can be useful, if care is taken not to scratch the surface.

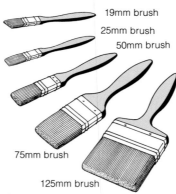

Orbital sander

Disc sander

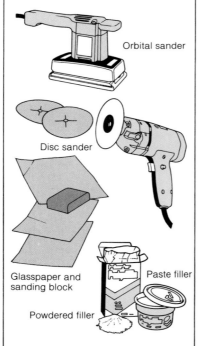

Glasspaper and sanding block

Powdered filler

Paste filler

Cleaning and storage
Remove dried filler with emery paper or wire wool. Store unused filler in a dry place. Wash silicon carbide paper thoroughly to remove particles and store all equipment in a cool, dry place.

Brushes
A range of brushes will be needed for painting an average room, in addition to a priming and dusting brush. The smallest, a 19mm cutting-in brush with angled bristles, is useful for painting window frames without smudging the glass. A 25mm size is also suitable for window frames and mouldings; a 50mm for skirtings; and a 75mm for flush doors and similar large areas of gloss. If you prefer not to use a roller or pad for large areas of emulsion, use a 125mm brush. A mini roller or crevice brush with a long, flexible handle is useful for painting behind radiators, pipes and other inaccessible places. Choose brushes with good length well-packed bristles.

19mm brush

25mm brush

50mm brush

75mm brush

125mm brush

Cleaning and storage
During short breaks of up to half an hour, wrap bristles tightly in cling film or foil, but clean thoroughly every night, immediately after use. Scrape off excess water-based paint with a knife blade on to newspaper, then wash in hot water and washing-up liquid. Rinse, shake and hang up to dry. For long-term storage, wrap in newspaper, taking care not to bend the bristles, and secure around the base (ferrule) with an elastic band. A brush used for oil-based paint should first be cleaned in white spirit or a proprietary brush cleaner. Work up and down on clean newspaper and manipulate in hot washing-up liquid, until all traces of paint disappear. Oil-based paints that prove particularly sticky can be removed by rubbing bristles with linseed oil after the initial cleaning in white spirit. Soften old hard brushes by agitating in paint stripper. Brush cleaners and white spirit can be used repeatedly if kept in a screw-top jar, but must be discarded when sediment builds up.

Rollers and pads
These allow large areas to be covered quickly and easily, but are more suitable for emulsion than for oil-based gloss paint. Solid emulsion is supplied in a block, but liquid paints need a roller tray or pad trough for an even coating. For a smooth finish, use a roller with a short pile; for a lightly textured look, a medium pile; and for a deeply textured finish, a long pile. Foam rollers with an indented pattern are available for textured paints, but for general use, lambswool and mohair produce a better result. Choose a paint pad that will fit into a 2½-litre paint can.

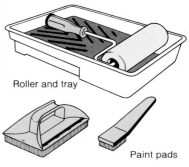

Roller and tray

Paint pads

Cleaning and storage
Scrape off extra paint. Then, if used with water-based paints, wash in warm detergent; wash in white spirit or in brush cleaner if oil-based paints have been used. Rinse, squeeze and shake out before hanging up to dry. When dry, cover the roller and tray to protect from dust. If lined with cooking foil, the tray will not need cleaning. Clean pads in the same way as rollers, and store flat and unwrapped.

Rinse and squeeze roller sleeve after use

Other equipment
Additional essential items include a paint kettle for decanting the paint, a bucket and sponge, and dust sheets.

The effects of colour on a room

Colour has the power to transform a room. It can raise and lower ceilings, it can expand and reduce walls, it can disguise and highlight individual features, and it can soothe or excite. A dark room can be lightened with a light-reflecting sheen, and warm, dark colours can make a large, cold room feel more cosy. Your decision may be influenced by existing furnishings, and in many rooms the paintwork may need to act as a neutral backdrop to more vibrant accessories. Remember that when applied, the accumulated colour will intensify the shade of the colour chart.

Using colour to disguise room shapes
Colour can influence the apparent size and shape of a room. Light shades will bring space to a small room and dark tones foreshorten a large one. A low ceiling will appear higher if it is painted a paler shade than the walls. For a more complete disguise of the room shape, a single dark background colour over the ceiling and walls can be applied, and can then be broken up with spot lights (above). The reflections produced by the lustre of a high-gloss paint deepen and enlarge a room, as well as adding pattern. A paler, receding background shade will lighten and open out a dark, poky room (right) and will help to conceal pipes, radiators and irregular window shapes. A co-ordinating furnishing colour will contribute to the enlarging effect.

Using colour to establish moods
Temperament and lifestyle influence choice of colour as much as the intended purpose of the room. Those who demand a stimulating home environment, for example, probably enjoy strong primary colours, broken up with neutrals; others who need a restful, relaxing atmosphere may prefer natural and more muted tones. The aspect of the room should also be considered when selecting paint colour. A burnt orange shade (top) on the wall – picked up in the furnishings – gives warmth to a large room with harsh light coming through the windows, and promotes an air of relaxation. Cool shades, such as the frosty blue, monochromatic colour scheme (above) lends a cool feeling of light and space to a sunny room. This crisp and vibrant effect is accentuated by the sparkling white woodwork and silver chrome accessories.

1

Preparing ceilings

First remove any light fittings that may impede the work, not forgetting to turn off the mains first and to seal any exposed wires afterwards. Then assess the condition of the existing paint and plasterwork. If it is sound, wash down the surface with diluted sugar soap and rinse thoroughly with clean water, taking care not to allow any drips to percolate fixed light fittings.

If the paint is discoloured by nicotine stains, apply a coat of aluminium sealer paint. Dried water stains, caused by a leaking roof or pipes, will show through emulsion, so these need to be coated with an oil-based primer sealer. Kitchen ceilings are often coated with accumulated grease, which will prevent the paint from sticking if it is not removed. Likewise, soot or dust deposited on the ceilings above coal fires must be thoroughly cleaned to prevent it discolouring subsequent layers of paint.

Fill any superficial cracks with cellulose filler. If deep cracks persistently develop between the wall and the ceiling, they are probably caused by the normal movement of the house and will re-open if filled, so consider fixing coving to conceal them (*see Jobs 38/39, p. 49*). In an old house, if distemper remains, scrape off the flakes and either wash off the rest or coat the ceiling with primer sealer before repainting. If paint dust has accumulated, seal with a coat of stabilizing primer.

Papered ceilings

Loose ceiling paper should be stripped off but any which is firmly attached can be left and painted. When removing paper, always wash off any remaining adhesive. If existing paper bubbles when washed, make a small slit when dry and re-stick the edges. Remember that a ceiling may have been papered because it is badly cracked though structurally sound or, in the case of a plasterboard ceiling, because the joints are conspicuous. (*For ladders, see Job 11, p. 24 and Job 14, p. 32.*)

Cover nicotine stains with sealer paint

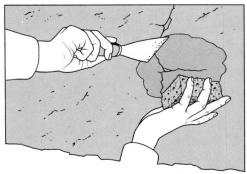

Remove distemper with a scraper and sponge

2

Preparing walls

More preparation is needed if a wall is to be painted than if it is to be concealed with wallpaper. Even a small hairline crack will show through paint, if it is not filled and carefully smoothed first. Where an otherwise sound wall has become a network of small cracks, try covering it with lining- or wallpaper for overpainting. (*For chips and small cracks, see opposite; for more extensive damage, see p. 93; and for stripping off old paint, see Job 6, pp. 18-19.*)

Sound surfaces

A new plaster wall should be left to dry for several weeks before sealing with a primer or a thin coat of emulsion prior to painting, and fresh plasterboard should be given a coat of plasterboard primer sealer. A previously painted wall must be washed thoroughly from the bottom up with diluted sugar soap, then rinsed.

Clearing the room

◇ Extract anything you may need from drawers, and move small pieces of furniture into another room.
◇ Take down curtains and pictures and remove door and window handles.
◇ Move large furniture to the centre of the room.
◇ Roll up the carpet and cover the floor with a polythene or cloth dust sheet, secured at the corners.

3

Preparing metal

Rust is the enemy of ferrous metals (those that contain iron and steel) and must be kept at bay with a rust-inhibiting primer and a sound coat of gloss. Even small chips in the surface paint can allow moisture to seep below the paint film and encourage corrosion, especially in window frames. First locate the areas of rust and remove all traces with an emery cloth or a wire brush. For larger areas, a wire cup brush or wheel fitted to an electric drill

will save time, but always protect your eyes with safety goggles. Holes caused by rust can be repaired using a glass fibre repair kit.

Primers

Rust re-forms rapidly, even overnight, so apply rust-inhibiting primer immediately. Zinc chromate is the most useful primer, since it can also be used for aluminium and galvanized surfaces, but red lead and zinc phosphate are also suitable. Non-ferrous metals such as aluminium and copper should be washed down with white spirit, abraded and primed.

Treating rust

Scrape off any rust and flaking paint with a wire brush, 1. When no trace of rust remains, apply rust-inhibiting primer, 2, before rust has time to re-form and give vulnerable points an extra coat. If the surface is sound and rust-free, simply wash it down.

1 *Remove rust or flaking paint with a wire brush*

2 *Seal metalwork with primer to inhibit the formation of rust*

How to fill cracks and holes

Time spent filling cracks and holes will be well rewarded in the final result. Standard interior-grade cellulose fillers are suitable for most inside plaster or wooden surfaces to be repainted. They come as ready-to-use paste in tubs or tubes, or as a powder to be mixed with water to a creamy consistency. Most small holes can be simply built up with filler and smoothed off. Corners in walls can be easily chipped when moving furniture. Apply thin layers of filler and when the surface is slightly raised, allow to harden, then sand down. Small, superficial chips in otherwise good paintwork can be filled with a fine surface filler, which is worked into the surface and spread with a broad filling knife, then sanded to produce an ultra-smooth finish. Badly crazed plasterboard ceilings can be concealed with thick, textured paint, which stretches with the normal movement of the ceiling to keep the crazing covered. (*For information on more serious cracks and holes, see Jobs 104-6, p. 93.*)

Applying filler
First score the crack with the side of a filling knife to widen the cavity for filler, and brush away any debris, 1, then moisten the crack, 2. Prepare the filler and pack it tightly into the crack. Push in the filler by drawing the filling knife across at right angles, 3. If the crack is deep, allow to dry and apply another layer. Then smooth off. If it will not lie flush, leave the filler slightly proud of the surface and leave for a few hours to harden. Finally rub with glasspaper, for a smooth finish, 4. To avoid waste when preparing paste, try not to make up more than you can apply within the setting time marked on the packet (usually about 30 mins). Unlike cellulose filler, resin-based fillers will not shrink as they dry and harden. This means they can be applied flush with the surface, instead of proud, and will produce a smooth surface with less abrasion.

1 Widen the crack below surface and brush out debris

2 Dampen the crevice with a water-soaked brush

Pour powdered filler on to a board for mixing

3 Apply filler and smooth it down with a knife

4 When dry, sand to a flush finish

4

Using wood-coloured stoppers

Where wood is to be given a clear varnish or lacquer finish, instead of a coat of paint, waterproof stopper that comes in a variety of wood colours can be used. One type of stopper comes as a putty-like material; another, which also dries to a natural wood colour and can later be stained to any shade, is sold as paste and separate hardener to be mixed together. Both stoppers should be worked well into the surface with a filling knife and allowed to set before sanding down and applying an oil- or spirit-based stain. Take care not to spread the stopping into the grain beyond the immediate split or nail hole. Small gaps that tend to form in window frames and at joints can be packed with stopper and pushed down with a finger before smoothing off with a damp cloth. Always use an oil-based stopper on chipboard, since it is very porous.

Use wood-coloured stopper under clear varnish

5
Preparing bare wood

Whether it is brand new or stripped of old paint, all bare wood to be painted needs a coating of primer, undercoat and gloss. To ensure a smooth finish, the surface should be first rubbed down with glass-paper or a power sander. Rough surfaces may call for coarse paper, but a final smoothing with a fine grade will ensure a good finish.

Sealing the surface
After filling any cracks with filler or stopping, knots in the wood will need a coating of shellac to prevent resin staining the paintwork. To seal the pores in the wood and to provide a sound, stable base for undercoat, a coat of primer is applied. Most woods will take a standard white or pink wood primer, but particularly resinous woods need aluminium primer. Universal primer may be used, although purpose-made products give a better result.

Undercoat
Since undercoat is heavily pigmented for hiding power, always select the colour recommended by the manufacturer for use under the chosen gloss. It might be necessary to apply more than one coat of undercoat, in order to leave a smooth finish for the gloss coat.

For a natural wood finish, use a transparent varnish or a varnish stain if the colour of the wood is to be changed.

Before applying gloss to wood
Sand and wipe the surface and fill any cracks before soaking wood knots and resinous patches with shellac. Dab the liquid on to each knot with a clean brush, 1, taking care to cover the edges. Leave to dry for a couple of days, then apply primer, 2. Brush in the direction of the grain and give end grain a second coating, before applying a coat of well-stirred undercoat, 3.

1 Brush a layer of shellac liquid on to wood knots

2 When the shellac is dry, brush on primer

3 Finally paint on a layer of undercoat

6
Stripping old paint

It is not always necessary to strip off old paint, for if the gloss on woodwork is sound and smooth, it will form an ideal base for fresh paint. Old whitewash and distemper on walls can often be removed by washing, but if the paint is loose and chips off easily, it is better to strip it off. Test the surface with masking tape; if it pulls paint away, strip the affected area.

Choosing the method
Dry scraping is hard work and can leave score marks, so unless the paint peels off readily, it is best to use heat or chemicals to loosen the coat. Heat stripping is the most economical way of clearing a large area, but a gas blowtorch, may scorch the surface. Chemical strippers, although expensive, are especially useful on intricate surfaces.

Peel-off stripper
This new generation of chemical strippers can be a great time- and labour-saver. Apply a thick layer of paste over the paintwork, 1, and leave it to eat through the layers of paint. After several hours, the layer can be peeled off, 2, leaving a clean sub-surface.

1 Apply the paste with a filling knife

2 Peel off the dried paste with gloved fingers

Cleaning paintwork

◇ Before applying a fresh coat to existing paintwork, the surface must be free from stains, dirt and dust, or the new finish will look pimpled and will soon start to flake prematurely.

◇ Remove surface dirt by brushing, washing or vacuuming and use a pointed handle or knife to clear dust particles from awkward corners.

◇ When washing down the area, use sugar soap, washing soda, a proprietary cleaner or a mild detergent, and prevent water dripping down behind electric fittings.

◇ Before painting window frames from inside, always ensure that outside frames are thoroughly clean, so that dirt is not picked up on the brush. Wipe down sills and other wooden surfaces with a lint-free rag moistened with white spirit.

◇ Allow all surfaces to dry before applying paint.

Chemical stripper

*Chemical solvents are most useful for removing paint from intricate mouldings or tight corners where the wood could be scorched by heat. They can be used on emulsion, cellulose and most oil-based paints, but a specialized type is needed for removing varnish. Dab on the liquid thickly with an old brush, **1**, and after a few minutes the paint will shrivel and can be stripped off, **2**. Scrape off any remnants, **3**. Follow the instructions and consult the safety tips (below).*

1 *Brush on a thick layer of stripper*

2 *Scrape off the shrivelled paint*

3 *Remove remnants with wire wool and white spirit*

Gas blowtorch

Modern blowtorches are simple to use and most suitable for removing large areas of gloss. Avoid using lead-based paints, which release toxic fumes; and take care around windows where the glass may crack, the draught may dissipate the heat, and billowing curtains may be a hazard. Hold the torch about 15cm to 20cm from the surface and, starting at the top, play it across the paint until it starts to melt. Using a sharp scraper, quickly peel it off into a tin tray, before it hardens. Gently sweep the flame over any remaining paint until it slides off, taking care not to scorch the wood.

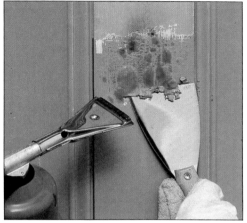

Remove softened paint with a scraper on flat areas

Use a shavehook for peeling paint off mouldings

Hot-air gun

Operating like an immensely powerful electric hair dryer, a hot-air gun blasts out a stream of heat which will melt the paint in its path. Direct the gun at an area of paint and when it softens after a few seconds, peel off the coat with a scraper. For stripping paint around windows and awkward areas, special nozzle attachments are available (below). Although effective, some hot-air guns are noisy and heavy to use, and all need an electricity supply.

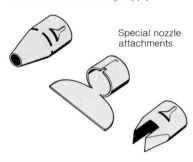

Special nozzle attachments

A nozzle attachment will shield the glass around windows

Safety tips

With chemical stripper

◇ Always wear goggles, gloves and protective clothing, to avoid skin burns, and don't smoke.
◇ Cover furnishings that may be splashed.

With heat stripper

◇ Keep buckets of water to hand.
◇ Never place fingers in the air stream.
◇ Catch burning peelings in a tin tray, never in newspaper.
◇ Always switch off the stripper when not in use.

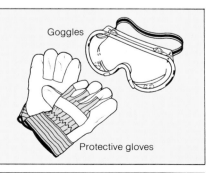

Goggles

Protective gloves

How to apply paint

Before you start work, check that you have: enough paint for the first coat; a spare brush and some brush cleaner; a rag and some overalls or an apron. Emulsion and other water-based paints will usually brush straight from the can, but half-full cans of oil-based paints develop a skin. To remove this, score around the inside of the can and lift off the layer of solidified paint, then stir thoroughly. Non-drip paints, however, should never be stirred. Before dipping the brush into the paint, flick the bristles to dislodge dust and loose bristles. Gloss and emulsion paints demand slightly different techniques as shown below. Thixotropic paints, designed to go on in one coat, should be brushed sparingly. There is no need to scrape off surplus paint, but try

Brushing on gloss
For a smooth, shiny finish, free from brush marks and runs, do not over-load the brush. First flick the bristles to dislodge dust and loose bristles, dip the ends into the paint, and wipe any excess on the side of the can or paint kettle, 1. Avoid dipping in too deep or the paint will trickle down the handle on to your hand. Begin with two or three strokes in the direction of the wood grain, covering a small area, 2. Without re-loading, change direction and spread the paint lightly to cover the sur-face. Then work back again with the grain, finishing with an upward stroke. Re-load the brush and, leaving a gap the width of the brush, move on to paint a parallel strip. Then paint across to fill in the area between strips, 3. At the join, allow the brush tips to gently skim the line, to avoid a thick ridge form-ing at each overlap.

Finally, brush vigorously over the whole area and lay off with vertical strokes, 4. Gloss takes several hours to dry, so leave surfaces clear until the paint no longer feels tacky. Sand the sur-face with fine-grade glasspaper after each coat, to make a key for the next one.

Brushing on emulsion
Since emulsion is used for large surfaces and dries faster than gloss, select a wide 10cm or 12.5cm brush, for quick application. Stir the paint thoroughly and pour enough into a paint kettle to cover half the length of the bristles. Coat the brush in a generous layer of paint and apply in horizontal bands, about 60cm wide, 1. Work away from the light and cover the area quickly to con- ceal joins before the edge of the painted section dries. Glossy emulsions, such as silk and satin finishes, dry more quickly than matt, so if you find it is drying faster than you can paint, you may have to modify the band system and work radially from a top corner. With matt emulsion finish off with criss-cross strokes, and with a silk or satin emul-sion, lay off with light, upward strokes, **2**.

1 *Dip the bristle tips into the paint and squeeze off the excess on the inside of the paint kettle.*

2 *Begin with downward strokes*

1 *Apply emulsion in horizontal bands*

3 *Then spread the paint across*

4 *Lay off with vertical strokes*

2 *Lay off with light upward strokes*

not to load too much paint on to the brush initially. Before applying a second coat of paint, dust the surface with a lint-free rag to make sure no specks spoil the finish. Complete each surface in one session to prevent dried paint lines forming.

Using a roller
*The fastest way of applying emulsion is with a roller. Pour some paint into the well of the roller tray, dip in the edge of the roller and run it up and down the slope to ensure an even layer of paint on the roller sleeve. Run the roller over the surface in a random, criss-cross pattern, **1**, taking care to fill any gaps and to keep the joins well merged. Be careful not to overload the roller or to jerk it, or a spray of paint will spatter the area. Finish off the edges with a small brush.*

With a roller, apply paint in a criss-cross pattern

Using a pad
*Dip lightly into the paint and wipe away the excess on the side of the can or paint kettle or use a special applicator to load the paint evenly on to the pad. Smooth on the paint in random directions, **2**, and re-load as soon as the layer begins to thin.*

Use a paint pad quickly in random directions

7
Painting flat surfaces

The first consideration when preparing to paint a large area is the light. Try to avoid starting in natural light and finishing in artificial, or you may find yourself covering the same area twice. You should also complete ceilings and individual walls in one session since, if you stop mid-wall for a meal-break or for the night, the dried paint line will show conspicuously through the final finish.

Working conditions
Before applying emulsion, close the windows to stop the paint drying too quickly and so give you time to join up the wet edges of each section. When the room is finished, open the windows to accelerate drying time. For ease of working, try to get as close as possible to the ceiling. Bare walls need a diluted coat of emulsion to prime the surface, before applying a first coat, but pre-painted surfaces need no primer. If the paint does not cover well, do not try to thicken the coat, but leave it to dry and apply an extra coat. For a perfectly smooth finish, you may need two or three coats. While painting, keep a damp cloth handy for removing dust or blobs. As a general rule, paint a room from top to bottom, so that disturbed dust does not fall on to wet paint and so that drips can be painted over later. If using a roller complete corners with a small brush.

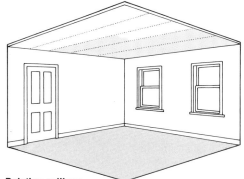

Painting ceilings
Always plan to complete a ceiling in one uninterrupted session, to prevent dried paint lines forming. Start at the window end, in a corner and work away from the light. Paint systematically from wall to wall in 60cm strips and ensure the edges are wet when joined.

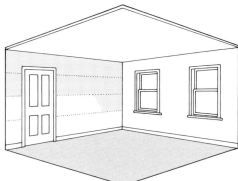

Painting walls
Start at the top corner of a wall nearest the window. Cover the wall in broad, horizontal bands and work down to the skirting board. Cut in with a narrower brush around windows and door frames. If using a roller, first coat the edges with a narrow brush.

Painting a mural

First design your image on grid paper, then divide the wall area into the same number of squares, but enlarged in proportion, to fill the allocated space. Sketch the outline on the wall, floor, ceiling or furniture in pencil, one square at a time, then fill in the colours, using masking tape and a thin brush for the edges.

Using masking tape
Fix masking tape to the outlines, then, apply the colour (right). Start with the paler shades and let each section dry before moving on to the next. Brush on the paint thickly to reduce the number of coats required. Finally, remove the masking tape, fill in any gaps in the colour and apply a thin, black line to the edges (far right).

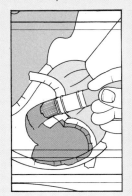

8

Painting doors

Always remove handles, keyhole plates, hooks and other door furniture before painting, to avoid smudges and runs and to speed up the work. Store them carefully with their screws and loosely refit between coats, to allow doors to be opened and closed. Give keyholes and the top edges of doors a thorough clean, so that specks are not picked up on bristles and spread over the surface. Complete any necessary repairs, such as fixing hinges and sanding down a sticking door before painting. (*For preparing surfaces, see Jobs 5/6, pp. 18-19.*)

Achieving a good finish

Aim to paint doors after walls and windows, but before skirting boards, and in one continuous session to prevent dried-paint lines forming. Doors need a gloss or oil-based silk finish for protection against normal wear and tear; they represent the largest area of gloss in most homes. An undercoat is necessary – even if the existing paint surface is sound and the new colour is darker than the old. Use two undercoats, however, when covering a dark or strong colour with a paler shade and sand between coats. There is no need to paint the top edge of a door, unless it is visible from stairs above. However, a painted edge will collect less dust than bare wood. If the door is to be painted in different colours each side, paint the hinge edge the same colour as the outer face and the lock edge the same colour as the inner face if the door opens into the room.

Painting skirtings

Use a 50mm brush for painting skirting boards. At corners, dab a lightly loaded cutting-in brush into the crevice and draw away the excess paint. Use masking tape or card to prevent paint smudging on to the walls.

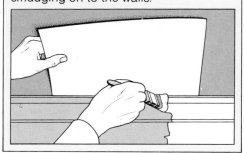

Panelled doors

*The following working sequence is designed to minimize the number of "wet edges" and so avoid ugly ridges. Using a 25mm brush, begin by painting the mouldings, **1**. Take care not to overload the brush or runs will spoil the finish. Then paint the panels, **2**, with a 50mm or 75mm brush, before moving on to the vertical centre sections, **3**. Next, cover the top, middle and bottom horizontal bands, **4**, then complete the vertical outside sections and edges, **5**, and finally the frame.*

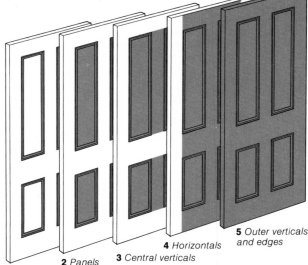

5 Outer verticals and edges
4 Horizontals
3 Central verticals
2 Panels
1 Mouldings

Paint the panels from the top down

Flush doors

To cover the area quickly, use a 75mm brush. Start at the top corner of the hinge side and work in 60cm² sections until you reach the bottom corner on the handle side. Begin with vertical strokes, then cross-brush to spread the paint and lay off with light, upward strokes, before moving on to the next section. When painting the edges, take care not to allow the paint to build up into ridges, and where possible, take the paint over the corners. You will find a small 50mm brush easiest for the edges (below). Try to avoid the common mistake of applying too much paint to the top of the door and too little to the sides. Work quickly so that the edge of each 60cm² painted section can be covered before it dries.

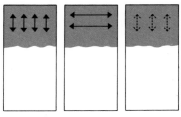

Which direction to paint

Begin with vertical strokes, then cross-brush the paint to fill in gaps. Lay off each section with upward strokes.

Use a small brush for edges to prevent ridges forming

Jamming the door open

Jam a flush or panelled door open by tapping a wedge under it. This exposes both the hinge and handle edges for painting. Allow each coat to dry thoroughly before closing the door.

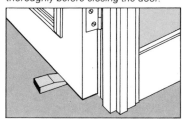

9
Painting windows

Window frames. which suffer both condensation and changes of temperature, are subjected to the worst conditions of all interior woodwork, so it is worth taking the time to ensure a good result. Repair any damage and prepare the surface before painting (*see Job 5, p. 18*). Paint any openable windows as early in the day as possible, to allow enough time for them to dry before closing in the evening. You will need a 25mm brush and, for precision work, a cutting-in brush; also, if you choose, a paint shield.

The order of working for individual parts of a window are determined by its construction. For the best results, follow the order given below for sash and casement windows, and always finish painting in the direction of the wood grain.

Cutting in
It is worth practising the cutting-in technique to get a fine line on glazing bars, frames and edges. Place a loaded brush about 3mm from the edge and carefully push it towards the join. Press lightly down and draw the brush swiftly along to make a long, clean line. Until you have acquired this skill, however, it would be wise to use a more foolproof method for painting around glass, such as a paint shield or masking tape.

Sash windows
*Push the bottom sash up and the top sash down, until there is a 20cm overlap. First paint the bottom meeting rail of the top sash, followed by the accessible vertical sections, **1**. Almost close both windows and paint the rest of the top sash, **2**, before covering the bottom sash, **3**. Leave to dry with the sashes almost closed and matchsticks inserted between them to prevent them sticking together, then paint the frame, **4**. Finally close the windows and paint the exposed parts of the runners, taking care not to get paint on the sash cords. Then paint the sill.*

 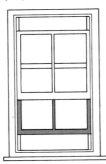 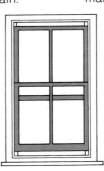 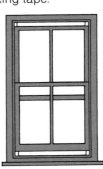 

1 Bottom of top sash   **2** Rest of top sash   **3** Bottom sash   **4** Frame   **5** Runners

Casement windows
*First remove catches and handles and store in a safe place. If one window is fixed, begin with the opening one. Paint the rebates first, **1**, next the crossbars, **2**, then the crossrails, **3**. Move on to the side verticals and edges, **4**, then the frame, **5**, and finally the sill. Always paint the sill last, or sleeves and clothing will smudge the wet paint. If paint overlaps on to the hinges, wipe it off before it dries and becomes more difficult to remove. Leave the stay until last to allow the window to be adjusted during painting.*

1 Rebates   **2** Crossbars   **3** Crossrails   **4** Sides and edges   **5** The frame

Tips on keeping paint off glass

To guarantee a neat edge around window panes, try protecting the glass with a paint shield (right) as you work, or apply masking tape (far right), before you begin. Press the tape firmly down to prevent paint creeping under the edges, and remove it before the final coat of gloss is dry, to avoid peeling a layer of paint off the frame. Alternatively, with experience and a steady hand, a clean line may be drawn using a cutting-in brush. Splashes and smudges can be scraped off when dry with a razor-blade and the surface cleaned with white spirit on a clean rag. Always allow the paint to overlap 3mm on to the glass to prevent moisture seeping through the join between the putty and the glass, and causing the wood to rot.

Hold the paint shield firmly against the glass

Alternatively, paint over masking tape

10
Painting stairs and stairwells

The stair area should be painted last, since halls and landings are likely to be scuffed when moving furniture from room to room; and, as the nucleus of the house, forms the main colour link between individual rooms and upper and lower floors. First set up a secure working platform for reaching even the least accessible parts of the stairwell (below). Remove carpet and fittings, clean the entire staircase and cure any faults such as creaking and uneven stairs, cracks, dents or splits. Follow the usual order of work, beginning with the landing ceiling, then the walls of the stairwell, working from the top down, and finally the stairs, banisters and the handrail. Throughout the work, keep the movement of doors and people to a minimum until the paint has dried, to reduce dust. If the wood is to be varnished and its colour changed, first fill any holes or splits and coat it with a woodstain. If it is to be painted, apply an undercoat.

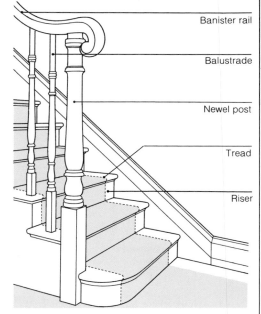

Banister rail

Balustrade

Newel post

Tread

Riser

Stairs and banisters
Staircases attract a great deal of dust, so when painting the treads and risers, ensure that working conditions are spotless. Wash the banister thoroughly and, working from the top, clean each tread and riser immediately. If carpet is to be fitted, paint the border only, allowing a 25mm carpet overlap.

11
Using ladders

Painting stairwells can prove perilous, so make sure your ladders are safe. A variety of convertible step ladders are now available, which will either slide or swing out into a straight ladder, for using against the wall (right). Ensure, however, that the connections will not allow the ladder to slip when extended and check for loose screws and jammed parts. If you are buying a new ladder, the aluminium types (right) are generally lighter and cheaper than the old wooden sort. Always ensure that it reaches at least 1m above the highest level at which you wish to stand, and never stand above the third highest rung. Face the ladder as you climb and do not lean over too far either side while painting. For larger areas, use a working platform (*see Job 14, p. 32*).

Convertible ladders

Clip-on shelf

A clip-on shelf
If your ladder does not have a built-in shelf, consider buying a clip-on one. It will serve as a useful platform for equipment.

Non-slip ladders
Ladders which will stand on two different levels are useful on stairs, provided there are suction pads on the feet.

12
Painting kitchens and bathrooms

Steam and condensation are the main problems to be solved when redecorating these rooms. Good ventilation in the form of efficient extractor fans will help to minimize the effect of moisture and a layer of emulsion on walls and ceilings will provide an easily washable surface, especially if it has a slight sheen. Anti-condensation emulsion paints containing insulating material are now available to help offset some of these problems. Cream-coloured, these paints can be overpainted to match a colour scheme. Avoid gloss on walls and ceilings since it exaggerates condensation.

Pipes
Copper pipes can be given a coating of undercoat and gloss and will not need primer. Normal gloss will withstand temperatures up to 90°C, although white and pale colours may yellow at over 70°C. Alternatively, a metallic paint can be used. These are corrosion and heat resistant and give lustre to hot and cold pipes. Avoid water-based paints, since they tend to soften and crack when heated. Never paint connections or fitting nuts on pipes; they could prove difficult to undo if they are sealed with a layer of paint. If you are repainting sound paint, simply wash down the surface and abrade it to make a key for the new paint.

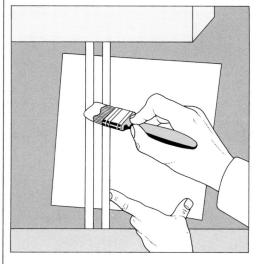

Painting behind a pipe
When pipes lie close to the wall, hold a card behind to shield the wall paint from smudges and splattering and start painting at the top.

13
Painting radiators

Radiators should always be painted when cold and allowed to dry thoroughly before the heating is turned on again, or the finish will be impaired. A strong smell usually emanates from a newly painted surface when heated but it soon fades. Old radiators may need to be treated for rust and primed, but new ones are delivered pre-primed, ready for undercoat and gloss. Any copper pipes connecting with the radiator can be painted in the same way. Use a 25mm brush for a panelled radiator and a crevice roller or brush for tricky areas. Work carefully to avoid runs, and do not paint the connections or they may prove difficult to undo if the radiator needs to be removed. Ordinary paints are usually satisfactory, but avoid paints with a metal pigment, since this will reduce radiating power.

Painting exterior walls

◇ Start at the top of the house and work down, to avoid dripping on to new paintwork.
◇ Divide the house into sections using natural breaks as demarcation lines. Begin with fascia boards, gutters and eaves, then tackle the walls, down-pipes and finish with the windows and doors.
◇ Work in horizontal strips one block at a time.
◇ Do not apply masonry paint in frosty weather, it may damage the paint.
◇ Porous surfaces, such as masonry and pebbledash absorb about 50 percent more paint than wooden surfaces.
◇ Try to work in the shade. and move around the house in the same direction as the sun.

Fault-finding

Painting faults can always be traced back to an error in preparation, poor working conditions, or incorrect application. Inadequate cleaning and abrading of surfaces, over-brushing or overthinning the paint, and over-loading the brush are some of the most common mistakes made by amateurs. In addition to surface textural problems, the paint colour may deteriorate. Lack of light will make some white paint yellow, and some red and orange pigments will bleed into a new coat if a barrier coat is not applied.

Brushmarks
A poor-quality brush will leave tell-tale marks. Other possible causes include overloading the brush and applying too thick a coat of paint, or failing to sand down an old surface sufficiently.

Loss of gloss
If a coat of gloss fails to retain its sheen, insufficient drying time between coats may be the cause. Overbrushing or overthinning the paint may also contribute.

No hiding power
Where a previous coat is still visible, either the wrong undercoat has been used or there are insufficient under-coats. Overthinning, overbrushing or understirring may also dilute the paint and cause transparency.

Flaking off
On woodwork, paint will peel if the surface is not correctly prepared. On emulsion, painting over dust, dirt or distemper is the cause.

Runs, sags and wrinkles
Unsightly tears and ridges form if the paint is applied too thickly or if it has not been adequately brushed out, particularly around fittings such as door handles and mouldings. Gloss paint has a greater tendency to sag and run than other paints.

Specks and pimples
Dust in the paint, either blown by the wind or transferred from the brush, or a badly sanded surface may leave a speckled finish.

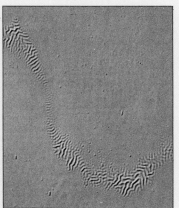

Blisters
Surface bubbles are caused by painting on a damp surface or on to old, soft or lifting paint.

Remedies

For all the above
Allow paint to harden for a week
Rub down with glasspaper
Clean the surface
Cure damp if necessary
Apply fresh gloss or emulsion

For blisters on woodwork
Cut out the bubble and fill with fine surface filler
Sand down, dust off
Apply fresh gloss
If excessive, strip off the paint and start again

Textures and finishes

A wide range of attractive paint finishes can be achieved by brushing, sponging, rolling or dabbing a design into a coloured glaze or stencilling on a shape, while textured paints can be rollered or combed into a raised pattern. These effects need no special skill and in many cases can be completed more rapidly than a standard painting job.

Decorative finishes

No specialized tools are needed beyond normal painting equipment, but you must use the correct paint for the base coat and the right glaze. For the ground coat, an oil-based paint with an eggshell finish produces the best results. Ordinary emulsion can be used, but it is more absorbent and so produces a less crisp finish. Glazes can be shiny, matt or transparent. Transparent oil glazes can be bought ready-made, to be tinted with universal stainer or artist's oil colours. Alternatively, a glaze can be made up from: one part linseed oil, one part turpentine, one part drying agent, a little whiting and some colour. Extra whiting will reduce the sheen. A third type of glaze is made from oil-based paint, thinned with white spirit.

Textured paints

Textured paints create a subtle decorative finish and cover a badly cracked surface. Some are also flexible, so that if a ceiling or wall "moves", the cracks remain covered. They are available in both a ready-to-use and powdered form for mixing to a gluey consistency. Some automatically leave a raised pattern when applied, while others are textured by hand after application, with combs, brushes or rollers.

Sponging
A mottled or stipple pattern can be produced with a large natural sponge and a little patience. Unlike dragging and ragging sponging usually involves adding colour to a neutral background, instead of removing patches of colour. First apply a coat of paint to the wall and leave it to dry for 24 hours. Then pour some thinned, coloured glaze into a shallow bowl. Dampen a sponge, dip it lightly into the glaze and dab on to a sheet of newspaper to absorb the excess. When the pattern becomes a delicate speckle on the paper, begin work on the wall. As the design begins to fade, refill the sponge with glaze. Allow the coat to dry, then fill in any gaps. For a softer effect, apply a second glaze colour (below).

Dragging
A fine, striped pattern is achieved by "dragging" a brush through a superficial coating of transparent oil glaze. First brush on the background coat to allow it to dry. Then brush on an even coating of coloured oil glaze in a broad band. While it is still wet, run the dragging brush down through the glaze to score straight lines. Then glaze and drag the next band of wall. You may find it easier to work with another person, so that one applies the glaze, while the other uses the dragging brush.

Ragging

The tucks and creases of a bundled-up rag, the woven design of hessian, or pieces of old net curtain can create an interesting textured pattern. When the base coat is dry, apply an even layer of glaze on to a small area of the wall, brushing thoroughly to even out the coverage. While the glaze is still wet, lightly roll a clean, lint-free, bundled-up rag in random directions on the colour, until a pattern forms. Use a dabbing and pushing action with a slight twist for a clear design (below). Apply the glaze to the next patch and continue, allowing a small overlap of pattern each time, and replace the rag when it starts to lose its effect. As with dragging, the job is most easily done with two people, one to paint on the glaze, the other to follow with the rag before the coat dries. If you find the colour is drying, moisten it with a damp sponge.

Stencilling

Stencils allow for more individual variations than other decorative finishes. Stencilling kits are available, complete with plates and brushes, but it is not difficult to invent your own design and cut out your own stencil. Draw or trace a picture on to graph paper, scale it up to size, and then transfer the pattern to a piece of stencil board or acetate. If you are using board, tape the picture on top with a piece of carbon paper behind and trace the outline with a pencil. If you are using acetate, insert the design underneath the transparent sheet, tape it down and trace the outline on to the acetate with an isograph technical pen. You can then cut along the lines with a scalpel. Tape the stencil to the surface to be decorated and fill in the colour with a stencilling brush (below).

Applying textured paints

Ensure the surface is clean, dry, sound, and free from flaking paint and distemper. If you are applying self-texturing paint, it will automatically create its own texture as you roller or brush it on. With ordinary textured paint, apply a coat first, then work the textured pattern into the smooth layer of paint. A variety of effects can be created with different implements, such as a plasterer's comb, a swirl brush (below), a stipple brush, and patterned rollers. Experiment on a piece of board before committing the pattern to the wall.

Wallpapering

Estimating time and quantities ◇ Types of paper
Tools and equipment ◇ Setting up safe
workstations ◇ Stripping off old wallpaper
Measuring and cutting ◇ Pasting and folding
Hanging lining paper and wallpaper
Papering awkward areas

Modern wallpaper is no longer simply paper – but includes a wide choice of synthetic and fabric materials, designed to wash, wear, strip and hang more easily than old-fashioned papers. Vinyls and washable papers are as easy to clean as paintwork, and "dry-strip" papers, that can be removed without water, make preparation quick, clean and simple when redecorating. Improved designs, colours and finishes have introduced a wider range of choice and most manufacturers change their collections every two years.

Once you have decided on the type of wall covering, measure the areas carefully, double check the figures and calculate quantities. Choice of pattern and colour will, to some extent, be determined by local availability, existing furnishings and price. Prices vary widely for the same paper, particularly as it is often cheaper to buy paper in stock than to order, so it is worth ringing round the stockists.

Unlike painting, wallpapering can be done gradually and will conceal minor cracks. Thorough preparation, however, is important to ensure a smooth finish.

Points to remember

◇ Always buy the type of adhesive recommended for the wall covering you have chosen.
◇ Check batch numbers on rolls before unwrapping them.
◇ Always paper ceilings before walls.
◇ Finish any paintwork before papering.
◇ Wear overalls or an apron with large pockets for holding scissors, a smoothing brush and other equipment.

For more information on types of wallpaper, see Choosing materials, pp. 118-21.

Estimating time

The figures below are a guide to the time needed to prepare and wallpaper an average 3m × 4m room with a normal number of windows, doors and other obstacles. If the surface needs extra preparation, allow an additional $\frac{1}{4}$-$\frac{1}{2}$ hour for sizing and 1-1$\frac{1}{2}$ hours for applying primer sealer.

Ceilings

Stripping old paper
(2)-(3) **hours**

Washing down a sound ceiling
(1) **hour**

Filling cracks and holes
($\frac{1}{2}$)-(1) **hour**

Hanging lining paper
(4)-(6) **hours**

Hanging paper
(4$\frac{1}{2}$)-(6$\frac{1}{2}$) **hours**

Walls

Stripping old paper
(2)-(3) **hours**

Filling cracks and holes
($\frac{1}{2}$)-(1) **hour**

Hanging lining paper
(6)-(8) **hours**

Hanging expanded polystyrene
(6)-(8) **hours**

Hanging wallpaper
(12)-(16) **hours**

Estimating quantities

Wallpaper quantities can be calculated more accurately than paint, since there are fewer variable factors. Use the chart (right) to calculate the number of rolls required, and remember to add on 10 per cent for waste, especially with a large or "drop" pattern. When completing a room, note down the number of rolls used as a guide for next time. Either jot down measurements and quantities in an unseen place, such as the top of the door frame, or keep a house "log book". Standard wallpapers come in rolls of approximately 10m × 53cm. Lining paper rolls are usually slightly wider and are available in both standard and economical large roll sizes.

Batches
Never skimp when ordering paper, since running out can cause considerable problems. Although you may be able to buy another roll with the same design, the colours in the pattern might be a remarkably different shade, which will show in bright light. This discrepancy occurs when the amount of ink used varies from batch to batch during printing. Each batch is given a code number, which is marked on the label supplied with each roll, so check that each roll you buy bears the same batch number. To avoid running out, consider buying a spare roll on a sale or return basis, but remember to keep the cellophane wrapper intact.

Unfortunately, the batch system is not infallible, since rolls of the same batch sometimes differ in shades of colour. "Shade before hanging" printed on the label means there may be some colour discrepancy within the batch. If there is a variation, hang darker colours nearer the window, but avoid using lengths of differing shades on the same wall.

Types of paper

When selecting wallpaper, it is important to match the colour, pattern and texture to the size, shape and general style of individual rooms (*see Colour and pattern for effect, pp. 30-1*). It is, however, equally important to choose a suitably practical material for the job. Some areas, for example, will need resilient papers, others demand easily sponged surfaces. Ease of hanging may also influence your choice, particularly if you lack experience.

Ease of handling
The hardest papers to hang are the thin, cheap types which tear easily when wet with paste, particularly when pulling round corners. Medium, heavyweight,

washable and vinyl papers are stronger, so tolerate rougher handling. Paste smudged on the decorative side of the paper can leave a stain, so the easily wiped vinyl-coated papers and paper-backed vinyls can be an advantage in this respect. Since they are non-porous, these papers are ideal for steamy rooms, such as kitchens and bathrooms, while heavy vinyls which resist stains and scuffs, are suitable for hallways, stairs and landings.

Convenience papers
Ready-pasted wall coverings save the time and trouble of mixing and applying paste (*see Job 17, p. 35*). Equally easy to use is a tough polyethylene

material which is hung directly from the roll after first pasting the wall (*see Job 21, p. 37*).

Lining paper
Usually hung beneath the wall covering as a sort of "paper undercoat", lining paper will camouflage the outline of carefully filled areas. There are several grades of lining paper, including off-white for normal use under wallpaper and a smoother pure white type – where the walls are to be painted later. A cold wall that has been prone to condensation should be lined with expanded polystyrene. This "warms" and insulates the wall and has the side effect of smoothing a poor surface.

Choosing patterns

Complicated patterns are usually best avoided by the beginner, especially in a room with lots of alcoves and corners. Simple, repeat patterns are equally problematic, since the eye will quickly pick up any mis-matching. These usually fall into two types; straight "set" patterns which have horizontal repeats, and "drop" patterns with diagonal repeats (below). There are, however, many "free match" designs now available, which will match automatically.

Patterns for problem areas
Vertical stripes emphasize out-of-true corners and a horizontal pattern should be avoided on a sloping ceiling, since the motif will gradually "disappear" as the ceiling line slopes down. In any difficult situation, a small, random pattern is the best solution.

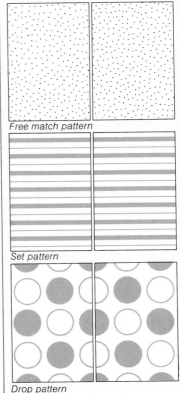

Free match pattern

Set pattern

Drop pattern

Calculating the number of rolls

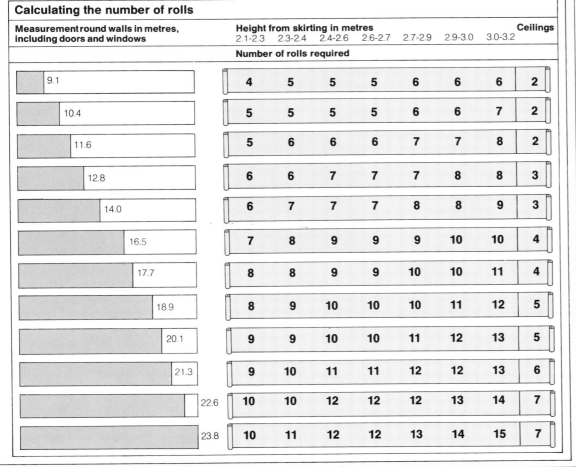

Measurement round walls in metres, including doors and windows	Height from skirting in metres							Ceilings
	2.1-2.3	2.3-2.4	2.4-2.6	2.6-2.7	2.7-2.9	2.9-3.0	3.0-3.2	
	Number of rolls required							
9.1	4	5	5	5	6	6	6	2
10.4	5	5	5	5	6	6	7	2
11.6	5	6	6	6	7	7	8	2
12.8	6	6	7	7	7	8	8	3
14.0	6	7	7	7	8	8	9	3
16.5	7	8	9	9	9	10	10	4
17.7	8	8	9	9	10	10	11	4
18.9	8	9	10	10	10	11	12	5
20.1	9	9	10	10	11	12	13	5
21.3	9	10	11	11	12	12	13	6
22.6	10	10	12	12	12	13	14	7
23.8	10	11	12	12	13	14	15	7

Tools and equipment

A full set of wallpapering tools is not a large investment, particularly since some general household items form part of the collection. The only expensive piece of equipment you might need would be a steam stripper for removing difficult papers; and this can be hired. Choose overalls with pockets large enough to hold brushes, scissors and a sponge.

Pasting tools
Essential wallpapering tools include a paste brush or an old 10cm or 12.5cm paint brush that does not shed bristles; a paste bucket, with a taut piece of string tied across it for resting the brush on, and a disposable pedal bin liner to save cleaning it; also a paper-hanging brush for smoothing down the paper. A 2m×60cm fold-away paste table is a good investment; it is cheap, takes up little space and serves as a work surface for cutting lengths and matching patterns. For ready-pasted paper, you will need a plastic water trough, instead of paste, a bucket and a pasting brush. A sponge is also recommended instead of a smoothing brush.

Scraping and cutting tools
You will need a straight and, possibly, a serrated scraper for removing wallpaper, and a pair of shears about 25cm long for making straight, accurate cuts. A trimming knife and a smaller pair of household scissors are also handy when making intricate cuts around complicated shapes.

Measuring tools
For marking an accurate guide line before hanging, you will need a plumb bob and a pencil for walls, and a chalked stringline for ceilings (or walls). When measuring out the paper, use a steel tape, a 60cm × 90cm folding boxwood rule or a straight-edge ruler.

Finishing tools
Finally, use a sponge for removing unwanted paste and, if necessary, a wooden seam roller for pressing down edges on untextured wallpapers.

Care and storage
A kit of decorating tools should last a lifetime. Just ensure that, at the end of the job, everything is cleaned of paste in warm, soapy water, dried and stored safely away. To save cleaning the paste bucket, simply insert a disposable pedal bin liner, which can be thrown away and replaced. Always store paper rolls on their side and leave them in their wrappers to keep them clean. Never stand them on their ends, since this can crumple the edges.

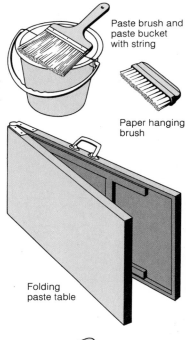

Paste brush and paste bucket with string

Paper hanging brush

Folding paste table

Straight scraper

Serrated scraper

Seam roller

Shears

Steel tape

Plumb bob and line

Sponge

Pastes
Always choose the paste recommended by the manufacturer for both lining and top paper or use a universal paste which can be mixed up to suit different types of wall covering. Modern cellulose paste is suitable for all types of wall covering except vinyl, which must be hung with a paste containing fungicide, to prevent mould forming on the wall. Ready-mixed pastes are only economical for heavy textiles, and cold-water paste is best used on heavier papers. Remember to buy sufficient quantities.

Pattern, like colour, influences the mood and shape of a room. Florals, for example, tend to be restful, while geometrics may create a more stimulating atmosphere. Designs can be used to play visual tricks: vertical lines help to "raise" a ceiling; horizontal lines "lengthen" a room; three-dimensional geometrics give the impression of depth; small designs give a feeling of space; large motifs diminish the size of a surface. Motifs have the power to focus interest on a feature or disguise irregularities when taken over an entire room. Try to avoid too many patterns in one room, do not combine florals with geometrics and always set off a pattern with a plain background, floor or furnishings.

Floral patterns
Fresh spring colours lend warmth and character to a bleak, angular room (above). Large sprigs have the effect of opening out a room and raising a ceiling, particularly when arranged in vertical strips. If the pattern is carried on to the blinds or furnishings, the warming and softening effect increases. In a small room with irregular shapes – an attic for example – a miniature floral in random sequences would be more suitable, since a regular line will highlight crooked walls or ceilings. The type of floral design may also suggest an era, a national style or the purpose of a room; a conservatory, for instance (right).

Large motifs
A large design continued over the walls and ceiling will help to conceal strangely shaped corners and will soften a series of harsh or irregular angles (right). A big motif, however, will only look comfortable if the room is broad or tall enough to accommodate it. It is not easy to mix floral designs, particularly if a floral forms a main feature or contains large shapes. The best effects are created by picking up the main colour of the pattern in other parts of the room, and using a neutral second colour, such as white, as a backdrop and to co-ordinate accessories.

Colour and pattern for effect

Geometric patterns

A geometric pattern instantly gives a room a clean and modern feel – particularly suitable for a bathroom (below). Ideally, the lines should complement any other verticals and horizontals, such as the grouting lines in tiles or the slats of blinds. The angles of the room, however, must be straight or the geometric lines will exaggerate any irregularities. A tiny motif within the geometric will help to soften lines and one or two colours should be repeated in other parts of the room.

A printed collage

Menus, wine labels, newspapers, magazines, catalogues and other printed matter, arranged into a collage, will form an unusual wall covering. This sort of montage is best pasted on to a small area to form a feature in a study, a bathroom, or a child's bedroom.

14
Setting up safe workstations

Always set up a safe working platform before attempting to decorate ceilings and stairwells. In most houses, this can be improvised using a combination of ladders and boards. If the stairwell is particularly high, however, a narrow scaffold tower, hired locally, may be the best solution. When using step ladders always ensure that they are fully open and that the shelf is pushed well down. When climbing ladders to reach the platform, remember to empty pockets of scissors and knives.

Stairs and stairwells
The exact arrangement of ladders, steps, boards and boxes will depend on your staircase, but the system shown (right) can be adapted for most stair shapes. Put a step ladder on the top landing and lean a straight ladder against the head wall with its foot firmly lodged against a stair riser. Then link them with boards. For the lower levels, put a step ladder in the hall and form a platform with planks resting on a ladder step and a stair. Keep equipment handy on the stepladder shelf or in a bucket hung from a ladder rung.

Ceilings and walls
Arrange a strong working platform across the room in the direction the paper is to be hung. Use two step ladders, some trestles or heavy tea chests, and a plank or a series of boards which span the complete room from wall to wall. In this way, the platform will only need to be moved once for each wall. Make sure you can reach comfortably, since stretching is dangerous.

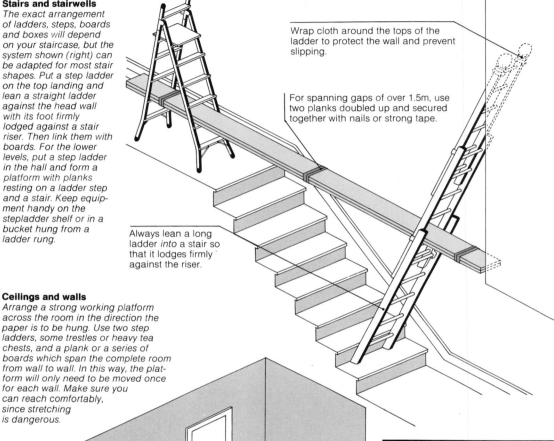

Wrap cloth around the tops of the ladder to protect the wall and prevent slipping.

For spanning gaps of over 1.5m, use two planks doubled up and secured together with nails or strong tape.

Always lean a long ladder *into* a stair so that it lodges firmly against the riser.

Ensure that step ladders are fully opened to avoid sudden jarring or toppling.

A single plank spanning more than 1.5m will need additional support.

Preparing the room

◇ Clear furniture away from the walls and leave space for the pasting table. If papering ceilings, remove *all* furniture to another room.
◇ Remove light fittings, curtains and, if necessary, picture rails.
◇ Spread a dustsheet or newspapers over the floor to catch drips, debris and paste.
◇ Lock any doors obstructed by ladders and keep dogs and children away from the work area.

Any existing wall covering should be stripped off to leave bare walls, since joins, peeling, blistering and a strong pattern in the old paper may show through the new. The fresh adhesive may also pull the old covering away from the wall, together with the new paper you have just hung. The key to stripping wallpaper is to take time and care over the job. The paper should not be scraped off too vigorously or lumps will be gouged from the plaster, leaving more holes to fill in later. Be patient with stubborn areas and continue soaking and scraping until the paper loosens. Standard wallpapers are removed by sponging with warm water until the paper is soft enough to scrape off. Easy-strip papers are simply peeled off. Washable papers which hold fast may need to be removed with a steam stripper.

Marking screw holes
When a fixture, such as a picture or shelf, is taken off the wall, put a matchstick in each screw hole, leaving about 5mm protruding. When the new paper is brushed on, the matchsticks will pop through to indicate the exact location of the screw hole.

15
Preparing surfaces

When all old paper has been removed, wash down the walls with hot water, to remove any traces of old paste and to loosen any final nibs of paper. Then fill any holes or cracks (*see Basic technique, p. 17*). When a wall covering comes

Basic technique

How to strip off old wallpaper

1 Soak the paper with warm water using a large sponge or brush

2 Scrape off the softened paper while it is damp

Stripping normal wallpaper
Most wallpaper is removed by soaking with warm water, **1**, using a large brush or a sponge, and then by scraping. Thicker papers may need an extra soaking: go right round the room once, so that by the time you get back to the starting point, the water will have started to loosen the old paste. Another soaking and the paper should scrape off easily as you work around the room. A little soap powder or liquid detergent added to the water will speed up the soaking process, and a handful of wallpaper paste will both thicken it enough to give it more time to soak through the paper, and will prevent water running down the wall. While scraping, keep the scraper as flat as possible, to avoid gouging out plaster, **2**.

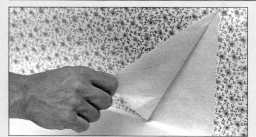

1 Gently peel back the bottom corner of vinyl paper

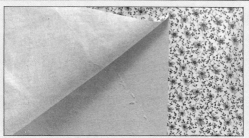

2 Remove the backing paper if it is damaged

Stripping vinyl wallpapers
Easy-strip wall coverings, now widely available, can be removed simply by releasing the bottom edge of the paper with your fingernail or a stripping knife, **1**, and pulling each length straight off the wall. Pull carefully upwards, not outwards, to avoid ripping the backing in uneven strips. With vinyls, a layer of thin white paper will remain on the wall as each length is removed. This is backing paper and can remain in position to act as lining paper for the new wall covering. If, however, the backing paper comes away in places, it must be removed completely, **2**.

1 Score the paper with a wire brush or serrated scraper

2 Hold the steam stripper plate to the wall, then scrape off the paper

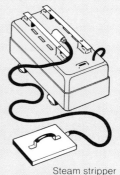

Steam stripper

Stripping difficult papers
Washable and overpainted papers are made to withstand water, so soaking the surface will have little effect. First score the surface using a wire brush, **1**, a serrated scraper or a sharp implement; this will break down the surface and allow the water to infiltrate and loosen the old paste. If the job proves hard going try hiring a steam stripper; it is simple to use and creates less mess than soaking and scraping. Steam generated by the machine passes through a plate held close to the wall, **2**. This loosens the paper so that it can be scraped off immediately with your other hand.

away easily – assuming it is not an easy-strip type – it indicates a flaking, dusty or damp surface. Scrape away any flaking paint then check and cure the cause of any dampness in the wall (see pp. 205-7) and apply a coat of oil-based primer sealer to provide a sound surface for the new wall covering. If papering over sound paintwork, wash down the wall first.

Applying glue size
Glue size is a gelatinous sealant that prevents a wall absorbing water from the paste. Diluted paste will serve the same purpose. Although it is not always necessary, it is wise to simply brush a coat over a wall to ensure that the wall covering sticks well, and to avoid ruining expensive paper. It also leaves the surface slippery, which makes it easier

to slide the paper over the wall when butting up adjoining lengths. Special formulations of glue size can be obtained, although it is now customary for diluted wallpaper paste to be used as size. Normally, a weak mixture of paste is made up according to the instructions on the packet and applied generously with a large brush. Within minutes, it will be dry and papering can begin.

Apply glue size liberally to the surface

Borders and friezes

Borders and friezes add an inexpensive finishing touch to a newly decorated room. Although traditionally fitted at ceiling or picture rail level, they can be used to good effect as a vertical wall surround or to trim a sloping ceiling, for example. A decorative strip can reduce the apparent height of a tall ceiling, elongate a short room, co-ordinate disparate colours, tone down a lively colour scheme, or enliven a quiet room. They should be applied at least 48 hours after hanging wallpaper.

A softening effect
In a simple, neutral room (right) a soft frieze adds a warm and friendly touch, particularly if it picks up a colour in the furnishings. In a room without pattern, a frieze can become a feature in its own right. It is important, however, to choose a design that is in tune with the mood of the room. A horizontal line will take the eye sideways and can help to broaden a narrow room, or lower the ceiling line in a tall one, particularly if the line is echoed by the arrangement of the furniture.

A co-ordinated effect
On a vibrant wall, the border needs to link with either the pattern or the colour of the wallpaper for a unified effect (far right). A patterned border, for example, can look stylish against a patterned wallpaper, provided the colours are co-ordinated and other surfaces or furnishings form a neutral background. A border design can give a splash of interest between two plain surfaces, and a single strip of colour can divide two patterns and so quieten the effect.

16
Measuring and cutting

Measure the height of each wall at both ends and in the middle to give you a maximum length for your strips of paper and allow an additional 100mm before cutting. This gives an extra 50mm at both ceiling (or picture rail) and skirting for neat trimming. Measure ceilings in the same way, and allow an excess of 50mm on ceilings for trimming on to the side and window walls. Unroll a few feet to check which way up the pattern should be. Trim off the end of the roll and either cut off lengths as you go or, to speed up the job, cut several lengths, so that one length can be soaking while you are hanging another. But mark consecutive numbers on the back, and make a note of which end is the "top".

Cutting to match
Use a steel tape measure to mark out lengths, then use wallpaper shears to cut your paper. When using a plain or a random-patterned paper, work from one roll of paper and cut equal lengths. With a diagonally matching "drop-pattern" paper, work from two or three rolls at a time, to minimize waste in pattern matching. Drape lengths over a table and align them carefully before cutting.

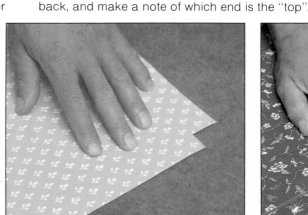

Measure out lengths with a steel tape measure, allowing 100mm extra for trimming

Cut equal lengths of set patterns or allow a small margin where necessary

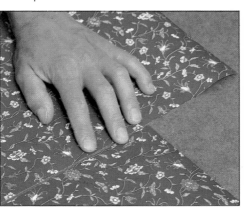

Carefully match up drop patterns before measuring and cutting lengths

17
Pasting and folding

After each length of paper has been cut, it should be given a good coating of paste, then folded and left to soak before hanging. Paste should be mixed until all lumps are dissolved and allowed to stand for a couple of minutes. If using thin paper, extra water must be added for a more dilute mixture. To ensure a good covering of paste, coat the brush generously, then paste systematically and in good light. Dry patches will form "bubbles" when the length has been hung.

Soaking
Some papers need to be left to "soak" for a few minutes before being hung. Medium-weight papers should be left for about 5 minutes, and heavyweight papers for about 10 or 12 minutes. If no exact guidance is given on the label, the best approach is to soak long enough to ensure that the paper is supple before it is hung. To "soak" the paper, simply leave it on a clean, dry surface after you have applied the paste, and continue pasting more lengths. Always keep the soaking time constant between lengths, to avoid variations in stretching and the resulting pattern-matching problems.

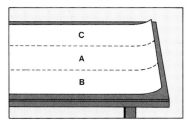

The order of pasting
First paste the central band of the paper, then the strip nearest to you and finally the far strip. When coating an edge strip, ensure that it overlaps the edge of the table, to avoid smearing paste onto the table and from there onto the decorative side of the paper. When half the sheet is completed, fold it and paste the other half.

Applying the paste
Place a length of paper decorative side down on the paste table. Allow the short edge of the paper to overlap the end of the table by 25mm, and let the long edge, nearest to you overlap the table edge by about 5mm. Divide the paper into three imaginary long bands. First, load the brush and paste the central portion, **1**, then work towards to the edge nearest to you – the one that overlaps the edge of the paste table, **2**. Push the paper across to the farther edge, again allowing the paper to overlap by about 5mm, then brush the paste outwards towards that edge, herringbone style (see below left). This should prevent the paste smearing on to the table. Keep the brush well coated with paste and continue feeding the paper along the table until about half the length has been pasted. Then fold the top edge over to the centre line, **3**. Paste the second half of the length, following the same sequence, then fold the other short edge over to meet the first in the middle, **4**, taking care not to crease the fold. Put this length aside to soak, while you paste the next or hang a soaked length.

1 Paste the central portion of paper, then the long edge nearest to you

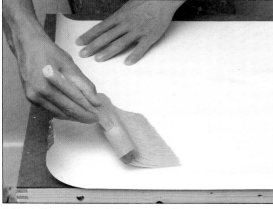

2 Brush the paste over to the opposite long edge

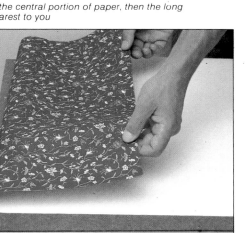

3 Fold over the pasted half of the paper

4 Paste the second half then fold it over and leave the whole strip to soak

Folding long lengths
When pasting a long length of paper, carefully arrange the pasted sections into concertina folds, pasted-side to pasted-side, taking care not to allow any paste to smudge on to the decorative side. Handle the lengths gently and do not crease the folds, since this will leave unsightly marks. These folds will make handling easier when working on ceilings or stairwells or when hanging lining paper.

1 Fold the paper, pasted-side to pasted-side

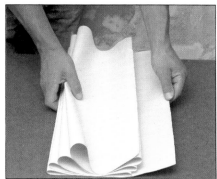

2 Arrange the concertina folds into a pile

18

Hanging lining paper on ceilings

It is advisable to use lining paper on previously painted or distempered surfaces or on new plasterwork. Without a lining, wallpaper may crease and stretch on uneven surfaces, paste may take a long time to dry on gloss surfaces, and gaps may form through shrinkage.

Lining paper is normally hung at right angles to the top covering on both ceilings and walls, so that the joins in the two layers do not coincide. Use the same paste as for the top wall covering, but hang the lining immediately, since there is no need to let it soak. However, once hung, leave it to dry for 48 hours before pasting on the top covering. When learning the art of paper hanging, it is worth practising with lining paper, even if you choose to paint rather than paper over it.

Marking a guide line

Having prepared the ceiling (see Job 15, pp. 32-3), a guide should be marked on the ceiling for the first length of paper. This can be made using a pencil and a long straight-edge, though a chalked string-line is better. The line is secured taut to the top of the walls and is then plucked to snap against the ceiling and leave a chalked impression. (For positioning, see below right.)

Cleaning shears

For neat trimming, stand paste-clogged shears and scissors in a jar of hot water from time to time to dislodge the adhesive and so guarantee clean cuts. If the paste hardens, it may need to be washed off in clean, soapy water.

Applying the lining paper

*Having set up a safe working platform, mark a chalk or pencil guide line on the ceiling, **1**, unfold the first portion of the paper and align it with the guide line. The remainder of the paper can be supported with a spare roll, **2**, or by an assistant standing on the floor and using a clean sweeping brush. Gravity is the enemy of papering ceilings. The paper will want to drop down, so brush each fold quickly, **3**, and keep the remainder of the length close to the ceiling so that it does not pull down the part already brushed into place. When the length is smoothed down, push the edges neatly into the wall-to-ceiling joint, **4**, and trim, **5**. If the walls are to be papered, leave a 5mm margin of paper on each wall. Successive lengths are hung similarly, ensuring that the edges of all lengths are neatly butt-jointed.*

To paper round a ceiling rose, cut a hole in the paper, pull the rose through and hang the rest of the length. Then make release cuts, press back the flaps and trim (see Job 29, p. 41).

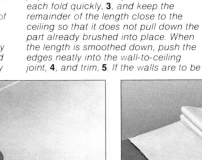

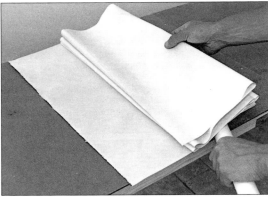

1 *Snap a chalk guide line on the ceiling and align the first length with it*

2 *Support the paper on a spare roll*

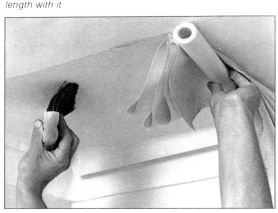

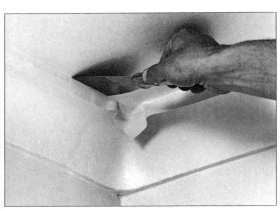

3 *Smooth the paper into position, eliminating air bubbles*

4 *Mark a crease line with a scraper*

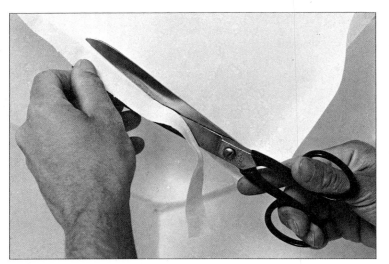

5 *Trim along the crease line with a pair of sharp, clean shears*

Where to begin lining on ceilings

The first length of lining paper is usually hung at right angles to the main window. In this way, the lining will also lie at right angles to the top layer of wallpaper, which is usually hung parallel with the window (see Basic technique, p. 39). Begin lining in a corner and allow about 50mm of paper to be turned on to the window wall for trimming. Also allow an extra 50mm for trimming on to the side walls.

19
Hanging lining paper on walls

Lining paper is hung horizontally, so each length must be as long as the wall's width. Joining short lengths is not advisable, since it is difficult to get a perfect join.

Mark a guide line for the first length (*see opposite*), start at the top of the wall and work downwards to the skirting. The first length should overlap on to the ceiling by about 25mm before being trimmed off (*see Job 18, p. 36*). Each length should also overlap around the corner on to the next wall by about 12mm. As you work down the wall, subsequent horizontal lengths should butt up closely to the previous length. Any overlaps, except in corners, should be avoided since these will be evident when the top covering is hung later.

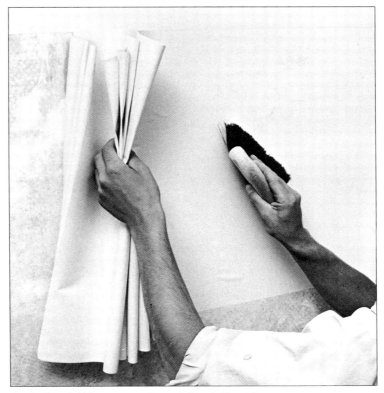
Gradually unfold the paper and smooth it on to the wall

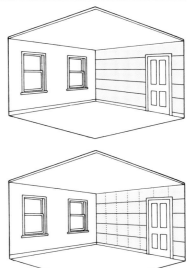

Where to begin lining on walls
Lining paper should be hung in horizontal layers on walls (top) unless the surface is bad enough to need a double layer of lining paper, known as cross-lining (above). The first layer is hung vertically and the second layer horizontally, so that the top wall covering will lie vertically. It is possible to hang the lining paper vertically if the joins in the layers do not coincide.

20
Patch lining

Where only a small part of the wall needs to be lined, try patch lining. Hang enough lining paper to cover the poor area with an overlap of a few centimetres, but do not stick down the edges. Allow the paste to dry, then tear off a rim of paper, to leave a softened feathered edge to the patch.

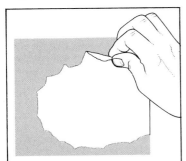
Tear around the patch for a soft line

21
Hanging expanded polystyrene

This "paste-the-wall" lining material can be hung in horizontal or vertical layers, though it is easier to hang it vertically. Just plan ahead to ensure that the joins fall between the joins in the wall covering.

Brush heavy-duty wallpaper paste on to the wall over an area to be occupied by one length of the material, and allow it to dry thoroughly. Position the end of the roll close to the ceiling then unroll the polystyrene down the wall, keeping its edge aligned with a vertical guide line drawn on the wall (*see Job 22, p. 38*). Smooth out the polystyrene using a wallpaper brush or a paint roller. Take care when trimming the bottom of the length into the skirting board, as the material will crack easily. The most reliable method is to press it gently into the top of the skirting to mark off a trimming line and cut before smoothing it back into place. Butt joint successive lengths, but do not try to take polystyrene around corners, as it is likely to crumble.

At skirtings, gently press the polystyrene into the angle, mark a cutting line, trim with scissors or a knife then smooth the paper into place.

22

Marking guide lines on ceilings and walls

Corners, door architraves and window frames rarely form true verticals. So, the first step when papering walls is to mark a vertical line on the wall as a guide to hanging the first length. The most effective method is to suspend a plumb bob on a chalked stringline from the top of the wall and snap it to leave a vertical line. Draw a new guide line as you come to each wall and after hanging a few lengths, use the plumb bob to check the alignment. Straight guide lines on ceilings are made by measuring equal distances from the wall at each end of ceiling and snapping a chalked stringline between the two points.

Where to begin on ceilings
The starting point for hanging ceiling paper is generally parallel with the main window, so that, as with painting, you will be working away from the light. In this way, accidental overlaps will not be cast in shadow. Draw your first guide line, to allow for about 50mm of paper to be turned on to the window wall for final trimming.

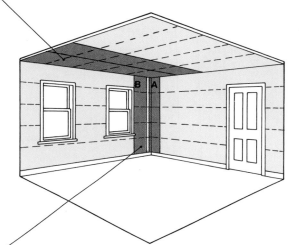

Where to begin on walls
When papering any room, the aim is to work outwards from the largest window, away from the light in both directions. The normal starting point is in the corner adjacent to the window wall (A). Draw your first guide line at a point which will allow a 12mm margin of paper to turn on to the window wall. Having papered the first side wall, go back and paper the window wall, then the other side wall and finally, the far wall. Alternatively, the first length can be hung next to the window (B) and from there to paper the rest of the window wall, followed by the side walls, working away from the light, then the end wall. Starting beside the window may prove easier, since it usually removes the need to cut awkward lengths around the window.

Where to begin on chimney breasts
A chimney breast forms a focal point in any room, so special planning is needed to create a balanced effect. If the paper has a large pattern, centralize the motif on the chimney breast (right). If the paper has a random design, mark a vertical line at the centre of the chimney breast and hang a length each side, so that two full widths can be used (far right).

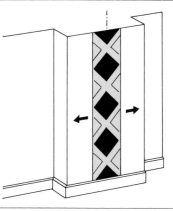

Using a plumb bob and chalkline
When the plumb bob stops swinging, press the chalkline into the base of the wall and pluck it, to leave a vertical line.

The secret of successful wallpapering is to be thorough, methodical and careful when matching patterns. When decorating, ceilings should be papered first to prevent paste splashing on to finished walls and woodwork. If the surfaces are in a poor condition, you will probably need to hang lining paper, on both ceilings and walls (see Jobs 18/19, pp. 36-7) before applying your top wall covering. Having lined the surface, cut and pasted lengths, established a starting point and marked straight guide lines, the paper is ready to hang. The first length is lined up precisely against the guide line, smoothed into place, then trimmed. Subsequent lengths are carefully brushed into place to form good pattern matches and neat butt joints.

Applying the paper
Open the step ladder close to the wall and drape pasted paper over one arm with the ends uppermost (below). Mount the step ladder, stand square to the wall and unfold the top half of the paper. Position the edge of the paper against the vertical guide line marked on the wall, 1, and leave a 50mm trimming edge at the top. Run the wallpaper brush firmly down the centre of the aligned length. Brush outwards to expel any air bubbles and smooth the paper neatly on to the wall, 2. If the top half of the paper is correctly aligned with the guide line, the lower half will follow it automatically. If it does not lie straight, peel the length off and reposition it. At the ceil-ing angle or picture rail and skirtings, run the back of the shears lightly along the paper, 3, peel back the edge of the paper and cut carefully along the crease line, 4. Brush the paper back into place to leave a neat finish, 5. Take the second length to the top of the wall, align the pattern where necessary and position the edge close to the first length. A slight push with your fingers will encourage the paper to slide across the wall until both edges touch and buckle slightly, 6. As the paper shrinks a little this will form a neat "butt" joint. Go over the joints with a wallpaper brush and finally press the edges with a seam roller unless the paper has a raised pattern.

How to carry a length of pasted paper
Drape the length over one arm, with the two ends uppermost (right). This arrangement will prevent you smearing paste on to your clothes, will enable you to mount the ladder easily with the paper, and will ensure that the length is not crushed. Long lengths of folded paper can be supported on a roll.

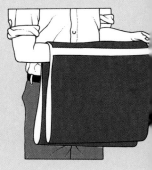

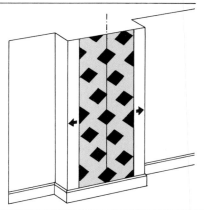

Basic technique

How to hang wallpaper

Hanging ready-pasted paper

1 *Align the first length of paper with the vertical guide line*

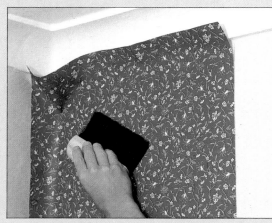

2 *Brush the paper flat to expel any air bubbles*

3 *Mark a crease line at the ceiling angle*

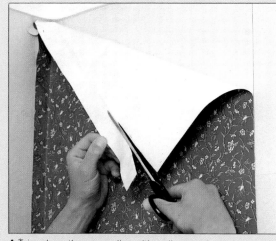

4 *Trim along the crease line with wallpaper shears*

5 *Smooth back the trimmed edge*

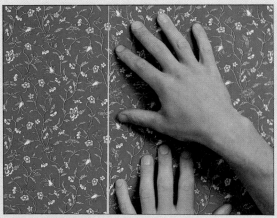

6 *Slide the new length to form a butt joint*

Ready-pasted paper has a coating of dried paste on the back which is activated by immersing the paper in water. Either buy a plastic water trough with the wallpaper or use any container which is long and deep enough to take a loosely-rolled length of paper – a plant trough, for example. Before starting work, lay plenty of newspaper or polythene sheeting along the skirtings.

Cut a length of paper, then roll it up loosely, with the pattern facing inward, to ensure the water reaches all areas of paste on the backing. Make sure the "free" end of the paper is the top edge to be fixed at the ceiling, then immerse the paper in the water for a full minute. Take hold of the top edge of the paper and slowly pull it upwards, allowing the water to run back into the trough. Then smooth it on to the wall using a clean, damp sponge, working from the centre to the edges, and sponge away any paste which may appear at the edges. If a wall has been lined with expanded polystyrene, hang lining paper before applying ready-pasted paper.

Activating the paste
Carefully pull up the top edge of the roll, allowing the water to drain back into the trough.

24
Papering stairwells

The height of most stairwells poses the problem of how to reach the top of the walls and how to handle very long lengths of paper. The first essential is therefore to set up a safe work-station (see Job 14, p. 32).

Although it runs against the normal procedure of working away from the light, it is easiest to hang the longest length first and work away from it in both directions.

When measuring lengths, mark the paper to allow for the slope of the stairs (see below). After pasting, fold each length concertina-style for ease of handling (see Job 17, p. 35) and, if possible, enlist a helper to support the length of paper as it is hung.

If you use a ready-pasted paper, always roll each length twice in the trough to ensure that water reaches all parts of the dried paste on the back of these long strips of paper. First immerse the length, pattern outwards, in the trough, so that the bottom end extrudes, then re-roll it until the end which will lie at the top of the wall emerges.

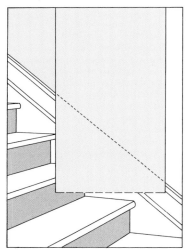

Measuring for the stair angle
Allow for the slope of the stairs when measuring lengths, so that the paper falls below the longest drop. Crease the paper along the skirting and trim.

25
Papering corners

Joins are less noticeable if they fall in a corner, so unless a width of paper conveniently ends in a corner, you will need to cut it into two strips. Internal and external corners are treated in much the same way. When less than a full width is needed to reach a corner, you should measure from the edge of the last length into the corner. Turn the paper face down to mark off the width needed, and double check that the strip is being cut from the correct edge, or the pattern will not match. Pencil guide marks to indicate which edges are to fall in the corner. When the first strip is in place, the off-cut is hung on the new wall, its edge covering the join.

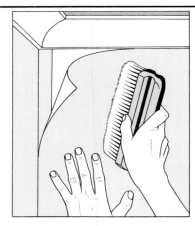

Internal corners
Hang complete lengths until a cut width is needed to reach the corner. Measure from the edge of the last length into the corner. Take three measurements, one at the top, one in the middle and one at the bottom, in case the corner is not true. Then add 12mm to the largest dimension for turning on to the next wall. Cut a strip this wide and paste it down. Then hang the offcut, ensuring that the "good" edge is vertical and overlaps for a good pattern match.

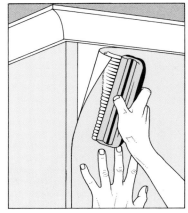

External corners
Measure from the edge of the last full width into the corner, as for internal corners. This time, however, add 25mm instead of 12mm to the largest dimension. Cut a strip this wide, paste it and hang it, smoothing the paper carefully round the corner. Use your judgement to decide where the offcut should lie for the best pattern match. Mark a vertical line on the next wall, the width of the offcut from this point, before pasting and hanging.

26
Papering around fireplaces

The way to tackle a fireplace surround depends mainly on the mantelshelf. If it reaches right across the chimney breast wall or to within about 25mm of the corners, treat the wall above and below the shelf as two separate areas. Hang the paper down to the mantelshelf and make a neat horizontal cut. Then hang the lower half of the length and make a neat butt joint where the pieces meet.

If the mantelpiece spans only a part of the wall, hang the length as one piece. Brush on the top half of the paper and cut along the rear edge of the mantelshelf. Then cut carefully round the contours of the fire-place surround, using sharp household scissors for intricate shapes (top right). When papering chimney breasts, try to make joins and overlaps on the side, recessing walls (bottom right).

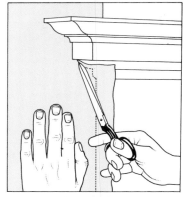

Use sharp scissors for intricate cuts

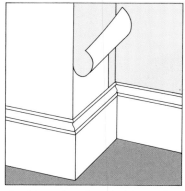

On chimney breasts make joins on the side walls

27
Papering doorways

Hang complete lengths until less than a full width of paper is needed to reach the door frame. Cut out an L-shaped piece of paper, leaving about 50mm excess all around for trimming. Hang the paper from the ceiling down to the top of the frame and trim along the line. Make a diagonal cut, about 25mm long, working away from the top corner of the frame to allow the rest of the length to be smoothed into place, then crease and cut.

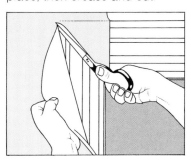

Cut diagonally up to the frame edge

28
Papering around windows

The shape of the window surround will determine the papering technique. In a window reveal, paper the inside walls first, cutting the paper to align exactly with the edge of the outer wall. Then hang a length on the outer wall, with a small margin overlapping into the papered reveal, and match the pattern carefully (top right). The trickiest rooms to wallpaper are in attics and lofts where there are unusual angles. Where dormer windows have triangular-shaped wall reveals, turn a 25mm margin of paper from the outer wall into the reveal. Cut triangular-shaped pieces to cover the reveal walls precisely and so overlap the margin (bottom right).

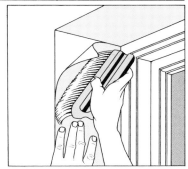

In a window reveal, paper the inside walls first.

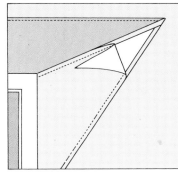

Cut triangular pieces to fit a dormer window exactly

29
Papering around light fittings

First switch off the electricity supply at the mains. Modern, flush-fitting sockets and switches are simple to trim around neatly. First loosen the cover plate, then hang the length of paper up to the electrical fitting. Cut a hole in the paper, about 5mm smaller than the size of the plate. Then smooth the paper on to the wall, and replace the plate.

Some older-style sockets and switches are fixed in a block. Press the paper against the switch and make small cuts, radiating from the centre of the fitting to about 12mm beyond its edges. Brush the paper around the block and trim the flaps (top right). With ceiling roses, make a series of radial cuts from the centre to the edge of the rose, then trim off the "tongues" (bottom right).

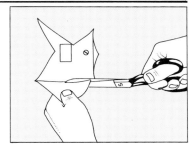

Make a cut to each corner then trim

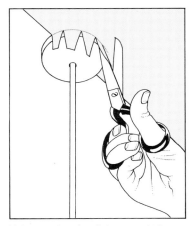

Make a series of radial cuts and trim

30
Papering arches

Paper the outer wall first and turn a 25mm margin into the arch. Make small cuts in the edge to allow for the curve of the arch. Fold the flaps around the corner and smooth them down. Paper the inside of the arch in two pieces, the exact width of the arch, making a neat butt joint at the top.

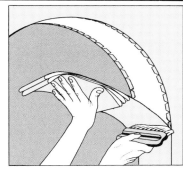

Carefully align the edges of the paper with the arch.

31
Papering around radiators

Some radiators can now be tilted forward for decorating, but most are fixed permanently in place. Either remove the radiator or tuck enough paper behind it to leave a "fully papered" look. Cut a slit to allow for the wall brackets supporting the radiator, and push the strips down behind. If the paper is visible below the radiator, butt join the strips at the base of the wall and trim carefully along the top of the skirting board.

Fault-finding

Symptom	Cause	Cure
Bubbles below the surface	Failure to brush out well.	If paste is wet, peel back the paper and rebrush. If dry, cut a cross through the bubble with a sharp knife and paste down flaps.
Failure to adhere	A damp wall, an unsized porous wall, the wrong paste, pasting too sparsely, insufficient soaking time.	Strip off paper and hang new material on a suitably prepared surface.
Loose edges	Insufficient paste or brushing.	Apply more paste and smooth edges with a brush or seam roller.
Pattern mis-matching	Stretching caused by differing soaking times or allowing lower half of roll to drop suddenly. Over-vigorous brushing.	Rehang, aligning design at eye level.
Open joints	Stretching then shrinkage caused by over-vigorous brushing.	Hang new length immediately if possible; re-paper if necessary.
Tears	Carelessness with thin paper.	Try to smooth down the torn edge to make an invisible join or hang a new length.
Bumpy surface	Poor preparation.	Strip off paper, smooth wall or hang lining paper.

Textured wallcoverings

Texture in furnishing fabrics influences the atmosphere of a room. Shiny surfaces, such as foils, reflect light and are cool to the touch and to the eye. Lustrous finishes, such as silks and satins, are elegant and cool but soft. Heavier, matt textures, such as hessians, tweeds and linens, absorb the light and give a warmer, more muted and relaxed effect. Many materials also act as heat or sound insulators and most wear better than paper.

Wall coverings are made in a wide range of textures and are sold by the roll or by the metre. Hessians, grasscloths and paper-backed types come in 91cm widths. Silks, foils and unbacked types come in 69cm and 76cm widths. Alternatively, a suitable fabric can be bought by the metre from a store.

Preparing the wall

Thick fabrics, such as hessian, linen and grasscloth, help to disguise irregularities in a wall, but thinner materials, such as foils, tend to exaggerate them. So, with the latter, thorough preparation is even more important than with traditional wallpaper. It is best to hang lining paper and then, if the covering is semi-transparent, apply a coat of neutral emulsion before hanging.

Hanging techniques

Coverings with a paper backing are usually easier to hang than those without and can be pasted like normal wallpaper. (*See Job 17, p. 35.*) With fine materials, such as silks, it is best to paste the wall not the fabric. Great care is needed when hanging any fabric to avoid stretching or staining it, even though many coverings are now made for easy hanging and can be spot cleaned.

Silk
Luxurious and long-lasting, silk wall covering suits a sophisticated decor. The material is delicate, so take great care when handling not to stretch or crease it. To prevent adhesive or water marks staining the face of the silk, it is usually best to apply the paste to the wall, but make sure there are no lumps in the adhesive before you start, or the bumps will show through. Measure the lengths required, allow 50mm extra for trimming, and cut carefully, using a sharp knife against a straight-edge. Always double check your measurements to avoid costly mistakes. If you need to divide a length to fit around a corner, you may find it easier to rough cut with scissors before scoring through with a knife for a neat and perfectly straight edge. Smooth the silk on to the wall with a soft roller and make neat seams as for hessian.

Hessian
This resilient fabric is available with or without a paper backing and in a wide range of colours and patterns. Paper-backed hessian is pasted and hung like traditional wallpaper with a layer of adhesive on the back. With unbacked hessian, you paste the wall before hanging cut lengths. Flatten each strip into place with a roller, and take care not to pull the material or it will stretch and leave an uneven surface. Overlap successive strips and complete all the walls before trimming, in case the hessian shrinks. Trim top and bottom with a sharp knife against a wide-bladed scraper. Make neat seams by cutting through each overlap with a very sharp knife held against a steel straight-edge. Remove the offcut and press down the join.

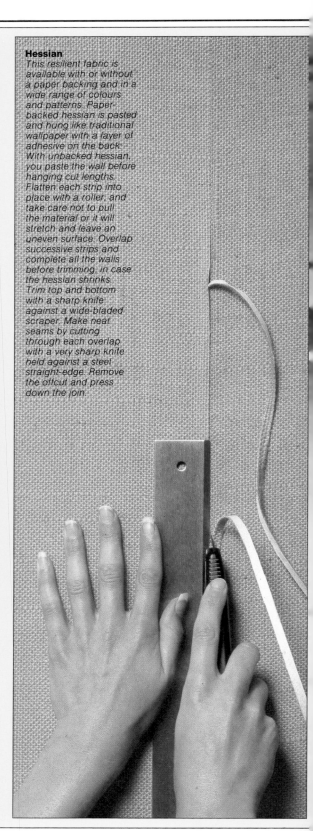

Fabric

Fabrics designed as wall coverings have a paper backing, but you can buy material off the roll from furnishing stores. Choose a colour-fast, shrink- and stretch-proof fabric and avoid ones that will attract dust – a slightly shiny finish, for example. Choosing an easily-matched pattern will make the job simpler, too. With most fabrics, it is best to paste the wall and then gently smooth the fabric into place with a paint roller. When the adhesive is dry, trim the edges with a sharp knife against a straight-edge, and make seams in the same way as for hessian.

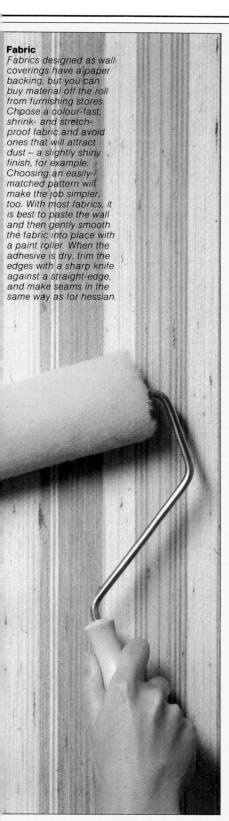

Foil

Made from metallized plastic film on a paper backing, foil provides a reflective surface. This makes it an ideal cover-ing for bathrooms, but only on walls that are perfectly smooth, as any irregularities will be exaggerated. Two types of foil are available; ordinary and ready-pasted. With the ordinary type, each length is pasted with a foam roller. The ready-pasted type is immersed in a trough of water to acti-vate the paste. Hang the foil from the top down and smooth it on to the wall with a clean sponge. Take care to match the pattern accurately and to get the design straight, since any mis-matching will show up glaringly. Trim the top and bottom edges, butt join the lengths and flatten the joins with a seam roller.

Grasscloth

Oriental in origin, this woven fabric is made from natural grasses woven with cotton and glued to a paper back-ing. To hang grasscloth, paste it in the same way as normal wallpaper, but cover the face of the pasting table first with a strip of lining paper, to protect the face of the fabric from adhesive and scratching. Do not fold the cloth or you will be left with hard crease lines. Apply lengths directly to the wall and smooth them down with a clean roller. Crease a trimming line at the wall-ceiling angle and at the skirting, using a piece of card. When the adhesive is dry, but not before, trim each length with a sharp knife against a steel straight-edge.

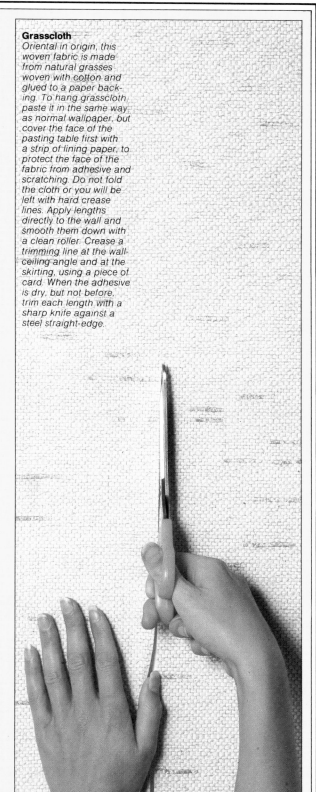

Tiling

Estimating time and quantities
Tools and equipment
Working out the tiling sequence
Fixing ceiling tiles and coving
How to apply ceramic wall
tiles ◇ Fixing mosaic, mirror
and cork tiles ◇ How to lay
ceramic floor tiles

Tiles are resistant to water, heat and most household chemicals. They are hard-wearing, easy-to-clean and demand little maintenance. Although time-consuming, the laying of tiles requires no special skill, particularly with modern adhesives and lightweight tiles. In many cases, tiles prove easier to fix than material from the roll and, since they may be bought in small quantities, result in less wastage.

Beyond the wide range of ceramics, tiles are now produced in a variety of materials. Cork, brick, mirrored glass, vinyl, polystyrene and steel tiles offer new textures and can be fitted in much the same way as ceramic. Transfer, mural and mosaic tiles have opened up new individual design possibilities, and heat-, frost-resistant and other special-purpose tiles have broadened their practical value.

Points to remember

◇ Always take time to plan the job carefully before fixing tiles. The position of the first tile determines the end result.
◇ Remember to allow for grouting joints when mapping out the tiling area.
◇ Choose adhesives and grouting to suit both the tiles and room conditions.

For more information on types of tile, see Choosing materials, pp. 122-5.

Estimating time

The time needed to tile a surface depends on the size of the area to be covered, the size of the tiles, the amount of preliminary preparation needed and, to some extent, your experience. A good result can only be achieved by careful planning, so always take the time to work out the best starting point and laying sequence. The times below give an approximate guide to the amount of time needed for each job. Remember to allow time for the adhesive to dry before grouting can be applied. The preparation time in each case will depend on the condition of the surface.

Ceiling tiles
(3m × 4m room)

Adhesive fixing (polystyrene tiles)
Preparation (washing and filling)
(1)-(1½) **hours**

Hanging tiles (incl. an average number of tiles to be cut)
(3)-(4) **hours**

Painting with emulsion (before hanging)
(1¼)-(1¾) **hours**

Stapling (fibreboard tiles)
Fixing battens
(4)-(6) **hours**

Stapling tiles (incl. an average number of tiles to be cut)
(2)-(3) **hours**

Ceiling cove

Polystyrene
(3)-(4) **hours**

Plaster
(4)-(5) **hours**

Wall tiles (2m long × 2.5m high wall)

Ceramic tiles
Planning and fixing battens
(1)-(2) **hours**

Laying tiles (incl. an average number of tiles to be cut)
(3)-(4) **hours**

Grouting
(½) **hour**

Finishing (beading, filling or edge pieces)
(1)-(1½) **hours**

Wall tiles contd

Cork tiles
Planning
(1)-(2) **hours**

Laying tiles (incl. an average number of tiles to be cut)
(1½)-(2) **hours**

Varnish (2 coats)
(1) **hour**

Mirror tiles
Planning
(2) **hour**

Laying tiles (incl. an average number to be cut)
(1) **hour**

Brick tiles
Planning
(1)-(2) **hours**

Laying (incl. an average number of tiles to be cut)
(2)-(3) **hours**

Filling joints
(2)-(3) **hours**

Floor tiles (4m × 3m room)

Setting out the floor (for all types of tile)
(1) **hour**

Laying (self-adhesive vinyl plastic tiles, incl. an average number of tiles to be cut)
(3)-(4) **hours**

Laying (ceramic tiles, incl. average number to be cut)
(8)-(10) **hours**

Grouting joints (for ceramic tiles)
(3)-(4) **hours**

Estimating quantities

The same method of calculating the number of tiles required can be used for all types of tile. First make a plan of the area to be covered and measure the length of each edge, then work out how many tile widths will fit into each. For example, a 4m × 3m room with 30cm square tiles will need 13½ tiles along the 4m wall and 10 along the 3m wall, so 13½ × 10 = 135 tiles are needed in total. For large areas with obstructions, divide the area into smaller squares, then add up a total. Since tiles are usually sold in boxes of a set amount, this may allow for wastage. If you are buying them loose, however, you should add an extra 5 per cent for accidental damage.

Tile size

10cm × 10cm
Mirror wall tiles
Ceramic wall tiles

15cm × 15cm
Mirror wall tiles
Ceramic wall tiles
Ceramic floor tiles

10cm × 20cm
Ceramic floor tiles

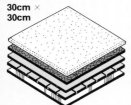

30cm × 30cm
Polystyrene ceiling tiles
Cork wall/floor tiles
Vinyl wall/floor tiles
Mosaic floor tiles
Mirror wall tiles

Calculating the number of tiles

Area to be tiled (sq m)	Number of tiles needed			
	10 × 10	15 × 15	10 × 20	30 × 30
1	100	44	50	12
2	200	87	100	23
3	300	130	150	34
4	400	174	200	45
5	500	217	250	56
6	600	260	300	67
7	700	303	350	78
8	800	347	400	89
9	900	390	450	100

Tools and equipment

For a good result, the correct tiling tools are essential; they cannot be improvised. Always ensure that you have the correct adhesive and grouting (if needed) for the type of tile and situation, and in sufficient quantities. A flexible waterproof sealant is useful to fill gaps around baths or sinks. Plastic spacer lugs are also available for ceramic wall tiles that are not already self-spacing.

Polystyrene tiles and coving
Polystyrene tiles are available in 30cm and 60cm squares and coving in 1m lengths together with special corner pieces. You will need a sharp knife and a straight-edge for cutting, an old paint brush for applying polystyrene adhesive, and a filling knife for finishing joints and the edges of coving.

Filling knife

Straight-edge   Cutting knife   Tile adhesive

Fibreboard tiles
In addition to the basic cutting tools, you will need a hammer for nailing the battens to the ceiling and a staple tacker for fixing the tiles to the battens.

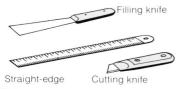

Hammer

Staple gun

Plaster coving
This is supplied in 2m lengths, which need shaping at corners if special corner pieces are not used. Use a small handsaw for cutting to size and apply plaster cove adhesive with a filling knife or trowel. Keep some glasspaper to hand for smoothing sawn edges.

Small trowel

Small handsaw

Ceramic wall and floor tiles
The essential tools for ceramic tiling include a trowel or spatula for applying adhesive to the wall or floor, and a notched plastic spreader which is drawn through the adhesive to leave a series of ridged lines on which to bed the tiles. Many types of tile cutter are available, some incorporating a measuring gauge for marking an accurate cutting line. For fitting around pipes and other awkward areas, tile clippers, pincers or a tile saw (see p. 218) should be used. A tile file is also available for smoothing rough edges. Finally, you will need a rubber grouter or sponge for filling the joints with grout, and a large sponge for wiping the tiles clean. With wall tiles, you will need a hammer, screwdriver and spirit level for fixing the support battens.

Adhesives
Always choose waterproof adhesive in damp situations, such as shower cubicles and sink splashbacks, where ceramic tiles are likely to be soaked regularly with water. There is no need to change adhesives half-way through a job, so continue with waterproof adhesive if this proves more convenient. Thin-bed adhesive, which is spread about 3mm thick, is normally used in preference to the thick-bed type, which is more difficult to use.

Grouting
Cement grout is supplied as powder to be mixed with water into a creamy paste. For colour add a powdered pigment, or use a ready-mixed coloured grout.

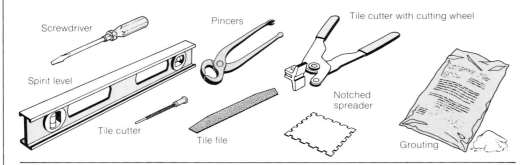

Screwdriver   Pincers   Tile cutter with cutting wheel

Spirit level

Tile cutter   Tile file   Notched spreader   Grouting

Mirror tiles
Since they are supplied with adhesive tabs, no equipment is needed beyond the basic measuring and cutting tools.

Cork wall and floor tiles
Measuring, marking and cutting tools are required in addition to a cork wall- or floor-tile adhesive.

Brick tiles
These tiles are difficult to cut so use an electric grinder, a circular power saw fitted with a masonry disc, or a tungsten-carbide rod saw fitted in a hacksaw frame. Use brick tile adhesive; and for pointing the joints, a dry mortar mix or a pointing compound and a pointing trowel.

Vinyl and plastic
You will need stringlines for marking out the floor, and a sharp knife or scissors and a straight-edge for cutting the tiles. Use vinyl flooring adhesive if the tiles are not self-adhesive. As with cork floor tiles, no grouting is needed, since the tiles butt up closely against each other.

32

Preparing the surface

All surfaces must be sound, level and dry before tiling begins. Strip off any wall or floor covering material and flaking paint. Rub down sound gloss to take off the shine and key the surface for tile adhesive. If a layer of old ceramic tiles is flat, firmly fixed and well keyed, new ceramic tiles can be applied on top.

Stripping off old tiles
If you choose to remove existing ceramic tiles, use a bolster chisel and club hammer or a small kango hammer with a chasing tool – all usually obtainable from a plant-hire shop, if you don't want to buy.

If necessary reline the surface – plaster or plasterboard on walls and ceilings and chipboard or plywood on floors.

Testing for a flat surface
It is difficult to align tiles unless the wall or floor is perfectly flat. Hold a long, flat piece of wood against the surface vertically, horizontally and diagonally to test for "see-sawing".

Tiles offer countless opportunities for individual style and pattern, since they are laid individually and come in a vast array of colours, shapes, textures and patterns. However, it is important not to 'overdo' it. The best effects are usually created with the clever combination of plain or textured tiles in one or two colours. In most cases, patterned tiles should be restricted to a single wall in an otherwise plain-tiled room, or interspersed individually or in rows among complementary plain tiles. Murals can be effective if the style and scale are well chosen.

33

Marking out a centre point on ceilings and floors

A well-planned room will have equal-sized tiles at edges and corners, to give the area a symmetrical look. To achieve this effect, you should start in the centre of the area to be tiled. If you simply begin from a corner, you may end up with whole tiles one side and narrow slivers the other. So the first task is to find the centre of each side of the square or rectangle to be tiled, then snap a chalked stringline between both pairs of sides, to form a cross. Where the two lines intersect is the central starting point. (*For a starting point on walls, see Job 40, p. 50.*)

Dealing with crooked areas
If the work area is an irregular shape, it is usually better to line up the first row of tiles parallel with the wall opposite the main door. Snap a chalked stringline parallel with this wall, then, using a compass to scribe arcs, snap a second at right angles to the first. Finally, snap a third at right angles to the second, in the centre of the room. This cross gives the position of the first tile.

Where to place the first tile
Once the centre point has been marked, the first tile may be laid in one of four positions (below). Before applying adhesive, plan out two rows of tiles at right angles to each other. If you are left with less than a half-tile gap at the edge, reposition the first tile at the centre point, using one of the other options, and try again. When the correct position is established, restrike the stringlines before starting to tile, to clarify the guide lines.

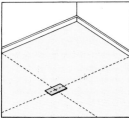

Centred on the cross

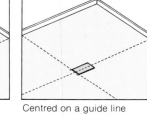

Centred on a guide line

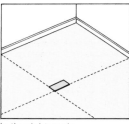

In the right angle

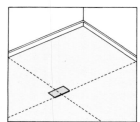

Centred on the other line

34

Working out the tiling sequence

It is best to tackle an area by dividing the job up into four segments sketched out by the chalklines. Fix the tiles diagonally across the square, to ensure that an equal number of cut tiles of the same size will be needed at each border. Work outwards in both directions from the first tile, to form a right angle and fill in the gaps as you go. If, however, the area is irregular, you may need to use a piece of wood to mark off the tile widths (*see Job 40, p. 50*).

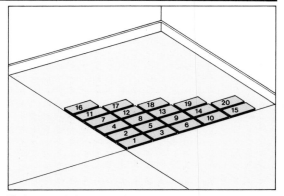

Work outwards in squares from the centre point

Decorative effects with tiling

Soft and sophisticated hallways

Cool to the touch, but warm to the eye, quarry tiles (top left) complement the soft neutral colours of an entrance hall and the natural pine finish of a kitchen, giving a warm continuity to the entire area. Traditional quarry and brick tiles in earth colours look particularly apt in country-style kitchens and patios. Stark black and white vinyl tiles (left), can look important, especially if laid diagonally. A bold, black and white floor, however, needs to be offset by low-key walls.

Increasing the space

An all-over mosaic design (above) taken over the floor, the walls and the side of the bath adds a touch of class to a simple bathroom, and gives a feeling of space. The muted effect helps to offset the white of the bath and basin and allows changeable accessories to create a splash of colour. In a small room, like a bathroom, use a single background colour, to avoid dividing the room into disparate blocks of colour. With patterned mosaic tiles, choose small designs for a small room.

Reducing the space

Warm, advancing colours help to make a large, airy bathroom feel more cosy (left). The cherry floor colour taken a short way up the walls helps to reduce the height of the room; and blue tiles interspersed in the tiled area help to break up the spread of colour and soften the monochrome effect. If a large expanse of single-coloured tiling is to be used, coloured grouting can relieve the effect and complement or contrast the basic colour.

35

Fixing polystyrene ceiling tiles

These tiles can be fixed to any structurally sound ceiling, provided the surface is clean, dry and stripped of paper or flaking paint. They are suitable for any room, but are ideal in kitchens and bathrooms, where condensation is likely. Since they provide good insulation, they also form a good lining to a ceiling without access from above. The normal starting point is in the centre of the ceiling, so find the midpoints of opposite walls and snap a chalked stringline in both directions (see Job 33, p. 46). The position of a fluorescent light or the shape of the room, however, may mean that this point has to be shifted to even up the cut tiles at the edges.

Gluing the tiles

Spread polystyrene adhesive all over the back of the first tile, then fix it so that its corner aligns with the crossing chalklines. Lay the remaining tiles by butting up their edges to adjacent tiles, and work progressively from the centre to the perimeter of the room. The tiles are lightweight and will stick firmly to the ceiling in seconds.

Overpainting tiles

Polystyrene tiles can be painted with emulsion if you want a coloured ceiling. They are awkward to paint, because of their texture and deep V-joints, so consider painting them a couple of days before fitting them to the ceiling. Remember, however, that you should never paint the tiles with gloss paint; it constitutes a fire risk.

Securing tiles
*Spread mixed adhesive on the back of the tile, **1**, making sure that the edges are also well covered. Then use a hardboard square, cut slightly larger than the tile, to press it carefully into position, **2**. This will prevent finger pressure leaving small dents in the surface of the tile.*

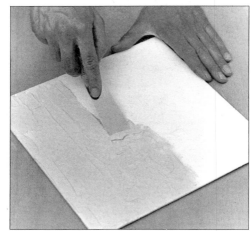

1 Apply adhesive to the back of the tile

2 Use hardboard to push the tile into place

36

Fixing fibreboard ceiling tiles

If a ceiling is in poor condition, though structurally sound, a new ceiling must be created with plasterboard, before polystyrene tiles can be fixed. Alternatively, tongued and grooved fibreboard tiles can be stapled directly on to 75mm × 25mm battens, nailed at right angles to the joists. Fix the battens at 30cm or 60cm intervals, so that the tile edges can be stapled through the flange of the groove into the batten. The tongue of the next tile then slides into the groove of the first and so on over the entire ceiling.

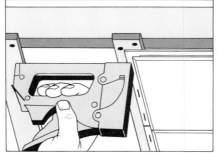

Staple through the tile flange into the batten

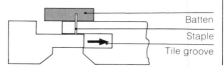

Batten
Staple
Tile groove

37

Cutting polystyrene tiles

On most ceilings, a number of tiles will need to be cut to fit the edges. For straightforward edge tiles, place the tile to be cut exactly over the last full tile in the row. Then put a marker tile on top and jam it hard up against the wall. Using a pencil or ballpoint pen, trace its opposite edge on the tile to be cut; this will form the cutting line. Lay the tile to be cut on a piece of wood and score along the line with a sharp knife. The cut tile should then fit perfectly into the gap. Extreme accuracy is less crucial where polystyrene cove is to be used to finish off the edges, since it should be wide enough to hide any marginal cutting faults (see Job 38, p. 49). When cutting around an awkward shape, such as a ceiling rose, make a cardboard template and transfer its shape to the tile and cut with a sharp knife.

Cutting border tiles
*Place the tile to be cut exactly over the last full tile in the row. Hold a marker tile on top and push it against the wall. Trace off its opposite edge. **1**. then cut the tile along the line with a sharp knife, **2**.*

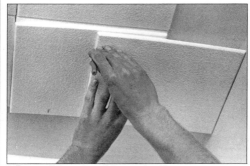

1 Trace off the edge of the marker tile

2 Cut the border tile with a sharp knife

38

Fixing polystyrene and cotton-fibre ceiling cove

Ceiling cove, fixed to the angle between the wall and the ceiling, will complement a tiled ceiling. It helps to take the square-ness out of a room and lends it a finished look. Moreover, the normal seasonal movement of a house may cause cracks to form at the junction of the ceiling and the wall, usually the weakest point of the house

Working out from the corners
Polystyrene cove is supplied with ready-cut corner pieces, so lengths are simply cut to butt up against them. First clean the angle between the ceiling and wall, and remove any wallpaper or flaking paint. Snap a horizontal chalked stringline on the wall for the lower guide line and trace the top line on the ceiling by holding the length in position. Then fix a glue-backed corner piece into place, following the guide lines, 1. Apply adhesive to straight lengths and push the first carefully into position against the corner piece to form a neat butt joint, 2. Continue fixing corners then straight lengths, and use a sharp knife to cut smaller lengths to fit.

structure. These cracks, although harmless, are unsightly and can be permanently concealed beneath ceiling cove. There are three types of cove: plaster, polystyrene and cotton-fibre. Polystyrene cove is supplied in 1m lengths, with special corner pieces for both external and internal corners.

Preparing the work area
Start by ensuring that the area to be covered is dry, clean and free from flaking paint and wallpaper. Then snap a chalked stringline on the wall as a horizontal guide line for the base of the coving. If you need

to remove only a small strip of wallpaper from a papered wall, use a sharp knife and scrape off the paper dry. Do not use water, since it may loosen the remaining paper.

Securing the cove in place
Brush a purpose-made adhesive on to the back of a corner piece and stick it in position. However, if either the wall or ceiling is uneven, use a thick, buttery ceramic tile adhesive, to ensure that the cove grips firmly. Continue fixing straight pieces along the wall, butting up the edges. To cut a length to fit, use a sharp knife against a steel straight-edge.

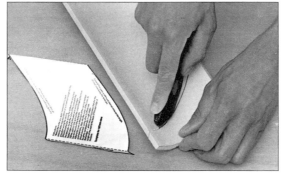

1 Use horizontal, chalked guide lines to position corner pieces

2 Straight lengths should butt up against corner pieces

39

Fixing plaster ceiling cove

Prepare the wall and ceiling as for polystyrene cove. Go round the room, cutting lengths to fit, and tap nails above and below each piece for temporary support. Ornate corner pieces are available; however, if these are not used, the end of the cove has to be mitred to form a neat joint at internal and external corners. For plain

Mitring corners
First snap a horizontal chalked string-line on the wall for the lower guide line, then, holding a length of coving in position, mark the ceiling guide line. Continue marking around the room. The point at which the lines intersect at corners will provide a position guide when mitring the cove. Use the template supplied with the cove to mark off a corner mitre, 1, cut it with a sharp knife and smooth off the edge with abrasive paper. Spread a thick layer of adhesive on to the coving, push it into position, 2, and tap in a support nail. Finally, fill any gaps with adhesive and wipe away the excess.

coving, a special mitre box can be obtained to ease the work, but a paper template is usually supplied with the cove. This is placed on the cove and the angle of the cut line marked out for an internal or external corner. Use a fine-tooth saw to cut the cove and a saw or sharp knife when mitring corners. Any rough edges can be smoothed off with sandpaper.

Applying adhesive
Mix up plaster-cove adhesive to a creamy consistency, layer it thickly on to the back

of the cove and press the length into place. If the adhesive does not grip firmly after a few seconds, insert some support nails as before and remove them the following day. Use any emerging excess adhesive immediately to fill gaps at the edges or between lengths and clean away the rest with a wet brush before it starts to dry. Continue to hang the cove, butting up the lengths and following your chalked guide lines. When the adhesive has set – usually after 24 hours – the cove can be painted with emulsion.

1 Trace the corner shapes with a template and cut with a knife or a saw

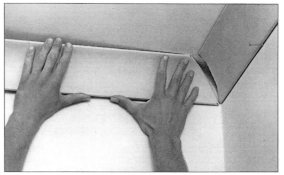

2 Slide the shaped cove into the corner

40

Marking out a wall for tiling

It is unusual to be able to tile a wall without having to cut some tiles for the edges of the work. So, to ensure equal-sized border tiles, plan out the job carefully. The simplest way is to mark out your tile widths (of, for example 10cm or 30cm) on a piece of wood, say 2m long. By holding the wood horizontally and vertically on a wall, you will quickly see how the tiles will end up from any given starting point.

Marking true horizontals and verticals
Since few rooms can claim to have perfectly true corners, window and door frames, these cannot be used as a guide for the first row of vertical tiles. Likewise, skirtings cannot be used as a horizontal base. Instead, you must establish a vertical pencil line, using a plumb line (*see Job 22, p. 38*), and set up a true horizontal, using a spirit level, by nailing a wooden batten to the foot of the wall. This will form a base for the first course of whole tiles.

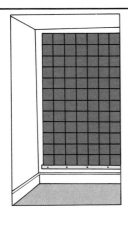

Outlining the area
Set up a true vertical and horizontal as a frame for the whole tiles. If a row of cut tiles is inevitable, these should fall along the skirting, in the space left by the batten and in the corners. Try to avoid using cut tiles for the top course of tiles, unless the ceiling is crooked. If the walls are crooked, you will have to use some cut tiles to compensate.

Basic technique

How to apply ceramic wall tiles

Having established vertical and horizontal guide lines, the outlined area can be filled with whole tiles. The tiles are applied in horizontal rows from the bottom up, working in areas of 1m². When the tiles have been in position for 24 hours, the horizontal batten can be removed and the borders filled with tiles cut to size. If plastic spacers have been used, they can also be removed at this stage and kept for re-use. After 24 hours, the joins between the tiles are grouted. Finally, the tiles are sponged clean and, when dry, are polished with a clean cloth.

Laying the first block of tiles
Beginning with the bottom left-hand corner, smooth a layer of adhesive over about 1m² of wall, with a trowel. Then draw a notched spreader horizontally over the area so that its teeth touch the surface, 1. This will create uniform ridge lines through the adhesive. Place the first tile on the batten, 2, lined up against the vertical line and press it firmly into the adhesive with a slight twist. Continue laying the tiles in horizontal strips. If the tiles are self-spacing, butt them up closely so that the lugs are touching. If not, insert plastic spacers for uniform grouting lines, 3. When the first 1m² is complete, check that the tiles are straight by holding a spirit level to the edges, 4, and make any necessary adjustments. Spread adhesive over the adjacent 1m² of wall and continue to tile as before.

1 *Spread adhesive over the first 1m²*

2 *Fix the first tile in the bottom corner*

3 *Insert plastic spacers if the tiles have no lugs*

4 *Check the tile courses with a spirit level*

41

Cutting ceramic tiles

When all the whole tiles are in position, you may need to cut tiles for the borders. The tile to be cut is offered up to the wall, measured up against the gap, and marked with a pencil for cutting. There are various tile-cutting gadgets available, some incorporating a measuring and marking gauge. A regular tile cutter has a sharp, tungsten carbide tip, which scores through the glaze so that the tile can be snapped in half along the score line. Another type of tile cutter contains a small cutting wheel to score the glaze, and jaws to hold the tile. When the handles are squeezed, the jaws close and break the tile. If the cut edge is rough, it can be smoothed down with a tile file.

Using a tile cutter
If you are using a regular tile cutter, place the tile on a flat surface, decorative side up, and score a single line through the glaze, using a try square as a guide, 1. Exert even pressure on the tile to ensure a straight cut through the glaze. Place two matchsticks under the tile, one at each end and in line with the scored line. Press downward on either side of the tile until it breaks cleanly, 2. With the clamp-like cutter, place the scored tile in the jaws and squeeze.

1 *Run the tile cutter through the glaze*

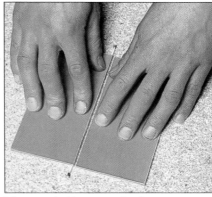

2 *Press each side to snap the tile*

42

Shaping ceramic tiles

Where a specially shaped tile is needed, make a cardboard template of the shape you want and then transfer it to the tile. To cut out an L-shape (around a switch, for example), a pattern of the shape is traced onto the tile. The tile is then scored deeply and evenly along the cutting line. To break up the glaze, criss-cross shapes are scored through the waste portion of the tile. These can then be chipped away with tile clippers or ordinary pincers. If you have a lot of awkward-shaped tiles to cut, it would be worth buying a tile saw, which cuts the tile while it is held in a vice. A tile saw will almost certainly be needed if slivers of tile (less than 10mm) have to be cut, although these should not be necessary if the job is well planned. To cut around pipes, the tile is split in two and an arc is nibbled from each half. Alternatively, use a tile saw.

Cutting an L-shape
To fit a tile round an obstacle, you may need to cut out an L-shaped tile. Either use a tile saw or make a template of the shape and trace the lines on to the tile. With a smooth motion, score deeply along the lines with a tile cutter, to pierce the glaze, 1. Then score criss-cross lines through the segment to be cut and clip it off in small pieces, 2. Trim to the deeply scored lines, then smooth the edges.

Cutting around a pipe
The easiest way to mark the position of a hole for a pipe is to make a paper template of the shape. Trace the outline on to the tile, then cut the tile in half. Chip or saw away an arc from each half, smooth the edge, then fit the tile.

1 *Score across the section to be cut*

2 *Chip away the waste section of the tile*

43

Grouting ceramic tiles

When the tiles have been in place for about 48 hours, fill the joints with grouting cement. Grouting is sold ready-mixed, but it is more economical to use powdered grout to which you add water and mix until it forms a creamy consistency. Coloured grout is also available – ready-mixed, as a dye to be added to the powder, or as a paint to be applied to the joints over old grouting.

Applying the grouting
Spread the grouting on to the surface of the tiles, and using a rubber squeegee-blade or a piece of damp sponge, 1, work it well into the cracks between the tiles. When the area is covered, draw a small rounded stick into each joint, 2, to press the grouting tightly home.

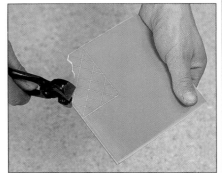

1 *Work grouting well into the gaps with a sponge or rubber squeegee-blade*

2 *Run a rounded stick between the joints for a neat finish*

44
Fixing mosaic tiles

Ceramic mosaic tiles are supplied as a sheet on a mesh backing and fixed to the wall with normal tile adhesive. Since the sheets may be as large as 33cm × 50cm, the main area of wall should be completed quickly, leaving borders and awkward shapes until last. As with normal tiles, meticulous planning and preparation are essential, and horizontal and vertical guide lines should be marked (*see Job 40, p. 50*). Having spread adhesive on the wall, press the sheets firmly into place, ensuring that any arrows on the back face the same way. To fit into corners and around obstacles, cut pieces to the required shape, and fix them to the gap. If protective paper covers the face of the tiling sheets, leave it on until they are securely fixed, then finish the job by grouting between the joints. Any small gaps may be filled with grouting.

Fitting border pieces
When the main area of the wall is covered by whole sheets, smaller pieces can be cut for the borders and to fit around obstacles. Measure the width and length of the area to be filled, then turn the sheet upside down and mark cutting lines on the back. Using a sharp knife, slice through the mesh backing, **1**, apply adhesive to the wall and fix the strip in place, **2**. Make sure the border piece is perfectly aligned with the adjacent sheet. If any small gaps remain at the edge, break off individual tiles from the sheet with a tile cutter and slot them into the space.

1 For border pieces, cut through the mesh backing

2 Align border strips with the main sheet

45
Fixing ceramic tile accessories

Tile accessories, such as towel rings, soap dishes and tooth-brush holders, are either screw-fixed or glued to the wall. Those with a ceramic base the size of one or two tiles are fixed using standard tile adhesive.

Adhesive fixing
Fix one or two tiles (the size of the accessory base) lightly in position. After 48 hours, remove the tiles, butter adhesive on the back of the accessory and push it into place. Secure it in place for 48 hours, using adhesive tape. Finally remove the tape and fill the joint around the edges with grout.

Screw fixing
To fix a screw into ceramic tiles, you will need a masonry drill bit for use in a power drill. Do not attempt to drill straight into a tile, since the bit may slide around erratically. Instead, stick adhesive tape over the hole position then drill.

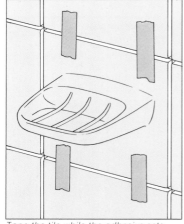

Tape the tile while the adhesive sets

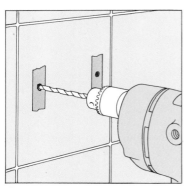

Drill a screw hole through tape to prevent the drill bit slipping

46
Finishing off

To prevent water seeping behind baths, basins and sinks, run a bead of silicone rubber sealant along the edges. This will remain flexible and so keep the gap permanently sealed despite any movement.

Smooth edging
At external corners, on a window sill, for example, a special plastic beading will form a neat, rounded finish to the edge tiles. The flat strip is bedded well down into the adhesive with the larger lip resting on the sill edge. The last course of tiles on the sill then butts up against the rounded lip. If cut tiles are inevitable on a window sill, these should lie at the back of the sill.

Over-tiling
If a wall has been half-tiled over existing tiles, the top rim needs to be smoothed off. The gap between wall and tiles can be filled with hardwood beading – either plain or L-shaped – which will need varnish.

Use sealant around baths and basins to produce a waterproof seal

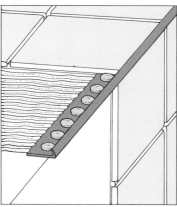

Add plastic beading to external corners for a neat finish

47
Fixing mirror tiles

Before applying these tiles, check that the surface is sound, dry and level. If it is of porous material, such as plaster or wood, seal it with a coat of oil-based paint, but do not use vinyl gloss. Leave it to dry for 72 hours. Remove any wallpaper from the area to be tiled and if the walls are cold, heat the room first, to ensure the tabs adhere firmly; newly plastered walls must be allowed to dry out. Tiles fixed to an un-even surface will produce a distorted reflection, so fix a sheet of 12mm chip-board or plywood, to ensure a flat wall (*see Job 78, p. 74*). The tiles must be per-fectly aligned to achieve a good result, so mark guide lines (*see Job 40, p. 50*). If the sticky tabs used to fix the tiles are not already attached, they will have to be bought separately. Avoid other adhesives; they may cause discoloration. Mirror tiles are cut in the same way as glass and do not need grouting.

Applying the tiles to the wall
Remove the protective paper from the adhesive pads, **1**, *and, following the guide lines, as for ceramic tiles, place the tiles in horizontal rows, from the bottom of the wall up. Try to align the tiles accurately first time and leave a narrow gap between them,* **2**.

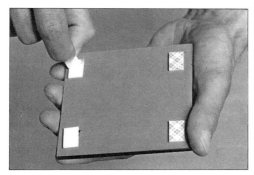

1 *Peel off the protective paper*

2 *Leave a paper-thin gap between the tiles*

48
Fixing cork wall tiles

Check that the wall is flat, smooth and dry before applying cork tiles. Fix a horizontal batten to the wall as a guide for the first row of tiles, draw a vertical guide, and proceed as for ceramic tiles (*see Basic technique, p. 50*). Using a special cork-tile adhesive, press the tiles firmly on to the wall, and butt joint them closely. If a tile has to be cut, place it on a flat surface and use a sharp knife held against a steel straight-edge. If the tiles are not pre-finished, apply a couple of coats of varnish sealer with a clean brush to leave an easy-clean surface. Allow the first coat to dry before adding the second. Where cork tiling is taken up to external corners, such as fireplaces, the exposed edges can be protected with wooden beading.

Cut cork tiles on a flat surface with a sharp knife held against a steel straight-edge

49
Fixing brick wall tiles

The secret of success with brick tiles lies in the careful planning of a realistic brick-bond pattern. The easiest way to plan the first few courses of brick is to draw them on to the wall. "Butter" the adhesive on the back of each tile, using a trowel or filling knife, and press the tile firmly on to the wall. As you lay each tile, insert spacers.

Cutting and pointing
To achieve an authentic look you will probably have to cut several bricks. Use either an electric grinder or circular power saw fitted with a masonry disc, or, though the method is slower, a tungsten-carbide rod saw fitted into a hacksaw frame.
When the tiles have been in place for 24 hours, remove the spacers and fill the joints with mortar or pointing compound. Use a small pointing trowel or a filling knife and take care not to stain the bricks. If you prefer to avoid the labour of point-ing, paint the wall with grey emulsion before fixing the brick tiles.

Arranging the tiles
Lay out several rows of tiles on the floor to work out the most realistic brick-bond pattern and pencil the pattern on the wall as a guide. Stagger the joins to imitate a brick wall, **1**, *and where available, use L-shaped corner tiles for authen-ticity. To prevent the tiles slipping and to produce uniform joints, insert small pieces of wood, about 9mm thick, between courses. Or saw up slabs of polystyrene packing material into small blocks.*

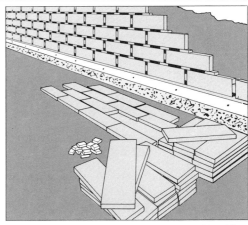

1 *Keep a sample pattern on the floor as a guide while you fix the tiles*

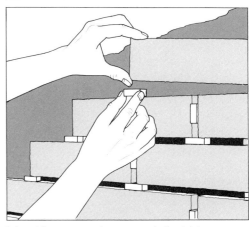

2 *Insert foam or wooden spacers in the joints*

50

Marking out a floor for tiling

When setting out and laying any type of tiled floor covering, always start in the middle of the room and work outwards to the skirtings where tiles are cut to fit. Since few rooms are square, if you begin tiling against one skirting, the tiles running along the adjacent wall will not run square. So mark the centre point (*see Job 33, p. 46*), adjusting it to leave at least half-tile widths at each skirting, then work outward, following the guide lines. (*For Preparing the surface, see Job 32, p. 46.*)

Testing the tile height

Once you have planned out the job, test the height of the tiles against the door. If thick tiles are to be used, the door may bind against the new flooring. In this case, either remove the door and trim its lower edge, or fix rising butt hinges, to allow the door to rise as it opens.

51

Laying cork floor tiles

Cork-flooring adhesive is spread over an area of about 1m² at a time and the tiles are laid in the same way as vinyl tiles. Some cork tiles are supplied ready sealed and waxed or coated with protective vinyl film and need no further treatment. Those sold without a protective, washable finish need to be sealed with wax or polyurethane before the room is used.

Use a template to trace the shape of architraves

52

Laying vinyl and plastic floor tiles

Most vinyl tiles are self-adhesive. The protective paper covering the adhesive on the backing should not be removed until the tile is ready to lay. If the tile is not self-adhesive, spread vinyl-tile adhesive over about 1m² of the floor and cover it with tiles before applying adhesive to the next area. Always lay the tiles in the correct order (*see Job 34, p. 46*) and butt up the edges closely, taking care to press down each tile firmly all over, to ensure that it is well secured in the adhesive.

Cutting tiles to fit

At borders, mark and cut the tiles, taking care to match the design of any patterns. Cut edge tiles in the same way as border ceiling tiles (*see Job 36, p. 48*). Place the tile to be cut over the last full tile in the row, then put a marking tile on top, with its edge hard up against the skirting. Using a marker, draw the opposite edge of the marking tile on the tile to be cut. Then cut along the line with scissors or a sharp knife held against a straight-edge.

For awkward shapes, such as around door architraves or pipes, make a cardboard template and transfer the shape on to the tile. When cutting a hole for a pipe, make a slit from the cut-out hole to the tile edge; it will then run from the back of the pipe to the skirting, and be barely visible.

Removing the backing from self-adhesive tiles
Leave the protective paper intact when working out the starting point and cutting tiles. Just before laying, pull off the backing and stick down the tile. Try to align the tiles correctly first time. If the tiles need to be lifted and re-laid, the adhesive may weaken.

Cutting an L-shaped tile
One side of the L-shape will need to be the same width as adjacent border tiles. So use a marker tile to scribe the outline on to the tile to be cut, 1. Then move the tile round the corner and, in the same way, scribe the outline of the gap to be filled on to the tile, 2. This line represents the second "leg" of the "L". Cut along the scribed lines, then fit the tile into place, so that it aligns accurately with neighbouring tiles, 3. Alternatively, use a template.

1 *Use a marker tile to trace the gap between the skirting and the last whole tile*

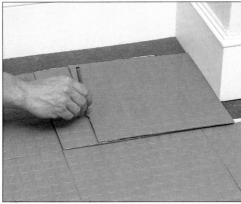

2 *Scribe the other side of the "L" on to the tile*

3 *Slide the tile into place*

How to lay ceramic floor tiles

The floor must be flat, dry, clean and stable before ceramic tiles are fitted. Timber floors should be well ventilated below and strong enough to support the tiling. The easiest way to provide a sound surface is to use either 12mm exterior-grade chipboard or 12mm plywood screwed to the floor at 30cm intervals. To ensure a good bond between the tiles and the floor, brush a primer over the whole floor and allow it to become "touch dry" before laying the tiles. (*For information on where to start, see Job 33, p. 46.*)

Applying floor adhesive
Ceramic floor-tile adhesive is supplied in large plastic buckets and should be prepared and applied according to the manufacturer's instructions. It is normal to stir the adhesive thoroughly and pour a thin layer over an area of about 1m² at a time.

Fixing and grouting
Press and twist each tile into position so that it is well bedded down. When the first m² is complete, clean away any surplus adhesive from the face of the tiles and clean out the joints, ready for grouting later. When the tiles have been in place for 24 hours, fill the joints with grouting. The tiles must not be walked on for at least 48 hours, however, so if grouting involves standing on the tiles, wait another 24 hours. It is best to tile a kitchen or bathroom in sections, so the room can be kept in use.

Fixing whole tiles
*First ensure that the floor is clean and level, and, if it is wooden, apply a coat of primer, **1**. Spread waterproof adhesive on the floor and, following your planned order of working (see Job 34, p 46), bed each tile firmly into place, **2**. Use chalked guide lines for positioning and work outward in both directions. Use spacer lugs if the tiles are not self-spacing.*

Cutting and fixing border tiles
*When all the whole tiles are in position and a narrow border remains to be covered, start cutting tiles to size. Lay the tile to be cut exactly over the last whole tile and half-cover them both with a marker tile, butted up against a spacer at the wall, **1**. Trace its other (non-wall) edge on the tile, score along the line with a cutting knife, then snap the tile with heavy-duty* tile cutters, **2**. *Comb adhesive on to the back of the cut tile, **3**, and carefully slot it into the gap, **4**. Continue cutting and fitting until no gaps remain. After 24 hours, apply grouting flush with the tiles, and when the grout has set after a couple of hours, wipe the new floor with a damp cloth. Do not walk on the freshly laid tiles for 48 hours or you may dislodge them before the adhesive has solidified.*

1 Brush primer on to a wooden sub-floor

1 Mark the cutting line for an edge tile, allowing for a spacer lug

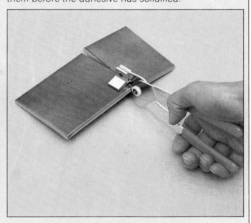

2 Use tile cutters for a clean break

2 Press each whole tile firmly into the adhesive

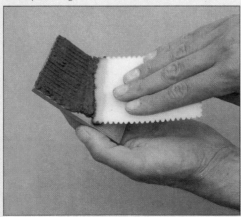

3 Apply adhesive to the back of border tiles

4 Press the half-tile into the gap

Carpeting

Estimating time and quantities
Preparing the floor ◇ Laying
underlay ◇ How to lay and
stretch carpet ◇ Laying carpet
tiles ◇ Laying stair carpet
Carpet repairs

Carpets are available in a variety of materials and are constructed in one of three ways. Woven carpets such as Axminster and Wilton are made from tufts woven in with the backing; tufted types have the tufts inserted into a pre-woven backing; and non-woven carpets are bonded, not woven, on to the backing. The best indication of quality, however, is not the construction method, but how long the carpet is expected to last (*see Identifying carpet quality, p. 57*).

Manufacturers produce carpet in roll form (broadloom), in strips (body), in large squares or rectangles (square) or as carpet tiles. The size and shape of the room will determine which type to choose. Carpet squares, for example, may have unbound edges if they are remnants from rolls and will be most suitable in a small room. Squares with bound edges, are intended for laying in the centre of a room with a large area of floor visible around the edge. Carpet tiles are easy to lay and trim, and can be taken up easily to clean.

Points to remember

◇ Be sure to choose a suitable grade carpet for the room.
◇ Cure any damp problems first.
◇ Lay stair carpet with the pile running downwards.

For more information on types of carpet, see Choosing materials, pp. 125-6.

Carpet types and widths

Broadloom carpet is the easiest type to lay in square or rectangular rooms. It is sold in roll widths ranging from 1.83m to 5.49m, but the most common widths are 2.74m, 3.66m and 4.57m. Body carpet is useful for oddly-shaped rooms and for stairs and is sold in 70cm and 91cm widths, although it can be professionally joined to form wider widths when necessary.

Underlays
All carpets need an underlay. Hessian- or paper-backed rubber is the best type for most carpets, but where there is an underfloor heating system, use a heavy felt underlay. Both are available in 137cm widths. Plastic foam underlay may be suitable in bedrooms, but it flattens easily and needs felt paper underneath to prevent the backing sticking to the floorboards. Felt paper, sold in 183cm or 91cm widths, is needed under foam-backed carpet and may also be used under rubber underlay, if there are gaps between the floorboards that are not wide enough to warrant a layer of hardboard.

Estimating time

The times shown here give an idea of the comparative lengths of time needed to lay different types of carpet in a 4m × 3m room. In addition, time should be allowed for preparing the floor. On average, a solid floor will take $\frac{1}{4}$-$\frac{1}{2}$ hour to prepare, and a timber floor, a little longer. Likewise, straight stairs may take about $\frac{1}{2}$ hour and winding stairs perhaps $\frac{3}{4}$ hour. Carpet tiles take about 3-4 hours to lay.

Hessian-backed carpet
Fixing grippers
(1)-(1½) hours

Laying underlay
(¾)-(1¼) hours

Laying and stretching carpet
(1)-(2) hours

Trimming
(2)-(3) hours

Stair carpet
Carpeting straight stairs
(3)-(4) hours

Carpeting winding stairs
(3½)-(5) hours

Foam-backed carpet
Laying foam-backed carpet
(2½)-(3½) hours

Estimating quantities for floors

Some retailers will measure and estimate free. If this service is not available or if you wish to forecast and check the supplier's estimate, mark the measurements on a plan of the room. Then choose a suitable carpet width for the minimum of waste and calculate the length required. If your room is 4.8m × 3.8m and if a 4m roll is not available, you would need a 3.66m width with a 0.3m strip (if your supplier can match the pile direction). Or, you will have to use a 4.57m width and waste a strip.

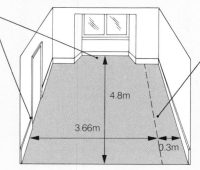

Drawing up a room plan
Sketch an outline of the room, including doors and windows. Measure the length and the width of the room, allowing for alcoves and doorways, then mark the maximum measurements on your plan. This will then act as a visual guide when you are calculating the most economic arrangement of lengths and joins.

4.8m
3.66m
0.3m

Where to position joins
If a standard carpet roll width will not fit conveniently into your room, or if you are using carpet squares, you will have to make at least one join. Where possible, run the pile to face away from the light and position seams by a wall and at right angles to the main window. Do not lay strips in a doorway.

Estimating quantities for stairs

Either make an accurate plan for the supplier, or if you choose to estimate for yourself, follow these instructions. Assume that the landing carpet will overlap the top riser. Then, measure from the top tread over each tread and riser to the foot of the stairs. Add 40mm to the total length of each tread to allow for the underlay and for tucking into the grippers. Add a further 50cm to allow the carpet to be moved up or down occasionally to even out the wear. To establish the width of your carpet, measure the width of the treads, and if the treads have one open side, allow 15mm for turning under at the edge.

Winding staircases
On winder stairs, measure along the outer edge for the longest length. Then allow 40mm for tucking in the underlay and an extra 50cm for moving the carpet, as with straight stair carpets. The pile should run down the stairs.

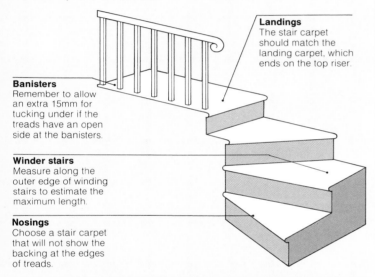

Landings
The stair carpet should match the landing carpet, which ends on the top riser.

Banisters
Remember to allow an extra 15mm for tucking under if the treads have an open side at the banisters.

Winder stairs
Measure along the outer edge of winding stairs to estimate the maximum length.

Nosings
Choose a stair carpet that will not show the backing at the edges of treads.

Identifying carpet quality

Many woven and tufted carpets are classified into various "wear factor" categories, according to their quality. In addition most manufacturers and/or retailers have their own quality-grading system, which indicates how well the carpet will wear. Always choose the grade recommended for the purpose, or a better grade, because an inferior grade will prove a false economy, since it will not stand up well to the wear.

Grade	Type of carpet	Use
1	Light domestic	Bedrooms and secondary rooms with light traffic
2	Medium domestic Light contract	Secondary rooms
3	General domestic	Lightly used living rooms
4	Heavy domestic General contract	Heavily used areas, such as living rooms, halls, stairs
5	Heavy contract	Extremely heavily used areas
L	Luxury use	Long pile, better quality than Grade 3, but not for heavy traffic

Tools and equipment

The number of tools required depends on the type of carpet being laid. Foam-backed carpet simply demands cutting and fixing equipment, and carpet tiles may only need trimming. Hessian-backed carpet, however, needs tools to ensure that it is stretched and securely attached.

Hessian-backed carpet
A knee kicker, which ensures that the carpet is stretched taut, is the most important tool and is available for hire. Its head consists of forward-facing pins which pass through the pile and grip the backing of the carpet. These are adjustable to suit the thickness of the carpet pile. At the other end is a padded plate. The head is placed on the surface of the carpet so that the pins engage in the backing; and the pad is kicked with the muscle just above the knee cap, to smooth and tension the carpet.

Fixing equipment
Carpet grippers hold the carpet taut after stretching, with an invisible fixing. The grippers, which are nailed around the perimeter of the room or on to stairs, consist of plywood strips through which a series of angled nails protrude towards the skirting. The strips, about 25mm wide and 6mm thick are usually available in 750mm, 1200mm and 1500mm lengths and can be cut to length with a saw. They come with ordinary nails for fixing to timber floors or with masonry nails for solid floors. Special angled grippers are also obtainable for stair carpets. Carpet tacks, driven down into the pile, can be used instead of grippers and are needed to tack down the edge of a carpet along an open landing. Use 19mm tacks where there is a double thickness and 25mm tacks at corners where there may be three thicknesses of carpet. Binder bars are aluminium strips, designed to give a neat and protective finish in doorways. Long lengths are available for finishing edges around stairwells, and double-sided bars can be used for the join between two carpets. Carpet tape, both self-adhesive and for use with adhesive, is used for joining carpet lengths.

Other essential tools
These include: a hammer and nail punch for fixing grippers; a trimming knife, a straight-edge and cutting board; and a flat scraper, flat bolster chisel or wedge of wood for pressing carpet edges behind grippers.

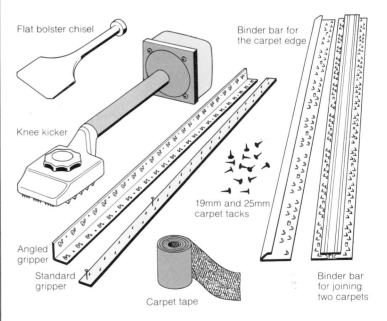

Flat bolster chisel

Binder bar for the carpet edge

Knee kicker

19mm and 25mm carpet tacks

Angled gripper

Standard gripper

Carpet tape

Binder bar for joining two carpets

Foam-backed carpet
For fixing down the edges, you will need double-sided adhesive tape or metal gripper strips with extra-large pins to penetrate the foam; also cutting tools and binder bars without pins.

Carpet tiles
In addition to cutting tools, you will need a chalkline for marking the room centre, double-sided tape for fixing at doorways and in the room centre; also binder bars.

Co-ordinating carpets

Choosing a carpet is an expensive decision, so it is tempting to "play safe" and settle for a plain carpet that will not "date" and will not need replacing with every redecoration. Nevertheless, a carpet can help to unify and bring life to a room; it can play visual tricks; it can suggest and reflect style; and it can bring interest to the flat expanse of the floor. But a carpet must be made to "work" with the decorating scheme. Its most important role is to co-ordinate with the walls, the furniture, furnishings and accessories. For good colour balance, a room should be divided into three: 60 per cent covered in a basic colour

Traditional designs
The rich colours of oriental carpets create an appropriate, dignified backcloth for a traditional setting (right). Warm reds and golds breathe life into a subdued room and bring a luxurious, cosy feel to a study. Smaller oriental carpets and rugs laid in simple rooms often reflect Islamic or Far Eastern culture and lend an ethnic touch.

Modern designs
Geometrics are cool, clean and allow you to play games with shapes. A carpet with parallel stripes (right) for example, draws the eye from wall to wall and appears to elongate the room. A diagonal stripe on a winding stair (below), creates an intriguing network of angles with the lines of the banisters, and harmonizes with the conflicting shapes.

Achieving colour balance
Traditionally, a carpet forms part of the basic colour or the second colour in a room, since it covers a large area. However, bright, accenting colours, introduced in the carpet can have an unusual and enlivening effect (right). The neutral charcoal grey background of the carpet co-ordinates with the grey furniture and furnishings, and offsets the plain white walls. This sombre base forms a perfect canvas for splashes of stimulating colour – vibrant, electric blue and pastels, bouncing between the carpet and the cushions. This focuses attention on the main living area of the room.

(usually the walls and floor), 30 per cent in a second colour (often furnishings) and 10 per cent in a third, accenting colour (accessories). A fourth, neutral colour (woodwork) forms a useful link.

53

Preparing the floor

Before laying carpet you should check that the floor is smooth, dry, clean and firm. Repairs undertaken at this stage will save taking up the carpet later.

Timber floors
For information on replacing floorboards, see Basic Technique, pp. 68-9; for laying hardboard, see Job 74, p. 72; for laying chipboard, see Job 78, p. 74.

Solid floors
Cement screed and concrete floors may be concealed beneath other surfaces, so ensure that the floor is dry and level. Undertake minor repairs where possible, but if the floor is uneven, apply screed.

Minor repairs
To ensure that the surface is level, you may need to remove the existing floor covering. Take up vinyl sheeting, for example, and scrape away flaking or crumbling sections, 1. Vacuum the floor to remove dust and fill any indentations with cement mortar or filler. A coating of diluted pva bonding agent before filling will improve adhesion, 2.

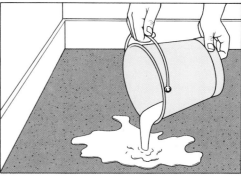

Applying screeding compound
Fill dents that are more than 6mm deep with mortar, remove grease and polish with wire wool soaked in white spirit. Apply a bonding and priming liquid to non-absorbent surfaces and
dampen absorbent surfaces. Mix the screed with water until creamy, pour it on the floor, and spread it roughly with a trowel, working towards the door. The screed sets quickly and can be covered by carpet after 24 hours.

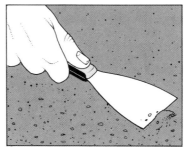

1 Scrape off lumps and flaking pieces

2 Apply a coat of pva bonding agent before filling

54

Dealing with damp

If damp is not detected and cured at an early stage, it will spread rapidly, and ruin any newly laid carpet. If you have noticed "tide marks" or if you suspect the room may be damp, test the area to see if the problem is caused by superficial condensation or rising damp. Before treatment for rising damp, ensure that the surface is clean and dust-free. (*For more information on the causes and treatment of damp and condensation, see pp. 204-7.*)

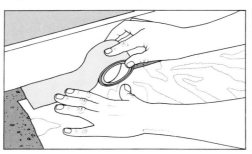

Testing for rising damp
Tape a square of polythene over the affected area of the floor, taking care to seal the edges. If moisture forms on the surface of the plastic, the
cause is condensation, and the cure is better heating and ventilation. If droplets form on the underside, you have rising damp, which must be cured.

Curing rising damp
If the surface is dusty, vacuum the floor then apply a coat of diluted pva bonding agent and fill any indentations. Remove the skirtings and
paint the floor with a damp-proof membrane. Take the membrane up the wall a short way to link with the damp course. Then replace the skirtings.

55

Fixing grippers

Before fitting underlay, secure grippers around the edges of the room with the pins angled towards the wall. Leave a gap of about 6mm between the grippers and the wall to allow the edge of the carpet to be tucked down neatly against the skirting. The strips should form a continuous line and shorter lengths can be butted together. On timber floors, grippers can be nailed into position, but on concrete, use either hardened pins or an adhesive recommended by the manufacturer. The alternative to fitting grippers is to use tacks.

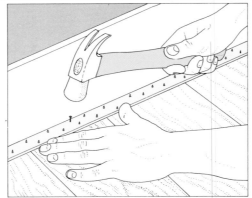

Nailing grippers
On timber floors, nail grippers around the edges of the room, using a hammer and nail punch. Position them 6mm from the skirting and angled to the wall.

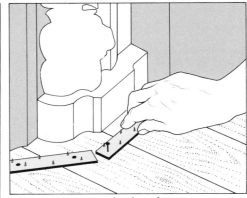

Fitting grippers around awkward areas
Around curving places, such as door architraves, fireplaces and recesses, saw a gripper into several short lengths and nail the pieces at each end.

56

Laying underlay

A good-quality underlay will improve a carpet's heat- and sound-insulating properties and will increase its life-expectancy. (*For information on underlays, see Carpet types and widths, p. 56.*) The two chief types of underlay are rubber and felt. They are fitted in slightly different ways because of their differing consistencies, and the fixing method is determined by the type of floor.

In most cases it is best to move the carpet into the room before fitting the underlay. In this way, the underlay is not disturbed when the carpet is dragged into the room. The carpet is then rolled back to allow the underlay to be fitted.

If you are laying carpet over thermoplastic tiles, always use felt instead of a rubber or plastic foam underlay.

Securing rubber underlay
Paper- or hessian-backed underlay must be laid rubber-side down. Cut the underlay roughly to size and start fixing it in a corner of the room, with the carpet half rolled back. Then fasten it just inside the gripper strip running along an adjacent wall. On a timber floor, secure the underlay with rustproof staples or tacks, at 30cm intervals, **1**. *On a solid floor, anchor it with spots of adhesive. Next roll back the carpet on to the underlay and fold back the other half. Then unroll the rest of the underlay and fix it down at the far wall. When all sides are in position, trim the underlay edges, so that they butt up against the gripper. If two pieces of underlay need to be joined, overlap the edges of both pieces. Using a steel straight-edge and a sharp knife,* **2**, *cut through both thicknesses then fix down the edges with adhesive, staples or tacks to form a neat seam.*

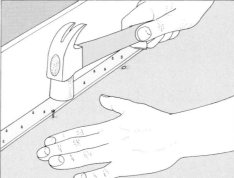

1 *Tack or staple the underlay on a timber floor*

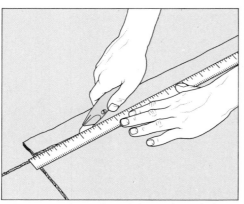

2 *To make a join, cut through the overlapped edges*

Securing felt-paper underlay
A layer of felt-paper underlay is essential under foam-backed carpet to prevent the foam backing sticking to the floor and for protection if the backing begins to disintegrate. To form the underlay, first join strips of felt paper with heavy-duty adhesive tape, **1**. *Then secure it to the floor. On a timber floor, fix down the paper with staples; on a solid floor, use adhesive,* **2**. *In either case, the underlay should stop 50mm from the skirting so that double-sided adhesive tape can be used to secure the carpet edges. If felt paper is used under rubber or plastic foam underlay to prevent dirt and dust rising from underneath the floorboards, it should stop at the grippers. There is no need to allow an extra thickness of underlay in areas of heavy wear: this would produce a bump in the carpet and result in uneven wear.*

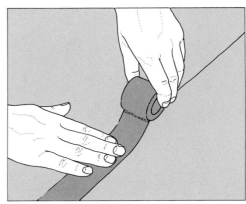

1 *Use heavy tape to join felt-paper strips*

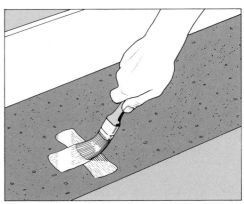

2 *On a solid floor, fix the underlay with adhesive*

Basic technique

How to lay and stretch hessian-backed carpet

When the underlay is down, the carpet can be rolled out on to the floor. It should be arranged so that the pile leans away from the light, to prevent uneven shading.

It will save trimming the carpet along all four walls, if it is positioned so that only about 10mm of material turns up against two adjoining walls. The carpet is then fixed to the grippers or tacked on one side, stretched across the room and hooked on to the rest of the grippers or tacked before trimming and finishing.

Fixing the carpet on to grippers
The first technique to master is how to secure the edge of the carpet on to the grippers. First bring the carpet to a corner and line it up so that it overlaps the grippers by 10mm on each wall. Push down the edge of the carpet with your fingers to hook its backing on to the gripper pins, 1, for about 30cm on each wall. Then rub along the gripper strip covered by carpet, with the side of a hammer or mallet, to ensure that the pins firmly engage into the carpet backing for a firm grip, 2.

Next, stretch the carpet across the room to an adjacent corner using the knee kicker and hook it on. Then complete the wall between the two corners.

Stretch the carpet across to the other corner and secure it on the gripper along the next wall. Finally, stretch and smooth the carpet right across the room, hook it into the corner and complete the last two walls, so that the surface of the carpet remains taut and wrinkle-free.

If you decide to use carpet tacks, insert temporary tacks about 15cm from the skirting. When the carpet has been stretched in all directions, fold the edge under and drive tacks through the double thickness well down into the pile, at 15cm intervals, and remove the temporary tacks.

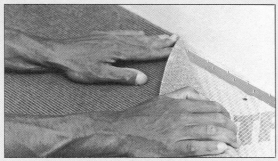

1 *Press the carpet edge on to the gripper pins*

2 *Run a mallet over the gripper to push the carpet home*

First corner
Hook the carpet on to the grippers in one corner so that the carpet is secured for 30cm along the wall each side.

Second corner
Connect the carpet on to the grippers at an adjacent corner. Then link the intervening wall. The carpet is now firmly held along the first wall.

Third corner
Stretch and smooth the carpet over to the corner immediately opposite the last and secure it on to the grippers along the wall that connects to the first corner.

Fourth corner
Stretch the carpet over to the last corner and secure it, then hook it on to the grippers on the last two walls.

Stretching the carpet
Place the head of the knee kicker on the carpet, and adjust the pins so that they engage in the backing without tearing the pile. Then kick the pad with the muscle just above your knee cap (not the knee cap itself), while smoothing the carpet with your hands.

Trimming off excess carpet
Crease back the carpet at the skirting board and mark a cutting line along the back. Then fold the carpet right back and cut long the line, with a cutting board protecting the carpet beneath. Roll back the carpet to try the fit and re-trim, if necessary.

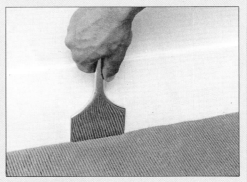

Finishing off edges
Once you have cut off excess carpet at the borders, trim it carefully against a straight-edge so that only 10mm rests against the wall. Press a paint scraper into the gully between the gripper and the wall, until the carpet is neatly tucked against the skirting.

57

Laying foam-backed carpet

Foam-backed carpet needs no stretching. You simply lay it on the floor, butt up two adjacent edges against the skirting and trim the other two edges to fit. Trim the carpet in position, or as for hessian-backed carpet (*see p. 61*). Gripper strips with extra large pins are available for foam-backed carpet, but it may prove easier to fix down the edges with double-sided adhesive tape or tacks.

Trimming foam-backed carpet
Hold a sharp trimming knife at an angle, with the handle pointing away from the wall to avoid over-trimming, and pull away the offcuts.

58

Fitting around problem areas

To allow the carpet to fit snugly in alcoves or around projections such as fireplaces, you must make vertical release cuts from the carpet edge to the floor. If the carpet has a tendency to fray, first coat the back with latex adhesive. To fit around pipes, cut a slit in the carpet from the front of the pipe to the edge of the carpet behind it. Ease the carpet around the pipe, making small release cuts where necessary, then trim to fit the wall. It will make the job easier if you cut off excess carpet first (*see Basic technique, p. 61*).

Door architraves
Make a series of release cuts in the carpet until it lies flat. Then trim the "tongues" as accurately as possible – with or without a template – until 10mm rests against the architrave. Push the carpet neatly behind the grippers.

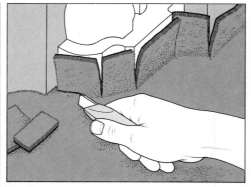

Fireplaces
Allow an overlap of 25mm, then make a release cut at each internal and external corner. Press down the carpet until it lies flat and trim off the excess allowing 10mm to ride up against the fireplace. Then secure the edges behind the grippers or tack them down.

59

Laying carpet tiles

The technique for planning out carpet tiles and the working sequence are the same as for floor tiles (*see Job 33 and Job 34, p. 46, and Basic technique, p. 55*). The first tile should be secured in place with double-sided adhesive tape, while subsequent tiles can be loose laid. If however, the tile manufacturer recommends securing the tiles at random intervals to prevent them moving and creating gaps, use a flooring adhesive or double-sided sticky tape. Working from the centre, butt up the tiles tightly against each other and ensure that the arrows on the tile backs point in the same direction, unless you prefer to lay them in alternate directions for a chequerboard effect. Cut border tiles on a cutting board and secure them in doorways with a carpet-tile binder bar.

60

Joining carpet pieces

If seams are unavoidable, the options are to seal the edges with 50mm wide carpet tape and latex carpet adhesive, or, if the join falls in a doorway, to use a binder bar with twin grooves (*see Tools and equipment, p. 57*).

Using binder bars
These aluminium strips have angled grippers to hold the carpet taut and a protective edge to prevent the carpet from fraying. Trim the edge of the carpet, tuck it into the binder bar and press it down flat. Then, using a piece of softwood to protect the bar, hammer down the lip to meet the carpet surface.

Using carpet tape
Brush a 25mm band of adhesive along a half-width of the tape, **1**, and along the back of a carpet edge. When the adhesive is dry, press the glued tape on to the glued carpet, leaving the other half of the tape free. Coat the remaining half-width of tape and the back of the other carpet. When the adhesive is nearly dry, join the glued surfaces, **2**, taking care to ensure a close joint without marks. On carpet squares, tape the entire border.

1 Glue a half-width of tape and one carpet edge

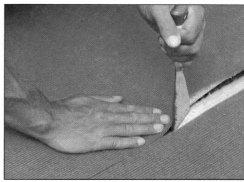

2 Hold back the pile when securing the second edge

61

Preparing the stairs

Before laying carpet, it is wise to examine the stair surface and make any minor repairs. Loose nails should be pulled out or punched below the surface, and any suspect holes treated with woodworm fluid. Any rotten treads or risers can be replaced by knocking out the glued

wedges, removing the old board and sliding in a new one. A creaking stair will be silenced by gluing and screwing a wooden block into the angle between the front of the tread and the riser below, working from below the stairs. If the stairs are boarded in, screws through the front of the tread into the riser below should cure the squeak. Finally, the stairs should be vacuumed and, to avoid taking up the carpet later, the entire staircase should be given a fresh coat of paint.

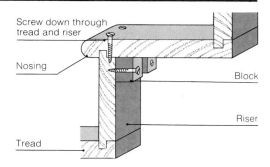

Screw down through tread and riser

Nosing

Block

Riser

Tread

62

Fitting underlay on stairs

There are two ways of fixing stair carpet: with grippers or with tacks. The method used will determine how the underlay is to be fixed. If the carpet is to be tacked, the

underlay must also be tacked.
If angled stair grippers are to be used to secure the carpet, a pad of underlay is placed over each tread and half-way down the next riser, then tacked into place. Angled grippers are then fixed on top of the underlay. If normal grippers are to be used, these are nailed directly on to the stairs in pairs, with the pins pointing into

the stair angle. The underlay butts up to the edges of the grippers, leaving a gap between each pair for tucking in the carpet. Whichever method is used, guide lines must be marked for the position of both carpet and underlay. However, if the carpet is to be fitted to the full width of the stairs, fit the grippers 20mm from the banister edge and 6mm from the wall.

Marking guide lines
On the first tread, mark with a pencil where the edges of the carpet will fall,
1, *taking care to ensure that the borders are equal. Then make a second pencil line 20mm inside each mark as a guide line for the underlay. Repeat this procedure on the bottom tread. Then suspend two stringlines from the two inner points on the top tread, pull them taut, so that they form a straight line, and secure them to the two inner points on the bottom tread. You can then use the stringlines to make pencil guide lines for the position of both the carpet and the underlay on each stair tread,* **2**.

1 *Mark the carpet position on the top tread*

2 *Use stringlines to mark the underlay position of each tread*

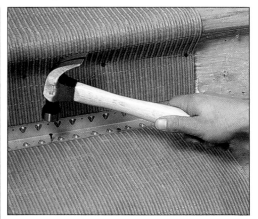

Using tacks
Position a pad of underlay over the nose of each tread, so that it covers the entire tread, and half the riser below it. Check that it is centred then, using tacks or wire
staples, secure the back edge of the underlay on to the tread, 20mm from the riser above, and fix the front edge on the face of the riser below. Insert the tacks or staples at 15cm intervals.

Using plain grippers
Fix one gripper on the back of each tread, about 16mm from the face of the riser. Fix a second on the riser below, 16mm above the next tread. This will leave a gap
between the two strips into which the carpet will be tucked. Then tack an underlay pad to the back of the tread, close to the gripper, smooth it down over the nosing, and tack it down on the riser.

Using angled grippers
Single gripper strips with two rows of angled pins are available for stairs. These are fitted into the stair angle on top of the underlay. First tack down the pads of underlay on
to the stairs, positioned as for the tack-down method (see far left). Then press the gripper down on to the underlay and nail it to both the tread and the riser on each stair.

63

Carpeting a straight staircase

Once the underlay is in position, the stair carpet can be fixed on top. The carpet *must* be securely held, or accidents may occur. The carpet can be fixed using either tacks or grippers, and this decision must be taken *before* fitting underlay. If the underlay is tacked, the carpet must also be tacked. If you have chosen to use plain grippers, the carpet is inserted into the gap between the grippers; the "teeth" or pins hold the carpet backing. If angled grippers have been fixed, the carpet is inserted between the two rows of teeth on each gripper. If the carpet is to be fitted to the full stair width, the grippers are fixed 20mm from the banister edge, to allow the cut edge to be turned and tacked. Although foam-backed carpet is not generally recommended for stairs, some types of foam-backed carpet are hard-wearing enough. Special gripper strips, without pins to tear the backing, are available, but tacks provide a firmer fixing.

Using carpet grippers
*Arrange the carpet with the pile running down the stairs and align the edges with the guide lines on the top tread, **1**. Push it firmly on to the gripper teeth and tuck the edge into the stair angle. A tack at each side will ensure that the edge does not move while you fit the carpet. Draw the carpet tightly across the tread, down over the riser below and on to the next tread. Push the carpet securely on to the gripper pins by hammering a wooden wedge or a thin, flat bolster chisel, **2**, into the gaps between gripper strips. Continue drawing the carpet over the stairs, **3**, and fixing it on to the grippers. If very thick carpet is being fitted, you may have to increase the gap slightly between the grippers. From time to time, check the alignment of the carpet, by ensuring that a row of tufts runs across the nosing in a straight line and that the uncarpeted borders are equal in width. At the bottom, turn under a 80-100mm hem of carpet and neatly tack or staple it to the bottom riser, **4**. Working from the centre out, attach it at 70mm intervals. This surplus will allow you to move up the carpet later.*

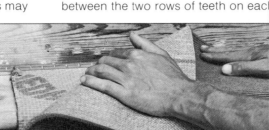
1 *Hook the carpet on the first gripper*

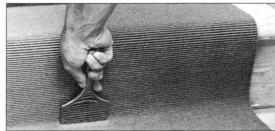
2 *Wedge the carpet firmly on the gripper pins*

3 *Smooth the material over each tread*

4 *Turn and back a hem on the bottom riser*

Using carpet tacks
*With the top edge turned under by about 80mm, align the carpet and tack it down on the top tread at 10cm intervals, **1**. The riser above will be covered by the landing carpet. Check that the carpet is correctly aligned and that the pile runs downwards, then begin fitting. Pull the carpet tightly over the first tread and down to the base of the riser below. Tack down one corner, into the base of the next tread down, stretch the carpet across the tread and tack the other corner. Insert tacks at the back of the tread, at 10cm intervals between the two holding tacks, **2**. Repeat this process of securing, stretching and tacking down the carpet, until you reach the bottom stair. Pull the carpet taut over the last tread. Fold under an 80-100mm hem of surplus carpet, so that the crease lies in the angle between the bottom riser and the floor, **3**, and fold the inner vertical edges under to give a neat single thickness. Tack or staple through both thicknesses on the bottom riser to encourage the hem to lie flat, **4**.*

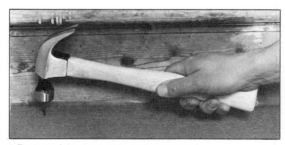
1 *Tack the folded top edge to the top tread*

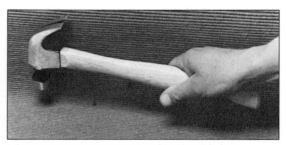
2 *Smooth the carpet over each stair and tack it down*

3 *Fold a hem at the base of the bottom riser*

4 *Tack through the double thickness*

64
Carpeting a winding staircase

The treads of corner stairs in a winding staircase are triangular, so it is best to use a separate piece of carpet for each tread with its riser. To ensure a good fit, it is wise to make a paper template of the stair shape. If grippers are to be used, two strips are fitted as for straight treads, to allow the carpet to be tucked down. But, in addition, a third is nailed along the wide, wall edge.

Ensuring a good fit
Fix two gripper strips in the stair angle and a third along the wide part of the step, 6mm from the skirting, 1. Then make a paper template for each tread and the riser below it, mark where the nosing of the tread falls on the template, 2, then lay the template on the carpet. Ensure that the noseline coincides with a row of tufts, then cut the carpet slightly oversize. Secure it on to grippers, stretching it tight, or tack it.

1 *Use a third gripper along each tread*

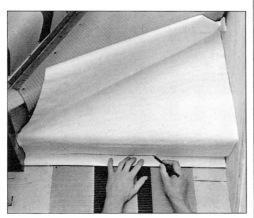

2 *Make a template and mark the nosing line*

65
Carpeting a landing

A landing carpet should be fitted in the same way as a floor carpet (*see Basic technique, p. 61*). On an open landing, the edge bordering the stairwell should be turned under and held with tacks or a binder bar. Take a flap of carpet over the first step to cover the top riser. Either fold under the edge and tack in to the base of the first riser, or hook the carpet on to the gripper on the first riser and tuck the edge into the stair angle.

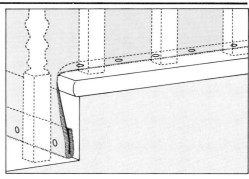

Finishing open landings
If the landing is not boxed in, fold and tack the edge at the banister. Take a flap of carpet over the first riser and secure it at the base.

66
Carpeting open-tread staircase

Since these stairs have no risers, each tread should be individually wrapped in carpet. When measuring, allow 40mm for hemming. The underlay is flapped over the tread and tacked or stapled to the underside, 50mm from the edge of the stair. The carpet is then laid on top so that the tufts line up with the nosing. The edges are then folded under by 20mm and tacked at the centre of the tread on the underside.

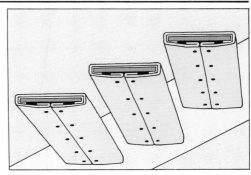

Securing the underside
Lay the carpet over the tread and tack down the folded edges under the tread, at the mid-point. Insert the fixing tacks 10cm apart.

67
Patching carpet

If the carpet has a woven (as opposed to foam) backing, the back of the damaged section must be coated with a band of latex carpet adhesive along the cutting line, to prevent fraying. When the adhesive is dry, the old patch is cut out from above. This is then used as a template for matching size, pattern and pile. The adhesive treatment is repeated before cutting the new piece, and carpet tape, fixed around the edge of the hole, on the back of the carpet, will hold the new patch in place.

Patching hessian-backed carpet
Spread a band of adhesive on the back of the carpet, around the damaged area. Place a cutting board under the carpet and cut through the backing from above.
1. Place the old piece upside down on the back of a new piece and match the pattern and pile direction. Then apply the new piece and carefully cut out around the outline of the old one. Fix 50mm wide strips of carpet tape around the edge of the hole and press the new patch down into position, 2.

1 *Cut around the damaged area from above and remove the old piece*

2 *Press the new patch on to the adhesive tape*

Wooden flooring

Estimating time and quantities ◇ Tools and equipment ◇ How to remove and re-lay floorboards ◇ Filling gaps between boards Securing loose boards ◇ Replacing skirting Laying hardboard ◇ Sanding a floor ◡ Laying chipboard ◇ Laying woodstrip flooring Laying mosaic flooring ◇ Laying parquet flooring

Wooden floors have a warmth, colour, and subtlety of texture that cannot be matched by imitations. They look rich, are hardwearing, blend with both traditional and modern furnishings, and are comparable in price with other floorcoverings.

Wooden floors of all types are best for living rooms and areas where there is little damp. Hardwood floors can be laid in kitchens and bathrooms, but there are more suitable types of floor for these rooms. Wooden floors are easy to maintain. Maintenance involves washing and occasional polishing with a wax emulsion polish. Rubbing the surface with a dry mop will improve the sheen. If the finish deteriorates, rub the floor surface in line with the grain with medium or fine wire wool soaked in white spirit to remove the old polish; then reseal the floor. Treat minor scratches with paraffin wax applied on a small cloth. You may be able to disguise large scratches using a wax repair crayon of the type used on furniture. Or you can sand the affected area and reseal it.

Points to remember

◇ Make sure the existing floorboards are level and that gaps are filled before fitting a new floor on top.
◇ Punch nails below the surface before sanding boards.
◇ If floorboards are loose for no apparent reason, check the joists underneath.
◇ Condition flooring materials by leaving them in the room where they are going to be fitted.
◇ Leave an expansion gap around the edges of woodstrip, mosaic, and parquet floors.
◇ If your room is not square, allow for the discrepancy at the edges.

For more information on types of wooden flooring, see Choosing materials, pp. 126-9.

Estimating time

The times shown here are for a floor area approximately 4m × 3m. The actual time taken will vary according to your own skill and experience. It will also depend on whether the room is exactly square (if it is not, you will have to allow extra time for dealing with irregular-shaped areas) and on how many obstructions there are. Remember that you may have to carry out floorboard repairs before laying woodstrip or wood-block flooring.

Floorboard repairs

Replacing a floorboard 4m long
 hour

Re-laying a floor
 hours

Replacing skirting
 hours

Sub-floors

Laying hardboard
 hours

Laying a chipboard floor
 hours

Woodstrip and woodblock floors

Laying a woodstrip floor using nails
 hours

Laying a woodstrip floor using glue
 hours

Laying a mosaic floor
 hours

Laying a parquet floor
5 - 7 hours

Finishing off a woodblock floor (one coat of sealer)
1 - 2 hours

Estimating quantities

Hardwood flooring comes in packs, and manufacturers usually specify the floor area that each pack will cover. They also produce ready-reckoners that enable you to calculate easily how many packs you will need for a particular room size. With both woodstrip and wood-block types there is very little waste, even in odd-shaped rooms, because you can easily split up the panels into small units to work round obstructions and fill corners.

Types of wooden floors

To create an attractive wooden floor you may be able to renovate and seal the existing floorboards if they are not too badly patched, split, or uneven. Alternatively, you can lay a hardwood floor over any dry, level sub-floor. This can be made of timber, chipboard, hardboard, or concrete. The most hard-wearing of the woods commonly used for strip or block flooring is maple. This is followed by merbau, iroko, oak, teak, and mahogany. But with reputable brands, all the timbers are selected for their hardwearing qualities. So base your choice mainly on the colour and grain pattern of the wood.

Decorative effects with sanded floorboards

Even the simplest of wooden floors can have a powerful influence on the character of a room. Floorboards that have been sanded, sealed, and polished can give a room an atmosphere of luxury, especially when combined with other polished wood surfaces and matching rugs and carpets. A natural-coloured stain can bring out the richness of colour in the wood.

But boards can also blend well with a simple decorative scheme, complementing a cottage interior. Because they wear well and are easy to clean and maintain, they are especially appropriate for living rooms, halls, passages and other areas of the home that have to stand up to heavy use.

Light, natural colours
Wooden flooring is particularly appropriate in this simple country interior. Its light colour looks good with the white painted walls and the room does not look bare with even a minimum of furniture, because there is enough visual interest in the texture of the stone and the grain of the wood. An extra layer of wood seal lends added warmth to the colour of a pale timber and enhances the pattern of the grain.

Rich, warm tones
In this children's room the natural wood colours of the door, window frame, cornice, and floor harmonize to create a warm atmosphere. A wooden floor has other advantages for a children's room – it is both hardwearing and easy to clean. A good quality and well-maintained hardwood strip floor may also prove cheaper in the long run than other floor coverings, which may lose their quality finish.

Tools and equipment

For most jobs you will need a minimum of at least one hammer and one saw. In addition, a number of other items will be required, depending on the job you are doing. As well as the tools illustrated, a bolster chisel is invaluable for levering up floorboards. For sanding wooden floorboards, you will need to hire specialized equipment (*see Sanding equipment and abrasives, p. 72*).

Saws
For cutting along the tongue before lifting floorboards you will need a circular power saw. A hand saw, designed specifically for floorboards is also available. It has a blade with a curved end to make it easier to start the cut. A circular saw with a tungsten-carbide blade should be used for cutting chipboard, which blunts normal blades quickly. A power jigsaw is useful if you want to cut across floorboards, but you can use a pad saw. You will need a drill to make starting holes before using these saws. Most need a hole about 1cm in diameter. For intricate cuts – for example, when you are laying flooring round obstructions – use a coping saw, while you can use a tenon saw for trimming by hand.

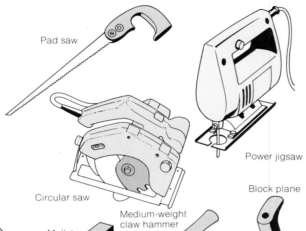

Pad saw

Power jigsaw

Circular saw

Block plane

Medium-weight claw hammer

Pincers   Chisel   Mallet

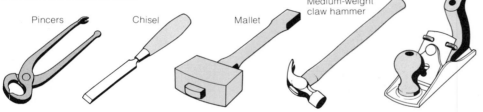

Other equipment
A pair of pincers is useful for removing old carpet tacks and nails. You will need a medium-weight or a lighter pin-type hammer for most flooring work. For hammering down nails use a nail punch. Some form of lever is needed for taking up floorboards. A bolster chisel is good for this, and you may also find a strong length of steel useful. Use a block plane when filling gaps between floorboards with thin strips of wood. A mallet and chisel can be used to chip away wood from the underside of a new floorboard, so that it matches older surrounding boards, and for jobs like taking out damaged blocks in a parquet floor.

Floorboards can have either square or tongue-and-groove edges, which are harder to lift up. Before you begin to lift

Removing square-edged boards
You can usually insert a wide bolster chisel or a strong metal lever into the gaps between the boards, 1. Use this to prise up each one, starting close to a convenient board end. Lift up the board until you can insert another chisel or lever on the opposite side, 2. Then work both levers along the board until it is free.
To help loosen the board, try working part of the way along it with a chisel and then place a strong metal lever under the floorboard, resting it on the adjacent boards, 3. When you press down on the free end it will be forced up farther along its length. Then move the lever along until you can lift the whole floorboard. If you cannot fit a bolster chisel into any of the gaps, saw across one of the joins.

1 *Insert a bolster chisel into a gap between the boards*

68

Fitting new boards

You may have to cut new boards along their length to make them fit a long, narrow gap in a floor. A bench-mounted circular saw is useful for making these long, straight cuts.

The new boards may not be exactly the same thickness as those that make up the rest of the floor. If they are slightly too thin, use pieces of wood as packing between the boards and joists. If the new boards are too thick, use a chisel to make them thinner at the joist positions.

You can fix most of the boards with 63mm cut floor brads or lost-head nails. Screw down any boards that may have to be lifted in the future.

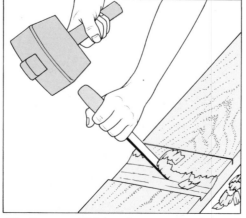

Chiselling away thick boards
Make two parallel saw cuts and chisel away the wood in between until the boards lie at the same height as the original ones.

69

Removing boards by cutting

If you want to lift only a short length of floorboard, or release a long board that is trapped under the skirting, it may be necessary to cut across the boards before levering them up. This may also be a helpful method for taking up tongue-and-groove boards. The first thing to do is to locate the joists which support the floorboards. Avoid cutting through the joists – cut alongside one of them. They will extend 25mm to 40mm on each side of the nails. Mark a cutting line to one side of a joist, cut through the board with a jigsaw, and lift it out.

Basic technique

How to remove and re-lay floorboards

either type, look for screwed-down boards. These are easy to lift and will tell you what type of boards make up your floor. Re-laying boards is straightforward. The main problem is getting them as close together as possible. To do this, use a pair of wooden wedges to press together the floorboards before nailing them down permanently.

2 *Use a second chisel or lever to prise up the board*

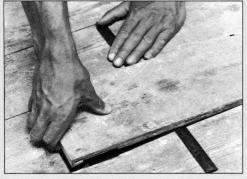

3 *With a lever under the whole board, force up the board farther along its length*

Removing tongue-and-groove boards
With tongue-and-groove floors the main difficulty is lifting the first board. When you have removed this, you can lever the others up fairly easily.
Start by cutting through the tongue by sawing along the length of the board. Use a circular saw, set to cut about 12mm deep. Retract the guard, tilt the saw forward and lower the blade. This will leave a small gap which will need to be filled later. Alternatively, you can use a floorboard saw, which has a specially curved blade, so that you can start the cut easily.

Re-laying floorboards
If there are large damaged areas or many gaps between the boards it is best to lift the whole floor and re-lay it, putting in new boards where necessary and closing up all the gaps. To ensure that you press the boards tightly together, use a pair of wedges made by cutting two pieces of board to a tapering shape. Lay four or five adjacent boards in position and nail a length of wood temporarily to the joists a short distance from the boards. Hammer the wedges into place between the boards and the fixed length of wood. This will tighten the boards. You can then nail them in place before removing the wedges and the temporary piece of wood. Repeat the process with further groups of boards until the floor is almost completed. At the end, you will probably be left with a narrow gap: cut a new floorboard to the right size to fill this space.

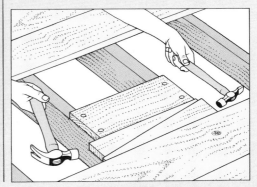

Cutting and lifting floorboards
With square-edged boards, insert a thin knife blade through the gap between the boards to help you find the joists. Drill a hole to take the saw blade at a position close to the joist edge. This hole should be about 1cm in diameter. Then draw a line along the joist edge, **1**. *Cut along the line with an electric jigsaw,* **2**, *or a hand pad saw. As you do this, tilt the top of the blade slightly towards the centre of the joist. This will create a chamfered edge, so that the board is supported when you replace it. Lift up the board, using a bolster chisel,* **3**, *as a lever.*

1 *After drilling a hole, draw a line along the joist edge*

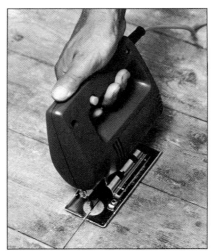

2 *Cut along the line with the blade angled towards the centre of the joist*

3 *Lift out the board, using a bolster chisel or lever*

70

Filling gaps between boards

If there are only a few gaps between the boards you can pack them using papier-mâché or wood filler. A better method is to use wood strips, planed along their length so that one side tapers. Apply pva glue to each side and tap the strip down so that it wedges into the gap. When the glue has dried, plane the wood level.

Filling with strips of wood
After you have allowed the adhesive to dry, plane each piece down to the existing floor level.

71

Dealing with gaps under skirting

It is possible to use papier-mâché or wood filler to seal gaps between boards and skirting, but they usually go on opening and closing as the room temperature varies. The best method is to nail moulding around the skirting to hide the gaps.

Fitting moulding
Press the moulding on to the floor and nail it to the skirting only, so that the floor can still move.

72

Securing loose boards

It is worth lifting loose floorboards to see if the joists beneath are also moving. Sometimes, particularly in old houses, joist ends

Fixing loose joists
If a joist has worked loose, pack the hole with pieces of slate, secured with mortar. An alternative is to use a joist hanger. This is a special galvanized steel joist support. With one type you screw the hanger firmly to the wall; another design must be built into the mortar joints in the wall.

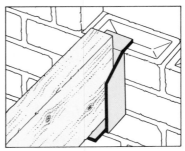

Built into the wall, a joist hanger provides firm support

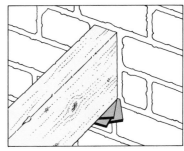

You can pack loose joints with pieces of slate and mortar

Renailing loose boards
Use 63mm cut floor brads or lost-head nails. Insert them slightly to one side of the original nail holes. Make sure that the nails go into the centre of each joist and use two nails at each joist position to ensure a secure fit. If the boards are split, or may need lifting in the future, screw them down with 50mm gauge 10 countersunk-head woodscrews.

work loose where they are built into the walls. If this has happened, pack them or support them on steel joist hangers. If the joist ends have rotted, either replace the affected joists or call in a flooring specialist to make the repairs. Secure loose boards by renailing them with 63mm cut floor brads, or by screwing them down.

73

Replacing skirting

If you need to replace skirting, you should use the method that was employed when the original boards were fitted. If the wall is

Skirting fixings
If the wall is a partition type fix the skirting with nails that pass through the plasterboard to the uprights of the frame. In older buildings the boards are often nailed to wood blocks. These may be set into the mortar joints between the bricks or simply nailed to the wall surface. With this type of construction, you should attach new blocks to the wall using screws and wallplugs. You can then nail the skirting boards to the blocks.

made of solid bricks, the skirting boards may be attached directly to the wall with masonry pins or nailed to wood blocks fixed to the wall. Pins should be long enough to penetrate the wall by 19mm. With hollow partition walls, the skirtings should be fixed with nails into the uprights that support the wall's internal frame.

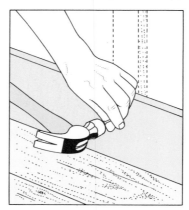

On a partition wall, nail into the uprights only

Attach wood blocks to masonry walls and nail into these

Effects with hardwood floors

Wooden floors can look effective in both traditional and modern homes. The most luxurious effects are usually obtained with hardwood floors, whether they are wood-strip or woodblock types. Narrow wood-strips can emphasize the length of a room, while woodblocks, laid in basket-weave form, provide an attractive yet unobtrusive pattern.

Another effect of this type of flooring is that it gives a room unity. Wooden floors set off a wide range of furnishings, from antique to ultra-modern, and help them look good together. An expanse of wooden flooring, for example, may echo the colour and grain in wooden furniture while it offsets brighter fabrics. A selection of ethnic or oriental rugs help to add colour, softness and comfort.

A modern interior
The large windows and empty central area of this modern room (left) would look stark and cold if it were not for the polished wood-strip floor. Its colour adds warmth, and its lines guide the eye from the furniture at one end to the rug and chair at the other, making it seem less empty. This type of floor is available in many different woods, so it is possible to get a good natural match, as here, between the colours of furniture and the floor.

A patterned effect
Parquet flooring creates a subtle pattern that does not dominate a room (above). Strongly patterned rugs can be placed on parquet without creating disharmony. The contents of this room encompass a wide variety of styles. Antique chairs, a modern table, and rugs of widely differing patterns are all included. But none of these items seems to clash because they all harmonize with the neutral wall colour and the rich wood of the parquet floor.

74
Laying hardboard

Hardboard creates the ideal sub-floor for many floor-coverings. Use standard hard-board, 3.2mm thick, or 4.8mm hardboard for very uneven floors. In kitchens and bath-rooms, use oil-tempered hardboard.

Before laying, condition the boards. Separate them and stand them on edge for 72 hours in the room where you are going to put them down. In kitchens and bathrooms they should be sprinkled with water. Fill any deep holes in the floor.

Fixing hardboard sheets
In new homes, kitchens, and bathrooms, sprinkle the rough sides with water, 1, and stack the boards flat, back to back. Leave standard board for 48 hours and tempered board for 72 hours. Cut each sheet in half to provide more expansion joints and cut some in half again. Use these pieces at the start of alternate rows, to give staggered joins, 2. Fix the boards smooth-side-down with ring-shank nails, hardboard pins, or flat staples. The fixings should be 10cm apart around the edges and 15cm apart over the rest of the board.

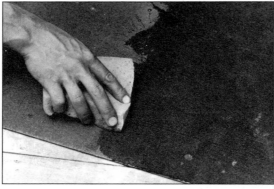

1 Sprinkle each of the 244cm × 120cm sheets with about 500ml of water to condition them

2 Stagger the joins between the hardboard sheets

Sanding equipment and abrasives

The main item you need for sanding floor-boards is an industrial drum floor sander. This will enable you to sand the main part of the floor. You will also need a smaller sander for the edges. You can hire both from tool-hire shops, which will also supply abrasives. One day's hire should give you plenty of time to prepare a large room. You will also need a dust mask, a nail punch and hammer, pincers for pulling out protruding tacks and nails, and a hand scraper for corners.

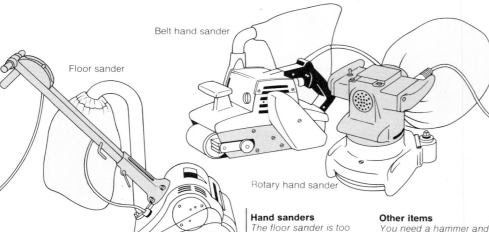

Belt hand sander

Floor sander

Rotary hand sander

Floor sander
This has a large revolving drum that takes the abrasive paper and is driven by a powerful electric motor. The machine has a vacuum action and a bag to remove most of the dust. The drum may be 20cm or 30cm wide. The smaller model is easier to handle and is suitable *for all but the largest rooms. If the floor is in reasonable condition, you should start by using medium-grade abrasive and finish with fine grade. Coarse-grade paper is available for very uneven surfaces and extra-coarse may be needed if there is a build-up of wax polish on the floor.*

Hand sanders
The floor sander is too large to go right up to the edges of the floor, so you also need a hand sanding machine. A hand belt sander is ideal, because it does not produce swirl marks on the wood surface. If you use a disc-type sander, take care not to score the surface. Both types of hand sanders should be fitted with a vacuum bag. A sanding attach-ment in an electric drill is not strong enough.

Other items
You need a hammer and nail punch and a pair of pincers for preparing the floor for sanding. A dust mask is also advisable, even with sanders that have a dust bag.

Dust mask

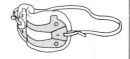

75
Preparing a floor for sanding

Make sure that all the boards are securely fixed. Look for split, damaged, or badly patched boards and replace them. (*For removing and re-laying floorboards, see Basic technique, p. 69.*) If the floor is badly damaged, it is best to lay new boards (*see Job 68, p. 68*). If there are a lot of gaps between the boards, take them up and re-lay them.

Pull out any protruding carpet tacks and nails using pincers. Then deal with the nails that fix the boards to the joists. If they protrude, they will tear the sanding belt, so drive them well below the surface using a nail punch.

Punching down the nails
Drive all the nails well down into the floorboards with a nail punch or another large nail that has had its tip filed off.

76
Sanding a floor

After you have prepared the floor, sand the main area with a large floor sander. Start with medium or coarse abrasive on the machine's drum, to strip away the surface,

before changing to a finer grade to get a smoother finish. You will not be able to get right up to the edges of the room with the large sander, so use a hand sander for these areas. With both machines, work in a direction parallel to the boards. Even a hand sander cannot get right into the corners of a room, so you will have to finish off these small areas, together with

places where there are other obstructions to the sander, using a simple hand scraper.

Although sanders have dust-collecting bags, these are not capable of picking up all the dust. So when you have finished sanding, vacuum the floor thoroughly. Then clean it carefully with a damp cloth and leave the surface to dry completely before sealing it.

Using sanding machines
Before you switch on a large belt sander, tilt it back so that the drum is raised off the floor, 1. Now switch it on and gradually lower the spinning drum on to the floor. The sander will tend to move forwards and you will have to restrain it so that it travels slowly. But be careful not to restrain it too much, or it will continue to sand the same small area of floor and start to gouge out a depression. Work the machine forwards and backwards in the same direction as the floorboards, 2. Overlap each pass by about 75mm and make sure you keep the cable out of the way by running it over your shoulder. If the floor is very uneven, make the first few passes at 45 to the boards. You can start working parallel to the boards when you switch to finer paper. Never run a floor sander at right-angles to the boards – it will not even out the bumps in the surface. When you have sanded the main floor area, tackle the edges with the hand sander, 3. Finally, finish off the corners and other confined areas with a hand scraper.

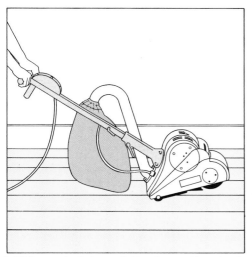
1 *Tilt the sander before switching it on and lowering it gently on to the floor surface*

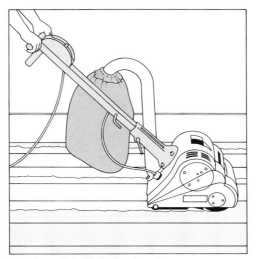
2 *Work parallel with the floorboards*

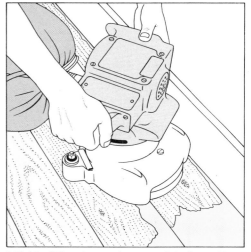
3 *Finish off the edges and corners of the floor with a smaller hand sander*

Tips for sanding
◇ Punch all nails well below the surface before you start.
◇ Use only sanders designed for floors – an electric drill with a sanding attachment is not sufficient.
◇ Let the drum sander move along the floor as soon as you lower it into position – if you do not let it move it will make an indentation in the floor.
◇ Work parallel with the floorboards, unless they are very rough.
◇ For floors in poor condition, start by sanding at 45° to the boards before sanding parallel with the boards.
◇ Do not sand at right-angles to the boards – the sander will not even out the surface and serious scratching will result.
◇ Finish off the corners with a hand scraper.

77
Sealing floorboards

When you have sanded a floor, you need to protect its surface so that it will resist wear and can be kept clean easily. To do this, use a floorboard seal. These come in two types. Polyurethane-based seals form a clear, gloss or matt coat over the wood surface. Oleo-resinous types soak into the wood and give a scratch-resistant, lustre surface. Both types usually have the effect of darkening the floor colour slightly, but if you want to change the colour of the boards more radically, you should apply a stain before sealing the floor.

When you are sure that the floor is perfectly clean and dry, apply the first coat of seal. Use a pad made from lint-free cloth, rubbing it well into the floor. As soon as the surface has dried (which will take

about 12 hours) apply another coat. Do not spread it too thickly, and brush it well out. After another 12 hours apply a third coat, and, within a further 24-hour period, perhaps a fourth. Applying the seal at these intervals will ensure that each coat bonds closely with the previous one.

Applying the seal
Rub the first coat on to the floorboards using a pad of lint-free cloth.

78

Laying chipboard

Chipboard is a cheap and hardwearing material that is ideal for flooring. It is increasingly used as an alternative to other forms of floorboards, especially in new homes.

Chipboard comes with either straight or tongue-and-groove edges and in 19mm and 22mm thicknesses. For most purposes, 19mm chipboard is adequate, but use 22mm chipboard for joists spaced farther than 45cm apart. For a smooth, strong floor, tongue-and-groove edged panels are best. These normally come in sheets measuring 244cm × 60cm.

If you use square-edged boards, nail and glue 50mm × 75mm timber between the joists so that all the edges are supported. This will cut down flexing. With tongue-and-groove chipboard there is no need for cross timbers. The edges of each panel should come halfway across the supporting joists. Fix the panels with 63mm lost-head wire nails. Leave screwed-down access panels over cables and pipes. Chipboard blunts saw blades, so if you are going to cut many panels use a circular saw with a tungsten carbide tipped blade, or a hard-point hand-saw. An electric jigsaw is best for intricate cuts.

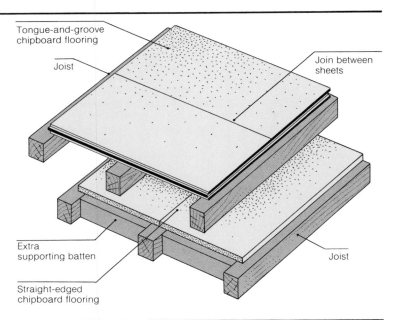

Tongue-and-groove chipboard flooring

Joist

Join between sheets

Extra supporting batten

Joist

Straight-edged chipboard flooring

79

Repairing chipboard

Chipboard floors require few repairs, but they can give problems when you have to lift a panel to gain access to cables, pipes, or joists beneath the floor. Sometimes a chipboard floor will flex as you walk across it, especially along the joins between adjacent panels. The best solution to this problem is to rest all the unsupported edges on lengths of 50mm × 75mm timber, glued and nailed into position between the joists.

Chipboard is a strong material, but it is sometimes softened and weakened as a result of damp from a water leak. The only cure for this is to replace the affected section of the floor. Only in rare cases will a whole panel of chipboard be affected, so the best method is to cut out the weakened area with a circular saw. It is then a simple matter to lever up the board. If you do need to take up a whole panel, punch down the fixing nails and prise it up. You can repair the floor by fitting a new piece of chipboard, supporting it if necessary on cross timbers placed between the joists and screwing it down with chipboard screws. You can fill gaps around a replacement panel with a layer of wood filler.

Lifting a panel
To stop the board crumbling, select the area you want to remove and make new cuts, rather than levering up an entire piece. First pencil cutting lines on the surface, 1. Run the lines alongside the nails, to avoid blunting the saw blade. Use a circular power saw and set the blade to cut 19mm deep (or 22mm with thicker board) so that you do not saw through the joists. A blade with tungsten-carbide tips is best for chipboard. Hold the saw firmly and keep your feet clear as you cut, 2. To remove a whole panel, saw round the join with adjacent panels to free the board if it has tongues and grooves. Then, using a slim nail punch, drive the fixing nails as deeply as possible below the surface and lever up the board.

Replacing a small panel
A chipboard floor that has been damaged by water will swell and crumble, and you may need to replace a small panel. After the water leak has been repaired, cut out the affected area of the chipboard (see left). If you used a circular saw for removing the board there will probably be a fairly wide saw cut round the edge of the panel. You should therefore cut the replacement piece of chipboard slightly larger than the original. Fit cross timbers between the joists so that all the edges are supported and then screw down the new small panel using 38mm chipboard screws at intervals of about 300mm round the edge, 1. If you still end up with gaps in the floor, fill them with a wood filler, 2.

1 *Mark lines for cutting alongside the nails to avoid blunting the saw*

2 *Keep a firm grip on the saw as you cut along the line*

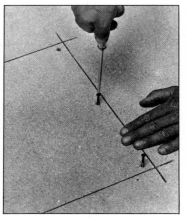

1 *Use chipboard screws to secure replacement panels*

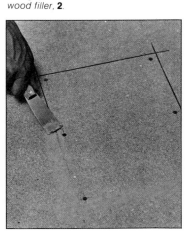

2 *If the panel is slightly too small, use wood filler in the gap*

80
Preparing a floor for woodstrip or blocks

If your existing floor is made of timber, make sure that any loose boards are secured (*see Job 72, p. 70*). If necessary, lay hardboard panels rough-side-up to give an even surface (*see Job 74, p. 72*).

If you want to insulate the floor at the same time, put foil-backed building paper over the floor before laying the hardboard.

For better insulation, and to give a sound-deadening effect, lay fibre insulation board under the hardboard. In kitchens and bathrooms, use boards impregnated with bitumen. Fix down the insulation board using the same method as for hardboard. Use ring-shank nails or screw-nails (with a gradual spiral at the point end) long enough to penetrate the floorboards

by at least 12mm. Stick the hardboard to the fibreboard with a bitumen flooring, contact, or pva adhesive. Make sure that the joints in the hardboard do not align with those in the fibreboard.

With solid floors you should also make sure that the surface is clean, smooth, and dry. If the floor is uneven, use a levelling compound, or smooth and insulate the surface using fibreboard and hardboard. Always use insulating boards impregnated with bitumen with solid floors.

81
Laying woodstrip flooring

Woodstrip flooring consists of narrow pieces of tongue-and-groove edged wood which come in random lengths. The grain colour can vary considerably, so it is a good idea to open the packs and check that the colours are consistent before you start to lay the floor.

Woodstrips often look best if laid in line with the doorway. But they can make long, narrow rooms seem wider if you lay them across the width of the room. It is best to put a few boards in position before you start, to see what looks best.

It is best to condition woodstrip flooring for at least 48 hours before laying it. Open the packs in the room where you are going to install the flooring and let the timber get acclimatized to the temperature and humidity levels of the room.

Laying woodstrip flooring involves preparing the existing floor so that it is clean, level, and dry. You can then lay insulating material to conserve heat and deaden noise. The woodstrips themselves are then attached using pins.

Underfloor heating can make woodstrip flooring shrink shortly after you have laid it. If you have this type of heating, you should consult the manufacturer of the flooring before laying the strips.

Fixing woodstrips
*If the room is square, lay the first strip parallel to the wall and 1cm away from it, to allow for expansion. The ends of the strips should also be 1cm from the walls. If the room is not square, use a stringline to position the boards. Fit the first strip with the groove facing the wall, **1**, at right angles to the floorboards. Attach it with pins 25cm apart close to the wall. Punch the pin heads down and fill them later. Drive pins obliquely through the shoulders of*

*the tongues using a nail punch. To finish the row, butt join the strips. After nailing, add the next row by pushing the groove of the new strip over the tongue of the previous strip. Hammer the strip into place, protecting it with an offcut, **2**. Nail the strip through the shoulder, **3**. Stagger the joints between strips.*

*You may have to saw the last strip along its length so that it fits. Leave an expansion gap. If the strips are sealed, finish off the surface by polishing, **4**.*

3 *Nail the strips in place using pins through the shoulder of the tongue*

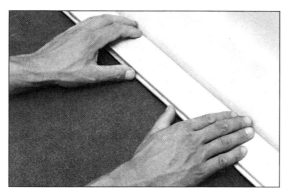

1 *Leave an expansion gap of about 1cm all the way around the room*

2 *Use an offcut to protect the strips as you hammer them into position*

4 *Finish off with an electric drill fitted with a lambswool bonnet attachment*

82
Laying mosaic flooring

Mosaic panels consist of small pieces of hard-wood shorter than those used in woodstrip flooring. They are glued to a flexible bitumen-felt backing. The blocks are usually grouped together to make up a larger panel of basket-weave pattern, although they can be separated so you can use individual blocks to fill small gaps and work round obstacles such as pipes and door architraves.

With mosaic flooring the conditioning of the blocks before laying and the preparation of the floor itself are the same as for woodstrip flooring (*see Job 80, p. 75*).

Fixing mosaic panels
Leave an expansion gap of 1cm around the edge of the floor area. Use a cork strip to help maintain the gap.

Start by fitting the whole panels. Leave gaps where you have to trim and fit smaller pieces. Stick the panels down with flooring adhesive, applied to the floor using a notched spreader, 1. Once you have laid the first row of panels, spread the adhesive in blocks of about ½ metre square and lay the next row. If the walls are not square, use a stringline to help position them.
2. Cut some panels to fit the gap. To make them less obvious, put them at the side of the room farthest from the door, or where a large piece of furniture will stand.

Tap the panels down firmly using a mallet, 3, and make sure that the edges butt tightly together.

For the small edge panels it is usually best to split up the large panels into sections to fill the gaps. To mark a panel for cutting, place it on top of the last complete panel in a row. Place another panel on top of this with its edge 1cm from the skirting. Using the opposite edge of this panel as a guide, draw a cutting line on the lower panel, *4. Cut mosaic panels with a tenon saw, a power jigsaw, or a bench-mounted circular saw or handsaw. You can also use this method for cutting parquet panels. To go round pipes and similar obstacles, separate individual sections from panels and cut these into even smaller pieces if necessary.*

1 Apply the adhesive directly to the floor using a notched spreader

2 Fit the mosaic flooring in panels that are about ½m square

3 Use a mallet to tap the panels down firmly, protecting the wood with an offcut

4 Mark the edge pieces for cutting by using the last complete panel as a guide

83
Laying parquet flooring

Parquet blocks are assembled in a basketweave pattern and look rather like mosaic blocks (*see Job 82, left*). But unlike mosaic pieces they usually have tongue-and-groove edges so that they interlock and form a very flat, good quality floor. Unlike mosaic panels, parquet does not require sanding.

Parquet flooring needs a good underlay. You can either lay it over a hardboard sub-floor or a special underlay. This consists of coarse paper impregnated with bitumen and covered with cork chips. It is laid cork-side-down over the original floor surface before the parquet panels are put down.

Parquet is usually loose laid. In other words, the panels simply "float" on the floor surface, and the interlocking tongues and grooves hold them all tightly together. Parquet flooring normally comes ready-finished, so there is no extra work to do once you have laid the blocks.

84
Repairing a parquet floor

To remove a damaged area, chisel out a central block. Once this is removed you can lift out any other affected pieces. The next stage is to scrape the floor surface clean. Then stick new matching blocks into place using flooring adhesive. The new blocks may be slightly thicker than the surrounding floor, especially if the original floor has become worn. Plane them down to the right level once the adhesive has dried.

Fixing parquet blocks

First lay a hardboard sub-floor, 1, smooth-side down (see Job 74, p. 72). Alternatively, put down cork-bitumen underlay, leaving a 1cm expansion gap around the perimeter. Cork expansion strips are available to prevent the blocks moving and to hold them tightly together. Join the small pieces together to form areas of basketweave pattern, 2. Lay these on the floor and knock together more panels, protecting them with an offcut, 3

Trim the edge blocks to fit the room in the same way as for mosaic panels. At the edges plane off the tongues to leave the blocks straight. You then slip these final sections into the gap between the main area of flooring and the wall, 4, and knock them into position. To do this you can use either a proprietary knocking-up tool, which you may be able to hire for the purpose, or a hammer, protecting the edge from its blows with a scrap of flooring. Do not forget to leave an expansion gap. To fit the last corner block, you will have to cut off the tongue and the lower part of the grooves so that it simply drops into place. This will give you a good place to start if you ever have to dismantle the floor.

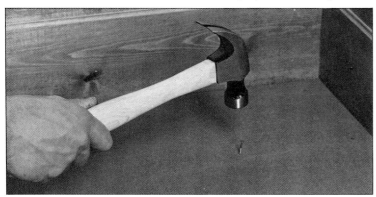

1 *Fit a hardboard sub-floor before laying parquet blocks*

2 *Join the small parquet pieces loosely together to build up large panels*

3 *Protecting them with a wooden offcut, hammer the pieces firmly together*

4 *After you have cut off the protruding tongue, drop in the final corner piece*

Chiselling out a block
To chip out a damaged parquet block use a chisel and start at the centre of the piece.

85

Finishing off a woodblock floor

To work round a door, saw horizontally through the base of the architrave at the height of the finished floor surface. Then push the flooring panels underneath. If you cannot do this, make a template and cut out the shape with a coping saw. Across the width of the doorway, finish off the edge with an aluminium binder bar or a hardwood strip that matches the wood of the floor.

Pre-sealed woodblock floors require no further treatment. Untreated types should be sanded smooth and sealed (*see Job 77, p. 73*). If there is a large area to sand, hire a floor sanding machine and use it with fine-grade abrasive paper. But usually only a light sanding is needed, and an electric belt sander, or even a smaller finishing sander, will be suitable unless the floor is very large.

Working around architraves
Cut the architrave away at the base and slide the flooring underneath.

Sheet vinyl

Estimating time and quantities
Tools and equipment ◇ How to lay
and trim ◇ Joining and patching

Sheet vinyl is a durable, easy-to-clean and attractive floor covering, particularly suited to kitchens and bathrooms. Once laid, it needs little attention, except sweeping and occasional washing and polishing. Abrasive cleaner may damage the surface, so use mild detergent to remove any spills before they stain. If a glossy vinyl fades, it can be recoated with a wipe-over liquid coating.

Unlike its predecessor, linoleum, sheet vinyl is relatively easy to lay. And although it takes longer to put down than vinyl tiles, it involves fewer joins and has the added advantage of offering a wider choice of patterns. The name vinyl derives from polyvinyl chloride (pvc), the flexible plastic from which it is made. Other materials are added, but the best-quality vinyls contain a high proportion of pvc.

Points to remember

◇ Never remove old vinyl by sanding or grinding; harmful asbestos fibres may be released into the air.
◇ Roll widths vary according to the brand, but 4m, 3m and 2m are the most popular. The supplier will cut the length you require from the roll but check your measurements first.

For more information on types of sheet vinyl, see Choosing materials, pp. 130-3.

Types of vinyl

Sheet vinyl comes in a wide range of qualities, textures, patterns and colours. The cheapest types are pressed on to a thin backing and have a clear, resilient coating. Most vinyls, however, have a cushioned backing, which makes them quieter, warmer and softer underfoot.

Lay-flat vinyl
The easiest type to put down is the "lay-flat" variety, which is stabilized with a glassfibre mesh backing to ensure that it remains flat throughout its life. This means that it needs no adhesive, except on doorway edges and seams. The reinforcement minimizes the risk of tearing and also allows the sheet to be folded without cracking, so that it can be taken home in the back of a car.

Choosing patterns
Each type of vinyl is available in a variety of colours and designs. If your room is irregular, a random pattern, such as a marble or stone effect, can help to disguise the shape. If the perimeters of the room are straight, then a pattern with distinct parallel lines, such as a tile effect, may look good.

Since vinyl is normally used in small rooms, a small pattern is usually best. This creates a feeling of space, makes pattern matching easy, and tends to conceal joins.

If the room already contains some geometric patterns – on the walls or curtains for example – any geometric design on the floor should be a similar shape and colour scheme.

Avoiding seams
The latest vinyls come in roll widths of up to 4m, and in virtually unlimited lengths, so that, by careful planning, all but the largest rooms can be covered with one sheet, thus avoiding time-consuming joins. Most vinyls, however, are available in an easy-match pattern, so that if smaller widths are used, the seams will not be too obvious.

Tools and equipment

For laying sheet vinyl, you simply need cutting, measuring and adhesive equipment and a ballpoint pen. Other useful items include a small block of wood for making trimming lines and some thick paper if you are going to make templates.

Care and storage
Remember to clean any dirty equipment after use and store rolls of vinyl on their side. Never stand unsupported rolls on end or the vinyl may distort and crack.

Cutting tools
You need a trimming knife with some curved blades for roughly trimming the vinyl and a set of heavy-duty straight blades for accurate lines. A pair of large, sharp, unserrated scissors is also useful for cutting and trimming edges, and a large scraper for pushing the vinyl into corners.

Measuring tools
A steel rule, ideally 1m long, is useful both for measuring and to provide a straight cutting edge when trimming.

Adhesive equipment
Use either vinyl flooring adhesive or double-sided adhesive tape for sticking down at doorways and along seams. Only use tape approved by a flooring manufacturer, since some types damage the vinyl in time. A plastic adhesive spreader may come with the can, but durable metal spreaders are available from tool shops for large jobs.

Extra equipment
A binder bar will make a neat finish in doorways.

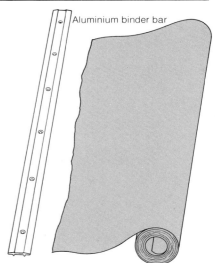
Aluminium binder bar

Thick felt paper for templates

Vinyl flooring adhesive

Strong adhesive tape

Estimating quantities

Measure across the widest part of the room, from the base of the skirting into the deepest part of door thresholds. Then measure the room length, allowing for any window bays and alcoves, and add 75mm for trimming in each direction. Draw up a room plan and decide how to lay the vinyl to look best from the main doorway into the room and without needing to butt join strips. The pattern should line up with the wall facing the door. Sheeting in the 4m widths should be suitable for most rooms, but in a small room, it may prove more economical to use the 2m width (or 3m where available) since there should be less wastage. When making your calculations, remember to allow for wastage caused by pattern matching.

A room plan
Draw up a plan of the room, including doors, windows and alcoves. Measure the maximum width and length, add 75mm on to each for trimming and note these on the plan. Then decide on the best direction to lay the vinyl, taking into account the roll widths available and the direction of the pattern. Aim to cover the main area of the room with one large piece of sheeting and try to position seams where they will be least noticeable.

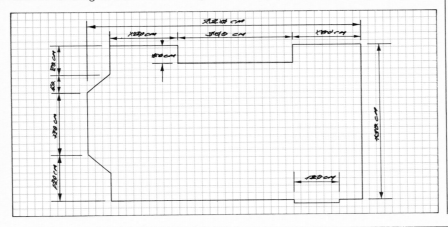

Estimating time

The most time-consuming element when laying sheet vinyl is the initial preparation of the floor. If this is minimal and there are few obstacles, a 4m × 3m room may be covered in under four hours.

Preparation
Sanding (with a floor sanding machine)

 4 hours

Laying hardboard

 4 - **5** hours

Making a template and cutting the vinyl

1 hour

Laying

 3/4 - **1 1/4** hours

Trimming

 2 - **3** hours

86
Preparing the floor and vinyl

Clear the room of all movable furniture and, to make the work easier, remove the doors. If you are fitting out a new bathroom, it may be a good idea to lay the vinyl before fitting skirtings or bathroom equipment. First screw down any loose floorboards (*see Job 72, p. 70*), and sand uneven areas (*see Job 76, p. 73*). If the floor is still distinctly coloured by wood preservative or anti-woodworm fluid and smells strongly, it should be left for several months to dry out. If this is not practicable, or if the surface is uneven or unsound, cover the floor with foil-backed building paper and tempered hardboard. (*See Job 74, p. 72*). Finally, vacuum the surface.

Conditioning the vinyl
Leaving the vinyl to adjust to room temperature allows it to "relax" so it is more supple, easier to lay and stable before laying. Lay the vinyl on its side, loosely rolled with the pattern facing outward, and leave it for 24 hours in the room where it is to be fitted. In cold weather, heat the room to a comfortable working temperature.

87
Making a room template

A template cut to the dimensions of the floor will simplify fitting, particularly in small or irregularly shaped rooms. The best material to use is thick paper felt sold as carpet underlay, which can be taped together to form the room shape. If replacement vinyl is being fitted, the old sheet can serve as the template. Outline the walls on the template, mark the position of any doorways and cut out holes to allow for awkward fittings. Lay out the template on the vinyl in a larger room or outdoors and centralize the pattern, then stick the template to the vinyl with adhesive tape. Transfer the outline of any obstacles from the template to the vinyl and cut a hole within the outline to allow for trimming. Then cut the vinyl about 50mm larger than the template.

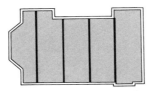
Join strips of paper felt and cut them to the outline of the room, allowing for irregular shapes

Tracing obstacles on to the template
Cut a line from the edge of the template to the back of the pedestal and rough cut a hole around it. Then, using a 25mm wooden block to trace the contour, pencil a line, 25mm larger than the object. **1**. *When transferring the shape to the vinyl, use the block to make the hole 25mm smaller than on the template,* **2**.

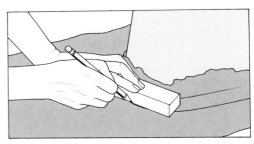
1 *Trace the outline on to the template 25mm larger than the object and make release cuts if needed*

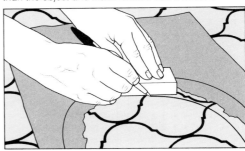
2 *On the vinyl, trace your cutting line 25mm within the template outline*

Basic technique

How to lay and trim sheet vinyl

If you have used the template method described on the previous page, lay the cut-out vinyl sheet on the floor, taking care to align the pattern with the walls. Smooth out the main area, eliminate any bubbles, and allow the surplus to rest against the walls. Fit the pre-cut holes around the fixed obstructions by making release cuts to the edge of the vinyl – if possible, follow the natural lines in the pattern to disguise the cut marks. When the sheeting is in position, first trim and fit the internal corners, then the external corners, and finally, the borders of the room. Pull back the vinyl at doorways and seams, spread a band of adhesive on the floor and smooth the vinyl back down into position.

If the room is too large to be completed with a single sheet, cut several lengths and join them (*see Job 88, opposite*).

Fitting internal corners
The corners of the room should always be fitted first. Gently push the vinyl into the corner with 50mm surplus riding up the wall. Fold it back and mark the position of the corner on the back of the material in a series of dots. Then join up the dots against a steel rule. Make a release cut down to the mark on the backing at the point of the corner, **1***. Then cut away small pieces to remove the surplus until the vinyl lies flat along one wall,* **2***, but work carefully to avoid overcutting. The vinyl will then need to be trimmed against the other wall.*

Fitting external corners
Make slanting release cuts from the edge of the vinyl to the point where it touches the floor at each protruding corner. Press the vinyl against the skirting, cut off the excess material and trim neatly to fit against one wall. Then trim the other side.

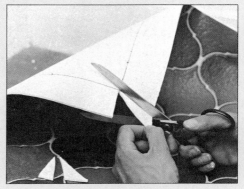

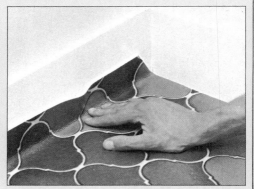

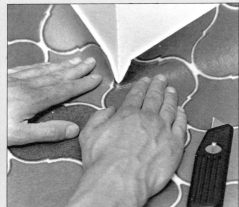

1 *Make a release cut to the point of the corner*

2 *Continue trimming the surplus until the vinyl fits against one wall*

Trimming with scissors
Having fitted the corners, the remaining edges need to be trimmed around the skirting boards. The easiest way is to use scissors. Press the vinyl into the skirting with a large scraper, fold back the surplus material and mark dots along the fold line, **1***. Pull the vinyl right back until it lays flat, join up the dots with a rule, and cut along the line with scissors,* **2***. If the vinyl buckles slightly at the wall when it is replaced, re-trim the edges until it lays flat. Always cut off less than you think necessary, or you may be left with a gap at the skirting. Take particular care with the last two edges, since there will be no surplus resting against the opposite walls.*

1 *Mark a series of dots along the fold*

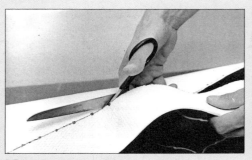

2 *Trim along the dotted line*

Trimming with a knife
The fastest way to trim the edges is to cut freehand, but this may need some practice to ensure a good fit. Press the vinyl firmly into the angle between the floor and the skirting with a broad paint scraper and cut to fit with a sharp trimming knife, held at an angle. Continue working around the room and cut off the remnant strips.

Marking trimming lines with a scriber
Another method is to use a block of wood and pencil to mark a cutting line. Pull the vinyl slightly away from the wall, keeping the line of the material straight. Lodge the block against the wall and trace the room's contours on the vinyl. Cut and fit, then repeat the sequence along the remaining walls.

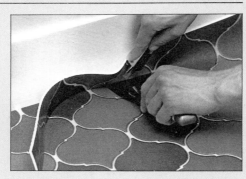

88
Joining sheets

Where more than one sheet is to be used, and joins are inevitable, add 75mm to each sheet for trimming on the overlap. You should mark a chalked guide line across the floor for the first length and try not to position seams in heavy-traffic areas.

Matching up the edges
The sheets are first fitted to the perimeter of the room, ensuring that the pattern matches and aligns exactly at the overlap. The edges are then trimmed. At this stage, if the vinyl is not the "lay-flat" variety, it can be secured to the floor with an overall coating of adhesive. Where the two sheets meet in the main area of the room, a cut is made through both sheets, along a suitable pattern line. When the offcuts are removed from above and below, the two edges are pressed down on to a band of adhesive on the floor, so that they form a neat seam. Any subsequent sheets are joined in the same way, and when the last sheet is in place, any loose edges can be secured with adhesive. Wipe surplus adhesive off the surface with a damp cloth.

Making the first join
When the first sheet is fitted in place, overlap the edge of the second sheet on top. Hold a steel straight-edge against a suitable pattern line, and, using a sharp trimming knife held vertically, cut through the double thickness of vinyl, **1**. Remove the top offcut strip, then fold back the edges of both sheets and remove the other, **2**. Spread a 20cm band of vinyl adhesive on the floor along the join line. Replace the edges and press down firmly, **3**, if necessary using a wallpaper seam roller to ensure a firm bond, **4**. Finally, wipe surplus adhesive off the surface with a damp cloth before it begins to set.

1 Overlap two sheets and cut through the double thickness

2 Remove the offcut from beneath the overlap

3 Spread a band of adhesive on the floor and press down the edges to form a seam

4 Finish with a seam roller for a firm join

89
Using binder bars

A threshold strip fastened on to the edge of vinyl in a doorway will protect the material from scuffing and will neatly cover the join between carpet and vinyl. It will also help to hide a bad join between two sheets of vinyl. Binder bars have evenly spaced, pre-drilled holes and are fixed in position with screws. They are available in aluminium, but a strip of hardwood could be used instead.

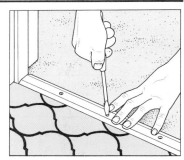
Screwing down the bar
Cut the binder bar to size, taking a little off each end to ensure the fixing points remain evenly spaced. Then screw it in the door threshold over the join between the two materials.

90
Patching tears

Any large areas of damage should be patched with an offcut. The new patch will need to be cut larger than the tear and adjusted to match the pattern. Having chosen a suitable line of pattern for the edge of the patch, you cut through both pieces of vinyl, using a sharp knife. The old piece is removed and the new patch coated with adhesive and pressed into place.

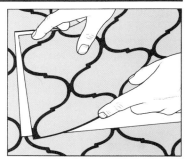
Fitting a new patch
Check the new patch for fit and pattern match, before gluing it into the gap left by the old piece. Use vinyl repair adhesive to "weld" the edges of the tear at the surface.

Panelling

Planning◇Estimating time and quantities◇Tools and equipment◇Preparing a wall for panelling◇How to put up board and sheet panelling
Panelling around corners and obstructions
Cladding ceilings

Panelling can form an attractive feature in a room. It provides a simple way of levelling an irregular wall surface and creates a permanent form of decoration that will require little attention in the future. You can also conceal insulating material and new wiring behind the panels. Panelling can be made of individual boards or of sheet material designed to imitate boards. Individual boards are easy to transport. But using sheet materials involves less work.

Two basic board types are available: tongue-and-groove, where the boards interlock, and shiplap, where each board rests over a lip on the previous one.

Sheet panelling varies greatly in cost and quality. Cheap boards often consist of a photographic reproduction of wooden panelling printed on to a thin vinyl sheet.

Points to remember

◇ Allow for overlaps when estimating quantities of panelling.
◇ Use battens or board offcuts to support the skirting.
◇ Start panelling at one corner of the room for the neatest result.
◇ Make sure all boards or sheets are exactly vertical.

For more information on types of panelling, see Choosing materials, pp. 126-9.

Planning

Apart from the panelling itself, you will probably need to attach supporting battens to the wall. These should be 50mm × 25mm and can be unplaned as they will be concealed under the panelling. If the battens are for an exterior wall, it is worth getting the timber treated with preservative so that it will not rot. If the panelling is intended to increase insulation, you should consider putting glassfibre, mineral wool, or expanded polystyrene between the boards and the wall.

For the panelling itself, a selection of colours is available. If you are choosing panelling for a small room, remember that dark panelling can produce a claustrophobic effect and make the room seem smaller and darker. Natural wood veneers normally come ready-sealed, so there is no finishing to do.

Estimating time

The figures give an estimate of the time it will take to panel a 4m × 2.3m wall with either individual boards or sheet material. The time for preparing the wall surface includes time for putting up battens. The total time for putting up the panelling will vary according to your own skill and experience. It will also depend on how many obstructions there are in the wall, and whether you have to panel around corners and into window reveals. But you can use these figures as a guide, converting them for your own wall sizes.

The other factor that will affect the time the job will take is whether you use boards or a sheet panelling material. Of course, individual boards usually take longer to put up than large sheets. But working round obstructions can be more time-consuming with sheet panelling since it is necessary to cut holes in the middle of sheets.

Ceilings usually take longer because you are working in an awkward position. The time shown here is for a ceiling 4m × 3m.

Preparing a wall
Basic preparation
④ - ⑧ hours

Fixing battens around a window
¼ - ½ hour

Putting up board panelling
Panelling a wall
⑥ - ⑧ hours

Panelling around a window
1 - 1¾ hours

Fitting panelling around a door
½ - ¾ hour

Fitting panelling around a socket
¼ - ¾ hour

Putting up sheet panelling
Panelling a wall
③ - ⑤ hours

Panelling around a window
1 - 2 hours

Fitting panelling around a door
¾ - 1 hour

Fitting panelling around a socket
¼ - 1 hour

Cladding a ceiling
⑧ - ⑫ hours

Estimating quantities

Measure the room width and height. Both tongue-and-groove and shiplap panelling are made up of individual boards that overlap (see right). So when you are using individual boards, take this into account when measuring. For vertical panelling divide the exact width of one board into the total room width. Then multiply the result by the room height. Add 10 per cent for wastage and joins.

For sheet materials you need pieces that are long enough to reach from floor to ceiling. So measure the room width to find out how many sheets you will require and allow for wastage. Most sheets measure 240cm × 120cm.

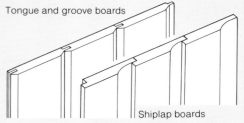

Tongue and groove boards

Shiplap boards

Tools and equipment

For sheet materials, use a circular saw with a fine blade or a cross-cut hand saw. One with eight teeth to 25mm is best. For cutting individual boards and battens, use a tenon saw. You will also need a pad saw or a power jigsaw for cutting holes. Other equipment includes claw and pin hammers, a nail punch, a drill, a steel tape measure, a spirit level, and a square. For panel adhesive, you will need a mastic gun and adhesive cartridges. For boards, panel clips are very useful.

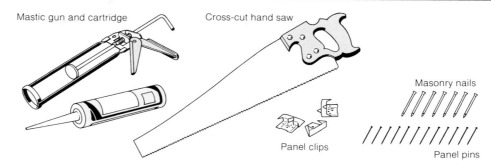

Mastic gun and cartridge

Cross-cut hand saw

Masonry nails

Panel clips

Panel pins

91

Preparing a wall for panelling

Adding panelling will hide the wall completely, so you should make sure it is well prepared and free of problems such as damp. Internal walls usually give no damp problems, but external walls must be perfectly dry. Do not worry if there is condensation on the wall.

You should also examine porous walls for damage to the pointing. Rake out and replace all loose and crumbling mortar and brickwork. Finally, treat the whole wall with a silicone water repellent. This will prevent water getting in, yet still allow the wall to "breathe". It is a good idea to fix a polythene sheet over the wall surface before attaching the battens. This will stop condensation forming.

To allow for the supporting battens, you will also need to remove the skirting board and any picture rail. If you are going to use insulation material under the panelling, this should be inserted after the battens are in position.

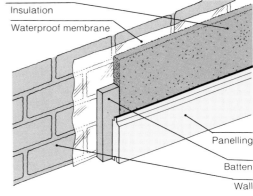

Insulation

Waterproof membrane

Panelling

Batten

Wall

Removing skirting boards
If you want to replace the skirting boards in front of your panelling, be careful not to damage them. Loosen a section of the skirting with an old chisel, and then slip the claw of a hammer under the board to lever it away. Pull out any nails in the skirting from the back – if you take them out from the front you will damage the face of the board.

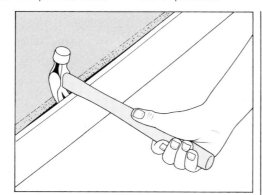

Removing picture rails
You need only take these away if they stand proud of the battens and obstruct the panelling. Make a cut in the rail close to one of the nails and break the rail away. It will be easier if you use a length of steel pushed under the rail to lever it up. By using this method you will avoid doing too much damage to the surrounding plaster.

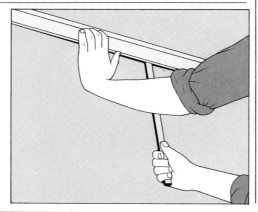

Fixing battens for vertical boards
For vertical boards, you should fix horizontal battens at intervals of approximately 40cm. Use a spirit level to get them exactly straight. Put hardboard packing pieces behind the battens if you need to level them. Secure the battens to the wall with masonry nails, or with wall plugs and screws, depending on the condition of the wall. At skirting board level fit short lengths of batten vertically, to support the skirting when you put it back in place. It is important to put these pieces at carefully set distances so that you can locate them easily under the panelling when you come to refit the skirting board.

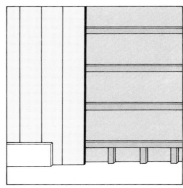

Fixing battens for horizontal boards
For horizontal panelling, the battens should be vertical and placed about the same distance apart as for vertical boards. The lowest board should go behind the skirting, but it need not go right down to the floor. If this is the case, support the skirting on short lengths of panelling attached between the battens and the skirting itself

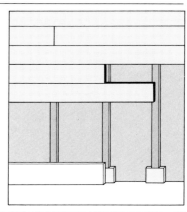

Basic technique

How to put up board panelling

At least a week before you start, take the panelling into the room where you are going to fit it. This will allow the timber's moisture content to adjust to the room. It is particularly important if there is a big difference between the storage and room conditions. If the wood has been stored outdoors and is then brought into a centrally heated room, it will shrink considerably, and if you put up the panelling too soon, unsightly gaps can open up between the boards.

There are two main ways of fixing boards. The traditional method is to drive pins through the boards into the battens. But clip systems are now available that provide invisible fixings for tongue-and-groove boards.

Fixing shiplap panelling

Position the first board in one corner of the room and make sure that it is exactly vertical. Then hammer the pins through the face of the board into the battens, just to one side of the rebated section, **1**. Sink the pins with a nail punch and take care not to let the hammer slip and bruise the wood.

Then go on to the rest of the boards. It is best to tap each board when you position it, to get it as near the previous one as possible. When you do this, protect the wood with a scrap of panelling to prevent the hammer bruising the wood. You should also check each individual board with a spirit level, to make sure that it is vertical. If you do not do this, you will repeat any error in every board. Pin each board to the battens at the same position as with the first board, **2**. The overlap will help secure the board. When you have finished, fill the nail holes with a matching stopper.

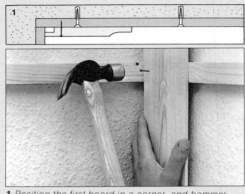

1 Position the first board in a corner, and hammer pins through its face into the batten

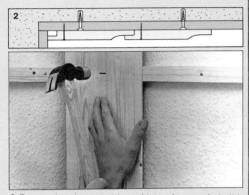

2 Tap each subsequent board into place and pin it in the same way

Fixing tongue-and-groove panelling using pins

Fit the first board with its groove pointing into a corner. Make sure the board is vertical, then pin it to each batten. Do not worry if there is a slight gap between the board and the wall – you can cover this with beading when you finish off the panelling. The pins should be about 12mm from the groove edge. Drive each pin below the surface with a nail punch. Then hammer pins through the shoulder of the tongue, angling them into the wood. The board is now held by two pins in each batten. Nailing in this way means that when you place the next board over the tongue, its groove should hide the pins.

When you add the second and subsequent boards, you only need to put one pin into each batten. This is because the interlocking tongues and grooves themselves help to secure the panelling. So for these boards you only need to hammer pins into the shoulder of the tongue, **2**. If your wood is slightly brittle, it is worth making start holes for the pins using a fine twist drill in a wheel brace. If you do split the tongues you will find it very difficult to slot it into the next groove, and will probably have to remove and replace the board.

When you have finished, go back and fill the holes made by the nail-punch in the first board, using a matching wood stopper.

Fixing tongue-and-groove panelling using clips

Different clip systems are available to fit particular board profiles. Some systems offer two types of clips – starter plates and standard clips. With systems that provide starter plates, begin panelling in one corner and, using the galvanized pins supplied, fix a starter plate to each batten. This should be level with the edge position of the first board. If the wall is not square, make sure the first board is vertical. You can conceal any slight gap with beading later. After stripping off the tongue from the first board, press the cut edge on to the starter plates, **1**. You may have to tap it into position. If so, protect the wood from damage with a piece of scrap batten held between the hammer and panel.

If you are using a system without starter clips, you should pin the tongue edge of the first board directly to the battens, hammering down the pins with a nail punch so that you can fill the holes later.

With the first board in place, you fit standard clips in the groove of this board and pin these clips to the battens so that the board is secure. Next place the tongue of the second board in the groove of the first, **2**, and press it home. Then fit another set of standard clips in the groove of the second board. You can cover the whole wall surface in this way.

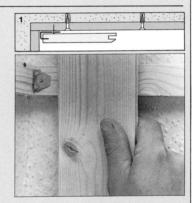

1 Fit the first board with a starter plate

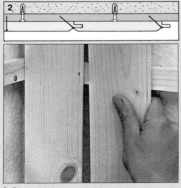

1 On the first board, insert clips 12mm from the groove edge

2 Pin all subsequent boards through the shoulder of the tongue

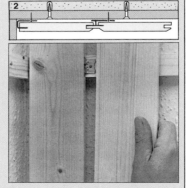

2 Fit clips into each groove and press in the next tongue

92
Fitting board panelling around corners

At an internal wall corner with tongue-and-groove boards, make a neat joint of two grooves. Tuck one tightly into the corner, and butt the next one up to it. Use clips only if they leave no gap between boards.

Work away from external corners for a neat result. If you are using clips, remove the tongues from the corner boards, secure them so that they just touch and fill the gap with beading. If you are using pins, bring two grooves together at the corner. Fill the gap with beading. With shiplap, you will get the neatest result with the squared ends in the corners.

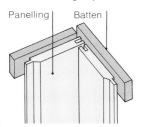

Internal angle using tongue-and-groove boards

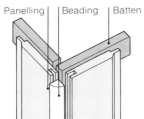

External angle using tongue-and groove boards

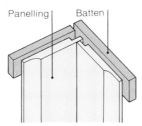

Internal angle using shiplap boards

External angle using shiplap boards

93
Fitting board panelling around obstacles

The main problems with panelling come when you have to work round obstructions such as doors, windows, and electrical fittings. Where possible, it is best to bring switches and sockets to the surface of the panelling – the most straightforward way is often to replace flush-mounted fittings with surface-mounted ones.

With windows, you can use beading to produce neat edges where the panelling meets the window reveal. With doors, you can also use beading to finish off, but you should remove the architrave and replace it over the panelling.

When you are panelling round electrical fittings you should cut a cardboard template to fit around the obstruction. Then transfer the pattern to the boards and use a pad saw to cut away the waste material. With surface-mounted switches you can then fit the panelling around the casing, but you have to raise flush-mounted units above the wall surface. If you put new wiring behind the boards, put it in conduit.

Doors
Carefully prise up the architrave that surrounds the door opening, letting the nails pull through the back so that the front is not damaged. Attach a vertical batten to the wall to support the edge of the panelling. When you have secured the panelling, choose a beading that will conceal both the batten and the join with the panelling. Then pin back the original architrave.

Windows
With windows, the main problem is turning the panelling into the reveals. This requires neat external angles (see Job 92, above). For most window reveals, it is easiest to stick the panelling to the wall, because there is no room to fit battens. Alternatively, you can stop the panelling about 6mm from the turn and finish it off with strips of beading.

Sockets and switches
After cutting the panelling to fit around the switch or socket, surround the unit with short pieces of batten, putting them as close to the fitting as possible and securing them with panel adhesive. If the unit is surface-mounted, you can then pin the panelling in place. With flush-mounted sockets and switches, raise the boxes behind, so that the top edges are flush with the panel surface.

94
Joining boards

If necessary, short lengths of board can be butt-joined, provided that the join is positioned over a batten. For a neat finish, cut the ends of butt-joined boards to a perfect right angle. Mark them with a set square, then use a mitre box for cutting a true angle.

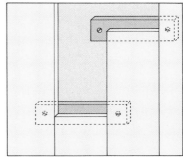

Butt joining boards
Where there is no batten on the wall, insert extra, short lengths at the join.

95
Finishing off board panelling

Cut your final board so that a gap of about 6mm is left between it and the wall. This is to allow for expansion. If you do not leave a gap, the panelling may bow if it expands. You can hide the gap later by fitting a length of beading or a piece of decorative moulding.

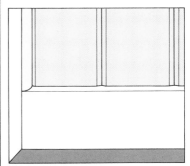

Using beading or moulding
These will hide the expansion gap and conceal any irregularity in the wall.

Basic technique

How to put up sheet panelling

For sheet panelling you need horizontal battens with additional vertical battens placed so that their centre lines correspond to the edges of the sheets. If, however, you are fitting this type of panelling on to a partition wall, the simplest method is to remove any wallpaper and stick the sheets directly on to the wall. If you prefer to use battens, you should find the timber uprights in the wall and nail the battens to these. The plasterboard itself cannot give adequate support for the battens.

If the walls are square, you can stick the panels on to them using panel adhesive and a mastic gun. Alternatively, fix horizontal battens at 40cm intervals. You will also need one vertical batten for each joint in the panelling. It is difficult to butt the sheets perfectly together. A good solution is to make a feature of the joint, either by hiding it with beading, or by leaving a slight decorative gap. If you do this, allow for the width of the gap when putting up the vertical battens.

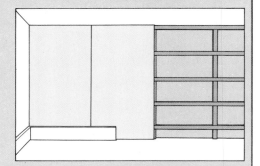

Battening for sheet panelling
For the large sheets that make up this type of panelling, you need horizontal and vertical battens.

Fixing sheet panelling using pins
When you have removed the skirting, start panelling from one corner. Make sure that your first sheet is vertical. If the walls are not square, leave a small gap in the corner. You can conceal this with quadrant moulding later. You should leave a gap – of about 6mm – at the bottom to allow for expansion. This will be covered by the skirting. If your panels are grooved, drive pins through the grooves and sink them slightly below the surface. If your sheet panelling does not have grooves, you will have to pin through the board. You should sink the nails with a punch and later fill the holes.

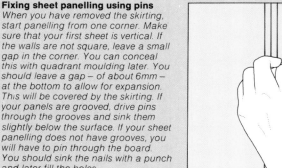

Fixing sheet panelling using adhesive
Panel adhesive can be used to glue sheets to battens or directly to the wall. It has slight gap-filling properties, so it will take up any small variations in the wall surface. If you are sticking the panels straight on to the wall, apply ribbons of adhesive on the back of the sheet at about 40cm intervals. Press the sheet on to the wall, working from the bottom to the top. It is important to work quickly. If the adhesive is losing its effect by the time you put the board up to the wall, try cutting up the boards so you are dealing with a smaller area at a time.

If the wall is very uneven, it is best to use battens. Pack the bat- tens with pieces of hard- board to allow for the unevenness in the wall. Apply the adhesive liberally to the relevant battens and, working quickly, press the sheet on to it, making sure that all the battens are in contact.

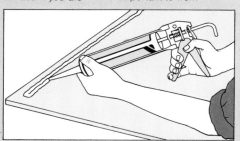

When not using battens, apply the adhesive to the boards themselves

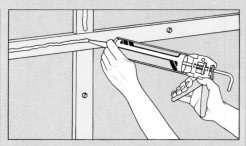

If you are using battens, apply a generous layer of adhesive directly to them

96

Fitting sheet panelling around corners

There are two basic problems when you are panelling up to a corner with sheet material – measuring (*see opposite*) and finishing off the corner (*see below*). With external corners you have to overlap slightly and sand one sheet back.

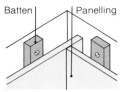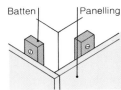

Internal corners
Take one piece right into the corner and butt the next piece over it at right angles.

External corners
Overlap slightly with one piece and then sand it back with fine-grade glasspaper.

97

Fitting sheet panelling around obstructions

The greatest problem with sheet materials is cutting holes of the right shape to fit around obstructions such as electrical fittings. The safest way is to make an accurate template in thin cardboard. Transfer the pattern to your sheet when you are sure it is accurate. If you are in any doubt, cut the holes on the small side – you can always enlarge them later.

To cut around doors and windows you should use the same method as for individual boards (*see Job 93, p. 85*).

98

Finishing off sheet panelling

If you have left small gaps between each sheet, you can either cover these with a wood or plastic strip, or leave them as they are. As an alternative to creating exact butt joints at the corners (*see Job 96, above*), you can leave a narrow gap to allow for variations in the width of the wall and finish off the corners with beading. You can also put beading at the top for a neat join with the ceiling.

Cutting sheet panelling to fit a corner

If your walls are perfectly square, you can measure the distance between your last sheet and the corner and draw a cutting line on the panelling with a set square and ruler. But if your walls are not square, you will probably have to mark the final panel for cutting, using a simple scribing block. This technique allows you to draw a line for cutting that corresponds exactly to the contour of the wall.

Cut a sheet about 10cm wider than you require, offer it up to the corner, and check with a spirit level that it is perfectly vertical, **1**.

Next, with a simple scribing block in contact with the wall, draw a pencil line on the sheet that will correspond to the contour of the wall, **2**. *Use a fine-toothed pad saw to cut along this line.*

When you have done this, put the sheet up to the corner to check that it fits. You should then mark on the other edge of the sheet the exact position of the adjoining sheet, **3**, *and join the marks with a straight edge. When you have cut to this line the piece should fit exactly in the corner space.*

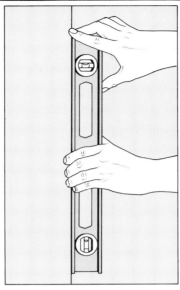

1 *Use a spirit level to ensure that the corner panel is vertical*

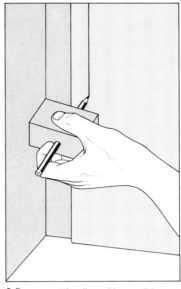

2 *Draw a cutting line with a scribing block held against the wall*

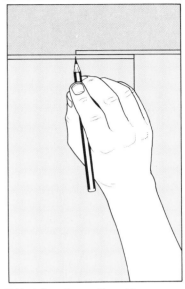

3 *Mark the edge position of the adjoining sheet*

99
Cladding ceilings

Panelled ceilings can look very attractive, and panelling is useful to disguise ceilings in poor condition. All ceiling panels – whether sheet or board – will need to be attached to battens; do not glue panelling to ceilings.

Drill and countersink your battens to take wood screws and fix the battens to the joists at 60cm intervals. Run them at right-angles to the celing joists, so that you have regular fixing points.

If you are going to make use of an existing light fitting, lower it to the same level as the new panelling. If you are not going to use it, you may have to replace it with a junction box from which you can take lengths of cable for new light fittings. Put in extra lengths of batten to take the light fittings.

Decorate the panels before putting them up. If you are putting up the panelling in a bathroom or kitchen, seal both sides of the wood so that it does not absorb moisture.

Start working from one wall and use the same techniques as for wall panelling. Clips offer the easiest method of securing the boards because you can put them in position before offering the panels up to them. If you use pins, make start holes in the wood first. If you are using cut pieces of board, arrange the joins over the batten centres.

Getting an exact fit around the perimeter of a ceiling is not easy, but any gaps can be concealed with a narrow decorative beading or moulding to finish off. Secure this with panel adhesive for the neatest finish.

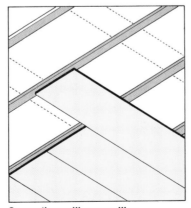

Supporting ceiling panelling
For ceiling panelling, attach supporting battens to the ceiling joists.

The effects of panelling in a room

Wooden panelling can transform a room. The wood's natural appearance and the strong lines created by the gaps between boards are the most important elements.

Using panelling in a bathroom
Panelling with boards can emphasize the length of a small room. In a bathroom, panelling the bath and other fittings, and building in a mirror, can add to this effect. The other advantage of the boards is that they conceal pipes.

Plastering

Estimating time and quantities ◇ Tools and equipment ◇ How to prepare the wall and the plaster ◇ Applying the floating and finishing coats ◇ How to fix plasterboard Plastering repairs

Plaster creates a perfect base for decorating with paint, wallpaper, panelling or tiles. Contrary to popular belief, applying plaster successfully is not a difficult skill to master, nor is it a closely guarded secret, known only to the professional. In fact, all that is really needed is the patience and time to practise the techniques first. You cannot expect to become an expert overnight, but master the basics, and you will be able to plaster as well as a professional.

Modern gypsum-based plasters have removed much of the labour of home plastering. They are quick setting and can be applied more smoothly than the cement-based types.

Fixing plasterboard requires less skill. It can be used to "dry-line" a solid wall, to cover a previously plastered wall, or to create a non-load bearing partition wall. Some types of board have a special fine finish intended for receiving paint or wallpaper, while others are designed to be a base for a layer of plaster. Plasterboard can improve the insulation and, like plaster, leaves a perfect finish for decorating.

In many cases, small cracks, holes and dents can be repaired with small quantities of plaster or pieces of plasterboard.

Points to remember

◇ When mixing plaster, always use a clean bucket, batten and trowel.
◇ Take plenty of time to practise the plastering technique before tackling a wall.
◇ Always leave a gap of 12mm at the foot of the wall when fitting plasterboard.
◇ Always key the floating coat of plaster before applying a finishing coat.
◇ An angled "screed bead" will protect plastered corners from damage.

Estimating time

A plastering job may not take as long as you think. The most time-consuming element is removing old plaster. If you are applying plaster to a smooth, medium-sized wall it may take only five hours to complete. However, if the old plaster is to be removed, it could take 12 hours. There is little difference between the time it takes to apply plaster and that needed to put up plasterboard over the same area. The times given below give an approximate idea how long it would take to apply plaster or plasterboard to a 4m × 2.3m wall.

Plaster

Preparing the wall
 ½ hour

(if old plaster to be knocked off)
 3 - 6 hours

Applying floating coat
 2½ - 4 hours

Applying finishing coat
 1½ - 2½ hours

Plasterboard

Preparing the wall and fixing battens
 4 - 8 hours

Nailing up plasterboard
 2 - 3 hours

Finishing joints
 ¾ - 1½ hours

Estimating quantities

Plaster is sold in a range of small bags – between 2.5kg and 10kg – for small jobs and general patching work, and in 50kg bags for larger jobs. The figures below are a general guide but coverage will depend on your skill in applying a coat of the right thickness. To plaster an area of 9m², you would probably need one 50kg and one 10kg bag of a base plaster and two 10kg bags of a finishing plaster.

The standard plasterboard size is 2.4m × 1.2m, but a number of smaller sizes are available. Baseboard is usually sold in smaller sizes – 1.2m and 91cm are common. Draw a plan of the area, take the measurements, then calculate how many whole boards you will need.

Browning plaster A 50kg bag will cover a 7.5m² area in a coat 10mm thick.

Bonding plaster A 50kg bag will cover an 8m² area in a coat 8mm thick.

Finishing plaster A 50kg bag will cover a 25m² area in a coat 3mm thick.

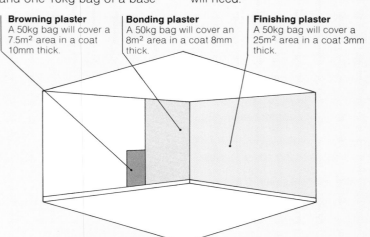

Types of plaster

Two main types of plaster are in common use today: one based on a mineral called gypsum, the other made from cement. Cement-based plaster can be used on internal walls but it may take days to dry out, and if the mix is not measured out accurately, it may not adhere well to the masonry beneath. Gypsum-based plasters are quick setting. They are sold pre-mixed, so all you have to do is add water. Those that contain lightweight aggregates, such as vermiculite are also easier to work.

Coats of plaster
Walls are usually plastered in two layers. The first, known as the backing, browning or floating coat, is applied thickly to mask any unevenness in the surface. The second (finishing) coat, is applied thinly and is smoothed over to give a perfectly flat surface for decorating. The most widely used gypsum plaster is made in various grades to suit walls of differing absorbency. High-suction surfaces such as brickwork absorb moisture rapidly, and need a base coat of browning plaster. Engineering bricks, concrete, dense blockwork and plasterboard, which are less absorbent low-suction surfaces, are sealed with a bonding plaster. A finishing coat is used in both cases. To test the absorbency of the wall, splash some water on to the bare masonry. If it soaks in immediately, the wall is high-suction; if it runs off, the wall is low-suction. If in doubt, treat it with pva bonding agent to make it low-suction.

Types of plasterboard

Plasterboard is a layer of gypsum plaster sandwiched between two layers of heavy paper. The paper extends over the long edges of the boards, but not over the short ends. There are two main types of plasterboard: baseboard, which has grey paper on both faces and is intended for plastering over; and wallboard or dry lining board, which has one ivory-coloured paper face for painting or papering and one grey paper face, like base-board, which can be plastered.

Wallboards
The most popular type of wall-boards come in two thick-nesses – 9.5mm and 12.7mm – and have either square or tapered edges. Tapered edges allow the joints to be reinforced unobtrusively with tape and joint finish, when fixed ivory-side out. The standard board size is 2.4m × 1.2m, but a number of other sizes are available which are useful if you want to match unusual stud spacings.

Other types
Baseboards are used mainly on ceilings to replace areas of old lath and plaster. Other types of composite wallboard are available for special jobs. These include insulating plaster-board; vapour-check plaster-board; and thermal wallboard, another insulating board.

Wallboard
The white paper face on wallboard can be painted or papered without plaster. The grey face can be coated with a thin layer of plaster.

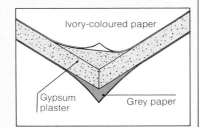

Ivory-coloured paper

Gypsum plaster — Grey paper

Tools and equipment

The only specialist tools needed for plastering are a hawk, a trowel and a float; and for plasterboard, 30mm nails and hessian scrim. For preparing the surface, you will also need a bolster chisel and a club hammer to remove old plaster, battens for marking out the area and "screed beads".

Plastering tools
For mixing up plaster, you will need a clean bucket and a batten; and to dampen the wall before you start, use an old paintbrush. Use a hawk about 30cm square to carry small quantities of plaster to the wall. The most important tool for applying plaster is a trowel with a rectangular steel blade, roughly 25cm × 12cm. For levelling off the floating coat, you will need a planed length of soft-wood, about 75mm 25mm and 1.5m long. Drive three or four nails into a wooden float for "devilling" surfaces.

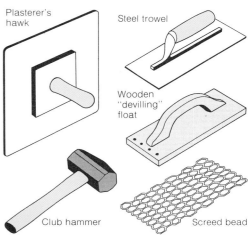

Plasterer's hawk

Steel trowel

Wooden "devilling" float

Club hammer

Screed bead

Plasterboard tools
You will need a sharp knife and a pad saw to cut the boards; a "foot-lifter" to raise them; 30mm-long galvanized nails to secure them; a sponge and fine hessian scrim for finishing.

Hessian scrim

Joint filler

100

Preparing the surface

Before you begin any plastering job, it is important to prepare the background thoroughly. On an old wall, hack off the old plaster with a bolster chisel and club hammer, rake out the loose plaster and dust it off, then repoint any crumbling pointing with mortar. Smooth surfaces, such as concrete and timber – need keying before the plaster will hold. On concrete, hack a series of criss-cross lines in the surface with a cold chisel and apply a coat of pva bonding agent. On timber, nail on a piece of expanded metal mesh, cut to fit the shape of the lintel.

Removing old plaster
If the wall is covered with a layer of old plaster, you should take it right back to the brick. Knock off the old plaster, using a club hammer and bolster chisel. If the pointing is crumbling, clean it and fill the holes with mortar.

101

Dividing the job

When plastering an entire wall, you will get the best results if you divide up the area into a series of bays. This is done by pinning three or four 10mm thick timber battens vertically to the full height of the wall, approximately 1m apart. The fixing pins are driven into the mortar, not the bricks, for easy removal. When the first bay has hardened, the first batten can be prised off and used to mark out the next bay. The gap left by the batten is then filled in with more plaster. Check that the battens are vertical and pack behind them if they "see-saw" noticeably. Since they act as guides for levelling off the plaster, it is worth taking care at this stage to ensure a flat finish. Before you apply any plaster, it is a good idea to fix angled "screed beads" to reinforce vulnerable corners.

Measuring out the bays
Pin vertical battens to the wall at 1m intervals.

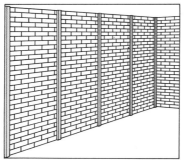

Protecting corners
Nail or staple angled screed beads to external corners.

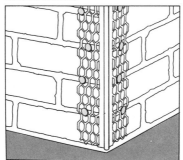

Basic technique

How to work with plaster

The success of any plastering job depends on the consistency of the plaster and its smooth application. The first essential is to mix the powder with water until the plaster resembles thick porridge without lumps. Cleanliness is all-important, since any dirt or chunks of hardened plaster could spoil the finish. To improve the workability of the plaster and to feel at ease with a hawk and trowel, it is worth practising the loading and applying technique several times. This involves scooping a mound of plaster on to the hawk, playing it between the hawk and trowel, then spreading it on the surface. When you feel confident with the technique, scrape off and discard the plaster, then apply the floating coat.

Mixing the plaster
The first time you mix plaster, tackle just a bucketful. Fill a clean bucket halfway with fresh tap water, and add an equal volume of plaster, sprinkling it into the water through your fingers to break up any lumps. When the water has soaked into the dry plaster, stir the mix slowly but thoroughly with a batten until it is smooth and fairly stiff. Tip the bucket on to your spot board, then chop and knead the plaster, using a clean plasterer's trowel. If the mix seems too sloppy, sprinkle on some more plaster and mix again. For larger quantities, use a bath-sized trough.

Working the plaster
Scoop some plaster from the spot board on to the hawk and push the plaster into a neat mound in the centre. Then place the trowel on the hawk with its blade at right angles to it. Push the trowel forwards towards the mound and tilt the hawk forwards at the same time, 1. When the hawk is vertical, push the trowel upwards to take off the plaster, 2. Keep the trowel horizontal, return the hawk to a horizontal position and tip the trowel over to return the plaster to the centre of the hawk from a height of a few inches.

1 *Press the trowel against the mound of plaster on the hawk*

2 *Tip the plaster on to the trowel*

Using the trowel
With a rounded mound of plaster on the hawk, move to the wall. Face the first bay and take about half the hawkful of plaster on to your trowel. Rest the right-hand edge of the trowel blade on the right-hand batten and tilt the blade up until its face is at about 30° to the wall surface, 1. Using even pressure, push the trowel upwards and tilt the blade more steeply as you press the plaster on to the wall in a sweeping, squeezing motion, 2. Scoop up the rest of the plaster from the hawk and repeat the technique.

1 *Apply the trowel to the wall and tilt the blade back 30*

2 *Squeeze the plaster on to the wall with an upward sweep*

102

Applying the floating coat

Plaster is applied in two layers: a thick "floating coat" to form a base; and a thin, skim coat for a smooth finish. Having practised the basic technique of using a hawk and trowel, and applying plaster to the wall, the floating coat can be trowelled on. You should start in the bottom, right-hand corner of the first bay and work across systematically to the left-hand batten before applying a second row above the first and so on up to the top of the wall. Once the bay is smoothed off, then keyed for the finishing coat, move on to the next bay. As each bay is finished, you can remove the right-hand batten and use the raw edge of plaster in place of a left-hand batten in the second bay. Alternatively, wait until all the bays are complete, remove the battens and fill the gaps.

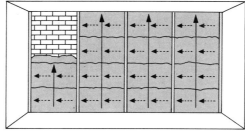

Apply the base coat from right to left in each bay

Covering the first bay
Brush the wall surface and sprinkle some water over it with a brush. Reload the hawk and spread trowel-loads of plaster on to the bottom of the wall, working from right to left within the bay, 1. Continue building up the rows, 2, using a trestle to reach the top of the wall. When the plaster begins to solidify, take a rule, rest it on the battens and draw it upwards slowly, 3, with a side-to-side motion, and dump excess plaster back in your bucket. Fill any hollows and rule off again as before. To key the surface, when it has almost set, run the devilled float across the bay in a series of swirls, 4. Plaster the other bays in the same way.

1 *Spread trowel-loads of plaster side-by-side on the wall, working from the right batten*

2 *Add a second row above the first*

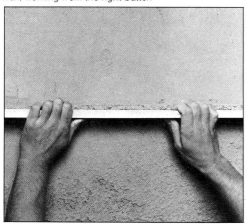

3 *Draw a rule through the plaster to level off the bay*

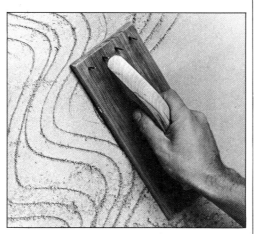

4 *Use a devilled float to key the surface*

103

Applying the finishing coat

As soon as the floating coat has dried – after about two hours – the finishing coat can be applied. You will first need to mix up the finishing plaster to the consistency of melting ice cream. When applying the plaster, it is important to keep the coat very thin, and to overlap each previous band. Begin at the bottom left-hand corner of the wall. Spread the plaster in a series of long, vertical sweeps, until you have covered an area 2m wide, then cover the top 2m of wall by continuing the bands up to the ceiling. When an area 2m wide has been covered, a second, thinner coat is applied, and any ridges smoothed off with a wet trowel. When hard, the plaster can be polished with a wet trowel.

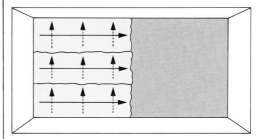

Divide the job into 2m widths and work from the left

Spreading the plaster
Take some plaster on to your hawk, then scoop half on to your trowel. Spread this thinly on to the wall in a long, upward sweep. Then take up the rest of the hawkful and apply it in a parallel sweep, just over-lapping the first. Continue in this way, until you have covered an area about 2m wide, from floor to ceiling. Then go back and apply a second, even thinner coat over the same area. Finally, sprinkle some water on to the trowel blade and scrape off any ridges or splashes using light, downward strokes, with the blade angled at 30 to the surface. Then move on to the next area.

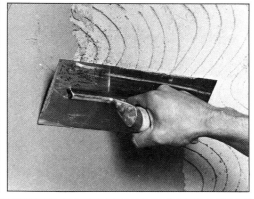

Basic technique

How to apply plasterboard

Plasterboard should be nailed to timber framing (for a stud partition wall) or to timber battens (for dry-lining a solid wall), so that vertical and horizontal joints between boards can meet over solid timber. To minimize cutting, try to obtain boards of the correct height and width. Some boards are intended to match the standard stud spacing of 60cm or 45cm. In rooms with high ceilings, try to use boards 2.4m long; or you may have to use two panels, one above the other.

Dealing with a solid wall
First remove skirtings and architraves and then position battens to coincide with the board edges. But if the wall is flat, stick the boards directly to the surface.

Dealing with a partition wall
You may need to cut the boards to match the position of the stud framework.

With both types, you should trim the sheet to allow a 12mm gap at the foot of the wall, to aid fitting. The boards can then be fixed, the joints covered and the skirting board added.

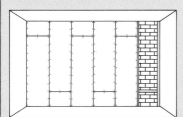

Covering high walls
Arrange the boards in two tiers and stagger the joints.

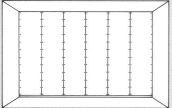

Covering normal walls
Where possible, use boards of the correct length and trim off 12mm.

Cutting boards to size
Unless you are fortunate enough to find boards that are the exact height of your room and that fit into the bay widths precisely, you will have to use cut pieces. Scribe along the cutting line with a sharp knife to cut through the paper. Stand the board on edge, with the cut line vertical, and grip the top end of the waste piece. Then slap this section with your other hand, while pulling it back slightly with your first hand. This should break the core and leave the paper intact the other side. Fold the board to 90 , then run a knife down the fold to cut the paper and free the offcut. To fit around obstacles, however, use a pad saw. At external corners, arrange for a paper-covered board edge to overlap a cut one.

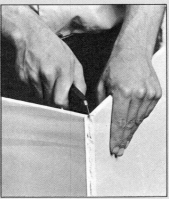 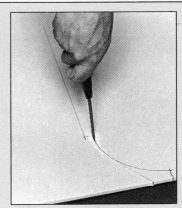

Break the core of the board, then bend it and slice through the paper

Use a pad saw to cut around awkward shapes.

Securing the boards in place
*Manoeuvre the cut-to-size board into position against the wall. It needs to fit tightly up against the ceiling, and to finish below the skirting height, so use a "foot-lifter", made from offcuts of timber. to lever it up and leave both hands free to drive in the fixing nails, **1**. Use galvanized 30mm long plasterboard nails, and insert them into the timber studs or battens at 15cm intervals and no closer than 12mm from the board edge, **2**. Hammer them in until the head just grips the surface of the paper, then tap in another 1-2mm so the hammer head just dimples the board surface without bursting it. You can fill the dimple with plaster later, for an invisible fixing. Fix subsequent boards in the same way, and push each one closely against its neighbour to form neat butt joints.*

 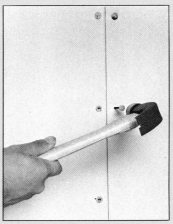

__1__ Use a "foot-lifter" to ensure a close fit at ceiling level.

__2__ Insert plasterboard nails at least 12mm from the board edge

Finishing off
*When all the boards are nailed in place, apply a narrow band of plaster or joint filler along the joint. Then cut lengths of fine hessian scrim to cover each joint from floor to ceiling. Press each length of scrim into the plaster at the top of the joint, **1**, and draw a filling knife downwards to bed the scrim smoothly and evenly in the band of plaster. With tapered-edge boards, apply more filler until the joins stand flush with the surface. Moisten a jointing sponge and wipe off the surplus. When the filler has set, apply a thin layer of joint finish with a trowel and feather the edges with the jointing sponge, **2**. With square-edged baseboard, apply a skim coat of "board finish", then a finishing coat (see Jobs 102 and 103, p. 91). Finally add the skirting board.*

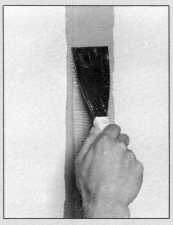 

__1__ Cover joints with scrim over a bed of joint filler

__2__ On tapered boards, feather the edges of the joint filler

104
Filling holes in plaster

Plastered walls which are basically sound, but damaged in patches, can be repaired

Repairing holes in solid walls
Score around the edges of the hole with an old nail. Brush out the dust and moisten the surface with a small brush. If you are using dry filler or plaster, mix it up to a stiff consistency. Then push it into the hole and allow it to harden. Add a second layer, and when this has set, sand the repair flush with the surface, or use a broad-bladed scraper to remove the excess. (For small holes and cracks, see Basic technique, p. 17.)

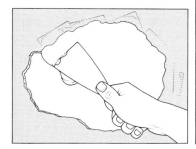

without plastering. Interior filler or finishing plaster can be used, but a plaster that dries in two stages leaves the best finish and will remain workable for up to two hours. Before filling holes, consider the extent of the repair. If a solid wall sounds hollow when tapped, the plaster needs to be entirely replaced.

Repairing holes in lath and plaster
Cut away the loose plaster to expose the laths, and brush out the dust. If the laths are damaged, bridge the gap with a small piece of expanded metal mesh wedged into the base of the hole. Then fill to just below the surface. Cross-hatch the plaster with your knife-edge and leave it to harden for 30 minutes. Mix more plaster, wet the patch and fill it completely. Add a finishing coat and sand when dry.

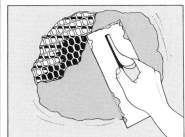

105
Repairing chipped plaster at corners

Plastered corners are particularly prone to damage. To ensure a straight line and a true angle at the corner, it is

Using a batten
Pin a batten to one side of the corner, its edge flush with the other side. Fill the hole on one side, with a trowel or filling knife, so that the plaster lies flush with the batten. When this has set, remove the batten and fix it over the filled patch. Repeat the process on the other side and finally sand the corner.

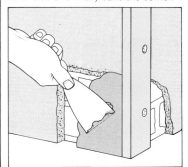

best to fit a batten first to one side of the corner, then to the other, while you fill the damaged area with plaster. If, however, the corner already has a reinforcing angle bead, simply patch the hole between the edges of the damaged area and the nosing of the beading on each face of the corner, and level off against the angle.

Patching a reinforced corner
If an angled "screed bead" was inserted when the wall was plastered, patch the hole by filling over the damaged area. Draw the trowel or knife upwards and smooth off against each face of the screed bead. When the filler is dry, sand the corner. (To fix an angled bead, see Job 101, p. 90.)

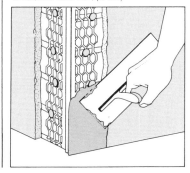

106
Patching plasterboard

Since a cavity lies behind each piece of plasterboard, holes have to be patched rather than filled. A piece of plasterboard is cut to fill the gap and is secured in place with plaster or nails. The plastered area is then finished with a skim coat.

Patching small holes
Cut a piece of plaster-board slightly wider than the hole in both directions. Make a hole in the middle of the piece, feed in a short length of string and tie a nail to one end. Dab some freshly mixed plaster on the face opposite the nail. Holding the string in one hand, guide the

piece into the hole, with the plastered side facing you, **1**. Pull the string to wedge it back against the inner face of the board. Hold the string and press more plaster into the hole, **2**, until it lies 3mm below the surface and leave it to harden. Cut the string, dampen the patch and fill the hole flush.

Patching large holes
Holes larger than 75mm across are best patched from the outside. Cut out a rectangle of plaster-board back to the studs on each side. Then cut a new piece to match the cut-out and nail it to the studs on each side with

plasterboard nails. To support the top and bottom edges of the patch, tape scrim around the joins. Or use a plasterer's trowel to force some finishing plaster into the gaps before smoothing a skim coat over the patch.

1 Insert the patch into the hole

2 Hold the string and fill the hole with plaster

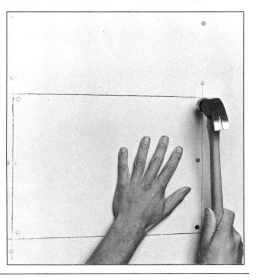

Windows

Estimating time◇ Types of window and glass◇Tools and equipment◇Removing broken glass◇Cutting glass◇How to replace a window pane◇Glazing doors◇Fitting a new window frame◇Easing a sticking window Preventing window rattle◇Replacing sash cords◇Double glazing

Windows perform three important functions: they let in light, they enable you to look out, and they provide ventilation. To fulfil these functions, not all the panes need to be openable, and many windows are made up of a combination of fixed panes (or "lights"), which you cannot open, and opening panes. These opening panes are usually either sashes, which slide up and down or from side to side, or casements, which are hinged at one side.

For improved insulation, there are double-glazed equivalents of most types of window. You can fit some designs yourself, while others are installed by the manufacturer.

The type of glass used also varies. Standard "float" glass is the most common type, but there are also various kinds of toughened glass, as well as patterned and tinted glass.

Points to remember

◇ Always wear stout gloves when handling pieces of glass.
◇ When measuring a window for a new pane, take measurements at several points along the frame.
◇ The larger the size of the pane, the thicker the glass you should use.
◇ When glazing a window, leave the putty for about two weeks before attempting to paint over it.
◇ Measure carefully for replacement frames – fit frames that are no more than 5mm smaller than the existing opening in the wall.
◇ If one sash cord in a window has broken, replace the others too.

Casement windows are the most common type. They usually consist of a fixed light, a side-opening casement, and a smaller, top-opening pane called a ventlight. Larger windows can have more than one casement. The panes may also be joined together in a curved shape to create a bow window, or in a rectangular or angled shape to make a bay.

Sash windows are very common in older buildings. They consist of two sliding sashes, one in front of the other. Each sash is counter-balanced by a hidden weight or a spring-balance system.

Pivoting windows are usually made from wood and have a single pane that pivots about a central point on the frame. Their main advantage is that you can clean both sides of the glass from the inside.

Traditional French windows consist of a pair of full-length glazed and hinged wooden doors opening outwards. The edges of the windows that meet in the middle are rebated so that one closes on to the other.

Replacement windows
If you have to replace a window there are two alternatives: an exact copy of the original window, or a double-glazed replacement window. Many double-glazing firms will provide only made-to-measure windows which they install for you. But replacement windows that you fit yourself are also available. These come in four different materials: timber, which you can stain or paint; aluminium, available in silver-grey, in anodized colour finishes, or with a factory-applied acrylic colour; unplasticized polyvinyl chloride (upvc), which is usually white; and steel – either galvanized or in a white finish.

Estimating time

The times shown here are based on a window measuring 1m × 1.5m. Most of the jobs will take longer if the window is larger, and times will also vary according to your own skill and experience. With large windows and those reached from a step ladder, you may need help, particularly when removing sashes and replacing large panes of glass.

Removing broken glass
(½)-(1) hour

Cutting glass
(¼) hour

Replacing a window pane
(½)-(1) hour

Replacing a leaded light
(½)-(1) hour

Glazing a door
(1½)-(2½) hours

Removing an old frame
(1)-(2) hours

Fitting a window frame
(1½)-(2) hours

Freeing a sticking window
(½)-(1) hour

Preventing window rattle
(½)-(1) hour

Replacing sash cords
(1½)-(2½) hours

Adjusting a spiral balance
(½)-(1) hour

Types of window

Casement windows
Most widely available with wooden frames, these windows come in a large number of standard sizes. There are also casement windows that have steel frames within an overall wooden surround. These have a thinner section, and therefore provide poorer thermal insulation than window frames that are made completely of wood.

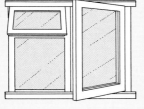

Sash windows
These windows are elegant, easy to clean, and allow good control over ventilation. Their main disadvantages are that the sash cords can break and the windows can rattle and stick. Modern sash windows use spiral spring balances rather than weights and are therefore more reliable. They also often have double-glazed panes.

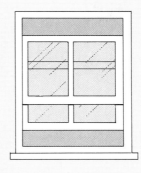

Louvred windows
These windows consist of thin horizontal slats of glass that are usually set in a metal frame. They are connected to a mechanism that enables you to open all the louvres with a single pull of a lever. Louvred panels often come as part of modern, double-glazed windows. Sometimes, the louvred panel is the only openable part of the window.

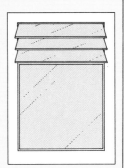

Pivoting windows
Because they are easy to clean from the inside, pivoting windows are very convenient, especially on upper floors. But they have one safety drawback. They are very easy to push open, and therefore should not be fitted where a small child could open them and crawl through.

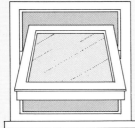

Sliding windows
Some modern windows slide horizontally. This is a design that is particularly popular for full-length patio windows, which are available in a wide range of materials including wood, aluminium, and upvc. Modern sliding windows usually have double-glazed panes.

French windows
Glazed double doors are often known as French windows. They are normally fastened by top and bottom bolts, with one door's inner edge overlapping the other, to give a good fit.

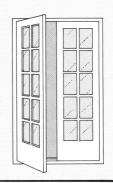

Types of glass

Most glass sold today is "float" glass, so-called because the method of manufacture involves floating the glass out of the furnace on molten tin. This gives a good surface finish and a distortion-free appearance. In addition, there are various types of safety glass.

When choosing which type of glass to use, first decide whether the area you are going to glaze is a "high-risk" one. Glazing within 80cm of the floor, doors or windows that might be mistaken for holes in the wall, and large expanses of glass that could get broken accidentally, all constitute a high risk.

Choosing the right thickness
Another important factor is the likely wind loading on the glass. The greater the exposure to wind, the thicker the glass required. In areas where the risk is not high, avoid 3mm glass except for very small panes. Use 4mm glass for windows up to 1m wide. For anything larger use 5mm or 6mm glass.

In a high-risk area you should not glaze an area larger than 0.2m² with 4mm glass; with 5mm glass the largest area is 0.8m²; with 6mm glass the largest area is 1.8m²; and with 10mm glass you can glaze an area up to 3.3m². For larger panes than this, use toughened or laminated glass.

Patterned glass
This type of glass can provide privacy as well as decoration. There is a wide choice of designs and some patterned glass is also tinted.

Wired glass
The wire grid does not make the glass stronger, but it holds the pieces together if it is broken. It also makes the glass more visible. It is available in both clear and opaque forms.

Toughened glass
This type of glass undergoes a special heat treatment that makes it four to five times stronger than float glass. The treatment also makes it impossible to cut once it has hardened.

Laminated glass
This consists of a thin layer of plastic sandwiched between two layers of glass. This strengthens it and also means that if it does break, the fragments of glass are held by the plastic.

Solar-control glass
To prevent rooms getting too hot in the summer, use plain or tinted solar-control glass. A self-adhesive reflective film, stuck on to an existing glass pane, will give a similar effect.

Glass bullions
In Georgian panes, glass bullions give an old-fashioned appearance. Other decorative effects can be achieved with stained and engraved glass.

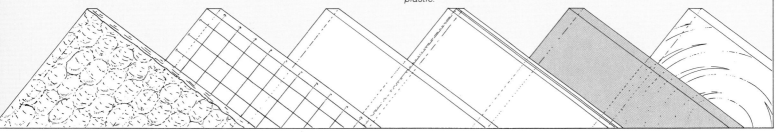

Tools and equipment

There are only a few specialized tools for glazing. If you intend to cut glass yourself, you will need a glass cutter and possibly some glazier's pliers.

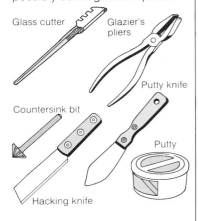

Glass cutter | Glazier's pliers

Putty knife

Countersink bit

Putty

Hacking knife

Equipment for working with glass
Use glazier's pliers to snap off small pieces of glass from the edge of a pane, or to remove a long, narrow strip of glass after you have scored it with a glass cutter. The hacking knife is useful for removing broken glass and old putty from a window frame. When replacing a window frame, use a countersink drill bit, so that you can conceal the screw heads.

107
Removing broken glass

Before starting to remove any glass, lay newspaper on the floor and, if possible, on the ground outside, to catch any falling pieces of glass. Wear thick gardening gloves to protect your hands and stout shoes to protect your feet. A pair of goggles is also useful – it will prevent flying fragments of glass getting in your eyes.

If possible, start by removing the large pieces of glass. Take care, because they may break up as you handle them. Then gently pull or knock out the smaller pieces.

If you have to break the glass in the frame in order to remove it, put strips of adhesive tape over it to hold the fragments together, and cover the glass with a cloth. The remaining pieces, together with the old putty, can be removed with an old chisel or a glazier's hacking knife. Pull out any glazing sprigs or clips that were used to hold the glass in place. Keep the clips from a metal window frame and mark their positions, but discard the sprigs.

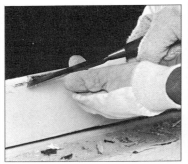

Removing putty
Use a glazier's hacking knife to remove small pieces of glass and old putty.

Taking off beading
To prise off beading, begin in the middle of the length.

For most types of window, you will need putty. 1kg of putty will be enough for about 3.5m of frame. There are different types of putty for metal and wooden windows, while solar control glass needs a special non-setting compound. You will also need glazing sprigs (for wooden windows) or clips (for metal frames) to hold the glass in place. Some windows use different fixing methods. Modern double-glazed windows have gaskets to hold the glass in position. Replacing panels in louvred windows is simply a matter of sliding in a piece of glass of the correct size. To cut down the security risk with this type of window, you can glue the pieces into place.

After you have removed the old pane, prepare the frame Clean out the rebate that holds the glass. If the frame is wooden, next apply the appropriate primer. If you have a steel frame, remove any rust and apply a rust inhibitor.

108
Cutting glass

Glass merchants will normally cut glass to size for you and this is always best, especially with irregular shapes. But if you do have to cut glass yourself, you will need a glass cutter, a firm, soft surface (such as a table covered with a blanket), and a straight edge.

If you are cutting glass for a replacement window pane, check the width and the height of the window at several places.

The size of the glass should be 3mm *less* than the smallest measurement. If the window is so badly out of true that you need an irregular-shaped piece of glass, either remove the window and take it to the glass merchant or make a paper template of the shape.

Making a straight cut
Make sure the glass is clean. Put it on a firm, soft surface and, using a straight-edge and a glass cutter score a straight line on the glass, 1. Pull the cutter towards you, using firm, consistent pressure. To help make a clean cut, apply white spirit. Tapping lightly with the cutter will also help keep the cut clean. Break the glass over a wooden rule, a batten or a dowel placed under the scored line, 2.

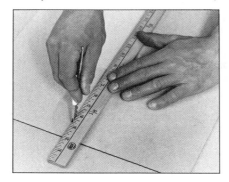

1 *Pull the glass cutter towards you along the straight edge and keep the pressure even*

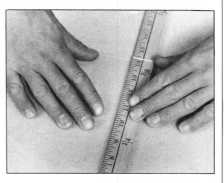

2 *Place the glass over a long dowel to break it*

109
Replacing a leaded light

The glass in leaded-light windows is held in by strips of lead which are bent over the glass and then soldered at the corners. If the shape of the pane you want to replace is irregular, it is best to make a card template and take this to the glass merchant, rather than trying to cut out the shape yourself. To remove a pane, first break these joints and bend back the lead. When you have cleaned out the strips of lead and inserted a new piece of glass, the lead should be bent back and the joints soldered back into place.

Basic technique

How to replace a window pane

Glazing a door

Applying putty and fitting the glass

After preparing the frame, apply a 3mm or 4mm layer of putty to the rebate. The best way to apply putty is to hold a ball of it in your hand and squeeze it out between the thumb and forefinger, 1. When you have done this, push the glass in gently on top of the putty. Press the glass only at the edges, not in the middle and, to get the correct clearance all round, support it on matchsticks at the bottom, 2. Next put in the glazing sprigs or clips and remove the matchsticks. Put in sprigs every 15cm using a small hammer or a glazier's hacking knife and sliding it along the surface of the glass, 3. If you are using metal clips, put them back into their original holes. Finally, apply a second layer of putty to the outside and smooth it off to the correct angle (about 45) using a putty knife, 4. When smoothing putty always use firm pressure and smooth strokes. If the knife sticks, moisten it with water. Finish it off with a paintbrush moistened in water. Remove any excess putty with a knife, and clean any finger marks from the glass with white spirit or methylated spirit. Leave the putty for about two weeks before painting it. When you do paint it, make sure that the edges are sealed by overlapping the paint on to the glass. If you do not do this the putty will dry out and crack.

1 Push the putty into the rebate with your thumb and forefinger

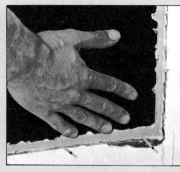

2 Support the glass on matchsticks to keep it in the right position

3 Use a hacking knife to tap in the glazing sprigs

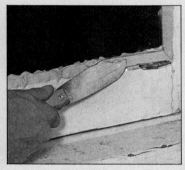

4 Smooth off the external layer of putty to give an angle of about 45

Fitting wooden glazing beading or quadrant moulding is a good idea if you are glazing a hardwood door. It is also a useful method for a window that you want to finish with a clear preservative woodstain. Glazing beading comes in long strips, which you can cut into mitred lengths. Check all the measurements carefully if you are glazing an old door or window – it may not be exactly square. A mitre box will help you get the corner angles exactly right.

Interior doors can be glazed in this way without any putty. Exterior doors should have a thin layer of putty on both sides of the glass to keep out the damp. Use coloured putty if your door is made of hardwood.

Fixing the beading

Attach the glazing beading with nails. To avoid splitting the beading, blunt the nails before putting them in. And, to reduce the risk of damaging the glass, hammer the nails part of the way into the beading before putting it in place. To get a neat finish, punch the nails below the surface. Clean any excess putty off the pane and protect the beading with paint or varnish.

Fitting the pane

Using a sharp knife or an old chisel, break the bottom two joints and ease back the lead, 1. Next remove the broken glass and clean out the old putty from the lead strips. Use an old chisel and a wire brush, 2. The new piece of glass should be about 2mm shorter than the opening.

You will need a small amount of putty – either the type made specially for leaded lights, or metal casement putty. Put a thin layer of putty inside the lead strip and insert the new piece of glass from the bottom, gently pressing it into position and squeezing out the putty, 3. Fold the lead strips over the glass and clean the lead with fine glasspaper. Resolder the joints, 4, using a soldering iron with a fine point.

1 Gently prise away the lead at the bottom of the pane you want to replace

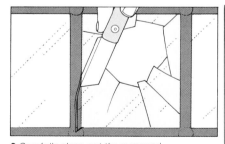

2 Carefully clean out the surround

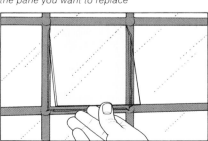

3 Surplus putty will squeeze out as you put in the piece of glass

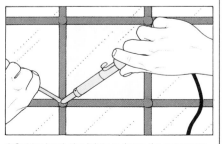

4 Solder back the joints to keep the new pane in place

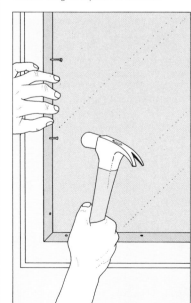

111

Removing an old frame

First unscrew and remove all the opening parts and take out the glass from the fixed lights. Cut through the nails or the screws with a padsaw fitted with a hacksaw blade. With a metal frame, find the lugs that secure the frame in the mortar joints on each side. Cut through these or chisel away the mortar around them. Once they are free, the whole frame can be tapped out a little at a time from the inside using a heavy hammer.

Cutting and levering out the frame
When you have cut through the fixing nails or lugs, make pairs of angled cuts through the horizontal parts of the frame, 1, so that you can remove the middle sections. When making these cuts, take care not to damage the internal window ledge or the sides of the reveal. Remove the horizontal sections of the frame, using a heavy hammer to tap them out if necessary, 2. Then take out the side parts, using a lever against the brickwork, 3. A crowbar is the best tool to use as a lever, while a club hammer is also useful for taking out the frame.

When you have taken out the frame. clean up the sides of the opening, removing any loose mortar and the remains of the fixing nails, screws, and wallplugs. Fill the holes left by the protruding "horns" of old wooden window frames, using pieces of brick and mortar to give a smooth opening.

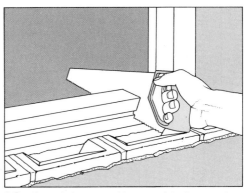

1 *Cut through the top and bottom of the frame to free the middle pieces*

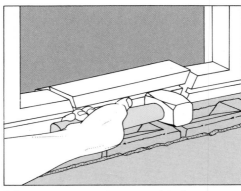

2 *Tap out the horizontal sections of the frame using a heavy hammer*

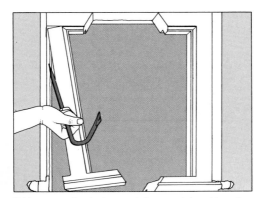

3 *Use a crowbar to lever out the remaining sides of the window frame*

112

Fitting a window frame

In most cases you will be able to keep the existing internal window ledge and fit the new frame against it. Conceal the screw heads by using a countersink drill bit. You may be able to use the original outside window sill, although most replacement windows come with a new sill.

Before fitting, give the frame an extra coat of primer (if you are going to paint it) or wood preservative (if you are going to varnish or stain it). Wooden windows come with protruding horns. Cut these off before putting the frame roughly in position.

To get the frame in position, knock in wooden wedges along the top, bottom, and sides. You will have to experiment with wedges of different sizes, constantly checking with a spirit level that the window is straight. Then you can mark the fixing holes.

Countersinking
A countersink drill bit allows you to recess screw heads so that they are flush with the surface of the wood.

Fixing the frame
Wedge the frame in place and check that it is square, 1. When it fits properly, number the wedges, mark their positions, and remove them. Then take out the frame and drill holes for the screws.

Next put a layer of mortar at the bottom of the opening with the correct thickness for the sill to rest on and replace the frame and wedges, 2. With the frame in position, drill holes in the wall through those in the frame. Fit frame plugs and secure the frame with zinc-plated screws, 3. For a neat finish, countersink the holes slightly and fill the hole over the screw head with external wood filler.

When fitting new steel frames, cut slots in the mortar joints to take the fixing lugs, and apply fresh mortar.

When the mortar has set, it may have shrunk a little. Fill the gap around the window with mastic, 4. If the gap is larger than 1cm, insert wooden quadrant moulding to cover the mastic. Fit the windows and glass.

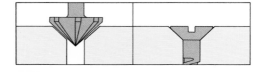

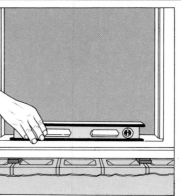

1 *Wedge the frame in position and make sure it is level*

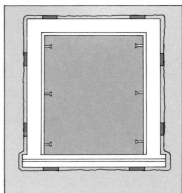

2 *Put a layer of mortar in the base of the opening*

3 *Insert zinc-plated screws into the window frame*

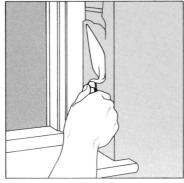

4 *Use mastic to fill the gap between the frame and the wall*

113
Freeing a sticking window

Windows can stick because of an excessive build-up of paint or because damp has made them swell. Stripping or planing is the best cure for this. Loose joints are another common cause. Re-gluing the joints and clamping them together can solve this problem. Loose hinges can make casement windows stick. Curing loose hinges may simply be a matter of tightening the fixing screws. If they continue to work loose, drill out the holes, glue in pieces of dowel and make new holes for larger screws. Sticking sash windows can be caused by loose sash cords (*see Job 115, p. 100*).

Stripping and planing
If the problem is too much paint, remove the paint using stripper or a hot-air gun (see Job 6, pp. 18-19). Do not use a blowlamp as this can damage the glass. Then rub down the frame with coarse glasspaper. If this does not give enough clearance, or if there is swelling, plane down the window. Use a primer on the bare wood before repainting (see Job 5, p. 18). If it is not obvious where the window is sticking, insert a piece of carbon paper between the window and the frame. The area where the paintwork is marked will indicate the place where the wood should be removed.

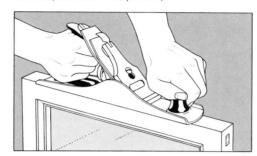

Tips for repairing gaps and leaks

◇ Foam-strip draught excluder can stop leaks and is easy to apply.
◇ For uneven gaps, try silicone draught excluder, which comes in a tube.
◇ When there are gaps between the window and brickwork, seal them with mastic, applied with a special applicator.
◇ When using a mastic gun, apply firm and steady pressure to the trigger as you move along the gap, and try to keep the resulting strip of mastic straight.
◇ An alternative method is to use the type of silicone sealant normally used around baths and kitchen worktops.
◇ Fill internal gaps with crack filler after you have applied the mastic.
◇ Check that the drip grooves on the undersides of window sills are clear.
◇ Replace flashing around roof windows with self-adhesive flashing.

114
Preventing window rattle

Casement windows rattle if the catch does not hold them tightly. The solution is to fit draught excluder around the window frame. If the window is distorted, straighten it by closing it on to a thin sliver of wood which forces it in the opposite direction to the way it is twisted. Repeat the process, gradually increasing the thickness of the wood until the frame has been reshaped.
    Rattling sash windows are caused by wear creating too much space around each sash. Fit the type of draught excluder with a nylon pile, so that the sash slides along it.

Fitting draught excluder
The simplest type to fit is self-adhesive foam strip, though this needs replacing regularly. The strip comes in different thicknesses to cope with different sizes of gap. If the gap is uneven, put one layer on top of another where the gap is at its largest.

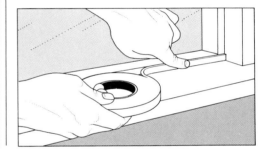

Types of window fastening

On most casement windows there are two types of fastener. The cockspur handle is attached to the window and engages with a metal stop screwed to the frame to hold the window closed. The casement stay at the bottom holds the window open. Both are easily fitted with screws.
    Sash windows are secured by a simple fitch fastener, or a Brighton catch, which has a threaded bolt and is more secure. Again these are easy to fit – you simply screw them to the rails of the sashes.
    The traditional catch for French windows is the Espagnolette bolt, which stretches the entire height of the closing door and shoots into holes in the top jamb and bottom sill.
    These basic handles and stays are not locking devices. If you want more security, fit fastenings that are lockable.

Casement fastenings
The cockspur handle holds the case-ment window tightly closed against the

frame. The arm of the casement stay has several holes to hold the window open at different positions.

Fitch fastener
Simply rotating this catch allows you to open the sash window.

Brighton fastener
This sash window fastener is opened by unscrewing the bolt.

115

Removing a sash cord

Fitting a new sash cord involves removing the window from its frame – a fairly big job and one which damages the paintwork. So it is sensible to replace all the sash cords at the same time – if one cord has broken, the others will probably soon need renewing. Use rot-proof man-made sash cord rather than the traditional waxed hemp. If the window is a large one, you may need someone to help you when it comes to taking it out of the frame.

The job involves removing both sashes, cutting new cords to exactly the right length, and re-assembling the window with the new cords. When both sashes are replaced, you will probably have to paint the window frame.

Removing and refitting the cord
Carefully prise off the beading around the edge of the window with a screwdriver or old chisel, 1. Cut any unbroken cords in the sash nearest to you and let the weights fall down into their boxes. Then remove the inner sash. To take out the other sash, first prise out the parting beads that separate the two sashes. To give access to the sash weights there is a small panel, usually held in place by a screw. Remove the panel and pull out the weights and the remaining lengths of cord, 2. Untie the weights from the old cords and remove the cord from the sides of the sashes, where it will be nailed in place. It is important to get the length of the new cords exactly right. Judge the length either by using an undamaged cord from the same sash, or by ensuring that the weight is just clear of the bottom of the box when the window is fully up. Do this by marking the position of the end of the sash cord on the frame and cutting the cord to size once it is in place.

When replacing the cords and windows, start with the outer sash. To get the new sash cord over the pulley, tie a thin piece of string to the cord and attach a small lead weight or screw to this. When you pass the weight over the pulley, it will fall, taking the string and cord with it. After removing the string, tie the sash cord to the weight, cut it to the right length, and temporarily knot the free end to stop it going over the pulley. When you have repeated the process for the other cord, hold the sash up to the frame and nail the free ends of the cords on to the window with galvanized clout nails, 3. Keep these 25cm from the top of the frame. Make sure that the cords lie properly in their grooves and that the position of the weight is correct. Replace the parting bead and ensure that the window slides up and down as it should. Put back the inner sash in the same way and refit the staff beads. Nail them in position with oval-head nails and drive these beneath the surface of the wood with a nail punch.

1 Start by taking off the vertical staff bead, working from the middle

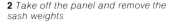

2 Take off the panel and remove the sash weights

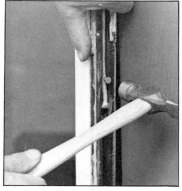

3 Nail the sash cord to the window

116

Adjusting a spiral balance

Modern sash windows are balanced by a mechanism that consists of a spiral rod inside a metal or plastic tube secured to the inside of the frame. Spiral-balance mechanisms are usually more reliable than sash cords, although the spring can lose its tension, which means that the mechanism needs adjusting. This is done by twisting the tube clockwise.

Spiral-balance repairs
Pull the sash down and unscrew the tube from the frame. Then twist the tube clockwise to tighten the spring. After a few turns, re-secure the tube. If this does not solve the problem, replace the whole mechanism. This involves taking out the sash (see Job 115, above) and the spiral balance. To fit the new balance, you first attach it to the sash and then lift it up to the window frame. With the sash in its middle position, tension the spring by turning the tube then secure the tube to the frame and replace the beading.

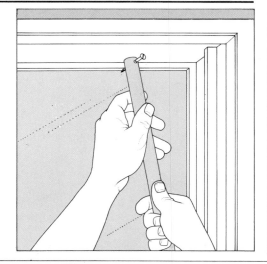

Windows are responsible for about 10 per cent of the heat loss from houses, while another 15 per cent is lost through gaps around windows and doors. As well as making a room uncomfortable, cold windows can cause condensation, which is produced when the warm, moist air inside the house meets the colder inner surface of the glass or the metal frame. Condensation looks unsightly and can lead to paint damage and rot.

Double glazing offers a solution to these problems. Double glazing is simply a way of fitting two panes of glass into a window instead of one. The second pane adds something to the heat saving, but it is mainly the air gap between the panes that gives the benefits. To be effective, this air gap should be at least 12mm wide. A gap of 18mm or 20mm is better still, but a larger gap will not give any further improvement. If you want your double glazing to act as a sound-proofing measure, the gap between the panes should be much larger – between 10cm and 20cm.

Types of double glazing
There are three main types of double glazing, sealed units, secondary panes, and secondary sashes and casements. Sealed units consist of pairs of glass panes that are hermetically sealed together in the factory and which simply replace the conventional glass panes. Secondary panes are fixed sheets of glass or plastic fitted to the inside of the windows. Secondary sashes are, in effect, framed windows fitted in front of the existing ones.

Most double-glazing systems are designed for use with 4mm glass. Toughened glass should be used for double glazing very large panes. As a cheaper alternative, use clear plastic sheets over the panes.

Types of double glazing

Sealed units

Sealed units have two big advantages: they are unobtrusive and, unlike other types of double glazing, they do not cause condensation. They are usually fitted into the window with gaskets made of rubber or synthetic material. Some units are gas-filled and have heat-reflecting qualities, and manufacturers make additional heat-saving claims for these. Some sealed units have a small unobtrusive air gap.

You can fit complete replacement windows with sealed units, which are available in standard sizes. A more economical method is to replace the existing panes with sealed units. The units are available in a range of different glass types in standard sizes or they can be made to measure. Units with a stepped profile are available if the depth of the window rebate will not take a normal unit.

Sealed inner frame
On this type, the inner metal frame is sealed to the outer frame of wood.

Outer pane

Inner pane

Sill

Drip groove

Gasket
Ensures a good seal, so that the sealed unit fits tight inside the outer frame.

Air gap
On sealed units, the air gap is usually very narrow. The result is an unobtrusive design with efficient heat insulation, but a narrow air gap is not very effective for sound insulation.

Wooden window frame

Secondary panes

The simplest form of secondary pane is a thin plastic sheet stretched over the window frame. Next in terms of simplicity is the type that is kept in place by a self-adhesive magnetic strip stuck to the edges of a sheet of rigid plastic. The magnet fits on to a strip of steel attached to the window frame. Finally, there is a variety of designs in which the secondary pane is surrounded by a plastic frame and attached to the window with clips, plastic strips, or other fasteners.

None of these panes can be opened easily for normal ventilation, although they can all be removed for cleaning or summer storage. But if the system allows you to fit the pane to an opening casement, both the original window and the secondary pane will open at the same time. You will need room for the casement catch when the panes are fitted.

Wooden window frame

Air gap
This type of double glazing allows for a generous air gap between the two panes.

Sill

Drip groove

Outer pane and frame
These are the pane and frame of the original window, which you can still open when the inner pane is not in place.

Inner pane
This can be made of glass or plastic. On this design, the metal frame surrounding the glass is held magnetically to metal plates attached to the wooden frame.

Secondary sashes and casements

These are more substantial double-glazing systems, which usually consist of sheets of glass or plastic with aluminium or plastic frames. They can either be fixed in position, or hinged or sliding so that they open independently of the main windows. Sliding panes are usually fitted in tracks attached to the reveal. They generally slide horizontally, but you can also get vertical sliding systems which are particularly useful for sash windows.

If your window sizes are not standard, you can get secondary casement or sash systems made to measure. You take the measurements and fit the system, but the manufacturer carries out the job of constructing the frame and fitting the glass.

Outer pane and frame
These are the pane and frame of the original window. They can easily be opened.

Sill

Drip groove

Wooden window frame

Inner pane and frame
This fits neatly to the original window frame and is opened by sliding the pane to one side.

Air gap
A large air gap for sound insulation can be obtained by fitting the outer panes to the inner edge of the original window frame.

Curing condensation

Condensation on the inside of the outer pane can be a problem on double-glazed windows. It can be alleviated by placing a moisture-absorbing substance (such as silica gel) in the gap. The crystals need replacing regularly. Draftproofing the inner window may provide a permanent solution to this problem. If this does not work, try ventilating the air gap between the panes by drilling downward-sloping holes in the outer frame and filling them with glass fibre.

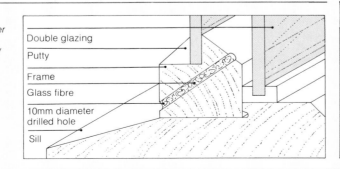

Double glazing

Putty

Frame

Glass fibre

10mm diameter drilled hole

Sill

Safety tips

◇ When fitting double glazing or strengthened safety glass, remember that windows offer important escape routes in case of fire.
◇ Provide opening windows at escape points.
◇ Leave keys for window locks where they are easy to find from inside in an emergency.

Curtains, blinds and shutters

Estimating time and quantities ◇ Tools and equipment ◇ Putting up curtain rails
Types of curtain fitting ◇ Making a roller blind ◇ Types of shutters

By day, window hangings and shutters are simply decorative, but at night they afford privacy, conserve heat, and muffle outside noise. Even if your windows are not overlooked, the glass at night becomes a cold, black, reflective surface, and drawing curtains or pulling down a blind will make the room seem much more hospitable.

When choosing curtains, blinds, or shutters, remember to check what they will look like from the outside as well as from within. Try to unify the decorative scheme from the outside, so that different windows on the same side of the house get a consistent treatment.

Points to remember

◇ When measuring for curtains, always allow extra material for hems, headings, and pattern repeats.
◇ Make sure that any curtain rails or poles you want to use are available in sufficient lengths – joins are not usually possible, unless you use an overlap arm.
◇ If you are using a batten to support curtain rail brackets, fix it securely to the wall using screws and, if necessary, adhesive.
◇ Buy roller blinds slightly larger than you need, so you can cut them down to the exact length required.
◇ Always use a spirit level to check that curtain rails and blind fixings are horizontal.

Estimating time

The time taken for putting up curtains will vary according to whether or not you have to put up a batten. Fitting hooks and sprung wire for net curtains is much quicker.

Curtains

Fitting a curtain rail

(½)-(1) hour

Blinds

Making a roller blind

(1)-(2½) hours

Estimating quantities

When measuring for curtains and blinds, use a wooden rule or a steel tape measure, and hold it at eye level.

Measuring for curtains
Two dimensions are required: the width of the rail and the length of the finished curtains measured from the point where the hooks are suspended. For floor-length curtains, measure down to 25mm above the floor; for sill-length curtains, measure to 10mm below the sill.

The heading tape will allow you to control the fullness of the finished curtain, so multiply the track width by $1\frac{1}{2}$ or 2 to give the fullness required. Divide this total width by the width of the fabric, to find the number of drops needed. Each drop should be the length of one curtain, plus a heading and hemming allowance of 25cm. Multiply the number of drops by the length of each drop. Add any extra you will need for matching tie-backs or pelmets, and round up the total to the nearest 25cm. Add extra for pattern matching.

Measuring for blinds
First decide whether you want your blind to hang inside or outside the window recess. If you are going to fit it inside, measure the width of the recess and then subtract an amount to allow for the blind fixings on either side. If you are installing the blind outside the recess, allow for an overlap of at least 5cm on each side. Measure the length from where you want to fix the blind to the bottom when fully lowered. To turn these measurements into fabric estimates, add 25cm to the length. The amount you add to the width depends on the type of blind. For a roller blind, you should not add anything to the width. With a Roman blind, add 5cm to give a 25mm seam allowance on either side. For a festoon blind multiply the width by the fullness required and add 5cm to give a 25mm seam allowance on either side.

Tools and equipment

For curtains, you will need rings, hooks, or clips to suit your rail or pole. Heading tape for the curtains will also be required. Equipment for making a roller blind usually comes in kit form with roller, fittings, pull cord, and fabric.

For more information on types of curtain fabric, see Choosing materials, pp. 134-6.

Effects with curtains

For a dramatic effect, or if paired curtains would overpower a narrow window, a single, asymmetrical curtain can be very effective. A flat curtain suspended from hooks through eyelet holes in the fabric can be attractive, and tie-backs can create interesting shapes.

Other interesting effects can be created with net curtains. While their main purpose is to prevent people seeing in, you can use them more imaginatively by draping them elaborately or gathering them on the type of headings used on conventional window curtains.

Matching fittings
Curtains, tie-backs, pelmets, and cushions (top left) made of the same fabric create a harmonious effect in this bay window.

Combining curtains and blinds
This combination (bottom left) gives great flexibility – the blind lets in some light, while the curtains act as light shields.

Using net curtains to diffuse light
If you have a large window that lets in a lot of bright sunlight, you can diffuse it with full-length net curtains. In this room (above) the striped and textured effect of the full net curtains is picked up by the reflective glass surface of the coffee table.

Types of rail, pelmet and heading

As well as the fabric that you choose, there are a number of other factors that will influence the way your curtains look. Particularly important are the type of curtain heading you use, the rail or pole on which you hang the curtains, and whether or not you fit a pelmet. Different degrees of fullness and types of pleating are possible with different headings. Some poles and rails are highly ornate, while others are invisible when you close the curtains. Pelmets can act as a simple way of concealing the curtain rail, as a means of unifying two windows in the same wall, or they can have a much stronger decora-

Types of curtain rail and pole

Whichever type you choose, make sure it is available in long enough lengths for your windows; joins are impractical. It must also be strong enough for the type of curtain you want. If you have curved or bay windows, choose a rail that can be bent around corners. Check also whether a cording set can be fitted to your rail. Most types of straight rail accept pull cords, so that you can close and open the curtains from one side. But some types of curved rail will not take pull cords. The traditional brass curtain rail has been largely superseded by nylon, plastic, and aluminium rails, together with wooden poles.

As well as the traditional brass rails, those intended for use with a pelmet include aluminium and plastic types with nylon runners. These are strong and easy to bend round corners, which makes them ideal for bay windows. Most can also be fitted with cords for drawing the curtains.

Rails designed for use without a pelmet are usually made from aluminium or plastic. Most use large hooks, so that the curtains cover the rail when they are drawn.

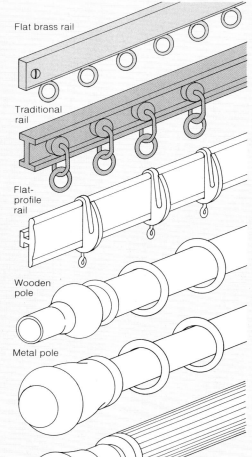

Flat brass rail

Traditional rail

Flat-profile rail

Wooden pole

Metal pole

Metal "imitation" pole

Types of pelmet

To hide the heading and give interest to the top of the curtain, you can use a pelmet. Pelmets allow you to fit the curtain track in two pieces with an overlap at the centre. They are also useful to give two adjacent windows a unified look.

There are two basic types of pelmet – those made of wood and those made of cloth. Hardboard is a common material and is particularly suitable for bay and bow windows because it can be bent round corners. Pelmets can also be constructed out of plywood or softwood, while hardwood pelmets look attractive with windows that are made of hardwood or that are set in a hardwood sub-frame.

There is a variety of fabric pelmet designs. They can either take the form of a gathered valance or be treated with a stiffener. Valance pelmets can be hung from a shelf above the window or suspended from a second curtain track in front of the main one.

Another type of pelmet, sometimes known as a draped pelmet, is made up of swags draped across the top of the window and tails decorating the edge. This type of pelmet looks very effective on large windows, but takes up a lot of fabric. So before you commit yourself by buying material, it is best to experiment with a sheet to find out approximately how much you will need to get the effect you require.

It is also possible to combine the strength of a wooden pelmet construction with the elegance of a fabric design to produce a fabric-covered wooden pelmet. This can either have a simple rectangular shape or have curved edges to give an effect similar to a valanced pelmet. The fabric can either match or contrast with the curtain material.

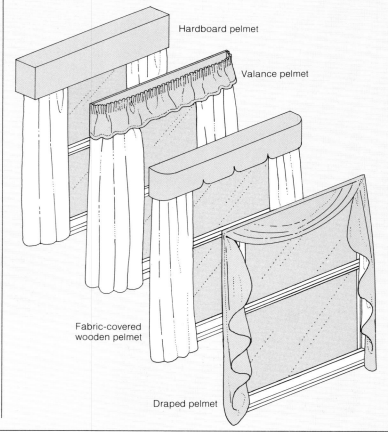

Hardboard pelmet

Valance pelmet

Fabric-covered wooden pelmet

Draped pelmet

Accessories for rails and poles

In addition to normal brackets for rails and poles, other types are available. Extension brackets hold the rail away from the wall, overlap arms allow one curtain to pass in front of the other where they meet, and return brackets enable the ends of the rail to turn in towards the wall and some allow for a dual track.

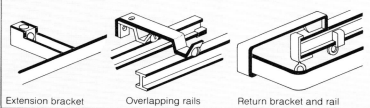

Extension bracket

Overlapping rails

Return bracket and rail

tive role, making use of gathered fabric, and swags and tails of material. You can also improve your curtains by fitting accessories such as overlap arms and return brackets.

Types of curtain heading
By using different heading tapes you can change the way your curtains hang. But different heading tapes also require varying widths of fabric. Standard tape gives a simple gathered heading. It makes the curtains look quite full and takes fabric that is about twice the total width of the track.

Pencil pleating creates a crisp, regularly pleated heading, but it takes more fabric – often $2\frac{1}{4}$ to $2\frac{1}{2}$ times the width of the track.

Triple pleating is more economical than this, requiring fabric about twice the width of the track. There are two types of triple pleating tape. With one, the pleats are made by drawing up a cord; with the other, you insert a pronged hook into the tape. The cord type is much easier to use.

Cartridge pleating gives a cylindrical pleat. To improve the roundness of the cylinder, the heading pleats are stuffed with tissue paper. This draws back tightly when the curtains are open.

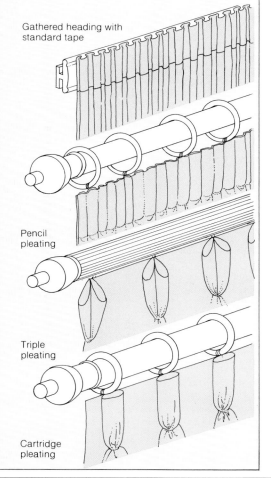

Gathered heading with standard tape

Pencil pleating

Triple pleating

Cartridge pleating

117
Fixing curtain rails to a wall

Most curtain rails are sold with the brackets you need to put them up, sometimes with the screws and wallplugs as well. Putting up poles involves the same techniques as putting up curtain rails. True poles only require brackets at either end. So they may not be the best choice for long windows, unless they are strong enough to take the curtains without sagging. Imitation poles allow you to put brackets at intervals along their length.

Curtain rails can be fitted to the window frame itself, but it is unlikely that there will be enough space in the reveal for anything except lightweight net curtains. So the most popular choice is to fit the rail to the wall above the window. Drilling the wall and inserting wall plugs should be simple with a hammer drill and a masonry bit unless there is a concrete lintel above the window that is too hard to drill into. In this case, the best solution is to fit a batten above the window.

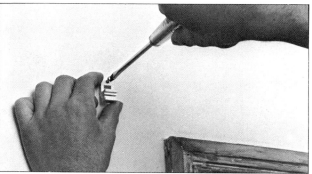

Fitting brackets to the wall
Drill holes in the wall at regular intervals to take the screws and wallplugs. When you mark the positions for the holes, use a spirit level to make sure that they are level. Use a screwdriver to ensure a tight fixing.

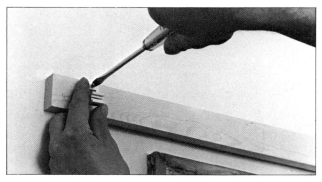

Fitting brackets to a batten
If the lintel above the window is too tough for a hammer drill, fit a batten of 50mm × 25mm timber to the wall and screw the brackets to that. The batten should be longer than the lintel so that you can drill into the brickwork at either end. Remove any paper from the area of the wall the batten will cover. Then attach it at either end with screws and wallplugs and secure the central part with contact adhesive. Paint or paper over the batten.

118
Fixing curtain rails to a ceiling

If the top of the window is very close to the ceiling, it may be easier to fix the brackets to the ceiling. Hollow wallplugs in the ceiling itself will not be strong enough. Find the positions of the joists above the ceiling and screw into these. They are usually about 40cm apart. On lower floors, the easiest way to pinpoint joists is to lift a floorboard in the room above (*see Job 69, p. 68*) and make a tiny marking hole through the ceiling next to the joists. On top floors, it is easy to find the joists by going into the loft.

Attaching brackets to the joists
If the joists run at right-angles to the wall, fix a bracket to each one. Use screws that are long enough to go through the full thickness of the ceiling plaster and into the joists themselves. If the joists run the other way, you will have to fit short lengths of batten between the joist and the wall to take the screws.

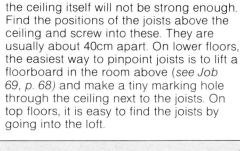

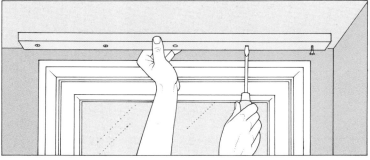

119

Making a roller blind

A roller-blind kit consists of a spring-loaded roller, a wooden lath or plastic bar for the bottom of the blind, a pull cord, and the necessary fixings and screws. The roller can be made either of aluminium or wood. The fabric for the blind is often bought separately. Kits are sold in a range of sizes – buy one slightly larger than you need so that you can cut it down to the required dimensions. Roller blinds can be fitted either inside the window recess or to the wall outside the recess.

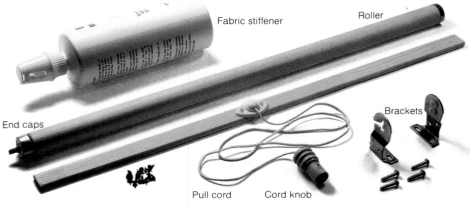

Fabric stiffener Roller

End caps Brackets

Pull cord Cord knob

Assembling and fitting the blind

First check the roller length that you will need. Take into account the projecting pins that fit on to the ends of the roller – they usually take up about 25mm at each end. Depending on the design of the brackets, you may also need a little space to allow for the fixing screws. Cut the roller to the correct length at the non-spring end. Make sure you cut it square by measuring the length in several places, marking it all the way round, and using a fine-toothed saw, such as a tenon saw, for wood, or a hacksaw for

aluminium. Smooth off the cut end with glasspaper and attach the fixing to the roller. On an aluminium roller this means simply pushing on the end caps. On a wooden roller, drill a pilot hole for the fixing pin to help keep it straight, push on the end caps, and tap the pin home, 1.

Mark the bracket positions on the window frame using a spirit level to ensure that the blind will be level, 2. When you attach the brackets to the frame, the one with the round hole should go on the right, the one with the slot on the left.

To prepare the material, cut it to the right size, iron it flat, and stiffen it. The easiest and quickest way to do this is to use an aerosol stiffener. With other types of stiffener, you have to make a solution with water and soak the fabric in order to stiffen it.

Fitting the bar at the bottom of the fabric is usually simple. Cut it about 1cm shorter than the blind and either glue it to the fabric or fit it into a pocket sewn along the bottom edge, 3. Screw the holder for the pull cord to the centre of the bar.

With aluminium rollers, the material

either fits into a slot in the roller or is secured with screw clips. With wooden rollers, the best method is first to glue the fabric to the roller to keep it in the right position and then to fix it permanently with tacks or staples, 4.

When the material is attached, all you have to do is roll it up tightly, put the roller on the brackets, 5, and tension the spring so that the blind rolls and unrolls properly. If the tension is wrong, unhook the non-spring end, turn the roller by hand to increase or decrease the tension, 6, and refit it to the bracket.

1 Push the end pieces into place on either end of the metal or wooden roller

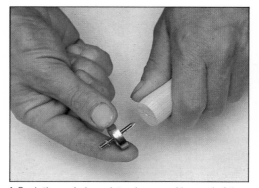

2 Mark the bracket positions and check them with a spirit level

3 Attach the bar to the bottom edge of the blind

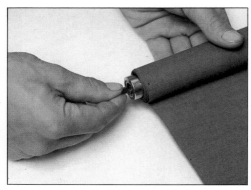

4 Staple the fabric to the roller after gluing it in place

5 Put the blind up and check the tension

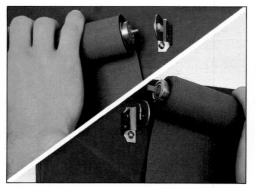

6 Adjust the tension by turning the roller around

Effects with blinds

The simple roller is not the only type of blind you can use. A number of other designs, such as Roman, festoon, and Venetian blinds, are available. They all have different decorative effects.

Roman blinds offer an unusual alternative to roller blinds. They look rather like roller blinds when pulled down. But the lifting mechanism draws the blind up in straight folds. This is achieved by a series of cords threaded through rings on the back of the blind.

Festoon blinds are gathered on a curtain heading and controlled by cords like Roman blinds. The result is a pretty blind that falls in gentle swags.

Slatted Venetian blinds will fit into a variety of decorative schemes. Their adjustments are very versatile – they can be angled to filter the light, closed to cut out all the light, or pulled up.

Venetian blinds
The horizontal blades of Venetian blinds (below) can form a strong design element in a room. In this room, the blinds have been continued all over the wall, on either side of the window, to make the horizontal lines even stronger. Slats designed to mimic the blinds below the window continue the effect.

Festoon blind
Combined with curtains of the same material, a large festoon blind can look striking (left). The ornate folds of the blind contrast with the other plain, flat surfaces in the room and add a rich quality to the otherwise simple furnishings.

Picture blinds
Matching picture blinds can provide an element of humour (above). Here, the picture shows a view through a window. The effect is enhanced by the "mirror-images" of the two blinds. The simplicity of this design is very effective in an uncluttered room.

Types of shutters

Shutters keep in more heat than curtains or blinds and if they fit well they can also help keep out window draughts. In addition, well-made shutters can help make the home more secure.

There are several different designs suitable for interior use. Folding types range from elegant Georgian and Victorian shutters that tuck into the window reveal when not in use, to plantation shutters, which are louvred and based on the type used on houses in the southern United States. There are also sliding interior shutters and both hinged and sliding exterior shutters.

Folding shutters

In Georgian and Victorian homes window shutters were common on the inside of the house. By day, they folded back into storage recesses at the side of the window. At night, or when the house was unoccupied, the shutters were unfolded and secured by strong iron bars. If you have a home with shutters like this, they are well worth restoring. To free shutters that have been painted shut use paint stripper and a knife. If the shutters have been removed, you may be able to find genuine old shutters that will fit your windows, from an architectural salvage firm. But it is more likely that you will have to make a set, or get them made by a local carpenter.

Georgian and Victorian shutters are usually panelled and fold back concertina-fashion. This is an idea that you can copy for any windows that are set in deep recesses. Although the shutters will probably not fold back fully clear of the window, they can be fitted so that curtains either side will hide them from the inside when they are not in use.

Plantation-style shutters, which also fold, can be bought ready-made. They are intended to filter light rather than to contain heat, and the slats are adjustable to let in more or less sunshine as you wish. They are usually made of stripped pine.

Sliding shutters

These come in two forms. One type slides within the window recess, guided by runners like those used for secondary double-glazing. With this arrangement, one shutter will slide behind the other and, when they are in place, only part of the window can be unshuttered at any one time. But it is easy to remove the shutters completely by lifting them out of their runners. The other type slides on runners fitted outside the window recess and can be pulled aside.

Sliding shutters can also be fitted from floor to ceiling using the type of track intended for use with sliding doors. The shutters can either run in a single groove or one behind the other.

Exterior shutters

On the ground floor, external shutters can be closed and opened from the outside and secured with a hasp and padlock. On the upper floors, external shutters are difficult to use unless the windows open inwards. One compromise is to fit working shutters downstairs and matching, decorative fixed shutters on the floors above.

Exterior shutters are available ready-made, but the choice is limited and, as it is important that the shutters match the style of the house, it is better to make your own. Tongue-and-groove board is a good material to use. You can make it up into panels and strengthen it behind with horizontal rails and diagonal braces.

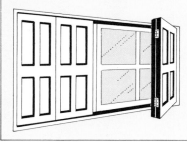

Effects with shutters

Louvred interior shutters form an effective alternative to curtains or blinds. They can have a natural wood finish, or be painted to match the windows and other woodwork.

The most versatile types are plantation-style shutters, which allow you to control the louvres to let in more or less light. Throwing them fully open gives you natural light from the whole window, while opening them partially, or opening some of the louvres, can provide a variety of lighting effects.

To get the best use of interior shutters, you need space on either side of the window and, ideally, a deep reveal. But shutters can work well in more confined spaces.

Plantation-style shutters
Opening the louvres in some panels and leaving others closed diffuses bright light and gives an interesting variety of surface patterns on the shutters.

Folding shutters
These fixed-louvre shutters fold neatly into the reveal when they are open. In combination with curtains, they make a simple window look more decorative.

Doors

Estimating time ◇ Types of door ◇ Measuring and cutting a door ◇ Fitting hinges ◇ How to hang a door ◇ Fitting a door handle ◇ Repairing faults in doors

Doors come in different materials (wood, metal, glass, and plastic), and in a range of styles (hinged, sliding, and folding). They are designed for a variety of uses – for example, internal and external doors are made to different specifications.

Most doors are made from wood and hung on hinges. The two most common wooden types are panelled and flush doors. Panelled doors have a framework of solid wood with the space between filled with solid wood, plywood, or glass. Flush doors have a much lighter framework which is covered on both sides with facing sheets of hardboard or plywood.

Points to remember

◇ Measure a door carefully before cutting it to size – check your measurements by holding the door in place.
◇ Strong hardwood and aluminium doors are best for exterior use.
◇ When planing a door, work with the grain and keep checking that the edge is straight.
◇ Use three hinges on heavy doors and bathroom doors.
◇ When hanging a door make sure that the hinge side of the frame is vertical.

For more information on types of door fitting, see Choosing materials, pp. 137-9.

Estimating time

The time shown here for hanging a door is for a conventional hinged door. You will need more time for double doors (add 2 to 3 hours) or for sliding and folding doors (add up to 2 hours). If your doors fit exactly, you should be able to hang them more quickly. Remember, you will have to allow extra time if you plan to paint or varnish the door.

Measuring and cutting a door
(½)-(1½) hours

Fitting hinges
(½)-(1) hour

Hanging a door
(4)-(5) hours

Fitting a door handle
(¼)-(1) hour

Curing a sticking door
(½)-(1) hour

Curing a sagging door
(¼)-(½) hour

Repairing a warped door
(½)-(1½) hour

Tightening a door or frame
(½)-(1) hour

Types of door

For exterior use, strong, hardwood panelled doors are best on older houses, while aluminium glazed doors blend in well with modern homes. Indoors, many homes have flush doors, although panelled doors often look more attractive. Fire-check doors are often required in flats and tall buildings.

Panelled doors
These are available in a wide range of designs. Outdoors, where strength and security are important, choose a door with a hardwood frame. The wood should be protected with a preservative stain. Safety glass should be used if the panels are glazed with single, large panes. If the panes are smaller, glaze them with bevelled-edge glass, to give a more attractive effect. Indoors, panelled doors with softwood frames are adequate. These can be made of redwood or Douglas fir.

Flush doors
These are much lighter than panelled doors. They vary greatly in cost, depending on the quality of the facing material and the internal core. Those with hardboard facing are suitable only for indoors, while plywood flush doors can be used either inside or outside.
Some flush doors have a moulded facing, to make them look like panelled doors. Others have an opening to take a pane of glass. Fire-check doors are usually flush doors in which the core is made up of fire-proof material.

Louvred doors
Available in a wide range of sizes, these doors are especially popular for cupboards. They can be painted or sealed for a natural wood effect.

Stable doors
These doors are split horizontally into two halves. By sliding a bolt, the top half can be opened independently of the bottom, providing light and ventilation.

Aluminium doors
Hinged doors made from aluminium are widely available. They usually have two glass panels and come ready-glazed with frosted safety glass.

Sliding doors
Any door can be made into a space-saving sliding door if it is combined with the appropriate sliding door gear. This is usually made up of rollers and tracks.

Bi-folding doors
These are made up of two parts connected by a hinge. As you open it, the door folds, and only half of it projects.

Concertina doors
This type of door consists of a number of vertical plastic or timber slats that fold against each other when the door is open.

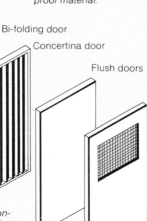

Panelled door
Panelled door
Louvred door
Stable door
Aluminium door
Sliding door
Bi-folding door
Concertina door
Flush doors

120

Measuring and cutting doors

Before buying a door, measure the width of the door frame and check it at several points. Then measure the height. The door should be 6mm less than the width of the frame, with a 3mm gap at the top and sufficient space at the bottom to clear the floor covering when the door opens.

If you cannot get a standard door of exactly the right size, remove some wood from a larger door to make it fit. Start by using a set square to check that the frame is square at the corners. The hinge side of the frame should be vertical. If it is not, the door frame should be removed and refixed, or replaced if necessary before you attempt to hang the door.

Do not rely on measurements alone when marking a door for cutting. Check them by positioning the door in the frame with supporting wedges underneath to raise it up and keep the hinge side vertical. Then mark the outline of the frame on the door. Flush doors are more difficult to cut to size than panelled doors because they often have only a very thin wooden frame. The best solution is to cut equal amounts from either side of the door.

Planing a door
If you need to remove only a small amount of wood from a door, use a plane. If you are going the full length of the door, use the biggest plane you have and work with the grain. On the top and bottom, plane inwards from the edges, so you do not split the timber. Check constantly that the edge of the door is square, except on the opening edge, where the outside of the door should be about 2mm narrower than the inside to allow for opening.

Sawing a door
If there is a lot of material to remove, use a saw. A circular saw is less tiring to use than a hand saw, and has a rebate fence, which helps you cut accurately. Cut just inside the line, so that you can finish off with a plane. You can cut up to 20mm from a panel door, but only half of this from a flush door. If you have to take a lot of wood off a door, try to remove equal amounts from both sides or from the top and the bottom of the door.

The most common type, the hinged door, is easy to hang provided that you can find a satisfactory method of holding it in the frame while you are inserting the screws in the hinges. A number of wedges and a lever that you can work with your foot provide the best solution to this problem.

Sliding doors are usually lighter and easier to lift into position. There are various types of sliding mechanism, and exact instructions for fitting are generally supplied with the door gear. But the basic principle usually involves fitting a wooden batten to the wall and attaching the track from which the door is suspended.

Folding doors
Bi-folding doors normally come with fitting instructions. Once you have trimmed them to the right size, fitting is straightforward. They have a track that fits along the inside of the door frame at the top. Pivot pins are inserted into holes drilled into the top two corners of the doors. One rotates, the other slides along the track.

A concertina door has a track that fits all the way around the frame. The width of the door frame is not as important for this type as it is for other types of door. If the door is already assembled, fitting is very easy. You simply fix the door into the track. With some designs, the door has to be assembled first and, to finish off, a pelmet is fitted to hide the working parts at the top. This has to be cut to the right length.

121

Fitting hinges

With a new door and frame, the hinge positions should be about 15cm from the top and about 20cm from the bottom. For heavy doors, a third hinge is required, which you should place centrally, equidistant from the other two hinges. When rehanging an existing door or using a frame that is already fitted, it may be simpler to use the existing hinge positions. For light internal doors use 75mm hinges. Use two 100mm hinges for other internal doors, and three 100mm hinges for heavy external and bathroom doors.

Cutting hinge rebates
First mark the hinge positions. Use a hinge itself to trace the dimensions and hole positions, 1, and a try square to draw the lines. Next cut recesses in the door and frame. These should be long enough for the inside face of the hinge to be flush with the door. The width of

the recess should allow the hinge pin to be just clear of the door. To make the recesses, first cut along the lines with a sharp knife, then use a sharp chisel and mallet to remove the wood, 2. Hold the chisel with the bevelled face down so that it produces a flat-bottomed recess. Take off small amounts of wood

at a time. Unless you are using the existing frame positions, fit the hinges to the door. Drill small pilot holes and fit the hinges using countersunk screws of the same material as the hinges, 3. Finally, holding the door in place, mark the hinge positions on the door frame.

1 *Score round the hinge and mark the positions of the screw holes*

2 *Chisel out the wood a little at a time*

3 *Use countersunk wood screws to secure the hinges*

Basic technique

How to hang a door

Fitting a door handle

Hanging a hinged door

After you have fitted the hinges to the door (see Job 121, opposite) and drilled pilot holes in the door frame, lift the door into place in the frame to check that it hangs properly. It is useful to have some assistance when doing this, but if you are hanging a heavy door on your own, you will need a way of moving it by small amounts without lifting it bodily. Wooden wedges under the door will help, **1**, *but it is also useful to put some sort of lever under the door and over a block of wood. Applying pressure with your foot will then lift the door until the hinges are in the right position. Insert one screw in each hinge,* **2**, *to check that the door fits.*

At this stage, if the door does not fit properly, you may have to deepen or enlarge the recesses, **3**. *Be careful not to deepen the recesses too much – or the door will bind: If you do cut them too deep, pack the recesses with card.*

When the door fits, insert the remaining screws, **4**. *Use wood filler for any gaps that you have chiselled out unintentionally. On external doors, fit a weatherboard along the bottom edge to throw off rainwater.*

When you are hanging double doors or French windows, both sides of the frame must be vertical. Most double doors come in standard sizes, so it is best to use doors and frames that match in size. Otherwise, the method for hanging double doors is the same as that for hanging single doors. It is easier if you glaze the doors after you have hung them – they are much easier to handle without glass.

1 *Wedges under the door will help you get it into position*

2 *Put one screw into each hinge to check that the door fits*

3 *If necessary, deepen the rebate on the door frame*

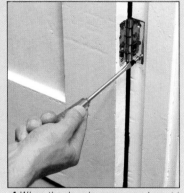
4 *When the door hangs properly, put in the remaining screws*

There are two types of handle that can be fitted to doors where a mortise lock has been installed. One sort, usually called a knob set, is secured by small grub screws to a square spindle that passes through the centre of the lock.

The other type of door handle is screwed to the door itself and fits over the spindle. The only problem with this type is that some doors are too thin to give a proper fixing for the screw and accommodate the mortise lock. With doors that are too thin, the solution is to fit a piece of wood to each side of the door, to which you can attach the handle. You can either glue it in place or screw it to the door beyond the line of the lock.

Fitting a knob set

Little extra work is required to fit the handles once the mortise lock has been installed (see Job 201, p. 212). The spindle must be cut to the right length to leave the handle in the correct position. It is then simple to slide the knob on to the spindle, **1**, *and insert the grub screws to secure it,* **2**.

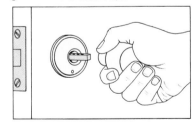
1 *Check the length of the spindle by sliding on the knob*

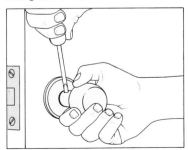
2 *Attach the knob to the spindle with grub screws*

Hanging a sliding door

First prepare the door opening. The door stop – the piece of wood against which the door opens – can be removed by levering it up with a chisel. This may damage the paint and reveal nails underneath which hold the door frame in place. Punch these below the wood surface and use filler to give a smooth finish before repainting. Next fill the hinge recesses. Use thin pieces of wood glued into place and finish off with filler. The architrave should also be removed from the side on which the door is to be fitted.

If you are using the existing door, you will have to reduce the size of the original opening so that the sliding door overlaps slightly when it is fitted. Fix thin lengths of wood to the frame, cut to the right width.

Fix a batten to the wall to support the track from which the door is suspended, **1**. *With hollow partition walls, the batten must be fixed to the internal uprights. Find these by tapping the wall – once you have found one, the next should be about 40cm away. The batten should be at least as long as the*

track, and longer if this is necessary to fix it to the uprights in the wall. If you are going to fit a pelmet, you should also allow space to attach this to the ends of the batten. The thickness of the batten should allow the door to clear the frame at both sides.

The instructions will tell you at what height to fit the track – there should

be enough space at the bottom to keep the door well clear of the floor. Make sure the track is perfectly horizontal, then fix the plates and bolts to the top of the door, secure the guide to the floor and hang the door on the track, **2**. *If a draught excluder has not been supplied with the door gear, fit a brush type to prevent heat loss.*

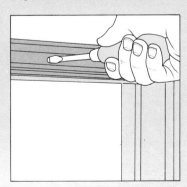
1 *Fix the track to a batten so that the door clears the frame*

2 *Hang the door on the track at the top of the frame*

123
Curing squeaking and sticking doors

Squeaking doors have two main causes. The hinges may need oiling, or part of the door may be catching on the frame as it opens. If neither of these things seems to be happening, the door may be warped (*see Job 126, below*). Squeaky hinges can usually be cured with a little household oil. But if they are very dry and stiff, it is worth removing them, applying a more penetrating oil, and working them free

before replacing them. Stiff hinges put a strain on the fixing screws.

If part of a door is catching on the frame, it may be that the hinges are recessed too far into either the door or the frame. If this is the case, remove the door and pack the recesses with cardboard.

Squeaks are often caused by protrusions on the hinge side of a door. Sand down any small high spots in the woodwork.

A door that sticks probably either has too much paint or has swollen because of moisture in the atmosphere (this is particularly likely if it is an outside or kitchen or bathroom door). In either case the solution is to plane off the swollen area.

Finding where a door is sticking
If you are not sure exactly which part of a door is sticking, close it on to a strip of carbon paper. This will rub on the door or frame where the door is sticking, and will leave a mark to show you which area to plane down.

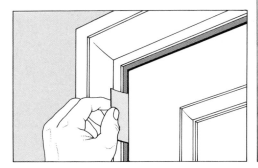

Refitting door hinges
If the hinges are recessed too far into the rebates, pack them out to the correct position. Use thin pieces of cardboard and build these up until the door hangs straight. It should then open and close easily without squeaking or sticking in the frame.

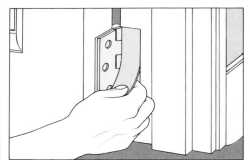

124
Repairing loose doors and frames

Door frames, especially internal ones, are often only loosely attached to the wall. If a door frame is loose, drill new holes and refix it to the wall. Doors rattle when they have shrunk and become too small for the frame. There are two solutions. Fitting foam draught excluder round the frame will probably cure the problem and keep out draughts. If this does not work, move the striking plate of the catch or lock.

Refixing a loose door frame
Remove the frame and drill new, deeper holes into the masonry with a masonry drill bit. Insert wallplugs of the correct size and put back the frame, attaching it with long screws that pass deep into the masonry to give a firm fixing.

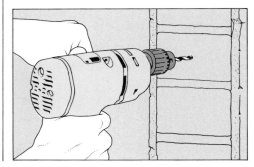

125
Curing a sagging door

A door will sag either because its hinges have got loose or because the joints of the door itself have worked loose. If the hinges are loose, you may be able to solve the problem by simply tightening the screws or fitting larger ones. If this does not work, the old screw holes may need plugging. In some cases the original hinges are too small, and they can become distorted. Replace them with larger hinges, or add a third hinge between the original two. Doors with loose joints should be strengthened using glue and dowels.

Refitting hinges
Tightening the screws of the hinges on a sagging door may only be a temporary solution to the problem. If the door starts to sag again, remove the old screws, drill larger holes, and fill these with glued dowels. When the glue has dried, fix larger screws.

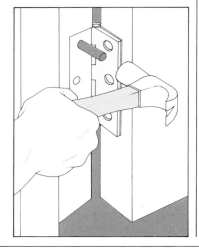

126
Dealing with a warped door

If the door has warped on the hinge side, you may be able to cure it by fitting a third hinge. But warping is more common on the other side, preventing the door from closing properly. Where this has happened and the top or bottom of the door will not fit inside the frame, push the door closed by inserting thin slivers of wood to force it into place. When it is the middle of the door that is preventing it from closing, fit temporary bolts to the top and bottom of the door and force it closed with a sliver of wood at the centre.

Bending back a warped door
Inserting thin strips of wood between the door and the frame will force a warped door back at the top or bottom. If you leave the door like this or repeat the process often enough, it will eventually be pulled back permanently into its original shape.

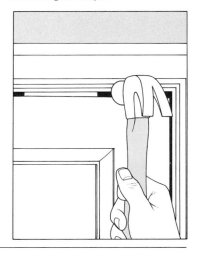

Choosing materials

Paints, stains and varnishes ◇ Wallcoverings
Tiles ◇ Wooden surfaces ◇ Floor coverings
Furnishing fabrics ◇ Door furniture

In all do-it-yourself work, successful and long-lasting results
depend on using the right materials. One of the first con-
siderations in making your choice is the room itself: is it
subjected to damp, dirt, splashes and spillages (kitchen,
bathroom) or heavy wear and tear? Are the surfaces in good
or poor condition? Another point to bear in mind is your skill;
if you are tackling a job for the first time, you may want to
to choose a material that is easy to handle. Finally, you will
need to compare prices and select a suitable colour, pattern
and texture for your own home. This section is a photographic
"buyer's guide" to decorating materials. It mirrors the topics in
the previous chapter, illustrating the range of paints, fabrics,
wallpapers, woods, tiles and so on, and compares the particular qualities and design features of different types. Each
colour "glossary" is backed up with detailed comparisons and
practical advice on choosing the right materials and
accessories for the individual job in hand.

Paints, stains and varnishes

Paint serves a dual purpose – to decorate and to protect a surface. Paints are available for both interior and exterior use, but it is outside where protection is of paramount importance. Paints can be divided into three categories: preparatory paints, such as primers and undercoats; top coats, including gloss and emulsion; and special purpose paints, such as masonry and floor paints. Most paints are made up of three ingredients: pigment, which provides colour; a binder, usually a resin, which causes the pigment to stick to the surface; and a liquid, either oil or water, which combines the two. Thus top coats are divided into oil-based paints, which are available in gloss, eggshell and matt finishes, for use on wood and metal; and water-based paints or emulsions, which come in matt, satin or silk finishes, for use on plaster, paper and brick.

Stains and varnishes also decorate and protect a surface, but provide a transparent covering. So, unlike paint, these natural finishes are used solely on bare wood; they can change its colour, while allowing the pattern of the wood grain to show through. There are three basic kinds of stain: water-based, oil-based and spirit-based.

For information on applying paints, see pp. 12-27.

Paints

Surface treatments

Knotting
A shellac-based liquid, applied to knots in wood before applying primer. It prevents resin oozing through and staining new paint.

Filler
For cracks and holes in wood and plaster, the best fillers are resin-based. These are sold as powder, and are mixed with water to form a paste.

Wood-coloured stopper
A paste that dries to a natural wood colour and is designed to fill holes in wood that is to be given a clear finish. It is sold as paste with a separate hardener to be mixed in.

Preparatory paints

Primer
A thick liquid designed to clog the pores of wood and so reduce absorbency. It also forms a uniform surface on wood, metal and masonry before painting. A multi-purpose primer is manufactured, but specific types are available for various surfaces, such as wood and metal.

Aluminium primer-sealer
Not to be confused with aluminium paint, this preparation is made from fine aluminium scales and seals off stains, such as water-damage marks.

Undercoat
Used under gloss, this paint is designed to obliterate other colours, and provide a good surface, prior to using a top coat. It does not weather well on its own.

Top coats

Emulsion
A water-thinned paint, based mainly on vinyl resins, and widely used for walls and ceilings. It is quick drying and is available in a matt or sheen finish. It is available in liquid, jellified or solid form.

Gloss
A solvent-based paint, based mainly on alkyd resins, and used on wood and metalwork. It is available either as a thin decorative coating, or as a jellified "non-drip" (thixotropic) paint.

Eggshell
Although similar in make-up to gloss paint, eggshell produces a sheen instead of a gloss finish and helps to conceal surface faults.

New paints
A new family of decorative paints is now on the market. They have no generic name, but provide a complete system, needing no undercoat and no primer on wood. They also allow the surface to "breathe", and are now available in white as well as a variety of colours.

Special paints

Enamel paint
A solvent-based paint that needs no primer or undercoat and gives a very high gloss finish, but is considerably more expensive than gloss.

Anti-condensation paint
Provides an insulating film between a cold surface and a humid atmosphere, and so reduces condensation.

Textured paint
More a coating than a paint, this is widely used on ceilings to create a pattern or texture. The design is added after the paint has been applied, although some types automatically form a stipple pattern during application.

Masonry paint
A durable emulsion for external use. It contains mica, nylon fibre, sand or other materials to add bulk for filling gaps and hiding cracks and to prevent erosion.

Floor paint
Tough epoxy resin paint often strengthened with rubber to withstand heavy foot traffic.

Aerosol paint
A solvent-based paint thinned down so that it can be dispensed through a fine nozzle. Several coats are needed to give good coverage.

Eggshell paint on lining paper

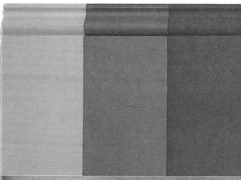

Primer, undercoat and gloss on wo[od]

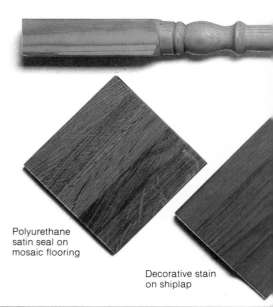

Polyurethane satin seal on mosaic flooring

Decorative stain on shiplap

Matt emulsion paint on woodchip paper

Silk emulsion paint on embossed paper

Matt emulsion paint on high relief paper

Enamel on metal

Masonry paint on brick

Teak oil on balustrade

Wood preservative (light oak) on trellis

Polyurethane gloss seal on woodblock flooring

Polyurethane varnish (teak) on wall panelling

Stains and varnishes

Oil-based stains

Linseed oil
Still available in many stores in both plain and boiled form. However, it tends to become gummy and attract dirt and dust. It is also hard to remove.
Teak oil
Gives an attractive, protective coating to wooden furniture.
Oil-stain preservative
This new family of decorative finishes offers the protection of paint with the transparent appeal of varnish.

Seals

Polyurethane varnish seal
Widely used for wood finishing, and available in matt or gloss. The matt type gives a more mellow, natural finish than the gloss.
Seal and stain combined
Many varnish seals are available in a range of wood colours, so you can decorate and seal at the same time. Each new coat darkens the wood.

Varnishes and lacquers

Varnishes
A range of tough finishes, sold as yacht varnish in DIY shops are suitable for exterior decorative wood, such as hardwood front doors and garden furniture.
Cellulose lacquer
Tough and resistant to abrasion. It is fast drying and available in clear and coloured finishes.
Two-part cold cure lacquer
Produces a tough, glossy finish, but is not easy to apply and can make timber look artificial.
Exterior preservatives
Available for use on exterior timber, such as garden fencing, these include creosote and a range of decorative pre-servatives in a limited range of colours.

Paints, stains and varnishes

Choosing the right paint

Price is not necessarily the best guide to quality of paint, largely because price wars between brands and trading groups have distorted price categories. The best advice is to buy a well-known make, or an "own brand" in one of the superstores or trading groups. Unknown, cheap paints, particularly emulsions, usually give an inferior result with little durability. Try to buy primer, undercoat and top coat from the same manufacturer, since they will have been formulated to be compatible.

It is best to estimate the quantities you will need and to buy the full amount in one batch to be sure of a good colour match. This is particularly important if you are having the paint custom-mixed by the supplier. Paints of the same type can be mixed, provided they come from the same manufacturer. If you are mixing your own paint, make a note of the quantity and names of pigments used.

Colour strengths

The small area of colour on a manufacturer's colour chart rarely gives a clear idea of how the paint will look in a room. The combined effect of the colour on the walls and the ceiling may intensify the shade as much as 50 percent above the paint colour chart. If you have a piece of fabric in a similar shade, try holding it up to the wall to gauge the colour strength. Alternatively, buy a small quantity and test it on a hidden area of wall.

Tips on buying paint

◇ Be sure to buy enough to finish a job with one batch. Pigments can vary slightly from batch to batch. Remember to allow for enough coats.
◇ It is cheaper to buy one large container than several smaller cans.
◇ Avoid mixing paints made by different manufacturers.
◇ Do not buy cheap paint with an unknown brand name.
◇ Consider the colour of the paint in relation to the rest of the decoration.

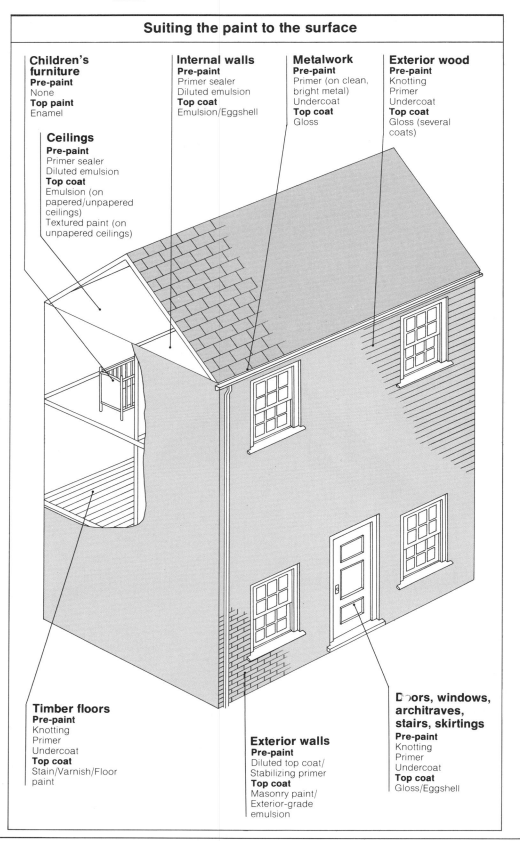

Suiting the paint to the surface

Children's furniture
Pre-paint
None
Top paint
Enamel

Ceilings
Pre-paint
Primer sealer
Diluted emulsion
Top coat
Emulsion (on papered/unpapered ceilings)
Textured paint (on unpapered ceilings)

Internal walls
Pre-paint
Primer sealer
Diluted emulsion
Top coat
Emulsion/Eggshell

Metalwork
Pre-paint
Primer (on clean, bright metal)
Undercoat
Top coat
Gloss

Exterior wood
Pre-paint
Knotting
Primer
Undercoat
Top coat
Gloss (several coats)

Timber floors
Pre-paint
Knotting
Primer
Undercoat
Top coat
Stain/Varnish/Floor paint

Exterior walls
Pre-paint
Diluted top coat/Stabilizing primer
Top coat
Masonry paint/Exterior-grade emulsion

Doors, windows, architraves, stairs, skirtings
Pre-paint
Knotting
Primer
Undercoat
Top coat
Gloss/Eggshell

When to use emulsion paint

Of all the top coats, emulsion is the easiest to apply. It spreads well and dries quickly to a smooth, even finish. On new plaster surfaces, it is usual to use a thinned paint and water coating as a primer. On previously painted or papered surfaces, it is advisable to apply the paint sparingly, recoating, if necessary, to ensure that paint covers well and seeps into any crevices. Emulsion is not ideal on bare wood, since the water content raises the grain, producing a rough finish.

When to use oil-based paint

Gloss needs to be more thoroughly brushed out than emulsion and should be applied in thin coats to avoid runs. Non-drip (thixotropic) gloss paint, however, is laid on in a thick layer, without much brushing. The gloss is simply a protective finishing coat, so previous colours must be obliterated by layers of undercoat. Generally gloss paints do not need to be thinned, unless for use in a spray gun.

Enamel needs to be brushed on extremely carefully, since the high gloss finish will show up irregularities. Like emulsion, it needs to be built up coat by coat, allowing each layer to dry. For small items, dipping is very effective.

Suiting the stains/varnish to the surface

Surface	Treatment
Woodblock Woodstrip	Polyurethane seal
Floorboards	Polyurethane or yacht varnish
Wall/ceiling panelling	Polyurethane seal
Interior joinery	Polyurethane seal and stain
Exterior joinery	Oil stain preservative Yacht varnish
Sheds Fencing	Decorative preservatives
Garden furniture	Oil stain preservatives
Timber cladding	Oil stain preservatives

Choosing the right stain and varnish

As with paints, it is best to choose a well-known brand to be sure of a quality finish. If you are treating exterior wood, it is particularly important to choose a protective, exterior-quality stain or varnish.

Colour strengths
It is not always easy to choose the right coloured wood stain for the effect you have in mind, because the final colour will be influenced by the initial colour of the wood and its rate of absorption. So, where possible, make a test on a small piece of the wood, remembering that additional coats will intensify the colour and that most stains will darken as they dry. To lighten the shade, water-based stains can

be thinned with water and oil, and solvent-based stains thinned with white spirit. Wood stains of the same brand can also be mixed to produce various colours.

Application techniques
Oil-based stains are the easiest to use, because their slow drying time produces a more even colour. Spirit-based stains need an expert hand as they dry very quickly. Water-based stains tend to raise the wood

grain, so need rubbing down after staining. This can be an advantage, however, if you wish to reduce the colour slightly.

Polyurethanes are best built up in a number of coats, the first rubbed into the wood with a lint-free cloth to act as a seal to the wood surface. It is lightly sanded when dry before subsequent coats are brushed on. If used outdoors, these stains will be affected by bright sunlight and the edges must be sealed against damp.

Tips on buying stain and varnish

◇ If using stains for the first time, choose an oil-based type.
◇ If you find your chosen stain is too pale, add extra coats to darken the wood. To lighten a stain, sand the surface of the wood and dilute the stain.

◇ Varnish will last longer on mahogany-type woods, than on coarser woods, such as oak and Western red cedar.
◇ If you plan to add a coat of varnish over a stain, check that they have a compatible chemical base.

Wall coverings

Modern wall coverings fall into three main categories: paper, plastic and fabric. Yet, within these three groups, the range of decorative styles and practical properties can be overwhelming, so, to limit the choice, it is usually best to consider the practical details first.

The most resilient materials are usually plastic – they will withstand wear and tear, scrubbing and scuffing. Some also have insulating and water-resistant properties. Wallpapers, whether designed to be painted after hanging or not, are less hard-wearing; however, they can help to disguise an imperfect surface. Some papers and fabrics such as silk are purely decorative.

Colour, pattern and design influence the style and proportions of a room (see *Colour and pattern for effect, p. 31*), so it is important to choose with great care.

Price may also influence your decision. The range is wide – from the cheapest printed paper to expensive silks, and it is worth "shopping around" for the best prices. It may not be possible to cover an entire room in an expensive fabric, so consider using one or two rolls as a panel against a less expensive, but harmonizing backcloth.

Most wall coverings are supplied in rolls, 10.05m long by 52cm wide, but wider rolls are sometimes available. You will usually find details of the sizes specified in the manufacturer's pattern book.

For information on applying wall coverings, see pp. 28-43.

Lining papers

White lining paper
A pure white paper specially made to provide a smooth surface for painting.

Off-white lining paper
Used as a base for wallpaper, the lining comes in three weights: lightweight, for use over non-absorbent surfaces, such as gloss paint, when a standard wall covering is to be used; medium-weight, for normal surfaces; and heavyweight, when a thick wall covering or a vinyl is being used. Brown lining paper is used under extra heavy coverings, such as flock wallpaper.

Reinforced linen-backed lining paper
A heavy white lining paper backed with fine linen scrim, used for very uneven surfaces and those subject to movement, such as tongue-and-groove boards.

Expanded polystyrene
Sold in rolls or thin sheets, this lining will seal a wall that is prone to condensation and will also help to smooth a poor surface before adding a top wall covering.

Wallpapers

Standard wallpaper
A roll of smooth paper with pattern and colour printed on it. Although inexpensive, this is the least resilient of the wall coverings.

Plain embossed wallpaper
A heavy paper, designed to be painted over. It has a texture pressed into it to form a whole range of patterns, from basketweave to imitation plaster. Some types, known as duplex, comprise two layers of paper.

Woodchip
Designed to be painted, this heavy paper is good for disguising mild imperfections on a surface. It consists of a heavy-paper base, with a surface layer of wood chips which creates a pleasant texture.

High relief paper
A variety of wall coverings with a pronounced relief pattern, imitating stone, pebbles, tiles, plaster daub or random relief patterns. Good for concealing a lumpy surface, high relief paper is also designed to be painted.

Hand-printed paper
Printed by hand (by block or screen methods) instead of machine, and available from specialist suppliers. Roll widths and lengths are not always standard.

Flock paper
A fine pile is added to selected areas of the paper to produce a flocked pattern. It needs careful handling to prevent paste staining the surface. Flocks with a vinyl base are more durable, easier to clean and some are ready pasted.

Borders and friezes
Thin ribbons of printed wallpaper, usually supplied in rolls and often in designs that co-ordinate with wallpaper ranges. Friezes are usually hung just below ceiling level, and borders are positioned around walls or doorways.

Plastic wall coverings

Washable paper
A thin transparent vinyl coating makes this paper easy to clean and resistant to stains but difficult to remove once hung. Some types are available ready-pasted.

Vinyl paper
Not to be confused with washable paper, this consists of a thick layer of vinyl bonded on to a paper backing.

Ready-pasted paper
A convenience paper: the backing is pre-coated with water-active adhesive and is dipped in water before hanging. This avoids the time-consuming job of pasting the paper and ensures an even covering of adhesive. Washable vinyl and woodchip papers come ready-pasted.

Foamed polyethylene
A lightweight material resembling a printed fabric, it is hung by pasting it to the wall. It is warm to the touch and easy to strip, since there is no backing paper.

Foamed vinyl
The pattern is raised or embossed by a heat process after printing. This provides a relief effect while retaining a smooth backing. Designed to be painted, it is tougher than embossed paper and cannot be spoiled by pressing out.

Relief vinyl
Using photographic techniques, these produce a realistic imitation of all kinds of tile, and are an inexpensive substitute for the real thing.

Metallic foils
A metallized plastic film, finely embossed with coloured patterns to reflect the light. A smooth wall is essential, since the shine tends to highlight any defects.

Fabric coverings

Hessian
Normally sold in 90cm-wide rolls and usually hung by pasting the wall. It is available unbacked, but the paper-backed version is easier to handle.

Grasscloth
A fragile fabric consisting of natural grasses woven into a fine cotton weft and bonded on to a paper backing. It must be hung carefully and with a special adhesive.

Silk
Plain or patterned silk stuck to a paper backing. It is important not to contaminate the face of the material with paste, since it stains easily.

Woven fabrics
A variety of fabrics are sold purpose-made with a paper backing. Alternatively, furnishing fabric can be cut into lengths and applied to a pre-pasted wall. Some fabrics are hung with special adhesives.

Cork
A thin veneer of cork mounted on to a painted paper backing to give a two-tone effect. Careful hanging is essential and a special, ready-mixed adhesive should be used.

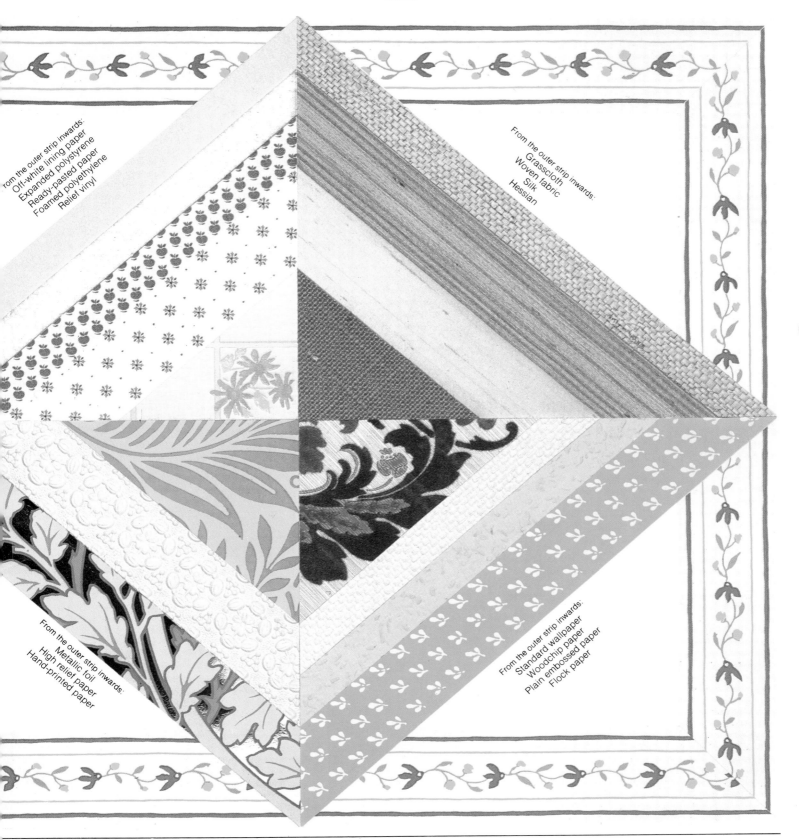

From the outer strip inwards:
Off-white lining paper
Expanded polystyrene
Ready-pasted paper
Foamed polyethylene
Relief vinyl

From the outer strip inwards:
Grasscloth
Woven fabric
Silk
Hessian

From the outer strip inwards:
Metallic foil
High relief paper
Hand-printed paper

From the outer strip inwards:
Standard wallpaper
Woodchip paper
Plain embossed paper
Flock paper

Wall coverings

Comparing types of wall covering

The durability of wall coverings varies. Vinyls and some of the thicker fabrics stand up well to wear and tear, while thin papers and delicate fabrics are more vulnerable. The emboss on a duplex paper is more resilient than a standard single paper, since the embossed texture is added in the factory while the two papers are still wet with adhesive.

Ease of cleaning
Some materials are also easier to clean than others. Papers divide into three sorts: spongeable types (which can be gently sponged clean); washable types (which can be washed with a wet, soapy cloth); and scrubbable types (which withstand washing with a mild abrasive). Fabrics are more prone to staining than papers, and vinyl less so.

Ease of hanging
The thicker and washable materials are the easiest to handle. Foamed polyethylenes and foamed vinyls, for example, hold their shape well when pasted and as the backings are smooth, they use far less paste than the traditional embosses. When pressure is applied to the pattern (when securing the edges with a seam roller, for example) the foam will flatten but recover, whereas an emboss will remain flat.

The most luxurious finishes are usually the most expensive, and often demand a slightly different hanging technique (see Textured wall coverings, pp. 42-3). Greater care is needed to keep paste off the surface, and to avoid expensive cutting mistakes. However, once hung, they usually have a long life.

Tips on buying wall coverings

◇ Check that you receive the exact design you ordered from the supplier and that all rolls display the same batch number.
◇ Generally rolls on display are cheaper than paper ordered from a pattern book, so shop around.
◇ Avoid thin, cheap papers; they will tear easily after pasting.

Comparing types of wall covering

Wall covering		Durable	Easy to clean	Easy to hang	Inexpensive
		In each case, a score of 5 indicates the highest score from an average sample.			
Standard paper		3	3	5	5
Wood chip (painted)		3	3	3	4
Plain embossed High relief		4	4	5	5
Hand printed		3	3	2	2
Flock		2	2	2	3
Plastics					
Vinyl		5	5	5	3
Washable		5	5	5	3
Ready-pasted		5	5	4	3
Foamed polyethylene		4	5	5	3
Vinyl flock		3	4	3	2
Relief vinyl		4	5	4	2
Metallic foil		3	4	4	2
Wallcovering fabrics					
Hessian (paper-backed)		3	2	4	2
Grasscloth (paper-backed)		2	1	1	1
Silk (paper-backed)		1	1	1	1
Woven fabrics (paper-backed)		2	2	2	1
Cork (paper-backed)		3	2	4	3

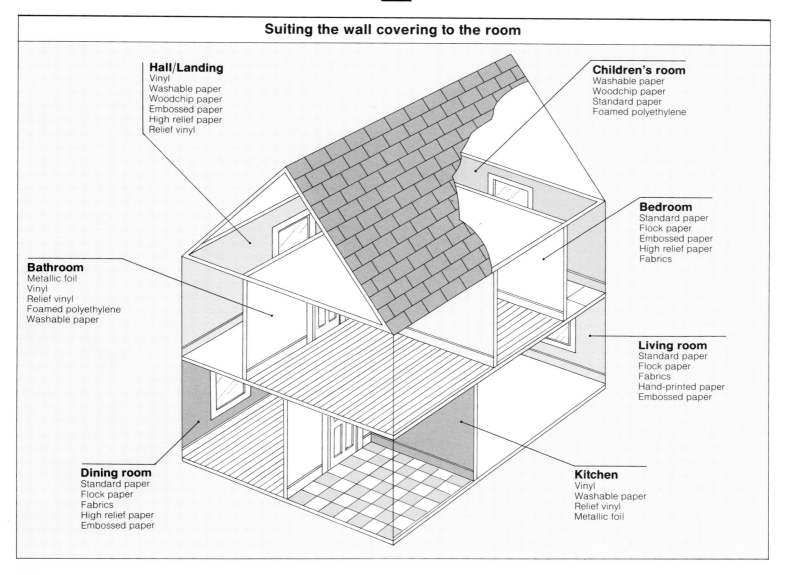

Suiting the wall covering to the room

Hall/Landing
Vinyl
Washable paper
Woodchip paper
Embossed paper
High relief paper
Relief vinyl

Children's room
Washable paper
Woodchip paper
Standard paper
Foamed polyethylene

Bathroom
Metallic foil
Vinyl
Relief vinyl
Foamed polyethylene
Washable paper

Bedroom
Standard paper
Flock paper
Embossed paper
High relief paper
Fabrics

Living room
Standard paper
Flock paper
Fabrics
Hand-printed paper
Embossed paper

Dining room
Standard paper
Flock paper
Fabrics
High relief paper
Embossed paper

Kitchen
Vinyl
Washable paper
Relief vinyl
Metallic foil

Choosing the right adhesive

It is vitally important to choose an adhesive compatible with your wall covering, or it may ruin your decoration. So, it makes sense to choose your wall covering before buying adhesive. If in doubt, consult the store staff. For wallpapers, there is a choice of powder adhesives designed to be mixed with cold water. As a general rule, the heavier the paper, the thicker the paste should be.

Using glue size
It is still good practice to "size" walls prior to decorating (see Job 15, p. 33). This improves adhesion and makes positioning easier, allowing the wall covering to slip into place. Many pastes can be used as size, and instructions about quantities are usually given on the packet.

Specialist pastes
For vinyl and heavyweight papers, there are, in addition to powders, a number of ready-mixed pastes used straight from the tub. For vinyls and other impervious materials, it is essential to use a paste which contains fungicide, on both the top covering and the lining, to prevent mould growing under the surface. Fungicides are poisonous, so always wash your hands after using these pastes. Some materials, such as hessian and grasscloth, demand a special heavy-weight paste.

Most paper-backed wall coverings expand when pasted. It is therefore important to allow the paper to "soak" until expansion is completed, before applying it to the wall (see Job 17, p. 35).

Pre-applied pastes
Some wallcoverings are available pre-pasted, and the adhesive has to be activated by immersing the wall covering in a water trough. A compromise has to be made by the manufacturers as to how much paste is applied, and on some impervious surfaces, there may be a surplus of paste which will have to be wiped away.

Tiles

Ceramic wall tiles, available from DIY shops, supermarkets and special tile shops, come in a wide range of colours, patterns, textures and shapes. The range of ceramic floor tiles is less extensive. Plain tiles are often coloured to match standard bathroom fittings, and can be combined with complementary patterned tiles. Some patterned tiles carry an individual pattern and can be used as random cameos within plain tiling, while others, such as tile murals, are designed to be used in groups to complete a motif. Both smooth and textured finishes are available – also hand-painted tiles which are very expensive but can be used sparingly in strategic places. Heat-resistant and frost-proof tiles can also be used where required. Other materials, such as cork, metal, glass and vinyl, offer an additional range of design effects and practical properties.

Ceramic tiles are sold singly, by the square metre or, more economically, in boxes of 25 and 50 or 16 and 36. However, prices vary enormously so it is worth shopping around. Other types of tile are usually sold in packs, but some suppliers will break a pack to give you the exact number you require. Take care to measure and estimate accurately (*see Estimating quantities, p. 45*) and allow a few extra tiles for breakages, and for future repairs.

For information on applying tiles see pp. 44-55.

Ceiling tiles

Polystyrene tiles
The least expensive ceiling covering after paint, these tiles are available plain for over-painting or with a design embossed on to the surface. Avoid using polystyrene above cookers, since it may constitute a fire risk. Only use water-based emulsion paints for over-painting polystyrene tiles; oil-based paints can also be a fire hazard. Use the recommended adhesive.

Fibreboard tiles
Made from compressed wood or mineral fibres, and thicker than poly-styrene tiles. Some have tongue-and-groove edges which allow them to interlock together and to be stapled invisibly to the ceiling joists. Others have straight edges and are fixed with adhesive. Both types come with either a plain or an embossed surface.

Wall tiles

Ceramic tiles
Modern ceramic wall tiles consist of slabs of clay, decorated on one side with a coloured glaze. They are fired to produce a durable, stain- and water-resistant surface.

Cork tiles
Manufactured from pressed layers of tree bark, and available either sealed or un-sealed, these come in a variety of natural colours, sometimes with a slight grain direction. Cork is warm to the touch and a good heat and sound insulator, but the surface must be sealed with a polyurethane varnish if it is to be cleaned easily. Some are also treated with a washable and steam-proof finish.

Mosaic tiles
These consist of tiny ceramic tiles – square shaped or interlocking – mounted on a mesh backing sheet. They are laid and grouted in the same way as ceramic tiles and have the same qualities, but are more expensive.

Mirror tiles
Square or rectangular pieces of clear or tinted mirrored glass. They are easier to work with than mirror sheets, but the wall surface must be perfectly smooth before the tiles are laid or the reflection will be distorted.

Brick tiles
Thin slices of real brick or man-made brick

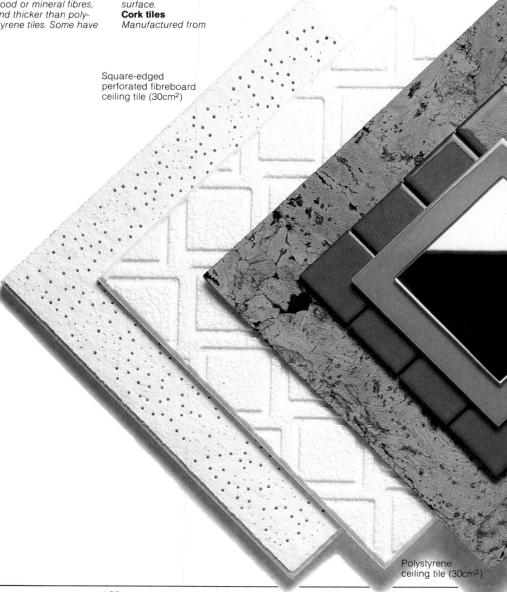

Square-edged perforated fibreboard ceiling tile (30cm²)

Polystyrene ceiling tile (30cm²)

construction, available in several colours and cut to the same size as real bricks to give the wall an authentic appearance.

Metallic tiles
Usually coloured gold, silver or copper in a matt or shiny finish, these provide a heat-proof surface. They are washable, but any splash marks must be cleaned off immediately. They have hollow backs, can be cut to shape with scissors, or bent around corners, and are fixed with self-adhesive pads. Since metal conducts electricity, these tiles should be trimmed around light switches.

Vinyl and plastic tiles
Made from thin plastic or vinyl sheet, these are warm to the touch and help reduce noise. Like metallic tiles, they have hollow backs, can be cut with scissors, and are fixed with self-adhesive pads.

Floor tiles

Ceramic floor tiles
Slightly thicker than ceramic wall tiles and fired at a higher temperature, so that the particles fuse, making the tile almost unbreakable when laid. They may be bought glazed or unglazed in a variety of earth colours. Glazed tiles may be cold and noisy underfoot but the slip-resistant types are less dangerous when wet. Unglazed tiles should be sealed before use.

Quarry tiles
These are unglazed and therefore rougher in finish and cheaper than ceramic tiles but they have the same properties. They are laid in a mortar bed, then sealed and polished. Colours are normally restricted to earth reds and browns.

Vinyl tiles
Solid vinyl, latex-backed tiles are durable and comfortable, but can be slippery when wet. They are easier to lay than sheet flooring and less wasteful, especially in awkward-shaped rooms. A choice of plain colours and patterns is available, some imitating other materials, such as stone and wood.

Vinyl-coated tiles
Smooth and easy to clean, these tiles are much cheaper, but less comfortable and durable than vinyl tiles.

Rubber tiles
Quiet and comfortable, rubber tiles are expensive but hard-wearing. The colour range is limited, but studs and other embosses can create a "high tech" style.

Marble tiles
Durable and luxurious, marble tiles come in slabs of the natural marble colours – pink, green, grey and black, and are laid on a bed of mortar.

Stone tiles
Like marble, stone tiles are enduring and expensive floor coverings. Slate is available in grey, green and blue squares or rectangles and is laid on a cement bed.

Cork tiles
Cork is comfortable to walk on but not very durable. Some types are supplied with a polyurethane or thin vinyl finish, others have to be sanded and sealed after laying to prevent water penetrating between the tiles.

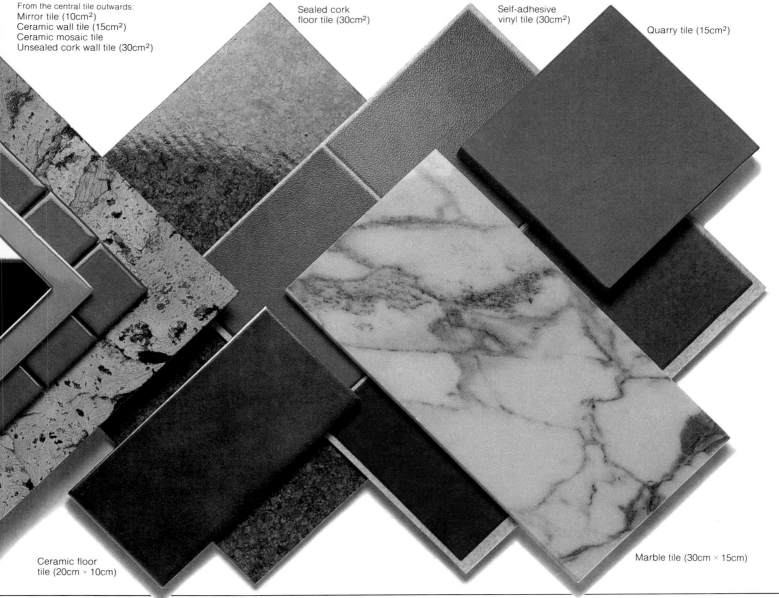

From the central tile outwards:
Mirror tile (10cm²)
Ceramic wall tile (15cm²)
Ceramic mosaic tile
Unsealed cork wall tile (30cm²)

Sealed cork floor tile (30cm²)

Self-adhesive vinyl tile (30cm²)

Quarry tile (15cm²)

Ceramic floor tile (20cm × 10cm)

Marble tile (30cm × 15cm)

Tiles

The range of tile shapes

Most ceramic tiles are either square or oblong, but a range of interlocking circular, hexagonal and Provençale-shaped tiles are also to be found. Square and rectangular shapes, however, are generally less expensive and easier to lay. The most common type of tile, known as a "field" tile, has square edges, sometimes with spacer lugs to allow space between the tiles for grouting. Some manufacturers also produce "universal" tiles which have one or two glazed edges for finishing exposed edges. Quadrant tiles are round-edged slivers for use as border tiles on corners, such as window sills. Other types of tile, such as cork, vinyl, mirror and plastic, come as squares or rectangles, and brick tiles are the same shape and size as natural bricks. Ceramic wall tiles usually come in 10cm² or 15cm² sizes, ceramic floor tiles come in 15cm × 20cm sizes, whereas most other tiles are 30cm².

Choosing the right adhesive

As with wallpapers, it is crucial to choose the correct adhesive for the type of tile, the conditions and the area in which it is to be used. Ceramic tiles should be fixed with ceramic tile adhesive, which is sold ready-mixed or in powder form.

Waterproof types are available for shower cubicles and sink splashbacks; frost-proof types for use on patios or balconies; and heat-resistant ones for kitchens and fireplaces. There is also a flexible adhesive for tiling over a surface which is prone to movement, such as hardboard and chipboard: it often comes in two parts to be mixed before use. A thick-bed adhesive should be used on uneven surfaces.

Cork tiles should be fixed with either non-flammable cork wall or floor adhesive, or a water-based contact adhesive, depending on the instructions supplied. A specific adhesive is also available for brick tiles. Mirror, plastic and metallic tiles are secured in place with sticky tabs. For each square metre of tiling, you will need about 1 litre of adhesive.

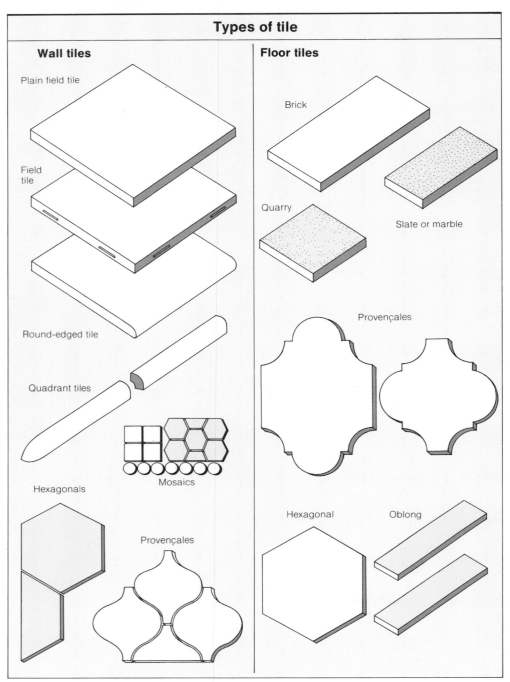

Types of tile

Wall tiles

Plain field tile

Field tile

Round-edged tile

Quadrant tiles

Hexagonals

Mosaics

Provençales

Floor tiles

Brick

Slate or marble

Quarry

Provençales

Hexagonal

Oblong

Tips on buying tiles

◇ It is cheaper to buy tiles in boxes than singly.
◇ Count part tiles as whole tiles for estimating purposes, but remember that with large cork or vinyl tiles, one tile can be cut into several border pieces.
◇ Always check tiles for chips and colour differences when you get them home.
◇ Allow a few extra tiles (about five per cent) for breakages and for future repairs.
◇ When cutting tiles, always exert even pressure and keep the tile supported, to be sure of a clean break.

Suiting the wall tile to the room

Type	Qualities	Room	Adhesive
Ceramic	Hard-wearing, waterproof, stain-resistant	Kitchens and bathrooms	Ceramic wall tile adhesive – waterproof adhesive in areas likely to be splashed by water
Mosaics	Hard-wearing, waterproof, stain-resistant	Kitchens and bathrooms	As for ceramic tiles
Cork	Warm, reasonably hard-wearing and stain-resistant	Anywhere except excessively wet areas, e.g. showers	Cork wall tile adhesive. Non-flammable emulsion types are safest. Contact adhesive is an alternative
Mirror	Hard-wearing, stain-resistant Ideal for small feature areas Gives a feeling of space	Anywhere except excessively wet areas	Adhesive tabs
Brick	Hard-wearing, ideal for complete walls or feature areas	Any room but avoid areas where bricks could be affected by grease, excessive steam or water splashes	Brick wall tile adhesive
Plastic and metallic	Fairly easy to clean but some can be damaged by abrasive cleaners. Reasonably hard-wearing	Kitchens and bathrooms but avoid using plastics near heat, and metallics near steam	Adhesive tabs or contact adhesive

Suiting the floor tile to the room

Type	Qualities	Room	Adhesive
Ceramic	Hard-wearing, waterproof, stain-resistant but cold and noisy	Kitchens, bathrooms and halls	Ceramic floor tile adhesive
Quarry	As above	Kitchens, bathrooms and halls	Ceramic floor tile adhesive or (for thicker types) mortar cement
Cork	Very comfortable, warm and quiet. Not very durable. Reasonably able to withstand water	Any room	Cork floor tile adhesive as recommended by tile manu-facturers
Vinyl	Very comfortable, warm and quiet. Durable on well laid sub-floor. Reasonably able to withstand water	Any room but mostly kitchens and bathrooms	Some are self-adhesive. Others are laid with vinyl floor adhesive
Marble	Hard-wearing and waterproof	Kitchens, bathrooms and halls	Mortar cement

Wooden surfaces

Wood forms a warm, smooth and attractive surface. It is extremely durable, has acoustic and insulating properties and, thanks to modern wood finishes, is easy to maintain. It therefore forms an ideal covering for walls and ceilings in any room and for floors in all but kitchens and bathrooms.

Wooden panelling for walls and ceilings is available as boards or as sheets. Tongue-and-groove boards are made from planed planks which are designed to interlock together to form a broad, gap-free area of panelling. Most have chamferred edges to form a decorative "V" joint. Man-made sheet wallboards, designed to simulate boards, are usually sheets of thin plywood with a real wood veneer or a printed plastic or paper surface, simulating various types of decorative wood. Embossed panels, printed with deeply textured wood effects, are also available.

Most wooden flooring is solid hardwood laid over an ordinary sub-floor, such as chipboard, plywood or hardboard. Some types, however, consist of a hardwood layer bonded to a plywood backing. Flooring comes as either long strips of wood (wood strip) or blocks arranged into patterns (wood block or mosaic panels). Wood blocks can be arranged into a variety of patterns and basketweave mosaic panels can be laid square or diagonally across the room.

For information on fitting wooden panelling and flooring, see pp. 66-77 and 82-87.

Panelling

Board panelling

Tongue-and-groove boards
These are usually available in whitewood (spruce) and knotty pine (deal, Scots pine and Red Baltic pine) and often in a good range of more unusual decorative species (see chart overleaf). They usually come with chamferred edges, to form a decorative "V" joint and with either a flat or a decorative face – channelled or scalloped, for example. The standard thickness is 13mm, although 19mm and 9.5mm thick boards are readily available. The nominal width is generally 100mm (the actual covering width is 85mm), but 150mm tongue-and-groove boards are not uncommon. The most usual length is 2.4m, although some suppliers stock longer random lengths.

Shiplap boards
These are similar to tongue-and-groove, except that the top edge of each board fits under a rebate in the edge of the previous board. When fixed horizontally, the water will run down the face of the boards without penetrating the surface. Shiplap boards are usually available only in deal and in two sizes: 19mm × 120mm and 25mm × 150mm.

Sheet panelling

Wallboards
These thin plywood or hardboard sheets come with a variety of surfaces. The best quality sheets have a veneer of real wood, which may also be grooved to simulate tongue-and-groove boards. Cheaper varieties have a photographic image of a wooden surface printed on paper or plastic and bonded on to the plywood backing. Both types come in sheets measuring 2440mm × 1220mm, and 4mm or 6mm thick. This height is usually sufficient to cover a wall from floor to ceiling in one sheet without horizontal joins.

Flooring

Wooden sub-floors

Chipboard
This man-made material consists of resin-coated wood chips compressed under heat and pressure into a board. Standard chipboard is usually used as a self-contained sub-floor, but an extra-strong type has tongue-and-

Tongue and groove board (Pine)

Pine veneered wallboard

Walnut veneered wallboard

Shiplap board (Pine)

From the central piece outward
Chipboard (18mm)
3-ply plywood (12mm)
Hardboard (3mm)

groove edges and can be used as a top floor covering.

Plywood

Plywood is composed of thin sheets (veneers) of wood glued together. The grain runs alternately along and across the wood, giving the composite sheet greater uniformity of strength than wood. There are two basic types of plywood: timber ply, which is made from a single type of timber and is used as a sub-floor; and veneered ply, which is made from a variety of woods and can be used as a substitute for timber flooring. Tongue-and-groove plywood is available for this purpose

and the wood is graded according to the quality of the surface veneer and the glue. There are also special surface finishes, such as plastic, metal and varnish. For exterior use, choose boards made with moisture- and weather-proof glue.

Hardboard

This is made from pulped wood fibre, hot-pressed into thin sheets, and since it bends easily, it is generally used as a sub-floor over timber boards. There are a variety of types and finishes, but standard and water-resistant tempered hardboard are usual floor coverings. Standard hardboard has one smooth face and a

textured back. Medium hardboard has a softer surface for lining walls and ceilings. Double-faced and plastic-coated hardboards are also available.

Woodstrip flooring

Hardwood woodstrip

Solid tongue-and-groove boards about 19mm thick and in random lengths slot together to form narrow floorboards. They are laid at right angles to the sub-floor and come in a range of solid timbers to form a luxury floor.

Plywood woodstrip

Some woodstrip floors are made from plywood

strips overlaid with hardwood. The strips are either slotted together with tongues and grooves, allowing them to "float" on the sub-floor as one piece; or, the plywood has interlocking "ears" which are pinned to the floor. The floor thickness can vary from 8mm to 14mm overall.

Bitumen-cork underlay

A coarse paper, impregnated with bitumen and coated with cork chips, this underlay is used under parquet panels.

Woodblock flooring

Wood mosaic panels

Each panel is made up

of five or seven hardwood "fingers" in four parts (20 or 28 pieces overall), which are glued together on a bitumen-felt backing. The panels are usually either 300mm or 470mm square and the individual "fingers" in each panel are arranged to build up a basket-weave pattern. This type of floor usually requires sanding and sealing after laying. Some hardwood mosaic floors are supplied tongued-and-grooved, pre-sealed and finished in rigid panels, which are strengthened with soft aluminium pins or a plywood backing.

Parquet panels

A parquet panel floor consists of shallow

blocks, about 220mm × 70mm and 20mm thick, which are interlocked with tongues and grooves into panels, to create a flat, solid surface. They are available in a range of hardwoods. Traditional blocks can be laid in a variety of patterns – usually basket-weave, but also traditional herringbone, brick-pattern and others. Unlike wood mosaic panels, parquet panels are pre-finished and simply float on an underlay of bitumen paper and cork granules. Traditional parquet blocks, however, are not tongue-and-groove, and must be both sanded and sealed after laying.

Parquet woodblock (Merbau)

Hardwood woodstrip (Light oak)

Straight-edged mosaic panel (teak)

Tongue and groove mosaic panel (Red oak)

Wooden surfaces

Comparing types of wooden panelling

Timbers vary dramatically in graining, colour and properties, so take time to choose a wood that is suitable for both the purpose and the style of the room. Remember that stains and varnishes can be used to modify the colour and the gloss of the surface, although nothing can be done to change the grain. Hardwoods are generally more durable and decorative, although more expensive than softwoods. However, the quality is more variable and they are not always as readily available.

Price differences

Whitewood panelling is about one-third of the price of hardwood and red cedar, and just under half the price of hemlock and Douglas fir. Knotty pine is slightly more expensive than whitewood – almost exactly half the price of hemlock and Douglas fir. Wood veneer wallboards allow luxurious hardwood finishes to be used at reasonable prices. The prices are roughly equivalent to panelling in traditional knotty pine, although rosewood is about twice the price of other types. Flame-retardant treated panels are also available at about twice the price of conventional veneered boards. Embossed hardboard wall panels are in the same price bracket as real wood veneer panels, while printed face wallboards are about half the price. Some timber merchants charge on a sliding scale for cutting, so it may work out cheaper to buy a full-size board.

Choosing between sheet and board panelling

Individual tongue-and-groove boards offer the widest choice of pattern. They are also more versatile than sheet panelling, since they comprise smaller units. Wallboards, on the other hand, are usually large enough to stretch from floor to ceiling and will cover a wall in a few sheets butted side by side, and so involve less work. For a large area, tongue-and-groove boards are usually best, because the end joins can be neatly staggered and so form part of the overall pattern.

The range of timbers for wooden panelling			
Wood type	**Description**	**Comments**	**Price** **A** = High **B** = Medium **C** = Moderate
Solid boards			
Cedar (Western red)	Reddish tan, pronounced straight grain	Will withstand high temperature	Ⓐ
Knotty pine (Deal, Scots pine, Red Baltic pine)	Pale yellow/cream, pronounced knots	Quality of finish varies	Ⓒ
Whitewood (Spruce)	Creamy white to light golden yellow	Tools must be sharp	Ⓓ
Douglas fir	Gold, reddish brown, pronounced wavy grain	Tools must be sharp	Ⓑ
Hardwood (Mahogany type)	Reddish brown, open grain	Some timbers may need sanding	Ⓐ
Veneered sheets			
Cherry	Medium, wavy grain		Ⓒ
Sapele	Reddish-brown, straight open grain		Ⓒ
Rosewood	Dark brown, wavy black grain		Ⓐ
Teak	Reddish brown, attractive graining	Resists acid, fire and rot	Ⓒ
Elm	Light brown, close grain		Ⓒ
Knotty cedar	Golden reddish brown, wavy grain		Ⓒ
Oak	Beige/brown, long straight grain	Durable, needs sharp tools	Ⓒ
Ash	Creamy brown, wavy grain	Bends well	Ⓒ

Tips on buying timber

◇ Many DIY shops, supermarkets and hardware stores sell timber panels, strips, blocks and sheets, pre-cut in packs, complete with a coverage guide. Always check that there is a good mixture of light and dark grains.

◇ Timber merchants sell wood planed and ready cut to standard sizes, and most will cut hardwood to a special size if given a few days notice.

◇ Timber merchants are often cheaper than DIY shops, especially for larger quantities, and will usually give good advice.

◇ Before buying, check boards for defects and avoid those that are bowed, cupped, twisted or heavily knotted. It will be impossible to straighten a distorted board. A few knots can look attractive, but always check that they are sound and show no sign of loosening.

◇ Prices vary according to the outlet and the availability of timber, so shop around.

Choosing between strip and block flooring

Woodstrip flooring is a glorified form of floorboard, but with the range of attractive grains and colours afforded by natural timbers and wood stains, it can become a high-quality floor. Woodstrip is quicker and easier to lay than woodblock. However, it may shrink when underfloor heating is used, so always check with the supplier first. Woodblock flooring is the most popular wooden floor. It is more versatile than woodstrip, giving more opportunity for pattern and texture, and produces a smoother, more luxurious finish. Both parquet and wooden mosaic floors need to be sealed and sanded after laying, unless they have been pre-sealed.

Woodstrip flooring is at the top of the price range, followed by parquet, then wooden mosaic panels. Solid and pre-finished woodstrip is more expensive than plywood overlaid with hardwood and unfinished woodstrip, that needs to be sanded and sealed after laying.

Some man-made softwood boards, such as chipboard and plywood, can be used as a top floor covering, provided they have a special veneer or finish, although the result can never compete with solid timber.

The range of timbers for wooden flooring					
Wood type	Description	Parquet	Woodstrip	Mosaic	Price A = High B = Medium C = Moderate
Merbau	Rich red brown Good for heavy traffic	◇	◇	◇	Ⓐ
Iroko	Warm golden brown Very hard-wearing	◇		◇	Ⓑ
Mahogany	Reddish brown Hard-wearing			◇	Ⓐ
Tasmanian oak (Eucalyptus)	Cream, straight grain Fairly hard-wearing			◇	Ⓒ
Light oak	Light straw colour. Hard-wearing	◇		◇	Ⓑ
Dark oak	Rich brown Hard-wearing			◇	Ⓑ
Maple	Cream. Exceptionally hard-wearing	◇	◇		Ⓒ
Ash	Pale cream. Hard-wearing		◇		Ⓑ
Beech	Creamy brown, light grain. Hard-wearing		◇		Ⓒ

Comparing types of wooden flooring

Wooden flooring receives more wear than panelling, and the timbers need to be more durable. The availability of timbers for different floor types varies. Mahogany and oak, for example, are usually only available for mosaic panels, while ash and beech are generally only found as wood-strip flooring.

Price differences
Prices of timbers vary, and Merbau, the most hard-wearing, costs a little more than oak and ash. Beech and maple are less expensive. In parquet flooring, all timbers cost the same, but ordinary parquet costs a third of the price of pre-finished parquet. In the mosaic panel range, Merbau again is the most costly, followed by Iroko and dark Oak; Eucalyptus is about three-quarters of the price of Merbau. Thus, one of the most expensive floors is Merbau woodstrip, and one of the cheapest, Maple mosaic.

Comparing types of man-made boards

Man-made boards, such as plywood and hardboard, are cheap, hard-wearing and form excellent sub-floors over old boards. Plywood is the strongest of the three types and is not prone to splitting or warping.

Hardboard is more brittle and needs to be cut and fitted carefully to avoid damaging the edges. Chipboard is coarser and even less expensive and can be fixed directly to the floor joists.

Chipboard
Standard chipboard for sub-floors is supplied with sanded faces, but sealed chipboard is available for finishing off with gloss and timber-veneered types for a top floor covering.

Plywood
The thinnest types of plywood are 3-ply, but multi-ply boards are also available with up to 11 layers. Plywood strips with a surface veneer of a decorative hardwood are available for a quality finish.

Hardboard
Standard hardboard has one smooth face and a coarse, mesh back face. Tempered hardboard is impregnated with oils for extra strength and water-resistance and medium hardboard is less coarse.

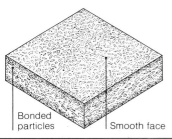

Bonded particles — Smooth face

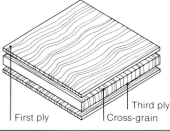

First ply — Third ply — Cross-grain

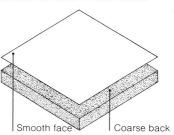

Smooth face — Coarse back

Floor coverings

Any new floor covering represents a major furnishing buy, and the choice can be bewildering, so it is important to know what to expect for your money.

Each type of covering performs a slightly different function. Carpeting provides luxury underfoot – it is warm, comfortable, sound-proofing and comes in a wide range of colours, patterns and qualities to suit most rooms in the house. For kitchens and bathrooms, sheet vinyl makes an excellent waterproof barrier, and is softer, quieter, cheaper and less slippery than tiles. Matting is a budget-priced alternative to carpets – useful for rented flats and if you are planning to move house soon. Rugs which include pieces of carpet under 4m square hide worn carpet and form a soft and decorative accessory over carpet, tiles or wooden flooring.

Carpets can be broadly divided into the following categories. There are tufted, woven and bonded types, which refers to the construction method; there are cut, looped cord and twisted types, which refers to the pile; and there are hessian-backed and foam-backed, which refers to the backing material.

For information on laying floor coverings, see pp. 56-65 and 78-81.

Underlays

Felt
This traditional type of underlay has been largely replaced by hessian-backed rubber underlay, but it absorbs underfloor dust more efficiently.

Rubber
Hessian-backed or paper-backed rubber are the best quality under-lays for most carpets and are essential for stairs.

Foam rubber
Only suitable for use in areas of light wear, it should have a layer of felt paper beneath.

Felt paper
Used under foam-backed carpet and foam rubber underlay to prevent them sticking to the floor.

Other types
Other materials include hard-wearing jute, waterproof pvc, and felt-substitutes.

Foam rubber

Felt paper

Rubber

Latex

Felt

Carpets

Standard short pile
A standard pile carpet is available in either a woven form (such as Axminster and Wilton carpets, named after the looms on which they are woven) or in a cheaper tufted form. The pile is cut short.

Loop pile
In this case, fine or coarse yarn is woven into the carpet, but left uncut to make a series of loops.

Sculptured pile
A woven or tufted carpet that is a mixture of cut and looped pile. Some loops are cut and some left looped, to produce a three dimensional effect, which, though attractive can be difficult to clean.

Hair and woolcord
The yarn is woven into the backing, pulled tight and left uncut, to give a hard-wearing surface.

Twist
Before the carpet is woven, the yarn is twisted to give the carpet a textured, springy and very hard-wearing surface.

Velvet
The pile is extremely dense, deep and smooth and is cut to produce a luxurious finish, with a definite right and wrong way. It will shade and track when walked on.

Shag
A luxurious carpet with a long cut pile of 25mm. The pile treads down easily and needs to be raked and cleaned regularly.

Berber
These carpets have a dense, looped pile and are made from undyed sheep wool.

Foam-backed carpet
Usually a tufted carpet with a foam backing. It is easier to lay than hessian-backed types, but normally it does not wear as well.

Carpet tiles
Available in woven, tufted, cord and bonded carpets in a variety of fibres. Most are loose laid.

Standard short pile

Foam-backed

Carpet tile

Berber

Twist pile

Velvet pile

Woolcord

Loop pile

Shag pile

Rugs and matting

Ethnic rugs
Available in cotton and wool, ethnic Indian, African, European and American rugs are generally flat weave. The price varies according to the fibre content and the intricacy of the design. Cotton rugs may "bleed" if laid over a pale carpet, so it is best to line them with fabric or paper and dry-clean.
Flokati rugs
Some cultures have used different weaving techniques to produce unusual rugs. Greek Flokati rugs, which have a luxurious, deep pile, are made from woven wool fleece. They are machine washable.
Rush matting
Usually woven in 30cm squares, rush matting can be sewn together to form larger pieces. It is available in a variety of designs, can be loose laid directly on to wood or concrete without an underlay and is easily rolled up to take with you when you move. However, it collects dirt, and should be regularly lifted to sweep away the dust. It can be gently scrubbed with a soapless detergent.

Coconut matting
This is the coarse matting found at front and back doors, and is available in a variety of sizes for use in areas of heavy and dirty traffic.
Coir matting
A more refined form of coconut matting, coir comes in a variety of

thicknesses, colours, textures and weaves, from simple crossweave to a heavier, tighter loop with a non-slip backing.
Split cane matting
Similar to rush matting, but more rigid, split cane is likewise inexpensive and hard-wearing, but attracts the dust.

Sisal matting
This tough, naturally white fibre makes a good floor covering in halls and passageways.
Plastic matting
Useful in kitchens and bathrooms, plastic matting is cheap, easy to clean and comes in a range of bright colours.

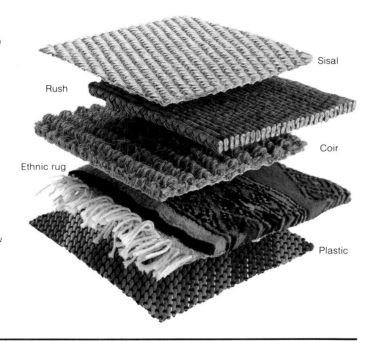

Rush

Ethnic rug

Sisal

Coir

Plastic

Sheet flooring

Sheet vinyl
Some types, known as "lay flat vinyl", can be loose laid, others need to be stuck around the edges to the sub-floor with double-sided tape. The better qualities, known as cushioned vinyl, have a layer of foam between the vinyl and the backings, making them soft, quiet and very comfortable to walk on. Vinyls come in a wide variety of colours, designs and textures, including imitation tiles. Vinyl is impervious to water, oil, fat and most household chemicals, but most grades are not immune to burns.
Rubber flooring
Usually made from a mixture of natural and

synthetic rubber, this type of flooring is hard-wearing, quiet and water-proof; but is not as easy to lay as vinyl and marks more easily. Modern designs feature ribs, studs and squares to give a smart, non-slip surface. Rubber floors can be cleaned with soapy water, but must be rinsed well.
Linoleum
Made from a mixture of wood, linseed oil, ground cork, flour and resins, linoleum comes in various thicknesses. It is hard-wearing, but is inclined to rot if water gets underneath. In recent years, it has lost in popularity to vinyl but modern designs are now appearing in tile form.

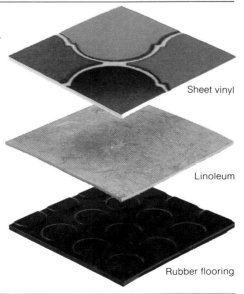

Sheet vinyl

Linoleum

Rubber flooring

Floor coverings

Comparing types of carpet fibre

Carpet fibres are divided into three basic types: pure wool, synthetics and mixtures of the two: the fibre content should be clearly labelled together with other details on every carpet.

Any carpet which bears the "Wool-mark" will have passed stringent tests for fading, wear and shrink-resistance. Wool, the traditional carpet fibre, is expensive but warm, hard-wearing, dirt-resistant, naturally fire-resistant and easy to clean. Synthetics include the following materials: acrylic, which is closest to wool in feel and appearance; nylon, which is cheap and hard-wearing, but attracts dirt and dust; and polyester, which is soft and reasonably water-resistant for bathrooms, but less hard-wearing. Mixtures are a blend of two fibres to combine the best properties of each. The most popular combination is 80 per cent wool, 20 per cent synthetic, since it reduces the price of the carpet, but looks, feels and wears like wool.

Suiting the underlay to the carpet

Underlay plays an important part in the life of your carpet, increases its heat- and sound-insulating properties and gives it a softer tread, so be sure to choose the right one. Carpets with a woven backing need to be laid over a good quality rubber underlay with a paper or hessian backing or over felt underlay. Foam rubber underlays are also available, but are only advisable in areas of light wear. They need a layer of paper underneath to prevent them sticking to the floor. Most cheaper carpets have a built-in foam backing and should be laid over felt paper underlay.

Hessian-backed carpet
You will need paper-backed or hessian-backed rubber underlay for most rooms. Alternatively, use felt, especially in rooms with underfloor heating. For rarely used rooms, a foam-rubber underlay will be adequate.

Foam-backed carpet
The only underlay appropriate to a foam-backed carpet is a felt paper one.

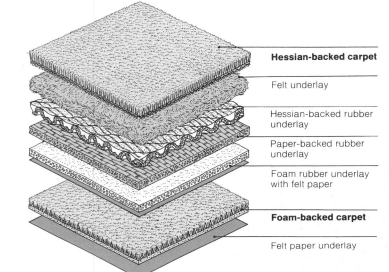

Hessian-backed carpet

Felt underlay

Hessian-backed rubber underlay

Paper-backed rubber underlay

Foam rubber underlay with felt paper

Foam-backed carpet

Felt paper underlay

Comparing types of carpet construction

There are three different ways of connecting the carpet fibre to its backing: by close interweaving; by stitching and gluing; and by simple glue bonding. Woven, tufted and bonded carpets are all available in a variety of fibres, pile lengths and roll widths. When you are looking at carpet samples, bend them back to see how dense the pile is, and how it has been connected to the backing. Then tug at a few tufts to check that the fibre is securely fixed to the backing.

Woven carpet
All woven carpets are made by either the Wilton or the Axminster method. These are two different weaving techniques, not brand names. Axminster carpets are woven one row of tufts at a time, so that the loom anchors the U-shaped tufts into the backing

material as it weaves each row. Wilton carpets are woven in one continuous length, and the pile and backing are closely interwoven for extra strength and thickness. Wilton backings are usually flatter than Axminster, and denser, with 10 or more rows of pile to the inch.

Tufted carpet
These are not woven at all. The yarn is stitched into a pre-woven "primary" backing to give a looped or cut pile. The backing is then coated with latex to secure the tufts and a second backing is added for strength and easy handling.

Bonded carpet
This is a relatively new manufacturing process in which the pile fibre is bonded on to a pre-woven backing. Bonded carpets will not fray when cut, but are available in plain colours only.

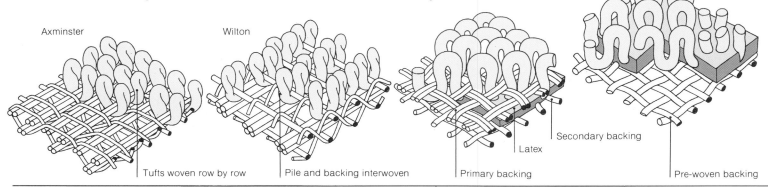

Axminster

Wilton

Tufts woven row by row

Pile and backing interwoven

Secondary backing

Latex

Primary backing

Pre-woven backing

Suiting the floor covering to the room

Before choosing a floor covering, it is important to consider the demands that will be put on it – whether it will be subject to splashing, scratching, spillages or heavy traffic. The first decision is the type of floor covering – carpet, vinyl or matting; the next is the quality. Price will naturally be a controlling factor, but when selecting carpet, it is essential to choose a grade that will withstand the wear and not to make false economies. (*For carpet grades, see p. 57.*) Once you have chosen the most appropriate type of flooring, it is worth buying the best quality you can afford: it will last longer.

Room	Carpet	Sheet flooring	Rugs and matting
Kitchen	Short pile nylon or synthetic for easy cleaning or loose-lay carpet tiles	Perfect	Rush mats give a country feel; plastic fits a modern style.
Bathroom	Only if recommended since it must have a waterproof backing. Preferably a polyester	Perfect. Sheet vinyl is water-resistant	Plastic mats or loose-lay washable cotton rugs
Living room	Choose a hard-wearing grade	Not the best choice	To brighten a large expanse of carpet or to hide worn areas
Dining room	Choose a medium grade	Not unless the dining area runs into the kitchen	Add a rug or mat over a vinyl floor for comfort
Bedrooms	The lightest and cheapest grades make economic sense	Practical in a young child's room, but too hard for adults	Add rugs beside the bed for comfort
Hall	Needs to be very hard-wearing to stand up to heavy traffic	Practical if you have children, dogs – or both	Coir is hard-wearing. Durries make a bright and cheap covering over tiles, vinyl or plain carpet

Comparing types of sheet flooring construction

The quality of sheet flooring is determined by its construction. Sheet vinyl consists of an outer "wear" layer, a filling and a backing. The most comfortable vinyl has a "cushioned" filling layer; the cheaper types have a pattern layer instead of foam cushion; while in the more durable solid vinyl the design is integrated in the material. Rubber flooring consists of layers of natural and synthetic rubber, compressed under high pressure and temperatures into a strong sheet.

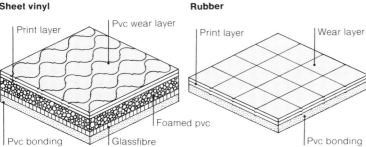

Sheet vinyl

Print layer
Pvc wear layer
Pvc bonding
Glassfibre
Foamed pvc

Rubber

Print layer
Wear layer
Pvc bonding

Tips on buying floor coverings

◇ A new floor covering should see you through several changes of decoration, so choose colours with care.

◇ Remember that dark colours show up fluff and dirt more quickly than muted tones.

◇ Small homes can be made to appear larger by using the same colour carpet throughout the ground floor and up the stairs; and sheet vinyl with a small pattern in the kitchen.

◇ "Lay flat" vinyl is easier to lay and transport than other types.

◇ All carpets should carry a label indicating the widths available, the construction method, the fibre content and any special laying and cleaning instructions.

◇ Buy the correct carpet quality grade for the room in which it is to be used (*see Identifying carpet quality, p. 57*).

◇ If one supplier does not stock the roll width of carpet or sheet flooring you require, shop around to avoid unnecessary joins and wastage.

◇ For stair carpets, choose a strong underlay and a resilient carpet that will not reveal the backing on the treads.

◇ Vinyl and plastic sheeting is widely available from DIY shops but carpets and matting are best bought from carpet shops, who will measure and estimate free.

Furnishing fabrics

When choosing fabrics for curtains, blinds and upholstery, it is important to select colour, pattern and texture to suit the style of the room and choose practical properties that suit the area to be covered. Some designs are available in a wide range of fabrics, so that furnishings can be co-ordinated. The price, of course, will also be a significant consideration, and it is always better to buy a slightly cheaper fabric, and use it lavishly, than to skimp on a more expensive material. Curtains, for example, need to be about 2-2½ times the width of the window, and will never look good if they are not full enough. Moreover, if you run out of furnishing fabric before you finish a job, you may have difficulty matching it exactly, so always measure and estimate carefully, and allow for wastage.

For information on curtains and blinds, see pp. 102-7; for care and repair of fabrics, see pp. 140-3; and for making curtains and upholstery, see pp. 150-7.

Curtain and upholstery fabrics

Cotton
This natural fibre is made into a number of fabrics and can be blended with synthetic fibres. Cotton and cotton mixtures come with a variety of finishes, such as crêpe, chintz and seersucker, or with a pattern woven into the fabric – herringbone or gingham, for instance. Cotton takes printed patterns well, and is easy to work with and to launder, although it may shrink when washed and fade in harsh sunlight.

Wool
This hard-wearing, natural fabric is usually made up into worsted or crêpe fabrics. Most are too heavy for curtains and are better used for upholstery. Wool tends to attract the dirt and stain easily, and may shrink.

Silk
Luxurious, soft, smooth and easily dyed, pure silk is extremely expensive. Silk blended with other fibres is more reasonable, and 100 per cent synthetic silk substitutes cost a fraction of the price, while offering a comparable look.

Moiré
This finish gives a wavy, watermark effect to silk, triacetate and acetate fabrics at the printing stage. It looks shiny and luxurious and lends itself to generously gathered, full-length curtains or festoon blinds, although synthetic types tend to fray and are slippery to work with. Moiré must be dry-cleaned, or the pattern will disappear.

Velvet
Any cloth with a pile shorter than 3mm is known as velvet. It is available in cotton, silk, and synthetic fibres in a broad range of prices. All velvets dye well and can be used for formal curtains and upholstery.

Canvas
This heavy, tough fabric is usually made from cotton or linen yarns and comes in plain colours or simple stripes. It can be used to make straight, simple curtains, but is usually used for loose covers or for upholstery.

Synthetics
Unlike natural fibres, synthetics are all made entirely from chemicals. Different chemical combinations produce acetate, viscose, acrylic and polyester, each of which has its own properties. They can be blended with more expensive natural fibres, to reduce their price.

Corduroy
A hard-wearing cotton, woven with extra weft threads to produce cut-pile ribs of varying widths. Suitable for upholstery.

Velvet cushion

Chair border

Tassel

Fringing

Braid

Gimp

Moiré

Cotton/polyester

Cotton

Silk

Acrylic

Quilted cushion cover

Corduroy

Wool

Sheer fabrics

Lace
Lace used to be hand-made, but is now almost exclusively made by machine. Available in nylon, cotton or viscose in a range of elaborate designs, lace is expensive and its crisp texture is best suited to gently gathered curtains. Lace should be given a lining – a net backing will accentuate the design. Lace and other sheer fabrics can be difficult to sew and may slip on a sew-ing machine so put tissue paper under it.

Net
The fibres are knotted, instead of woven or knitted together, to form a mesh. Usually made from synthetics, such as nylon or polyester, net is not expensive and comes plain, patterned or with a patterned border. Like loose weaves, net will diffuse the light coming through the window and coloured net will soften the effect.

Loose weaves
These will add texture to lined curtains and filter harsh sunlight through a window. They are made from most natural fibres and come plain or with a simple design woven in.

Cheesecloth
A soft cotton or cotton/polyester blend, this gauzy fabric is loosely woven to give a sheer texture. Naturally cream coloured, it can be dyed and is cheap enough to be used generously.

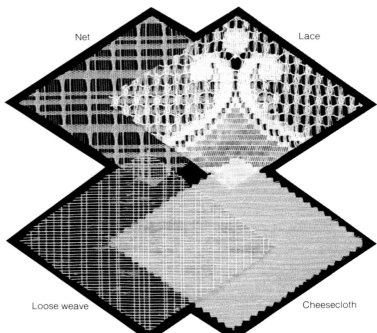

Net

Lace

Loose weave

Cheesecloth

Quilted fabrics

Quilted fabrics consist of light terylene or polyester wadding, sandwiched between a top layer and backing of fabric – usually cotton, silk, and linen. Double-sided quilts are also available to make a reversible quilt fabric. Quilts are too rigid for curtains, but are good upholstery, curtain and bedcover fabrics.

Upholstery accessories

There is a wide range of braids, bobbles, fringing and piping to trim the edges of upholstery or curtains in co-ordinating colours. The trim should be colourfast and non-shrink, unless it is to be hand stitched, so that it can be unpicked when the fabric is cleaned. Piping cord usually shrinks, so it is best to wash it before making it up. Cord should be covered with bias strips in a similar weight fabric to that of the main upholstery. Buttons should also be covered in fabric. Narrow braid, known as "gimp", is available for covering tacks and raw edges of newly upholstered furniture. It is more expensive than normal braid, since it is designed to fit smoothly round corners. When buying fringed curtain pulls, check that the stitching is strong – inferior qualities tend to unravel.

Furnishing fabrics

Choosing the right curtain fabric

Fabrics vary widely in their natural properties and decorative effects, so the choice of curtain material for each room must be considered individually.

Practical properties
Curtains act as both insulators and light shields, so the first consideration is the weight of the fabric. A heavy, textured fabric, such as velvet or brocade, is suitable for winter curtains. It will form a barrier against draughts and will also act as a sound-proofing agent. A light, sheer fabric is a good summer fabric. It will let in the light and give a fresh, airy feel. In south-facing rooms, exposed to bright sunlight, however, you should choose a fabric that will not fade. For kitchens, a flame-proof finish is an advantage.

Lining fabrics
A lining protects curtains against dirt and fading, makes them hang more elegantly and increases their warmth. The most usual lining material is cotton sateen, but there are more expensive types, such as aluminium-backed insulating lining.

Choosing the right upholstery fabric

Not all upholstery receives the same amount of wear, and you should take this into account when making your choice of fabric. Everyday dining chairs, for example, need a tougher fabric than a bedroom chair, and those exposed to spills, stains and pets every day will need to be easily cleaned. If the fabric is chosen to be durable, the pattern should likewise blend easily with other furnishings and be adaptable to a change in decoration. If you are using a pattern, you should aim to centre it on the back and the seat.

Suiting the fabric to the furnishing

Situation	Fabric	Design
Curtains		
Formal, full length curtains	Heavy fabrics: silk, brocades, velvet	Richly patterned, textured or with a large, dominant pattern
Sill length curtains	Light fabrics: sheer, silk or synthetic	Plain or textured with a small design
Blinds		
Roman blinds	Firm fabrics: cotton twill, cotton/linen blend	Plain or lightly patterned
Festoon blinds	Soft light fabrics: light cottons, moiré, silk, synthetics	Plain or lightly patterned
Roller blinds	Tightly woven fabrics: firm cotton, cotton blend, canvas	Plain or lightly patterned
Upholstery		
Loose covers	Colourfast, non-shrink, washable fabric: cotton, synthetic, canvas	Any. Small prints are easiest to match
Upholstery	Heavy, tough fabrics: heavy cotton, wool, corduroy, canvas, leather	Any. Plain or muted pattern
Cushions	Soft, smooth fabrics: silk, acetate, velvet polyester	Use a small design on small cushions

Tips on buying fabric

◇ When buying fabric to co-ordinate with an existing colour scheme, bring offcuts of wallpaper, furnishing fabrics and paint cards to compare shades.
◇ Take material to the daylight to see its true colour, and ask to see the fabric unrolled to check that the colour is even, and that there are no flaws. Check that the grain is straight – the horizontal and vertical threads should lie at a true right angle. Also check that the pattern lines up with the grain, or the final result will be crooked.
◇ When choosing curtain fabric, it is worth buying lining at the same time; it will extend the life of the fabric.
◇ Before buying, check whether the fabric is washable or must be dry cleaned; if it will fade, bleed, shrink or stretch; and if it can be ironed. Always buy a little more than you need for wastage and future repairs.
◇ When home sewing for the first time, a medium- or light-weight cotton in a plain or easy-match pattern is the easiest to handle.
◇ When buying patterned fabric, allow a little extra for pattern-matching, and when buying linen and cotton, allow extra for shrinkage.
◇ Choose a thread in a slightly darker shade than the fabric.
◇ A layer of inter-lining between the curtain and the lining increases insulation.

Door furniture

Door fittings including handles, hinges, knobs, knockers and catches allow a door to fulfil its function as a means of entry and exit. If it is to work properly, it needs the correct accessories. They are available from DIY, furnishing and specialist shops, where the range is usually on display. Alternatively, you may prefer to consult several manufacturers' catalogues to make your choice. Always check that your measurements are correct and that both the size and material of all the fittings are compatible with each other. Remember that the door fittings should be fixed into place after the door surface has been painted, stained or varnished. It is wise to lubricate metal catches and hinges with a drop of oil from time to time. If nylon fittings squeak, loosen the screw heads a fraction. (*For more information on the range of materials, see overleaf.*)

The range of door handles

There are two basic types of door handle: a turning handle that forms an integral part of a catch; and a static handle, which is used for pulling and pushing a door with a lock or an independent catch. Turning door handles come in two forms – as levers or as knobs. Both operate by rotating a square metal spindle, which passes through the door and the catch. If the door is very thin, you may need to cut the spindle. (*For fitting a door handle, see Job 122, p. 111.*)

A knob set
On one side of a knob set sits a knob attached to a rosette, which is nailed to the face of the door. A long, square-shaped spindle fits into the knob through the rosette, and passes through a hole in the door and the catch. On the other side of the door, a knob, attached to a rosette, slides over the spindle and is secured to the door face.

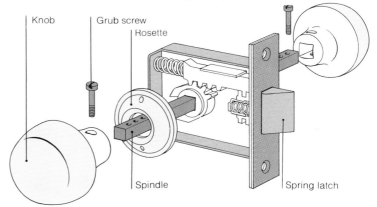

Knob Grub screw Rosette Spindle Spring latch

The range of door hinges

Hinges must be strong enough to support the weight of the door and must allow it to open wide enough. The best qualities are metal, but plastic types are adequate for small doors. A variety of hinges are designed for specific types of door and it is important to choose a suitable type in the correct size. You will generally need a 75mm size for internal flush doors, and a 100mm size for panelled and external doors, and smaller sizes for cupboards and cabinets. You will have to decide how wide you would like the door to open. The standard hinge opens to 95°, but 110° types are available for wider opening, and 170° hinges will allow the door to lie flat against the adjoining surface. If you want your door to remain shut without a catch, you will need a "sprung" hinge. Finally, you should check that the hinge will allow the door to open the way you intend. If you wish the door to open towards you with the hinge on the right, you should ask for a right-hand hinge; if you wish the door to open towards you with the hinge on the left, ask for a left-hand hinge. Most internal room and furniture doors need two hinges; heavy doors benefit from a third fitted half-way up the door. (*For fitting door hinges, see Job 121, p. 110.*)

Butt hinges
The standard hinge for most doors, the butt hinge is fixed first to the door, then to the door frame. The hinge is either recessed into the door, or into both the door and the frame. The pins on both hinges must be perfectly aligned with each other and with the door edge, for the hinge to work efficiently. The rising butt hinge, which allows the door to rise over a carpet as it opens, is fitted in the same way.
Lift-off hinge
For use on cabinets, this hinge allows the door to be removed easily for cleaning or painting. It is available in a butt or cranked shape and comes as either a left-handed or a right-handed hinge.

Flush hinge
For lightweight doors, a flush hinge is simply screwed on to the surface of the door edge and frame without cutting a recess. This is possible, since one flap closes within the other.

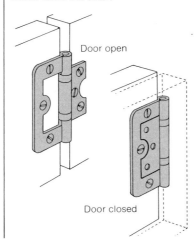

Door open

Door closed

Spring hinge
To encourage a door to swing closed of its own accord, a spring hinge can be fitted. A single hinge allows for one-way opening, and a double hinge allows a door to swing both ways.

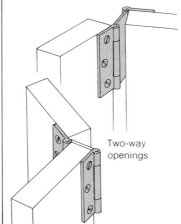

Two-way openings

Concealed hinge
Useful for cabinets, when room space is short, this hinge allows the door edge to remain flush with the frame when opened. It is only visible on the inside face of the door and may be recessed or fixed to the surface and the door can be adjusted after fitting to ensure accurate alignment.

Door closed

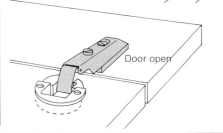

Door open

Door furniture

The range of door and furniture fittings is huge. Your choice of materials for knobs, knockers, handles, and other fittings, is largely an aesthetic decision, although the size and type will be determined by the door's function. Newly painted or varnished doors may show up scratches and wear on old door furniture, so to set off new decoration to advantage it may be worth the relatively small expense of a new set of door furniture. Shiny brass or gold-plated fittings usually look best on gloss-painted or varnished doors, particularly front doors, while wood, china or plastic lend themselves to interior and cupboard doors. Try to use clean-cut, modern-style fittings in a new home and more traditional styles in an older house. If choice is governed by price, you may find that many synthetic and plated materials now provide good imitations. However, brass, gold-plate, zinc and aluminium hinges supply stronger support for heavy doors.

For information on fitting doors, see pp. 118-21. For more information on types of door furniture, see previous page.

Brass door knob

Surround for cylinder door lock

Large brass door knocker

Cylinder lock cover

Porcelain handle and escutcheon

Glass handle

Brass handle

Satin chromium-plated pull handle

Chromium-plated pull handle

Stainless steel pull handle

Plastic pull handle

Brass knob

Porcelain knobs

Wooden knob

Plastic pull handles

Knobs, knockers and handles

Front door furniture

Door knobs
Knobs, knockers, letter-boxes, key plates and key covers fixed on to front doors are primarily decorative, but retain a practical function. The range of designs and materials is huge and coordinating sets are available. Front door knobs are usually made of solid brass, gold plate, bronze or steel. Some are lacquered for a protec-tive finish and these should not be polished with metal cleaner, which will abrade the surface. If, however, the metal begins to weather, you will need to strip off the surface and apply a new coat of lacquer.
Door knockers
Door knockers are also made of metal, to create a resonant sound on wood. Brass and bronze look particularly effective against a natural wood

finish. Black ironware is designed for an antique look and is best restricted to old and rural houses.
Keyhole plates
Keyhole plates (escutcheons) for front doors are usually brass or bronze and some come with a ledge for pulling the door closed. For added decoration, keyhole covers, bell pulls and house numbers can be chosen to coordinate with the rest of the fittings. Prices vary according to the metal used.

Internal door handles

Turning handles
Turning, or bolt-through handles, which operate a spring latch, come as round or lever handles. The choice of shapes and sizes is wide, and most come in a range of metals, including brass,

chrome, gold-plate and stainless steel, but wood, glass, porcelain and plastic will also stand up well to wear. Some turning handles are made with matching escutcheons. When replacing door handles, it is often advisable to take the old one with you, to check the size.
Pull handles
Used in conjunction with an independent catch, pull handles may be round or long, and come in the same range of metals as turning handles.

Furniture and drawer handles

Smaller knobs and handles, used for wardrobe, cupboard and cabinet doors and drawers are also made in a variety of decorative shapes and sizes, in wood, metal, glass and plastic.

Antique ironwork
door knocker

Hinges

Door hinges

Butt hinge
Widely used for room doors and windows, this hinge is especially suitable for solid timber doors. Available in 30-100mm sizes.

Rising butt hinge
Designed for doors that need to rise over carpets, the rising butt hinge is open-ended. Available in 30-100mm sizes.

Flush hinge
Used for lightweight doors, the flush hinge is designed to act like a butt hinge, but does not need to be recessed. Available in 38-100mm sizes.

Furniture hinges

Piano hinge
Originally for piano lids, this hinge is used where a continuous hinge is

needed along a door or lid. It is made in plastic or aluminium, in standard cut lengths of 84cm, and can be cut to size.

Concealed hinge
Popular for cabinets, this hinge is only visible on the inside face of the door and may be recessed.

Brass cylinder hinge
Even less obtrusive than the concealed cabinet hinge, the two halves of this hinge fit into holes drilled in the edge of the door and the frame.

Catches

Door catches

Ball or roller catch
Suitable for a light internal or cupboard door, this catch consists of a spring-loaded ball or roller inside a cylinder. When the door is closed, the ball or roller fits into a recess in the strike plate fixed to the door frame.

French window catch
An "espaniolette bolt" consists of two

long sliding bolts, which slot into recesses at the head and sill of the door frame. The bolts, which extend the full length of the door, are operated by a central handle.

Furniture catches

Magnetic catch
There are various types and shapes available, but all consist of a nickel-coated plate, which is fixed to the door, and a cased magnet, which is fixed to the cupboard or cabinet.

KD fittings

Block joints
Used to form an accurate right angled butt joint when joining two chipboard panels, this fitting is supplied as two square or rectangular blocks of plastic, a washer head, screw and retaining nut. Cam fittings, consisting of a cam and bolt section, may be used for the same purpose.

Plastic lever handle
and escutcheon

Brass lever
latch handle

Stainless steel knob

Plastic knob

Brass cabinet handles

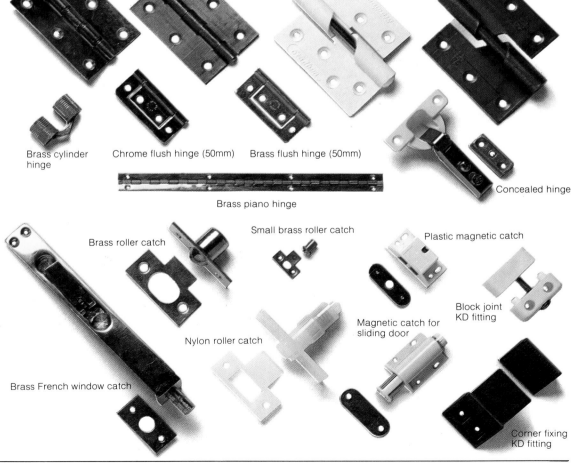

Brass butt
hinge (76mm)

Steel butt
hinge (76mm)

Plastic rising
butt hinge (76mm)

Steel rising
butt hinge
(76mm)

Brass cylinder
hinge

Chrome flush hinge (50mm)

Brass flush hinge (50mm)

Concealed hinge

Brass piano hinge

Brass roller catch

Small brass roller catch

Plastic magnetic catch

Nylon roller catch

Magnetic catch for
sliding door

Block joint
KD fitting

Brass French window catch

Corner fixing
KD fitting

Room-by-room guide

Before choosing colour schemes, decorative styles and textures, you will have to consider the practical requirements of individual rooms. Your choice of wall, floor, ceiling and window materials should be largely governed by the purpose of the room. There are a number of questions you will have to ask yourself, and the chart below divides these into categories, to aid the decision-making process, and offers some practical suggestions for choices you might make.

Hall/landing

	Easy to apply	Easy to clean	Inexpensive	Durable	To cover an imperfect surface	To cover a good surface	Luxurious
Walls	paint, woodchip paper, washable paper, vinyl paper	paint, washable paper, relief vinyl, vinyl paper, sealed cork	paint, standard paper	washable paper, vinyl paper	woodchip paper, relief vinyl, embossed paper, panelling	fabric, flock paper, hand-printed paper	fabric, flock paper, hand-printed paper, panelling
Ceiling	paint, standard paper	paint, standard paper	paint, standard paper	ceiling tiles, panelling	textured paint, ceiling tiles, relief paper, panelling	emulsion paint, standard paper	panelling
Floor	carpet tiles, rugs, matting	ceramic/quarry tiles, cushioned vinyl, rugs, matting	carpet tiles, matting, vinyl tiles	grade 4/5 carpet tiles, wooden flooring, vinyl/rubber flooring	hardboard, chipboard, screed	rugs	thick pile, high-grade carpet, rugs, wooden flooring

Living/dining room

	Easy to apply	Easy to clean	Inexpensive	Durable	To cover an imperfect surface	To cover a good surface	Luxurious
Walls	standard paper, woodchip paper, embossed paper, vinyl paper	paint, vinyl paper, sealed cork	paint, standard paper, woodchip paper, washable paper, murals	gloss paint, cork, hessian, vinyl paper, panelling	textured paint, embossed paper, woodchip paper	fabric, flock paper, hand-printed paper	fabric, flock paper, hand-printed paper, panelling
Ceiling	paint, standard paper	paint, standard paper	paint, standard paper	ceiling tiles, panelling	textured paint, relief paper, panelling, ceiling tiles	paint, standard paper	panelling, fibrous plasterwork
Floor	carpet tiles, rugs, woodstrip flooring	carpet, wooden flooring	cord carpet	grade 4 carpet, wooden flooring	hardboard, chipboard, screed	carpet, rugs	thick pile carpet, oriental rugs, woodstrip flooring with rugs

Bedroom

	Easy to apply	Easy to clean	Inexpensive	Durable	To cover an imperfect surface	To cover a good surface	Luxurious
Walls	paint, standard paper, vinyl paper, foamed polyethylene	paint, vinyl paper, foamed polyethylene, washable paper	paint, woodchip paper, standard paper	hessian, vinyl paper	smooth textured paint, high relief paper, woodchip paper	flock paper, fabrics, cork	flock paper, fabrics, cork
Ceiling	paint	paint	paint	relief paper, textured paper, ceiling tiles	textured paint, relief paper, ceiling tiles	paint, standard	mural
Floor	carpet tiles, rugs, matting	carpet, rugs, matting, cork	grade 1 carpet, matting	grade 2+ carpet	hardboard, chipboard, screed	rugs, carpet	high-grade carpet

Kitchen/bathroom

	Easy to apply	Easy to clean	Inexpensive	Durable	To cover an imperfect surface	To cover a good surface	Luxurious
Walls	paint, vinyl paper, washable paper, foamed polyethylene	vinyl paper, washable paper, foamed polyethylene, condensation paint	paint, washable paper, vinyl, metallic tiles	ceramic tiles, vinyl vinyl paper, relief paper, panelling	textured paint, ceramic tiles, panelling	metallic foil, mirror tiles	ceramic tiles, cork, mosaic tiles, panelling
Ceiling	paint, standard paper	washable paper, vinyl paper, anti-condensation tiles	paint, standard paper	textured paint, panelling, ceiling tiles	textured paint, relief paper, ceiling tiles, suspended ceiling	paint, standard paper	panelling
Floor	vinyl tiles, rush plastic matting	sheet vinyl, rubber, linoleum, vinyl tiles, ceramic tiles	rush matting, vinyl tiles, sheet vinyl	quarry tiles, ceramic tiles, sheet vinyl	hardboard, chipboard, screed	vinyl flooring, rubber flooring, sheet vinyl	ceramic tiles (polyester carpet in bathroom)

Home contents

Cleaning, care and repair ◇ Renovating wooden
furniture ◇ Renovating upholstery ◇ Lighting
Pictures and mirrors ◇ Storage and shelving
Appliance fault-finding

However well you decorate and maintain your home, it will
only look good and run efficiently if you care for the contents.
Stains on a carpet, a broken chair leg, or a marked dining
table, for example, detract from an otherwise attractive
interior, yet the solution is often quite simple, and the investment of time and effort minimal. This chapter is concerned
with the care, repair and cleaning of furniture, furnishings and
general household items, and with the arrangement of lighting, shelving and pictures. It ranges from soft furnishings and
glassware, through wooden furniture and electrical appliances, to storage space and lighting effects. You will find
step-by-step instructions on re-caning, re-rushing and re-
upholstering a chair, on framing and hanging a picture and
putting up shelves. The emphasis is on essential jobs that
require no specialist skills but demand a little know-how and
the correct tools and equipment.

Cleaning, care and repair

Cleaning and mending china, glass, metalwork and fabrics Sharpening blades ◇ Caring for plastics and leather Removing stains

Regular care, cleaning and repair extends the life and efficiency of the contents of any home. Having invested in your furniture and furnishings and perhaps a redecoration, it makes good sense to spend a little time ensuring that it continues to look and feel good. When buying anything for the home, you should find out how it should be cleaned. Modern products, including cleaning agents, polishes and glues, are designed for ease of use and for specific materials, so it is important to choose the right one. Valuable antiques and precious glass should be given to an expert for repair, but most small repairs of less valuable objects can be completed simply and quickly with the correct tools.

Points to remember

◇ Heat may weaken a repair, so wash any glued items carefully by hand, not in a dishwasher.
◇ It is often cheaper to replace than repair everyday items, particularly if you need an expensive adhesive.
◇ Always test dry-cleaning agents on an inconspicuous part of a fabric before use.
◇ Remove excess adhesive immediately after a repair.

Tools and equipment

For cleaning household equipment, you will need the usual range of brushes, mops, cloths, buckets and a vacuum cleaner; also washing-up liquid for china, metal and glass and detergents for fabrics. More specialist cleaning equipment includes dry-cleaning fluid, carpet shampoos and applicators, and upholstery shampoo. For removing stains you may need methylated, white or surgical spirit, ammonia, borax and peroxide. A variety of polishes, all applied with a soft cloth, is available for wood, metal, glass, plastics and leather. Whiting, a powdered white chalk, is used for polishing metal. To sharpen knife blades, use either an oilstone, a steel or a hand or electric sharpener. Use a slip-stone for scissor blades.

Repairing equipment
It is important to choose the right adhesive for repairs. Epoxy resins, used for china, metal and glass repairs, are strong, and heat and water-resistant. They usually come in two separate tubes, to be mixed together. Clear contact adhesive sets almost immediately, so there is no need to hold the pieces in place. Latex adhesive is used for patching fabrics and carpets. The glue required for mending plastics depends on the type of plastic (see Caring for plastics, p. 145). Masking tape and gummed paper strips are also useful for china and glass repairs. For darning upholstery fabrics, you will need a stout needle, thread and thimble, and a pair of needlework scissors.

Cleaning china and glass

Everyday crockery and glass, such as cups, mugs, plates and bowls, should be washed up soon after use and dried before storing.

Washing china
If you are leaving crockery to soak, use cold, soapy water. Hot water tends to "bake" some food, such as egg yolks, on to the china. If you have a dishwasher, load the crockery as you use it and pre-rinse if the machine has that facility. To remove tea or coffee stains, leave to soak overnight in a washing powder solution. Modern china, even delicate porcelain, may be dishwasher-proof, but always check before loading.

Handling ornaments
China and pottery ornaments should be dusted regularly with a light feather duster. If a layer of dirt has built up, soak in a bowl of warm, soapy water, then rinse and dry thoroughly. Bad stains can be removed with a damp cloth dipped in bicarbonate of soda or borax. Hard-water marks usually respond to vinegar and water, and hard rubbing.

Washing glass
If you cannot wash drinking glasses immediately, leave them to soak on their sides in warm, soapy water. Each glass should be washed individually with a long-handled, soft-headed mop in a large bowl of clean, soapy water. To clean the crevices of cut crystal, use an old, soft toothbrush. Rinse glasses well in clean, hot (not boiling) water for a sparkling finish and stand them upside down on a rack or a clean, folded cloth. When they have drained, dry thoroughly with a linen cloth. Glass tables and shelves can be cleaned with a cloth soaked in methylated spirit.

Removing stains from glass
Glass which is cloudy or stained should be filled with water and two teaspoons of ammonia, left overnight, then rinsed and washed. A badly stained glass may respond to soaking in a solution of one cup caustic soda to two litres of warm water, but be sure to rinse the glass thoroughly afterwards. To remove hard-water marks from vases, soak in distilled water or a vinegar and water solution. To remove spirit stains from the inside of a decanter half fill with vinegar and cooking salt, then add half a cup of uncooked rice or sand and swill around. Rinse it well in clean water and leave to drain. Tables and shelves can be cleaned with methylated spirit on a cloth.

Storing glass
It is best to store glasses the right way up, to avoid damaging the rim, and away from strong smells. Lavender bags, camphor balls and other distinct aromas will contaminate the glass and taint your drinks. Polish glasses with a clean linen cloth before you use them, rather than when you put them away.

Basic techique

Mending broken china and glass

Modern adhesives have greatly improved the results achieved by gluing broken china and glass. Epoxy resins, which are strong and heat-resistant, do not set immediately and therefore allow time for accurate positioning. Setting times vary, but will be quicker in a warm room and can be accelerated by placing the article near a radiator. Contact adhesives, which are less expensive, set almost immediately, so are more difficult to use, although the thixotropic type allows more time for repositioning. Special adhesives are available for clear glass. It is worth repairing cracks and chips in valuable items or to prolong the life of a favourite item; others are best thrown away in a newspaper wrapping and replaced.

Mending simple breaks
Clean, simple breaks in glass and china can be repaired more successfully than fractures and multiple breaks. Repairs in stems and bases will also be less noticeable than, for example, in the rim of a glass or mug. Before mending china or glass, ensure all pieces are clean. Wipe the pieces with a solvent, such as methylated spirits, white spirit or surgical spirit, ensuring that any old adhesive and grease is removed. Then rinse and allow to dry. Work out how the pieces fit together and use masking tape or gummed paper strips to hold them in position. Never use clear, adhesive tape, since it will be difficult to remove without dislodging the pieces. Then remove the pieces and roughen the broken edges with sandpaper before applying adhesive. Mix the adhesive according to the pack instructions and carefully glue the pieces together, removing any excess with methylated spirits. While the glue is drying, support the pieces in position. Use Plasticine to hold glass stems, 1, spouts or small pieces in place. With larger breaks, support the item with crumpled kitchen foil or a box of sand, 2. If the item is broken in more than two pieces, glue them one at a time, allowing the adhesive to set between the individual repairs.

1 Use two strands of Plasticine to support a glued stem

2 Support larger items in a bowl of sand

Mending multiple breaks
It is usually only worth mending multiple breaks on large or decorative pieces, such as vases and ornaments. Following the same technique as for simple breaks, use a solvent to clean each individual piece. Work out how the pieces fit together, using masking tape or gummed paper strips (never clear tape) across the breaks. Then number the pieces with a felt pen. Remove the tape, disassemble the pieces and smear a little epoxy resin along the side of the main item and along the side of the first piece to be attached, 1, and press together. Working from the inside piece out, secure each piece in place with masking tape, 2, and wipe away excess glue with methylated spirits. Use Plasticine, crumpled kitchen foil or a bowl of sand to support the item. When the first piece is dry, glue on the next, apply masking tape, allow to dry and so on until the broken object is complete. If you wish to speed up the drying process, use a hair dryer, or leave the item near a heater. When the adhesive has set, scrape off any ridges with a scalpel or razor blade until the repair lies flush with the surface and wipe away the dust. If a handle or stem also has multiple breaks, repair it as a whole, before sticking it on to the main item.

1 Smear epoxy resin along the broken edge of each piece

2 Hold the pieces together with masking tape, while the glue sets

Mending small holes and chips
Chips are difficult to disguise in clear glass, but you could take a favourite or valuable piece to a professional glass and china repairer to re-grind a chipped rim. It can be difficult to make cracks invisible, but a special epoxy adhesive is available for this purpose and is less noticeable than normal types. Chips in china can be concealed by filling out the surface and painting over the repair to match the rest of the piece. First clean the chip or hole with methylated, white or surgical spirit. Then make up a mixture of epoxy resin adhesive and titanium dioxide, a white powder available from artists' suppliers, **1**. *Press the filler firmly into the crevice with a smooth, rounded stick, eliminating air pockets as you work,* **2**. *When the cavity is well packed and the filler lies proud of the surface, remove any smears with methylated spirit. When the filler has set, rub it down with glasspaper, until it lies flush. If the chip is deep, apply the filler in several layers, allowing each to dry before applying the next. Then paint over the repair. To match a colour, mix in artists' powder colour until you reach the right shade and test it on spare filler. If the chip is large, support the piece until the mixture has set. Finish with a coat of varnish to match the glaze of the china.*

1 Make a filler from epoxy adhesive and titanium dioxide

2 Apply the filler to the crevice with a smooth, rounded stick

Cleaning metalwork

Everyday cutlery should be washed in warm, soapy water, as soon as possible after use, since food remains and even soaking in water will cause stains and pitting. A spoonful of mustard added to the rinsing water will remove fishy smells on silverware. Pots and pans should be soaked thoroughly to remove burnt food deposits, then washed (not scoured) in hot, soapy water. Leave to drain, then dry carefully, especially untreated cast-iron cookware, which tends to rust.

Dealing with corrosion
Regular cleaning and polishing will prevent rust forming on metalware.

However, if it does develop, use a proprietary cleaner to remove most of the corrosion, taking care to follow the instructions carefully. If iron or steel have rusted badly, scrape off the worst and use a rust remover. Badly corroded bronze should be scraped carefully with a knife or special brush or wiped with a 10 per cent solution of acetic acid in water. Never use a wire brush or steel wool, however, or you will damage the surface. Corrosion on brass may be removed by soaking for an hour in a strong, warm solution of washing soda. Wash off and repeat if one application is not successful. Corrosion on pewter can

be loosened by scraping gently or rubbing with wire wool or crocus powder (available from hardware shops) and finishing with whiting and polish.

Protective finishes
Most proprietary metal cleaners will protect against tarnishing to some extent, but an extra finish will provide greater protection. Brassware can be given a coat of varnish or lacquer; chrome will be protected by a layer of Vaseline; untreated iron or steel should be greased or primed and painted with a special paint; silver can be kept in tarnish-retardant bags or in a drawer with a soft lining.

Metal	Cleaning method	Metal	Cleaning method
Anodized aluminium (Trays, trolleys, light fittings)	Wipe off marks and stains with a damp cloth, then polish with a soft, dry one.	**Copper** (Saucepans, kettles, ornaments)	Rub with a piece of lemon, dipped in salt and vinegar, then rinse in hot, soapy water. Dry well, then buff up until it shines.
Brass (Saucepans, kettles, ornaments, door furniture)	Wash in hot water with a cupful of ammonia. Dry and polish with a cleaner recommended for brass. Lacquered or varnished brass tarnishes less quickly, but if marked, remove tarnish with acetone. Clean off the marks, polish and repaint or spray with lacquer or varnish. Finally buff up with a soft, clean cloth.	**Gold**	Wash in warm detergent solution with a cupful of ammonia. Then rinse and polish with a dry cloth.
Bronze (Door furniture, ornaments)	Wash in a hot detergent solution or rub with a cloth soaked in turpentine or paraffin.	**Pewter**	Clean regularly to prevent corrosion. Wash in warm, soapy water and dry with a soft cloth.
Chrome (Electrical appliances, door furniture)	Clean with a dry cloth and a little bicarbonate of soda, or wipe with a damp, soapy cloth then buff up with a soft cloth when dry.	**Silver**	Clean regularly to prevent corrosion. Clean with a proprietary dip or cleaner, then polish with a chamois leather. You can make your own silver dip by immersing a small piece of aluminium foil in boiling water with two tablespoons of washing soda. Rinse well in clean water, dry and polish.

127

Mending damaged metalwork

Most metal cleaners and protective finishes are designed to minimize the effects of minor scratches and knocks; and regular polishing should provide a good, sheeny finish and remove rust. Dents in pewter, copper and hollow brass can be removed, but dented gold or silverware will have to be taken to a professional repair shop. Broken metal will normally have to be soldered by an expert, but small holes and cracks can be fixed with acrylic or epoxy resin adhesive. Acrylic resin can be mixed with metal (such as brass) filings for a good colour match.

Removing scratches
On some metals, such as copper, scratches are impossible to remove. However, on most metals, a layer of the appropriate polish will help to disguise them (below). On brassware, try polish- *ing with a paste from powdered whiting, available from DIY shops. To remove silver scratches, apply methylated spirit, mixed with jeweller's rouge, available from jewellery makers' suppliers.*

Removing dents
Take a short length of wood and use a rasp and spokeshave to shape the end to fit the curve of the damaged item. Hold the wood in a vice and gently press and rub the metal *(pewter, copper or brass) against the shaped end until the dent is pushed out (below). Never try hammering – it usually increases the damage. Finally rub down with crocus powder, then with whiting, and polish.*

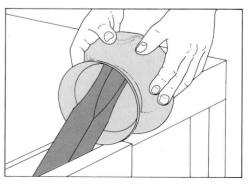

Basic technique

How to sharpen knives and scissors

Kitchen knives should be sharpened regularly, especially those with carbon steel blades, which blunt more quickly than stainless steel. Five types of sharpener are available from DIY shops – an oilstone, a sharpening steel, a hand sharpener, an electric sharpener and a fine slipstone. On each type of sharpener, the blade is sharpened gradually, at an angle of 30 degrees, working first one side, then the other. Saw-edged tools, however, need to be sharpened with specialist tools. Blunt scissors may be caused by a loose screw joint between the blades. To cure this, place the scissors with the head of the screw on a metal surface and hit the other end with a hammer. If the scissors are still blunt, you will have to use a slipstone. Never sharpen table cutlery or scissors with rounded ends designed for children's use.

Using an oilstone
Place the stone on a flat surface at hand level and cover it with a light oil. Draw one side of the blade away from you along the stone, then turn the blade and pull it back along the stone towards you. Repeat several times.

Using a sharpening steel
Hold the blade edge away from you and cross the knife and steel at right angles near the handles. Holding the blade at 30 degrees to the steel, draw it across, first on one side, then on the other and repeat about 10 times.

Using an electric sharpener
Follow the manufacturer's instructions and take care not to over-sharpen the knife. You can see if the blade is sharp by tracing a line of light reflected in the blade – dull patches or a broken line of light will show up blunt areas.

Using a slipstone
Draw the slipstone along the face of the blunt scissor blade, working at right angles to the blade. If the edge of the blade is damaged, run the slipstone, lightly oiled, over the inner face of the blade.

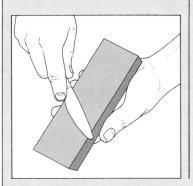
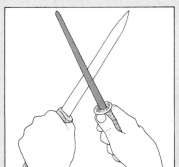
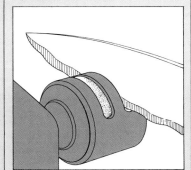
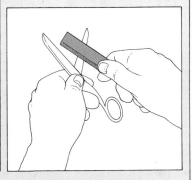

Caring for plastics

Plastic furniture and surfaces should be cleaned carefully with a damp cloth to prevent particles of grit scratching the finish. Use neat washing-up liquid to remove any stubborn patches, then rinse off and dry carefully. Plastic laminates can be wiped down in the same way, but should be rinsed well to avoid streaking. Cream cleansers are best on plastic baths to avoid scratching and plastic lampshades can be washed in a warm water and detergent solution. To remove stains in tableware, use denture cleaner or a bicarbonate of soda paste.

Mending broken plastic
Cracked and broken plastic tableware will attract germs, so they should be thrown away, never mended. Plastic furniture and toys, however, can be repaired successfully with the appropriate adhesive. Contact adhesive is ideal for ABS plastic (utensils, tool handles), rigid pvc (shower units, furniture) or decorative laminates (table tops). It is applied to both surfaces, left to dry, then pressed together. Clear adhesive is suitable for polystyrene (bathroom units, furniture) and flexible pvc (blinds, shower curtains). Epoxy adhesives are the most expensive and provide the strongest bond. They should be used for thermo-setting plastics (handles, switches), nylon (curtain rails) and acetal (taps).

Caring for leather

Leather needs regular care and attention, or it soon becomes hard and powdery. Before cleaning leather upholstery, test for colour fastness by rubbing a small hidden area with soap and a damp cloth. If the colour comes off on your cloth, the leather is untreated and needs to be cleaned carefully. The best way to protect treated leather is to rub in hide food regularly, or to polish it with a wax or cream.

Cleaning treated leather
Wash with warm water and pure soap, taking care not to make the leather too wet. To remove stubborn stains, rub gently with a soft nail brush. If the mark persists, use a mixture of three parts castor oil, two parts surgical spirit and leave for 24 hours, then wipe off with castor oil.

Cleaning untreated leather
Sponge off grease marks with a little white spirit on a soft cloth, then use soap and a slightly damp cloth. To remove bad stains, squeeze on a little rubber solution and leave to dry for 24 hours. The solution should absorb the stain and remove it.

Renovating leather
Restore faded leather by touching it up with a leather stain or coloured lacquer. Work saddle soap into stiff, dry leather until it regains its suppleness.

Cleaning furnishing fabrics

Regular care and cleaning of soft furnishings will help to prolong their life and keep them looking fresh. Dirt and dust can permanently damage the fabric, so it is worth vacuuming, brushing and shaking out the dust every week. Spills and stains should be treated immediately and fabrics should be washed before dirt becomes ingrained.

Protective treatments
Use a dirt-repellent spray on new fabric and re-apply regularly after cleaning. Slip covers will help to protect the arms and backs of upholstery and linings help to prolong the life of curtains.

Upholstery
Upholstery should be cleaned two or three times a year, with upholstery shampoo. Always test for colour fastness first by wetting a small area and pressing with a warm iron between two pieces of plain white cotton. If no colour comes off on the cotton, the fabric is colour-fast; if the colour smudges, the fabric will have to be dry cleaned.

Washable loose covers
Any tears should be mended before the fabric is shampooed. If it is not recommended for machine washing, you will need to launder it gently by hand in warm water and mild detergent. Iron while still damp, on the wrong side for matt finishes and on the right side for shiny ones. Fabrics with special finishes are best drip-dried; stretch covers can usually be machine washed and do not need ironing.

Curtains
All curtains should be washed or cleaned regularly to prevent the fabric wearing out quickly. Lined, interlined and heavy fabrics will probably have to be dry cleaned. Before washing or cleaning, remove hooks, ease out the gathers, and shake out any loose dirt. If washing, soak in cold water with liquid detergent for 10 minutes, then rinse, wash, drip-dry and iron while damp.

Fabric lampshades
Turn off the electricity, remove the shade and take off the trimmings if they are not colour-fast. Clean washable fabrics in warm, soapy water, rinse in clear, lukewarm water and allow to dry naturally. Non-washable fabrics should be dry cleaned.

Carpets
Regular vacuuming to remove grit and fluff will prolong the life of a carpet. For the first few weeks after laying a new carpet, however, use a hand brush or carpet sweeper instead of a vacuum cleaner to allow the pile to settle. After a while the carpet will need to be cleaned with carpet shampoo, using a hand-operated shampoo applicator or an electric carpet shampooer. Heavily soiled carpet should be cleaned with a professional carpet shampoo machine.

It is best to deal with spillages and stains as quickly as possible. Blot or scrape a spillage immediately, working

For solvent-soluble stains (Dry cleaning)
Use a dry-cleaning agent, but test it first on an inconspicuous part of the fabric. Follow the instructions carefully and leave for 15 minutes to check that it does not discolour the fabric. To treat a stain, place a wad of white tissues or cotton wool under the fabric, then apply the cleaner to the right side of the fabric with another pad. Take care not to soak the fabric too much, and work from the outer edge of the stain inwards to prevent it spreading. Change the pads frequently, and blot the stain dry after each application. When the stain has disappeared, wash or dry clean the fabric as normal.

For water-soluble stains (Shampooing)
Washable fabrics, except for wool, silk and non-colourfast materials, should be soaked immediately in a solution of the suggested cleaner (see right). To remove fresh stains on colourfast linens, stretch the fabric over the sink, sprinkle on some powdered detergent or stain remover, pour boiling water through, then rinse. If the stain remains, rub cleaner gently into it, rinse then wash.

With non-washable fabrics, stretch the fabric over a jug and pour cold water through the stain. If the stain remains, put an absorbent pad under it and work in the cleaning solution with a pad, then sponge with clear water and blot dry. Repeat if necessary.

128

Repairing torn upholstery

Small tears and holes in upholstery should be repaired as soon as possible to prevent them fraying. Burnt, worn and torn areas can be darned or patched with a small piece of matching fabric from inside a seam or hem. If the damage is bad, however, you will have to disguise it. Worn arms on chairs can be covered with a pair of simple arm caps, made from remnants. Bad stains can sometimes be disguised by appliqué motifs provided the fabric is the same weight.

Repairing small tears
Remove the damaged fabric from the chair and press it flat. Then cut a piece of "iron-on interfacing" 10mm larger than the tear. Place it centrally over the tear on the wrong side of the fabric and fix it in position with a hot iron. Then, using a length of thread to match the thickness of the original weave and small, neat stitches, darn across the line of the tear.

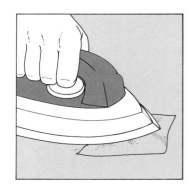

Patching large tears or holes
Snip off any loose threads and cut a small piece of matching fabric from inside the seam, hem or other un-obtrusive area, matching the design closely. Slide the patch under the tear and stick it into position with a latex adhesive. When it is nearly dry, press the edges firmly for a few minutes to ensure a strong bond. Alternatively, sew on the patch.

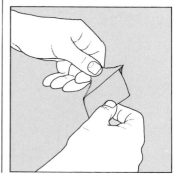

Removing stains from soft furnishings

from the edge to avoid spreading it. If the stain is greasy, sprinkle on an absorbent, such as talcum powder, leave for 30 minutes, then brush or shake and vacuum. Then dry-clean. If it is water-based, rinse immediately in cold water. Then wash or shampoo. To make up an ammonia or borax solution, mix one tablespoon of ammonia or borax in 600ml of warm water. For a peroxide solution, add one part of 20 vol peroxide to four parts cold water, and add a drop of ammonia.

Stain		Method of removal
Adhesive		**Clear and contact adhesive** Use acetone, amyl acetate or non-oily nail varnish remover. Then dry clean. **Latex and model maker's cement** Remove the worst with a spatula then use dry cleaner. **Epoxy resin** Cannot remove once hardened. Try acetone, amyl acetate or lighter fuel before the stain dries.
Ballpoint and felt pen marks		Use methylated spirit and a dry cleaner.
Candle wax		Scrape off as much as you can with a blunt blade. Place slightly damp blotting paper or tissues over (and if possible under) the fabric and press quickly with a warm iron. Repeat until the wax is absorbed. On furniture, chill with an ice cube then scrape off. Alternatively, use dry cleaner.
Chewing gum		Chill with an ice cube to harden then scrape off before using dry cleaner.
Cream, ice cream		Use dry cleaner. For washable fabrics, try biological detergent or borax solution first.
Beer		Use detergent or shampoo. For dried stains, add one egg cup of white vinegar to 600ml of water.
Blood		Soak fresh stains in cold water – never boil, this sets the stain. For dried stains, sponge with salt water ($\frac{1}{2}$ tsp salt to 1 pint water) or use biological detergent or carpet shampoo.
Coffee, tea and chocolate		Use borax or peroxide solution or carpet shampoo. With dried stains, loosen with glycerine first.
Fruit juice and jam		On white table linen, pour salt on the fresh stain to stop it spreading, then rinse with boiling water. Otherwise, use peroxide, borax solution or carpet shampoo.
Gravy browning		Use biological detergent.
Ink		Rinse in cold water and wash.
Lemon juice		Use borax solution then wash.
Mildew		Brush off excess then use upholstery shampoo.
Milk		Rinse fresh stains in lukewarm water. For dried stains, use borax solution or carpet shampoo.

Stain		Method of removal
Gravy		If it contains grease use dry cleaner.
Grease		Remove as much as possible with an absorbent, then use a dry cleaner. On wallpaper, dab lightly with baby powder on cotton wool or try holding blotting paper over the stain and press quickly with a warm iron but take care not to scorch the paper.
Mustard		For non-washable fabrics, use methylated spirit or dry cleaner. Soften old stains with glycerine, then rinse with lukewarm water and dry before using dry cleaner.
Nail varnish		Use acetone, amyl acetate or non-oil nail-polish remover.
Nicotine		Use eucalyptus oil or methylated spirit.
Oil and paraffin		Soak up as much as possible with absorbent then use dry cleaner. For bicycle or motor oil, try eucalyptus oil.
Paint and varnish		For enamel and oil paints use paint remover or turpentine. For cellulose paint, use an acetone or amyl acetate. Fresh emulsion can be rinsed off with cold water. Dried stains cannot usually be removed, but try methylated spirit.
Mustard		For washable fabrics, try detergent.
Nicotine		As an alternative to the dry-cleaning method, try detergent or peroxide solution.
Soft drinks		Rinse with boiling water then wash.
Soot		On washables and carpets, vacuum the excess then try detergent or shampoo before dry cleaner.
Urine		Use biological detergent or carpet shampoo, adding one egg cup of white vinegar to 600ml of water to the shampoo solution.
Vomit and faeces		If necessary, use an absorbent first, then biological detergent, borax solution or carpet shampoo.
Water		Rainspots on felt, velvet and taffeta can be removed by holding in the steam from a boiling kettle, not too near the spout. Remove alkaline drinking water marks by sponging one teaspoon of white vinegar to 600ml warm water solution.
Wine		Use an absorbent to prevent the stain spreading, sponge with clean warm water then use upholstery shampoo on non-washables. For washables, soak in a solution of borax for about half an hour before washing.

Renovating wooden furniture

How to finish wood
Repairing chairs and tables
Repairing table tops and
drawers ◇ Re-caning and
re-rushing chairs

However well you care for your home, sooner or later most pieces of furniture will need renovating, repairing or replacing. Replacing some items, particularly large pieces of furniture, can be very expensive, so it is always worth considering renovating articles you are fond of. A fresh coat of varnish on a fading table or a freshly caned seat on an old chair, for example, can make it feel like new.

A number of basic furniture repairs can be effected without specialist skills or equipment and prove cheaper and more satisfying than buying a replacement. Any valuable antiques, however, should be taken tc a professional restorer.

Points to remember

◇ When sticking wooden sections together, remove traces of old glue.
◇ Keep wooden furniture away from fires and radiators, or the joints may shrink.
◇ Polish wood regularly and treat it with an extra coat at the beginning and end of winter.
◇ To identify a wood finish, rub on a drop of turpentine: if it reveals bare wood, the surface is coated with oil or wax; if the sheen persists, a stain, varnish or polish has been applied.

Tools and equipment

For everyday care of wooden furniture and simple repairs, you do not need a full set of woodworking tools. You will, however, need a few specific tools for some repair jobs, and special equipment for rushing and caning chairs. Use a sharp saw to shorten chair legs or a rail, to cut a new drawer base and to remove dowel ends. To repair a joint, you will need a vice, a hand drill and dowel bit to make holes, and dowels to insert in them. You may also need a plane if you are fitting a new drawer base to size or building up a short chair leg. You will need pva woodworking adhesive for a variety of furniture repairs. To clean wood, keep a plentiful supply of soft cloths and use burnishing cream or metal polish for removing stains. A small paint brush will be useful for applying wood finishes.

Caning equipment
You will need one bundle of No. 2 split cane for the chair seat and a bundle of No. 6 split cane for edging, one bundle of 4.5mm plugging cane; also some pva woodworking adhesive to hold the pegs in place. Caning tools include a large bodkin to help thread the cane, and about 20 small wooden pegs (or golf tees). You will also need a sharp trimming knife, a drill or twist bit to clear holes in the seat frame, a small hand-sprayer to keep the cane moist and a hammer to insert the pegs.

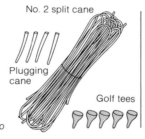

No. 2 split cane

Plugging cane

Golf tees

Rushing equipment
Seagrass, a twisted, rush-like material, is normally used, since genuine rushes are difficult to obtain. Real rushes produce a more attractive colour and texture but you will have to twist them while you weave. For an average chair seat, you will need a large bundle of rushes. Use a sharp knife or secateurs for cutting the seagrass and a hardboard or cardboard winder for holding the lengths of seagrass. A mallet and a scrap of wood are used to keep the seat tightly packed.

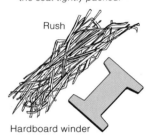

Rush

Hardboard winder

Caring for wood

Polish wood regularly to give it a protective coat. Cover the surface of dining tables with mats and cloths and try to remove spills before a stain develops.

Removing water stains
Dark rings and spots, which are most obvious on French polished or cellulose finishes, are usually water stains. Lay some blotting paper over the area and briefly press a warm iron over it once or twice, to dry out the wood. Alternatively, wipe burnishing cream or metal polish over the stain with a soft cloth.

Removing other stains
White rings and spots are usually caused by spilt coffee or alcohol or a scalding cup. Apply some burnishing cream or metal polish to a soft cloth and work it over the stain, in the direction of the grain, until the stain disappears. If you do not have either product in the house, try a mixture of lubricating oil and a sprinkling of salt. These stains are usually superficial, but if the mark has penetrated through the surface, the finish will have to be stripped off and a new finish applied.

129

Dealing with cigarette burns

A superficial burn can be treated like a heat or water mark, but if it penetrates the surface, strip off the surrounding finish and start again. You may, however, be able to treat the localized area of the burn.

Treating the burnt area
First scrape away the charred edges with a very sharp blade and rub the mark gently with fine-grade glasspaper. Then fill the damage with the appropriate finish. If the wood was treated with a clear coating, apply several coats of poly-urethane varnish or French polish. Then use fine-grade wet or dry glasspaper to smooth the repair, then apply metal polish with a soft cloth to restore the shine.

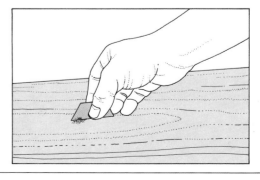

Basic technique

How to apply a wood finish

Wood can be given a variety of protective finishes – including stain, varnish, wax, polish and oil – to prevent moisture, heat, scratches and insects penetrating the surface. In each case the wood should be prepared carefully: stripped of old paint or varnish, filled with wood filler or stopper, sealed with knotting and smoothed ready for finishing (*see Jobs 4, 5 and 6, pp. 17-19*). Before applying a clear finish, you will need to smooth and seal the surface with a grain filler (a runny cream), which comes in different colours. You will need a natural wood colour for light and bleached woods, and the appropriate wood shade for darker woods. The grain filler is applied across the grain, with a piece of hessian or a coarse rag and left to harden overnight. If the wood is to be stained, the grain filler and stain can be mixed and applied in one operation. (*For more information, see pp. 114-7.*)

Applying French polish
French polish includes many different types of polish, all based on shellac and mixed with industrial alcohol. It leaves a good shine, but is not heat- or water-proof. First make a special pad. Spread out a clean, white linen handkerchief and put a lump of cotton wool in the centre. Pour some polish on to the cotton wool until it is soaked, then wrap over the linen to form a smooth, wrinkle-free, pear-shaped pad. Gently press the pad on to a spare piece of wood to remove excess polish,

and so prevent runs forming. Use a few drops of linseed oil to keep the pad lubricated and sweep the pad in figures-of-eight over the surface, taking in the edges. As the polish begins to fade, increase the hand pressure and when it is dry, open the pad and re-load it with polish. Apply several coats, allowing each to dry, and store the pad in an air-tight jar between coats. After six hours, make another pad with a double thickness of linen, dampen it with methylated spirit and work it gently along the grain to finish off.

Applying a seal or varnish
Seals and varnishes leave a tough surface. Apply with a good quality, clean paint brush, using a flowing action, and leave to dry for at least 6-12 hours in a dust-free atmosphere. When dry, lightly abrade the surface, remove the dust with a clean rag moistened with white spirit. For the best results, thin the first coat with 10 per cent white spirit and apply at least four coats.

Applying stains, oils and waxes
Using a soft, clean, lint-free rag, spread a first coat sparingly over the surface, working with the grain. Allow to dry and, if necessary, add a second coat. With a stain, if the colour is too light, add extra layers. If it is too dark, lightly sand the surface. With wax, apply two coats for a good finish. With teak oil apply a second thinner coat, leave it to dry for 24 hours, then rub with wire wool and polish.

130
Treating scratches in wood

A minor scratch should be gently rubbed away with fine-grade wet or dry abrasive paper. Metal polish or burnishing cream applied with a soft cloth will bring back the finish. Alternatively, try rubbing in some coloured wax or shoe polish of a matching colour. A severe scratch which has penetrated below the surface finish and into the wood can only be repaired by stripping and refinishing. A medium-depth scratch, however, can be disguised with a varnish stain.

Disguising a scratch
Thin the varnish slightly with methylated spirits and apply it with a small paint brush, working with the grain. Paint on several coats, allowing each to dry, until the repair stands proud of the surface. Finally, use fine-grade wet or dry abrasive paper to rub the varnish flush with the surface, wipe away the dust, and finally, to restore the shine, apply a thin coat of metal polish with a soft cloth.

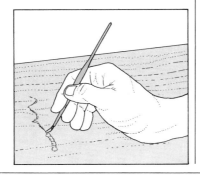

131
Treating bruises and dents in wood

A dent can be disguised by treating it with a clear or stained finish, although if it is deep, you will have to use wood filler or stopping of the appropriate colour first, to build up the surface. Bruises and small dents can be removed by using water to swell the wood. The finish is removed with white spirit, then water and heat is applied. After the wood has swelled, it must be allowed to dry before sanding, re-colouring, if necessary, with a matching stain, and re-polishing.

Using water to raise a dent
Place a damp cloth on the damaged area, and run a hot iron over the top, keeping the iron on the move to avoid scorching. Eventually the wood will swell to fill the dent. Alternatively, wrap a wad of cotton wool in clean linen and soak it in boiling water before applying it. Repeat several times. In either case, allow a few hours for the wood fibres to rise, sand and colour if necessary, then finish with wax or varnish.

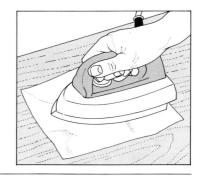

132

Preparing a chair for caning

Pre-woven panels of split cane for seats and chair backs are available, but are difficult to fix to an adequate tension, so it is best to use the traditional method, which will take about 6-8 hours for an average-sized chair. You will first need to cut out the old cane with a sharp trimming knife, keeping a small sample of the caning as a pattern guide. If necessary, drill out the old bits of cane from the holes in the seat frame. Check that the chair is sound and carry out any repairs. Meanwhile, leave the new cane to soak in water for about 15 minutes, then remove it, shake off the water and keep it in a polythene bag until the job is finished. Re-caning a chair involves fitting strands through peg holes, first lengthwise, then crosswise and building up criss-cross layers before finishing off with a series of woven diagonals. To be sure of a straight weave first mark out the chair seat with pegs. (*See Tools and equipment, p. 148*.)

Pegging out the chair
First insert wooden pegs or tees into the centre holes in the front and back rails of the seat frame. Put another tee in the back right-hand corner hole of the frame and count the number of holes between the tees in the back rail. Count the same number in the front rail and insert another tee. There will be more holes in the front rail than in the back if the chair seat tapers.

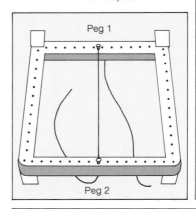

133

Fixing the first layer of cane

The first layer of cane consists of a series of parallel strands, running from front to back and from side to side. The canes slot into the peg holes.

Inserting the parallel canes
Push one end of the cane through the central hole in the back rail, until about 15cm protrudes underneath. Peg the cane in place with the flat, glossy side uppermost, then draw it forwards to the central hole in the front rail. Check that the cane is neither twisted nor too tight and peg it in place.

Then bring the first strand up through the next hole to the right and pull it back to the corresponding hole in the back rail, so that the strands are parallel. Continue in this way, until the right-hand side of the seat is filled with parallel canes, **1**. *Fill the left-hand side in the same way. Next take canes across the seat at right angles to the first line of canes,* **2**. *If the*

seat tapers, take the cane from extra holes in the front rail to holes in the side rails. Peg a cane into the back left-hand corner of the seat, keeping the corner holes free if possible, and take it across to the back right-hand corner then back across to the left-hand side and so on until the seat is filled with parallel canes running from side to side.

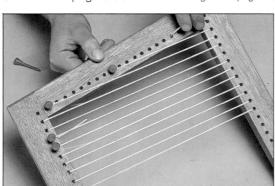

1 *Working from the centre, insert canes between the front and back rails*

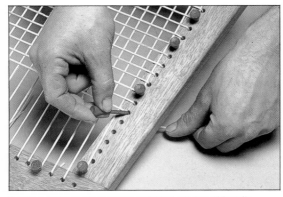

2 *Add a layer of cross canes between the two side rails*

134

Adding the second layer of cane

The second layer is built up in the same way as the first, so that the cross canes of the first layer are sandwiched between two rows of canes running from front to back.

Threading in the second set of canes
Now take a second set of canes from front to back on top of the previous layer, using the existing strands as a guide, **1**. *At this stage, the strands need to be slightly slack to allow for weaving in the second layer of cross-canes. As each length of cane runs out, instead of plugging in a new strand, you will be able to wind it around*

the loops that have formed on the underside. Where possible, remove the pegs holding in previous strands and tidy up the loose ends. When the second row of front-to-back canes is complete, the weaving can begin with the second row of cross canes. First moisten the canes by spraying with a mist of water, to prevent them cracking while you weave. Secure the first

cane in the back left-hand corner and weave it under and over both sets of canes running from front to back until you reach the back right-hand corner. Insert it into a hole, back through the next, and weave back from right to left. Continue weaving until the layer is complete, then use your thumbnail or matchstick to push the canes into neat double strands.

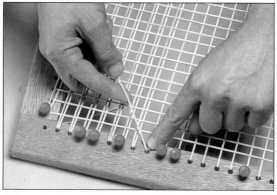

1 *Thread a second layer of cane through the holes in the front and back rails*

2 *Weave the second layer of cross canes through the strands running from front to back*

135
Weaving the diagonal layer

The top layer of cane consists of two rows of cane running diagonally across the seat – one from back left to front right, the other from back right to front left. They are woven through the intersecting canes to form an intricate pattern. Any weaving errors will be noticeable and can only be corrected by unthreading and reweaving, so work carefully.

Building up the pattern
Start at the back left-hand corner, this time using the extreme corner hole, and take the cane to the opposite corner, weaving it under each pair of cross canes and over each pair of front-to-back canes, 1. At the front corner, take the cane down into the extreme corner hole and up through the next hole to the left. Weave this strand diagonally back across the seat, keeping it parallel with the first.

As the holes become more crowded, you may need to use a bodkin. When the left-hand side of the seat is filled with diagonals, return to the back left-hand corner and continue as before, but working to the right to complete the seat. Working from the back right-hand corner to the front left-hand corner, weave a second set of diagonals, 2. This time take the canes over the cross canes and under the front-to-back canes.

1 *Weave a diagonal layer under the cross canes and over the front-to-back canes*

2 *Weave a second set of diagonals in the opposite direction*

136
Finishing off

The neatest way to finish off a cane chair seat is to plug alternate holes to lodge the canes in position, and fix a strand of beading over the peg holes.

Plugging
To prevent the cane slipping out of place, plug the holes. Cut the 4.5mm-wide basket cane into 20mm lengths, and smear each with a little pva woodworking glue. Using a hammer, drive the plugs into alternate holes all round the edge of the seat, until they lie just below the surface, but keeping the corner holes clear. If the plugs will not fit easily into the holes, taper the ends with a sharp knife. If you find a hole is plugged with a temporary peg, remove it, but hold the loose end of cane taut, while you insert the permanent peg. If you find that a hole you do not plan to peg has a loose end of cane, push the end into an adjacent hole and plug that instead.

Beading
Cut four pieces of edging bead (No. 6 cane) 50mm longer than each seat rail and cut one end of each strand into a taper. Take one strand and peg it into a corner of the frame. Then take a strand of ordinary (No. 2) cane, pass it up through the next unplugged hole, loop it over the beading cane and take it down the same hole to hold the beading flat against the seat. Take the securing cane along to the next unplugged hole and again up and over the beading cane, and so on until the front, back and each side of the seat have been separately beaded. Before tightening the last loop, tuck the end of the beading into a corner hole.

Finishing off
Finally, hammer cane plugs into each corner of the seat to secure the ends of the beading. Turn the chair upside down, apply glue to the remaining pieces of plugging cane and hammer them into the unplugged holes. Once the adhesive has set, trim off the untidy ends on the underside, and for a glossy finish, varnish the new cane seat. If the chair has a rounded seat, apply the beading in a single strip and when you reach the hole where you started, remove the peg and drive in the end of the beading strip. If the chair was dismantled to extract the seat frame before starting work, reassemble it, using pva woodworking adhesive for a firm bond (see Job 139, p. 152).

You will need No. 6 beading cane and No. 2 cane to secure it in position. If, however, the holes are very narrow or close together, use No. 4 cane for both. Alternatively, the canes can be fixed in place by plugging each hole with a permanent peg. Finally, the beading needs to be plugged into the corner holes and any loose ends trimmed.

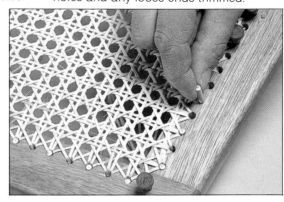

Insert glued plugs into the holes to secure the canes

Secure the edging bead with loops of cane

Use a sharp knife to trim off the untidy ends on the underside

137

Repairing loose chair joints

Chair joints are often heavily stressed, causing them to work loose. If the joint is covered in upholstery, you will have to remove it and take note of how it should be replaced. In this case, because the repair is to be concealed, joints can be repaired by screwing an L-shaped metal bracket to the inside of the frame. However, remaking the joint will produce a stronger repair – even though doing so will involve taking several joints apart and if the joint links the seat to a leg, removing a triangular reinforcing block. If the joint is visible, you will also need to take it apart to make a neat repair.

Remaking the joint
Unscrew the reinforcing block, then tap it sharply with a hammer or mallet to break the glue bond, **1**. *Separate the two pieces of wood and if the dowels have sheared off, use a drill to bore through and remove them taking care to stop short of the decorative side. Buy hardwood dowels to suit the diam-eter of the holes, measure the hole depth and cut a dowel 6mm shorter than the combined depth of the matching holes. Cut a groove down the length of each dowel, fill it with adhesive, then tap each into position with a hammer,* **2**. *Tap the joint together with a mallet, refit the corner blocks,* **3**, *and leave until the adhesive is dry.*

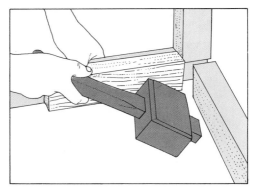

1 Knock out the unscrewed joint block with a mallet

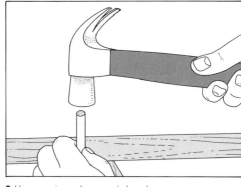

2 Hammer in replacement dowels

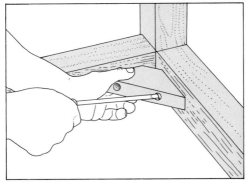

3 Screw in the new reinforcing joint blocks

138

Mending broken chair rails

If a rail used to reinforce chair legs dislodges where the rail enters the hole, you can usually fix a hardwood dowel through the leg and the rail end to secure it back in place. A clean break in the middle of a rail may be re-glued. However, in most cases you will either have to search for a matching rail or ask a carpenter to make up a new one.

Replacing a rail
Remove the old rail with a tenon saw, drill out the remaining stubs and clean the holes with a small file. Cut the new rail to length, allowing for the ends which enter the legs. Measure the diameter of the holes in the legs, **1**, *and draw a circle of the same diameter on the new rail, using a compass, then file the ends of the rail until they fit snugly in the holes. Apply pva woodworking adhesive to the holes and the rail ends. Then pull apart the* chair legs slightly, to allow the rail to fit into position, **2**, *but try not to dislodge the other joints. Finally, wipe off excess glue and wind a string or fabric tourniquet around the chair legs to hold the rail in place until the adhesive has firmly set. To prevent marks forming on the legs, however, insert cotton-wool pads under the tourniquet at the points of highest pressure. Finally, if necessary, stain the rail to match the colour of the rest of the chair.*

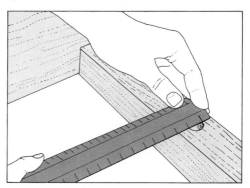

1 Measure the width of the holes in the chair leg

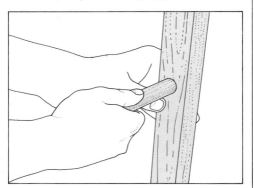

2 Insert the glued end of the new rail into the chair leg

139

Repairing uneven chair and table legs

A chair or table becomes unsteady when one leg is too short. The solution is either to trim the three longer legs or to add a sliver of wood to the shorter leg. To trim the legs, measure from the short leg to the floor and cut this off the other legs.

Building up a short leg
Stand the chair on a flat surface, making sure that the three longer legs are in contact with the surface. Then, by trial and error, plane down a scrap of wood until it fits snugly under the short leg. Glue and screw the packing block in place and allow it to dry.

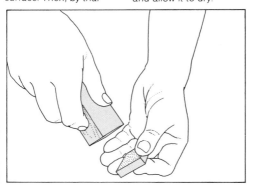

140
Repairing drawers

Drawers are often mis-handled. If they are used frequently and roughly, worn runners may cause them to stick; if they have been stored in damp or hot conditions, the sides may swell or warp, also causing them to stick. If they are over-loaded, the bottom panel may bow, making the drawer impossible to open or the panel may break away completely. Instead of runners, some older drawers have grooves cut in the side to allow it to run over rails. If the groove has worn, you will have to recut it with a circular saw, set to the correct depth, and chisel out the excess wood. If the rail is worn, it will have to be replaced.

Curing a sticking drawer
If the runners are worn, simply remove the old ones and replace them. If the sides are swollen, allow to dry out in warm conditions for a couple of weeks. Or, sandpaper the sides and runners and lubricate them with candle wax (below).

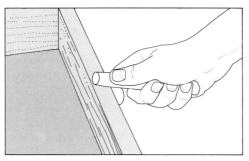

Rub candle wax along the runners to stop the drawer sticking

Curing a bowed drawer
Lever out the bottom panel with a knife or steel rule and apply fresh adhesive to the grooves before re-assembling. If the bottom panel is broken, cut a new piece of plywood of the same thickness and fix into the grooves. Or, weigh down the old panel.

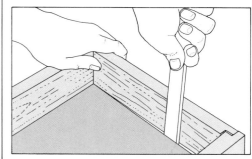

Insert a steel rule into the joints to lever out the bottom panel of the drawer

141
Mending castors

If the castors have become stiff, lightly oil them. If the screws holding the castor to the legs have worked loose, fill the worn screw holes with slivers of wood and replace the screws. If the wheel starts to buckle under the chair, tighten the shaft by tapping it lightly with a hammer and punch. In cases where the castor has simply snapped off, it must be replaced. Castors are fixed to the leg by a central screw or via a cup socket.

Replacing a castor
If the castor has a cup fitting, first remove the brass screws at the side of the cup and lightly tap round the base of the leg to release the castor. If it has a screw fitting, remove the wood screws and unscrew the castor by hand. Then check the new castor for fit. If the leg is too wide, trim it with a chisel or file; if it is too thin, pack it out with slivers of wood (below). If the fixing holes do not line up, plug the old ones and drill new holes, then insert new screws.

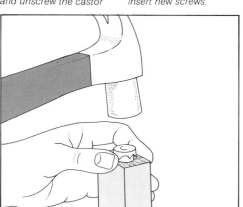

142
Repairing table tops

If the top has become warped, it can be straightened by screwing thick lengths of wood to the underside and tightening the screws connecting the top to the carcass. With a veneer, ensure that the top is well screwed down on to the carcass. A cracked top can be fixed by simply filling the opened joints with the appropriate shade of plastic wood filler or stopping. However, if the joints of a leafed table begin to open, it is best to remove the top and separate the pieces.

Closing the cracks
Remove the top and separate the pieces, then plane the edges absolutely flat. Check both edges with a spirit level or straight-edge. When the two pieces are identical, drill several matching holes in each edge, clean them out and fill them with glued dowels. Glue the two pieces together, cramp them firmly and leave until the adhesive sets. Finally replace the top on the table legs.

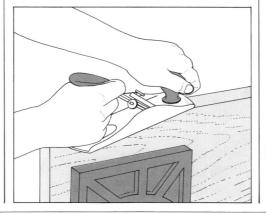

143
Treating veneer blisters

You may be able to remove a blister by covering it with a damp cloth and pressing it lightly with a warm iron, to extract moisture in the wood. This will soften the adhesive, so that if a heavy weight is left on the blister for a couple of days, the blister should deflate. If it returns, try injecting some pva adhesive behind the blister with a hypodermic syringe and weigh down the blister. If this does not work, you will have to make a slit in line with the grain, through the blister, to apply adhesive beneath the two flaps.

Slitting the blister
Use a very sharp knife to make a clean cut through the blister in the direction of the grain. If the blister is very small, make an elongated cross. Raise the flaps and clean out any old adhesive. Apply fresh pva adhesive to both surfaces, then weigh down the blister for 24 hours.

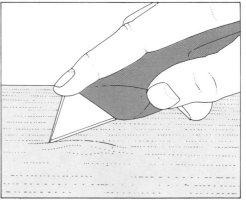

144
Preparing a seat for re-rushing

Genuine rushes are difficult to find, so you may have to use seagrass, a twisted, rush-like material of a slightly different colour (*see Tools and equipment, p. 148*). Rush or seagrass is normally quite flexible, but if it seems brittle, soak it in water for about 15 minutes, remove it and shake off the excess water before starting work. For a strong seat, it is best to have the minimum of joins, so wind as much as you can handle on to the hardboard winder. As a rough guide, allow 2-3 hours for re-rushing an average-sized chair seat.

To remove the old seat, you will have to cut through the old rushes with a sharp knife. This produces a lot of dust and rush splinters, so, if possible, work outside, or lay down a dust sheet.

145
Working out the sequence for rushing

The job involves winding the rushes around the frame from corner to corner. If, however, the seat is wider at the front than at the back, you will need extra turns around the front rail to keep the line of the weave running in a straight line from front to back. Likewise, with a rectangular seat, when the left and right segments are full, you will have to take extra turns over the front and back rails to fill the gaps.

Filling a square frame
A pattern automatically forms as a strand of rush is woven around the frame, and looped over
each corner. This gives the impression that diagonal seams divide the chair into four segments.

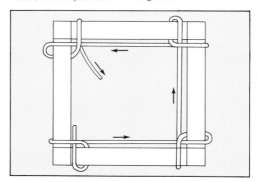

146
Weaving in the rushes

The first strand is fixed to the frame with a knot and is then wrapped around each corner in succession until it runs out. The second strand is then wrapped around the hardboard winder and tied to the end of the previous strand, on the underside of the seat. This process continues until the entire seat is covered. When you have used up all the rush on the hardboard winder, you will have to tie a new length to the old one with a simple knot on the underside of the seat.

Building up the pattern
Start in the front left-hand corner and tie the rush on to the frame, so that it exits from under a rail. Work around the seat in an anti-clockwise direction, taking the rush over the rail in the front right-hand corner of the seat. The strand is taken around this corner so that it exits from under the front rail and on to
the back right-hand corner. From here it is taken over the back rail, around this corner, and out from under the rail, 1. Continue winding anti-clockwise in the same sequence, building up the seat from the corners and working towards the centre of the seat, 2. As you pass strands over a rail, twist them, to ensure a neat finish and leave lower strands untwisted.

1 *Pass the rush under and over the rail at the corners*

2 *Continue working anti-clockwise so that a pattern builds up*

147
Tightening and packing the rushes

To ensure that the frame is well covered, and that the diagonals lie straight, the strands need to be pushed tightly and evenly together, after about eight rows have been woven in each corner. At this stage, you should also pack the cavity between the top and bottom layers with broken pieces of rush, to give the seat greater comfort and strength, and to prevent it sagging. This process should be repeated after every eight strands.

Filling up the gaps
To tighten the strands, use a scrap of wood and a mallet to drive them together, until the chair frame is not visible underneath. Insert the wood between the strands and tap firmly with the mallet. Alternatively, use your fingers to pull the strands firmly towards the frame. Take a few strands at a time,
lodge your knee against the frame and ease the strands together, 1. To pack out the seat, fold offcuts of rush in half and push them between the two layers of woven rush at the corners, using a blunt knife or scissors to ensure a tight fit, 2. Continue pushing in the offcuts until you can push no more in. Then continue weaving.

1 *Pull the strands towards the frame to tighten the weave*

2 *Push offcuts of rush into the space between the two layers.*

148
Finishing off

When the seat is filled, the woven rows will have to be eased apart with a blunt knife, to leave room for the last few strands. The last piece of rush is wound over the rail to the underside, or pushed through the central hole and secured with a knot. If the chair was dismantled before work started, reassemble it, using pva adhesive to ensure strong joints (see *Job 137, p. 152*). Finally, add a coat of wax or polish to give the rush a rich and protective finish and a lustrous sheen.

Securing the last strand
*Wrap the last strand over the rail to the underside of the seat. Pull it to the centre, and gently ease down a woven strand far enough to allow the final strand to be slipped underneath. Finally, tie a stopper knot in it, to prevent it slipping out of place and trim off any free ends. Alternatively, for a more secure finish, push the last two strands through the hole in the centre of the seat to the underside, **1**, and tie them both together with a firm knot, **2**. Then tidy up the loose ends, and, if you have removed the chair seat from its legs and back, glue the joints back together again.*

1 *Push the last strands through to the underside*

2 *Tie the strands tightly together with a secure knot on the underside*

Rush and cane furniture

Rush, cane, wicker and bamboo bring warm, natural colours and textures. Natural products are versatile and will blend well into a modern or traditional setting or may constitute the entire decor of a room, with furniture, blinds, matting, picture frames, flower pots all in rush, cane or wicker. The materials are hard-wearing, but attract dust, so should be washed regularly. A scrub-down with warm salt water will remove stains and bleach cane, and a coat of French polish will add a tinge of colour or a slight sheen to the surface.

A formal setting
Bamboo or cane blinds can be used to soften a cold, harsh light from the windows (right). Elegantly shaped cane furniture in an expansive setting gives a clean, sophisticated air in an otherwise cold and dark room.

A domestic setting
Golden cane and wicker give a warm, sunny feel in daylight and blend naturally with house-plants (below). The slatted and latticed patterns in cane can also be used to good effect in artificial light, and cast delicate shadows.

Renewing upholstery

Construction of an upholstered chair ◇ Renewing webbing, hessian and padding Replacing springs Re-covering a fixed seat

There are two basic types of upholstered seat: a fixed seat, which forms an integral part of the chair, and a loose seat, which contains no springs and simply drops into the chair frame.

If a chair seat is sagging or lumpy, it needs to be stripped, and the old webbing, padding and springs replaced. In many cases, however, the outer fabric wears before the inner padding. Nevertheless, when re-covering the seat, it is wise to renew the padding.

Although the same basic technique is used for all types of chair, a drop-in seat is easier to work on than a fixed seat, because it can be detached and turned to any angle, and because it contains no springs.

Points to remember

◇ Always use a strong cover fabric that is recommended for upholstery.
◇ Make sure the springs are sewn upright on the webbing, that they are not distorted, and that the new springs are the right size.
◇ When upholstering for the first time, avoid striped fabrics, since the stripes are difficult to align.

For information on types of upholstery fabrics, see Choosing materials, pp. 134-5.

Estimating time

The length of time needed to re-upholster a chair will depend on your experience and the complexity of the job. However, as a rough guide, an average chair will take about 6 hours to re-upholster completely. Allow 1 hour to replace the webbing, a total of 1¾ hours to replace the hessian, padding and calico, 5-10 minutes per spring, and ¾ hour for finishing off with braid and "bottoming". If you are only replacing the top fabric, however, allow about 1½ to 2 hours to re-cover a fixed seat and 1 hour to re-cover a loose seat.

Tools and equipment

Specialist upholstery tools and materials, available from needlework and DIY shops and upholsterers, are essential. Woven webbing, which comes in jute, linen or cotton mixtures, is used for traditional upholstery. Rubber webbing, used with foam rubber padding, is for modern furniture. The hessian should be the 16oz "tarpaulin" type. For traditional upholstery, horsehair and sheep's wool are best, but those mixed with other animal hairs are less expensive and more readily available. You will need a tack lifter to remove old tacks, and a sharp knife to cut the springs free from the webbing. Webbing is secured with 12-16mm tin tacks, hessian and calico with 16mm tacks and the covering material with 10mm fine-headed tacks.

Fixing equipment *Tacks are driven in with a small tacking hammer. The springs are attached with No. 1 upholsterer's twine and a 12.5-15cm spring needle; and the padding with light-weight upholsterer's twine and a 25cm stitching needle. Scissors are useful for cutting all materials and latex adhesive is needed for gluing the gimp over the tacks.*

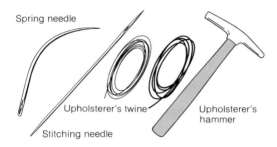

Spring needle · Upholsterer's twine · Stitching needle · Upholsterer's hammer

The construction of an upholstered chair

A traditional upholstered chair consists of a network of webbing at the bottom, which supports the springs; these are covered with a layer of hessian, which supports padding. This in turn is held in place with a covering of calico. The covering fabric forms the top layer and the bottom of the seat is sealed with black linen.

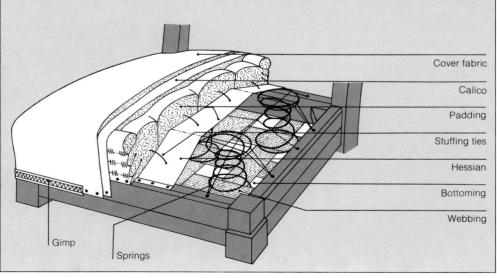

Cover fabric · Calico · Padding · Stuffing ties · Hessian · Bottoming · Webbing · Gimp · Springs

149

Renewing webbing

Before you start, you will have to turn the chair upside down and use the tack lifter to remove the tacks holding the layer of "bottoming" and the old webbing. You should also cut through the twine holding the springs to the old webbing. At this stage you should replace any broken or distorted springs. On a traditional chair, you will need woven webbing, which is fixed in a series of strips, first from front to back, then from left to right, until it forms a criss-cross network. It is best to keep the webbing in one long strip and to cut as you go, to be sure of the correct measurements. On a modern chair, you will need rubber webbing, which stretches when pulled, or sat upon, so it is important that each strip is fixed under the same tension. For dining and other smaller chairs, you only need to fix rubber webbing in one direction, but for larger chairs, you should interweave a second row for extra strength. With both types, you will finally have to attach the springs to the new webbing (*see Job 150, below*).

Using woven webbing
Fold under 10mm of webbing, position the folded edge halfway across the back rail of the seat and tack it just to one side of the old tack holes. Hammer in three tacks across the webbing 5mm from the fold, then add two more, evenly spaced below the first row. Pull the webbing straight across the chair frame, using a block of wood (150mm × 75mm × 25mm) to hold it taut. Then fasten it to the front rail, using three tacks as before. Cut off the excess webbing 10mm beyond the tacks, fold it back over the tacks and hammer in two more tacks to secure it, **1**. *Fix more strips in the same way, again just to the side of the old tack holes until you have a series of parallel strips running from the back to the front of the frame. Then fix more webbing in the same way, this time working from left to right and weaving in and out of the previous layer,* **2**, *to form a network.*

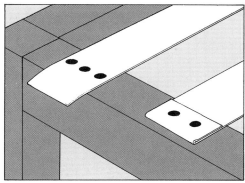

1 *Attach the webbing to the rail with three tacks, then turn and tack the surplus*

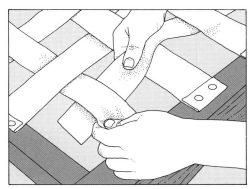

2 *Weave the second layer of webbing through the first*

Using rubber webbing
Measure the distance from the centre of the back rail to the centre of the front rail. To transfer this on to the webbing, first draw a line 10mm from one end of the webbing, then measure off the chair span from this line and draw a second line. Next mark a third line 2cm inside the second. Position the webbing on the chair with the first line lying half-way across the back rail and hammer in four tacks across it at equal distances, **1**. *Lay the webbing straight across the frame so that the third line lies half-way across the front rail. Then fix it in position as before and cut off the surplus,* **2**. *To ensure that each strip has the same tension, measure and fix each in the same way until equally spaced strips span the frame. On a large chair, add a second row in the same way, and stretched evenly but running from left to right and interweaving the first layer.*

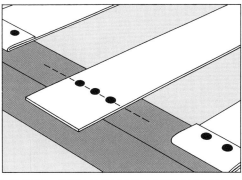

1 *Tack the webbing to the back rail, fold and add two more tacks*

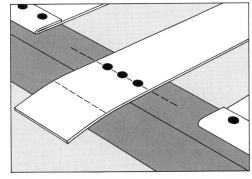

2 *Stretch each strand across the seat and tack along the tacking line*

150

Replacing springs

If you have just renewed the webbing, you will need to re-attach the springs. If you are not re-upholstering, but need to secure a loose spring or insert a new one, you will first need to remove the "bottoming", and release the webbing by prising off the securing tacks. To fix the springs to the webbing, cut a length of No. 1 upholsterer's twine and thread it to a spring needle. When you have secured the springs in position on the webbing, it is wise to lace the springs together and to the seat frame with a piece of string.

Sewing the springs to the webbing
Arrange the springs so that they are evenly supported by the webbing, and their ends face the centre of the chair. Then push the threaded needle through the webbing and make a stitch over the base of the spring, using a half-hitch knot to fasten it beneath the webbing, **1** *Make two more stitches, at equal intervals around the spring base and repeat the process for the other springs. Then connect the springs together and to the sides of the frame with cord.*

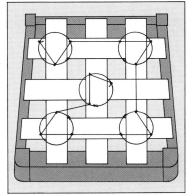

1 *Sew each spring to the webbing with three stitches*

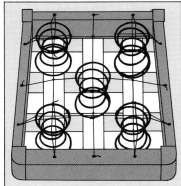

2 *Lace the springs to the sides of the frame*

151

Fitting new hessian

The springs need to be covered with a layer of strong hessian to support the padding and prevent it falling through the seat. You will need to mark position guide lines on the seat frame before tacking the new piece of hessian in place.

Positioning the hessian
Draw a line all round the top edge of the seat frame, 25mm in from the outer edge. Then mark the centre point of each rail. Measure the size of the seat frame and cut a piece of hessian to size, adding on 15mm all round. Centre the hessian over the frame and partially drive in tacks at the centre of each rail. On the back rail, fold the edge of the hessian to align with the line on the frame and tack in at the centre mark. Then stretch the folded edge to the corners of the back rail and tack the hessian in place, inserting more tacks along the folded edge at 25mm intervals, 1. Next pull the hessian to the front, fold the fabric and tack it in place then repeat on the side edges. Then sew the hessian to the springs, 2.

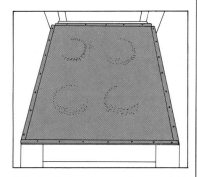

1 *Centre the hessian over the seat, fold the edges and tack them to the frame*

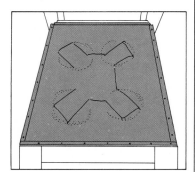

2 *Make three stitches through the hessian around each spring*

152

Replacing the padding

On traditional chairs, horsehair, wool or vegetable fibre padding is positioned on top of the hessian and is anchored with stuffing ties sewn across the hessian, then covered with a layer of calico. Modern chairs, however, are usually padded with foam rubber, which is fitted directly over rubber webbing. Foam rubber can be used on traditionally shaped chairs, provided the woven webbing is replaced with rubber for extra resilience. The foam rubber is cut to size with 15mm extra added all round and is secured to the frame with a calico surround.

Replacing traditional padding
Thread a spring needle with stitching twine and make a small securing stitch in the hem of the hessian at the front. Take the needle halfway to the back of the seat and make a 50mm back stitch through the hessian. Then take the needle to the back of the chair and make a small stitch in the hem of the hessian, leaving both loops of thread across the seat slightly loose. Take the thread over to the adjacent side and again make a back stitch halfway, so that the loops lie about 75mm from the edge of the seat. Continue around the seat until each side contains two loops, 1. To shape the filling, tease out the padding to make sure there are no lumps and tuck handfuls of it under all eight loops.

Most chairs take more padding than you would expect, so keep pressing it down firmly until the space is filled. When the loops are tightly packed with padding, fill in the centre. Tease out the filling with your fingers to spread it into a dome about 50mm high in the centre, 2 and taper it towards the back. Make sure the filling forms an even shape, then cover with a layer of calico.

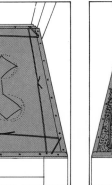

1 *Stitch twine to the hessian to create eight large stuffing ties*

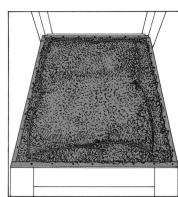

2 *Pack the padding under the ties and fill out the centre into a dome*

Replacing foam-rubber padding
Foam-rubber padding is secured on to the frame with a band of calico fixed around its edges. Measure the depth of the foam cushion, double it and add 25mm. Cut out four pieces of calico to this width and the length of one side of the chair seat. Fold each piece of calico in half lengthwise and spread fabric glue along one side of the fold line. Then stick one along the top edge of each side of the foam. Position the foam in the frame. Then pull the calico down tightly and tack to the frame at the centre of each rail. Insert more tacks at 25mm intervals, to within 50mm of the front corners, and drive home the centre tacks. Pull the fabric around the corners, cut off the excess and tack it firmly in place.

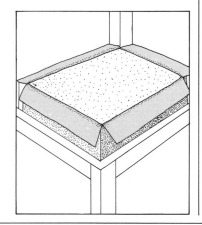

153

Making a calico undercover

Traditional padding, held in place with stuffing ties, needs to be completely covered with a layer of calico to preserve its shape before the final fabric is added. Foam padding is simply secured with a calico border (*see Job 152, left*).

Tacking on the calico
Cut the calico to the size of the seat, allowing 7cm extra all round. Centre it over the padding, pull it down at the sides and temporarily tack it at the centre of each side of the frame, 1. Stretch the calico at the corners, and insert temporary tacks, making sure that the padding is smooth. Then tack the calico to the frame along the back rail at 2.5cm intervals and drive the temporary tacks home. Repeat along the front rail then the sides. At the back corners, make diagonal release cuts, trim away the excess fabric to reduce the bulk, then neatly fold in the edge and retack. At the front corners, neatly fold the calico into a pleat and tack. Finally, trim the calico close to the tacks all round, with a sharp knife, 2.

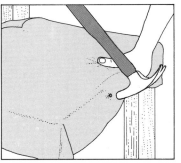

1 *Centre the calico and insert four temporary tacks*

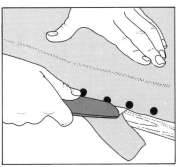

2 *Trim off the excess calico close to the tacks.*

Basic technique

How to re-cover chairs

When replacing the cover of a fixed, or a drop-in seat, the covering fabric will need to be resilient upholstery-weight material. It is cut to the size of the chair, allowing 70mm extra all round for turning and trimming. A piece of cotton wadding, cut to the exact size of the seat, is inserted underneath for extra strength and comfort. On a fixed seat, the cover is tacked on to the side of the chair frame, and a piece of black linen "bottoming" is fitted to the underside of the seat, then a length of braid or gimp is cut to fit the perimeter of the seat.

Re-covering a fixed seat

*Place the wadding centrally on the chair seat, then lay the new cover on top of it. Using fine-headed tacks, temporarily tack the cover to the frame, first at the centre of each side edge of the chair frame, then at 25mm intervals to within 50mm of the corners, keeping the fabric smooth and taut, **1**. Fold the corners back on to the seat, diagonally, then make a diagonal release cut from the corner of the fabric to the line of the fold. Take the resulting triangles down, either side of the upright, folding them in vertically to fit neatly against the upright. Trim away the extra fabric to within 10mm of the fold, press the folds in with your fingers and tack temporarily to the frame, **2**. If the front corners are square, fold the surplus fabric into a single pleat and tack it in place. With rounded corners, fold the fabric into a double pleat – one each side – before tacking, **3**. When the cover is wrinkle-free, hammer home the temporary tacks, then add an extra tack between them, so that they are spaced 10-15mm apart, **4**. Trim off the excess fabric, then turn the chair upside down. Take a piece of bottoming and turn in about 15mm all round. Centre it on the underside of the frame and attach it with tacks, at 50mm intervals, close to the folded edge, **5**. Fold in 10mm at one end of a length of braid. Insert a tack in the fold and tack the end of the braid to the chair. Spread adhesive along the braid and press it into position over the tacks, **6**, and secure the free end with adhesive and a temporary tack.*

1 *Secure the cover to the frame with temporary tacks at 25mm intervals*

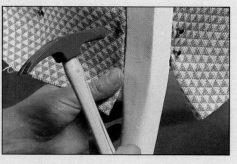

2 *Fold in the fabric each side of the back uprights and tack*

3 *At the front corners, make a neat pleat and tack*

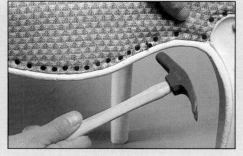

4 *Insert extra tacks between the temporary ones, at 10mm intervals*

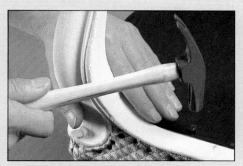

5 *Tack bottoming to the underside of the frame*

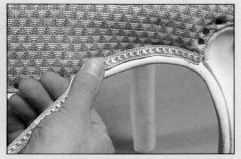

6 *Glue a length of braid over the tacks and the raw edges of fabric*

Re-covering a loose seat

*Lay the fabric upside down on a flat surface. Centre the wadding on top with the fluffy side down on the fabric, then lay the seat centrally on top, also upside down, **1**. Fold the fabric around the frame along the back edge and temporarily tack at the centre, on the underside of the rail. Working outwards from the centre, continue tacking at 25mm intervals, to within 50mm of the back corners. Smooth the fabric over the seat and attach it to the front edge in the same way. Repeat for the side edges, checking that the fabric lies smooth on the top side. To neaten the corners, pull the fabric down hard diagonally, and tack the corner to the underside of the frame, **2**. Fold the extra fabric on either side of the tack into a pleat and tack into place. If there are any wrinkles, remove the tacks which are pulling too tight and re-tack. Trim the fabric to within 1cm of the tacks. Finally tack a piece of bottoming to the underside of the frame, as for a fixed seat. Turn in a small hem, centre it over the pad, then tack it down every 50mm.*

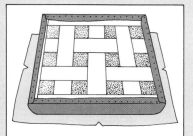

1 *Centre the wadding on the fabric and place the seat on top*

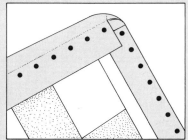

2 *Tack the cover to the underside of the frame at 25mm intervals*

Lighting

Types of light bulb ◇ Types of light fitting ◇ Suiting the lighting to the room ◇ Effects with lighting

Lighting needs to be both efficient and complementary to the contents of your home. If used well it can enhance, disguise, brighten, soften, highlight and reflect furnishings and decoration, while providing the right amount of light to see by.

Every room needs diffused general light to form a soft, shadowless backcloth. Sharper, directional light adds contrast and relief by creating dramatic high-lights and shadows. For reading, writing, sewing or working, how-ever, a specific bright light source is essential and must be planned for. These three types of light must be used in the correct balance for a harmonious effect.

Positioning fittings is as import-ant as choosing the correct types and can affect the dimensions of the room and the effect of its contents.

Points to remember

◇ Position switches within easy reach of the doors.
◇ Do not exceed the maximum watt-age recommended for the fitting.
◇ As a guide you will need 20 watts of light per square metre but dirty bulbs will reduce output.
◇ Fluorescent lights use half as much electricity as incandescent lights, but are more costly to install.
◇ Wall lights can make a room look smaller.
◇ Pendant lights can make a high ceiling seem lower.

For more information on wiring and electricity, see pp. 180-3.

Types of light bulb

Bulbs come in a variety of shapes and sizes. Most fittings take a pear-shaped bulb, but mushroom bulbs are designed for shallow fittings. Decorative shapes are made for chandeliers, wall lights and other special fittings. Larger bulbs are available for spotlights.

Finishes
Normal incandescent filament bulbs come in clear or pearl-white finishes and a few colours. Clear bulbs are best used with enclosed shades. Some directional fittings use reflector bulbs which are partially silvered to concentrate the beam. Some are coated at the base to cast the light backwards; others are coated behind the filament to project the light forwards. Some bulbs come with screw fittings, others with bayonet fittings.

Clear pear   Pearl-finish pear   Silvered pear

Mushroom   Globe   Silvered spotlight

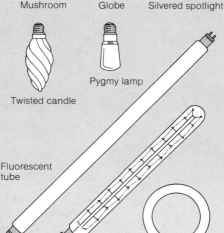

Twisted candle

Pygmy lamp

Fluorescent tube

Filament tube   Circular fluorescent tube

Light fittings fall into two groups: direc-tional fittings, such as spotlights, which give out concentrated beams of light in specific directions; and diffused fittings, such as pendants, which give a wide spread of general background lighting.

Pendant fittings
Traditionally fixed to the centre of the ceiling, these lights supplied light for every occasion in the past. Today, they form a useful back-up for more modern lamps and can be used with a dimmer switch and a rise and fall mechanism for use over a dining table. In confined areas, such as passages, hallways and stairs, pendants cast a useful general light and an attractive shade will add decorative interest. When fitted with trans-lucent shades, pendant lights provide diffused lighting, but an upward or downward pointing opaque shade produces directional lighting. Pendant fittings are available in many styles, including imitation Victorian and Edwardian oil, gas and early light fittings, and chandeliers. Shades for pendants come in glass, fabric, wicker, paper, wood, metal and other materials: and in a variety of shapes, includ-ing pyramids, cones, domes, bells, pleats and balls. Those with an enclosed base emit less glare than those with the bulb fully exposed. Pendant fittings need to be wired up and attached to the ceiling with a ceiling rose (see Job 160, p. 181).

Portable lights
Moveable lights include table and standard lamps and adjustable desk lamps. Traditional table and standard lamps with translucent shades throw a diffused light, while modern floor standard spotlights and desk lights all emit directional light for close work. The shape of the light shade will also influence the direction and intensity of the light beam. Desk lights can double as spotlights and if directed at a wall will cause the light to bounce off and spread into a diffused light. Desk lamps come in a variety of shapes, and with a stand or a clip-on fixing. Clip-on types save space on a crowded desk top. Standard and table lamps, like desk lamps, can simply be unplugged and moved to another part of the room or house. They also offer decorative flexibility, since the shade can be simply changed to suit new decoration or for variety and the base can be improvised from a bottle or jar.

Spotlights
Available in many shapes and sizes, these throw out directional light in wide, medium or narrow beams. The intensity of the light is determined by the type of bulb fitted: ordinary tungsten light bulbs for example give out a harsher light than internally silvered or crown silvered lamps. Spotlights can be wall or ceiling mounted, recessed into a ceiling, or, for more flexibility, they can be clamped on to bedheads, desks, workbenches or book-shelves, or clipped into a wall- or ceiling-mounted lighting track. Aluminium lighting tracks can be surface mounted or recessed into a ceiling or wall and wired to a single lighting point. Each track will then hold and power several spotlights. Each type of track is designed to carry compatible fittings, so be sure to choose the right ones.

Types of light fitting

Some, however, can be used for both. Directional fittings, for example, can produce background lighting if bounced off a light-reflecting surface. When choosing a light fitting, try to establish how much light it will emit, how much will be absorbed by the shade, what shape of beam it will give out, and whether it will shine upwards or downwards. It is always a mistake to buy a fitting merely because it matches the furnishings, particularly since many shades are changeable. Try not to pick a single fitting for the centre of a ceiling, except perhaps for a small kitchen or bathroom – it will lack interest and will not flatter the furnishings. It is best to choose a combination of fittings to create a good blend of general and specific light.

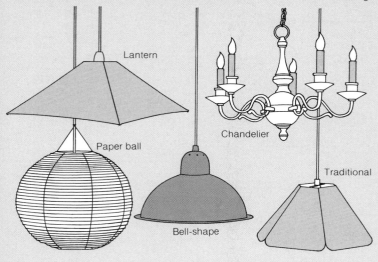

Lantern

Paper ball

Chandelier

Bell-shape

Traditional

Fluorescent fittings

Although widely used in kitchens, fluorescent light can be useful for decorative lighting – concealed behind a curtain pelmet to light the curtains, or fitted under a glass shelf to light ornaments. Fluorescent fittings, which consume very little power, are cheap to run and stay cool, so can be used in confined spaces. They also cast little shadow, so are useful in work areas. For an overall light source, fluorescent fittings can be fixed above translucent panel suspended ceilings.

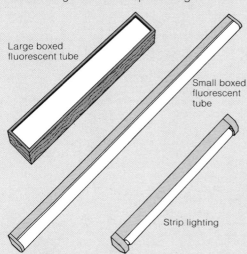

Large boxed fluorescent tube

Small boxed fluorescent tube

Strip lighting

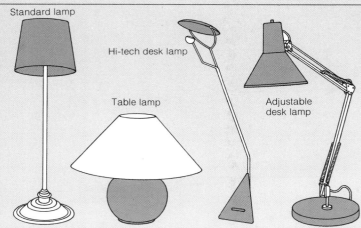

Standard lamp

Hi-tech desk lamp

Table lamp

Adjustable desk lamp

Wall lights

Traditional wall lights cast a diffused light, to be used instead of, or in addition to, a central pendant. They are best controlled with a dimmer switch and used in dark rooms, to illuminate dark halls and landings. Modern wall spotlights produce a concentrated beam of light which can be directed down on to a table or chair for specific work, or used to highlight a special decorative feature, such as plants or pictures.

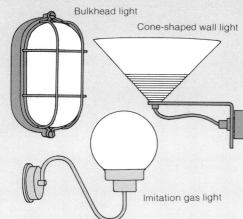

Bulkhead light

Cone-shaped wall light

Imitation gas light

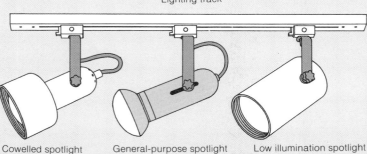

Lighting track

Cowelled spotlight

General-purpose spotlight

Low illumination spotlight

Uplighters and downlighters

Downlighters are square or cylindrical units, used to beam shafts of light downwards from the ceiling. They can be fitted fully recessed into the ceiling, semi-recessed or surface mounted. Narrow beams highlight specific areas, wide beams provide more general lighting. Uplighters are fitted in reverse, beaming light up from the floor.

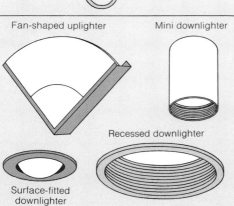

Fan-shaped uplighter

Mini downlighter

Recessed downlighter

Surface-fitted downlighter

Suiting lighting to the room

Different rooms have different lighting requirements to suit the conditions and the activities of the room. Living rooms, for example, need a soft combination of diffused, decorative and direct lighting, while kitchens need a brighter overall light for cooking. Evening meals are more relaxing in subdued lighting, so use diffused lighting and perhaps a dimmer switch or a pendant light in a dining room. In bathrooms and kitchens, ensure that all fittings are totally enclosed and have a shield or skirt to prevent anyone who is replacing a bulb from touching the metal bulb cap. If a small strip-light is to be used, ensure that it has a built-in switch and safety cut-out to isolate the holder when the tubular bulb is removed. For safety, you should use pullcord switches in rooms with a water supply, such as kitchens, bathrooms and washrooms.

Hall and passage lighting

Dark, confined spaces need to be clearly lit with pervasive lighting from wall lights or down-lighters bouncing off the walls. Halls should also have a warm, welcoming glow from diffused but clear lights inside, and a porch light at the door.

Bedroom lighting

Most bedrooms need soft general light, with a switch by the door, and bedside reading lights positioned above or beside the bed, with easily reached switches. It can be useful to have lights inside cupboards; for example a side strip-light, illuminating the shelves from above. For a child's night light, use a dimmer switch or allow the light from a landing or an adjoining room to filter in.

Bathroom lighting

For general light, surface-mounted closed ceiling fittings are best in most cases, especially plastic or glass types, which, unlike metal, are resistant to steam and condensation. Enclosed downlights or spotlights well out of reach of shower spray are also suitable. Fluorescent fittings can be useful, especially if hidden behind a suspended ceiling or a pelmet. In addition, you will need a light above a mirror. This should shine on to the face of the person in front of the mirror, not glaring on to the mirror itself. Remember that all lights in a bathroom should be controlled by pull-cord switches, and all fittings should be out of reach of the shower spray.

Living room lighting

Greater variety of lighting is needed in a living room than in any other room in the house. You will need a combination of general, diffuse lighting, supplied by wall washers or a pendant; directional lights, such as spotlights on a ceiling track or down and up-lighters; and portable lights for specific activities. For reading, you will need a light shining from behind the chair; for working, a concealed light reflecting on to the wall or an adjustable light will be suitable. A light shining from behind will cast shadows. Rise and fall lighting is useful over a dining table and an indirect light near the TV set will make it less tiring to watch.

Staircase lighting

Stairs must be well lit to avoid accidents. It is best to angle the light from the side and to keep the light constant. Light-sensitive switches which automatically turn the light on when the natural light dims to a set level are useful for stairs.

Kitchen lighting

You will need both strong lighting for cooking, and more subdued lighting for everyday use and mealtimes. Dimmer switches can be useful for this purpose, but remember they cannot be used with a fluorescent lights system. Fluorescent tubes are the traditional way of lighting a kitchen. In a small room up to 6m² a single tube mounted over the sink or working surface may be enough; in larger rooms, you will need at least two. They can be particularly effective under wall units, shining on to work surfaces. Adjustable spotlights offer good directional lighting over the cooker or sink.

Effects with lighting

Lights can create illusions. A broad flood of light over a pale ceiling or wall gives an impression of height and space, while light directed on the floor darkens and lowers the ceiling. Localized pools of light make a room seem smaller and more cosy and help to highlight good features, while the resulting shadows can be used to conceal bad ones. Dark colours and heavy textures absorb light and therefore demand a stronger wattage – up to three times as much as a lighter surface. A shiny and pale surface on the other hand may reflect up to 75 per cent of the light.

Complementary lighting
A large, pendant light (above) emits good general lighting, but casts shadows in corners. An additional selection of spot and fluorescent lights helps to provide clear lighting for working surfaces, and brightens up alcoves and shelving.

Clusters of light
Bulbs or spotlights grouped together and reflected in a mirror (left) can create a dramatic multiplying effect, such as this stage-dressing-room style.

Localized uplights
Illuminating a plant (right), sculpture or ornament from behind with an uplighter produces a halo with subtle upshafts of softened light.

Pictures and mirrors

Tools and equipment ◇ Types of picture frame and hook
Making a picture frame
Arranging pictures and mirrors

Pictures lend individuality to any room, but to look good they need to be well framed, well arranged and perfectly clean.

The easiest ways to frame a picture are to use a kit, to make a "frameless" (glass mount) frame, or to use a ready-made frame. However, with care and patience, a beginner can make a frame.

Paintings, prints and watercolours should be arranged to form an integral part of the room and to harmonize with the furniture.

Mirrors too play an important part in the decor of a room, beyond their obvious uses as an aid to dressing, but they must be positioned carefully and the glass must be good quality.

Points to remember

◇ Always take valuable pictures to a professional restorer for cleaning and repair.
◇ Make sure that all pictures and mirrors are securely fixed to the wall to avoid accidents.
◇ Keep all pictures out of direct sunlight, electric light or heat, and do not subject them to rapid changes in temperature and humidity.
◇ Dust oil paintings regularly and protect prints and watercolours with glass. Keeping them clean will prolong their life.

Tools and equipment

The basic elements of a picture include wooden or aluminium mouldings, 2mm thick picture glass, mounting card and hardboard backing board. To fit them together, you will need turnbuckle clips or glazing sprigs, and masking tape to seal the frame. When making a mount, use a sharp craft knife and a steel rule. Use stamp collector's gummed hinges for attaching the picture to a normal mount, and adhesive tape for a window mount.

Making a frame
To cut accurate mitred (45 degree) corners, you will need a mitre block and a fine-tooth tenon saw on wood and a fine-tooth hacksaw on metal. For assembling wooden frames, use pva woodworking adhesive and veneer pins to connect the four sides and a mitre clamp to hold them. On metal frames, you will need epoxy adhesive to glue the corners, and screws to fix the frame to the backboard.

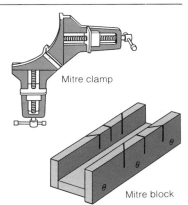

Mitre clamp

Mitre block

Types of picture frame

A frame should be chosen to suit the style of the painting, print or photograph it is to surround. Only oil paintings which are protected by varnish should be framed without glass. Ready-made frames come complete with glass and backing sheets. Framing kits usually come complete with a metal or plastic frame with pre-mitred corners, and clips, but without the glass and board.

Wooden frames
Picture frames made from wood can be painted, varnished or gilded. If you are making a frame, a wide variety of special frame mouldings are available. Carved and gilded mouldings, for example, can be bought from picture-framing specialists and art shops. In many cases these suppliers will cut the mitres (the 45-degree corner angles) to size, so that you glue and pin the frame together. DIY shops and timber merchants supply simpler mouldings, but will not cut mitres.

Frameless glass mounts
The picture is sandwiched between a sheet of glass or acrylic plastic and a similar-sized sheet of backing board. The three layers are held

together with simple metal clips or spring-loaded picture clips.

Metal frames
Polished aluminium is particularly popular for modern settings. However, it is best to buy these frames ready-made, since metal is difficult to work and join.

Old frames
Auctions, jumble sales and second-hand shops are a good source of picture-frame mouldings. Over-large frames can be easily dismantled and cut down to size. If parts of a moulding are missing, try casting a new section in plaster. Press dental impression compound on to a sound part of the frame. Remove it and pour plaster into it. When dry, glue the plaster shape to the frame.

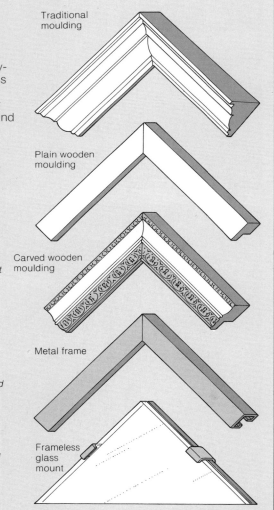

Traditional moulding

Plain wooden moulding

Carved wooden moulding

Metal frame

Frameless glass mount

Types of picture hook

The fittings you use on the back of the frame or backing board depend on the weight of the picture. The type of fixing used on the wall is chosen to suit either a solid or a cavity wall. Both fixings, however, need to be compatible.

Fittings for lightweight pictures
For small pictures with mouldings less than 20mm wide, use D-rings, 1, inserted directly into the backing board. The picture can then be hung on a lightweight picture hook or screw. If the mouldings are more than 20mm wide, a screw eye, 2, can be fitted to either side of the frame, joined with nylon cord, pulled taut.

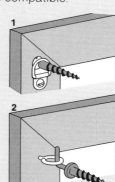

Fittings for heavy pictures
Heavier pictures need stronger fittings, such as picture plates, rings or battens, 2. Plates and rings are screwed to the thickest part of the mouldings, on each side of the frame, about one third of the way down. They can be linked with three-strand picture wire, twisted around the plate hole or ring and pulled taut, 1.

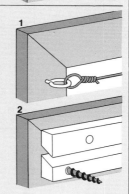

Solid-wall fixings
Solid walls will take picture hooks, which are fixed by hammering a thin masonry pin into the wall. Single hooks are suitable for lightweight pictures, 1, double-pin hooks for heavier ones, 2. If the wall is very hard, you may have to drill a hole, then insert a wallplug and screw.

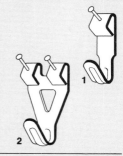

Cavity-wall fixings
On cavity walls, insert a dome-headed screw into a suitable wallplug, 1. You can hang the picture directly on to the screw head or hook the hanging wire over the screw head. Alternatively, screw a hook directly into a wallplug and hook on the picture fitting, 2.

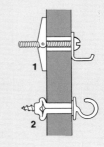

How to make a picture frame

To make a wooden picture frame, you will need four lengths of wooden moulding. If the supplier has not mitred the corners for you, you will have to cut eight mitres (45-degree angles) – two for each corner using a mitre box and a fine-tooth tenon saw. So remember to allow for wastage when buying the moulding. As a guide for calculating the length of moulding required, add the combined length of the four sides to the width of the moulding multiplied by eight, and add a further 50mm for cutting and waste. Once the mitred corners are precisely cut, they can be joined by glue and pins to form the frame. For a metal frame, the corners are mitred in the same way, but using a fine-tooth hacksaw.

Mitring the corners
Use a protractor to pencil in the 45-degree cutting guideline on the inside edge of the moulding. Insert the moulding in the mitre block; the slots in the block will guide the saw to cut an accurate 45-degree angle, 1. Cut from the top face of the moulding downwards, working carefully to avoid splintering. Keep the blade perfectly in line and always ensure that you are cutting on the waste side of your guideline.

To cut the matching mitre on the next piece of moulding, angle the blade in the opposite direction. If the moulding is thin, you may need to insert a piece of backing timber beneath the moulding to raise it sufficiently for the saw to reach it at the base of the mitre slot. This will also protect the wooden base of the mitre box.

Check the angle of the mitred joints after cutting: if the two adjoining pieces do not form a perfect right angle, use a bench sander or "shooting board" to make adjustments (see below right). A shooting board can be made from a wide, straight board of timber with battens secured at exactly 45 degrees to the edge.

When both pieces of moulding are trimmed to a perfect 45-degree angle, glue them together, to make a right-angled corner.

2. Then tap veneer pins into both mouldings to secure the join. To hold the frame in position, while the glue sets, use a mitre clamp which forms a true 90-degree angle, or Spanish windlass. A mitre clamp is best, since it allows you to pin each corner immediately after gluing, 3. While one corner is in the clamp, mitre the ends of the next pair of mouldings. A Spanish windlass consists of four corner pieces connected by string, which is twisted around a nail like a tourniquet. With this arrangement, you will have to glue all the corners and tighten the windlass with the frame held flat, then pin the corners when the adhesive has set. If the mitres set slightly out of position, break the bond and remake the joint. To check that the frame is square, measure the diagonals to check that they are equal. Finally, paint, stain, varnish or wax polish the frame.

Using a shooting board
Clamp the board to a work top and hold the moulding against one of the angled battens. Smooth a plane across the mitred corner against the edge of the shooting board.

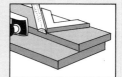

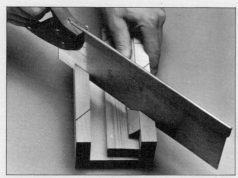

1 *Saw the end of the moulding to a 45-degree angle, using a mitre block*

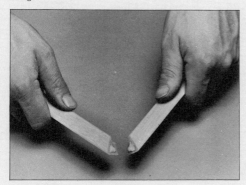

2 *When two mouldings form a true right angle, glue them together*

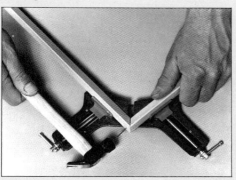

3 *Hold the two pieces in position with a mitre clamp, while the glue sets*

154
Mounting a picture

Before framing, a picture is mounted on to a piece of card. It may be stuck on to a card backing, larger than itself; or attached to a surround, which forms a "window" for the picture, and holds it away from the glass. If a backing is being used, the picture is normally attached to it at the top corners, using two stamp collectors' gummed hinges or a pasted strip of tissue paper.

Making a window mount
Use a sharp craft knife and steel rule to cut an opening bout 5mm smaller than the picture, with allowance for a wider bottom margin. Lay the picture face up on a table, so that it just overlaps the edge. Lay the mount over the picture, and secure the back of the picture to the bottom of the mount with adhesive tape. Then turn both over and tape the top of the picture to the mount.

155
Framing a picture

A framed picture consists of five layers: the outer frame, a layer of glass, the picture, the mount and backing board. It is best to buy 2mm thick picture glass and ask the glazier to cut it to 1.5mm smaller than the frame, then cut your backing board to the same size. The mount is attached to the backing board with a hinge of adhesive tape along the top inside edge, to form an assembly of picture, mount and backing board. Before the glass is slotted into the frame and the picture assembly secured on top, rings, plates or eyes must be screwed to the frame or the backing board (*see Types of picture hook, p. 165*). The glass is secured to the frame with turn-buckle clips or glazing sprigs.

Fixing the backing board
Lay the frame face downwards, clean the glass with methylated spirits, and slot it into the rebate of the frame. Then lower the picture, mount and board assembly into the frame, ensuring that the picture is centralized, *then secure the backing frame. If you are using turnbuckle clips (screws with a swivel "tongue") screw them into each corner and the middle of the frame. If you have glazing sprigs (wedge-shaped nails), press them against the backing board and tap them into* *the inner edge of the frame with a hammer,* **1** *or the edge of a chisel. To seal the frame from dust and dirt, stick masking tape around the back of the frame, over the join between the frame and the backing board,* **2**. *This will also protect the wall from the sharp* *edges of the clips or sprigs. Alternatively, glue brown paper over the entire back of the frame, and, if necessary, trim the edge with a razor blade. Finally, if you are using cord or wire, secure it to the picture rings, plates or eyes and hang the picture.*

1 *Tap glazing sprigs between the frame and the backing board*

2 *Seal the back of the frame with masking tape*

156
Hanging a mirror

Mirrors are available framed, like pictures, or unframed with polished edges. The best are made from good-quality float glass, which is flat and free from imperfections. Bathroom mirrors need a well-silvered backing to resist the steam.

Framed mirrors are hung in the same way as a picture, although in a bathroom you may need to drill through a tile (*see Job 45, p. 52*). Unframed mirrors can be screwed to the wall, if you ask your glazier to drill four holes at each corner of the mirror. Undrilled, unframed mirrors can be mounted on to timber backing board with mirror clips (which clamp the two layers together), or fixed directly to the wall with sliding clips.

Using a screw fixing
Hold the mirror up to the wall at the desired height, and make a pencil mark. Then mark where the screws are to fall in relation to the top of the mirror, using a spirit level. Drill the holes, *and fit wallplugs. Insert round-headed mirror screws, with rubber spacer or tap washers, to absorb irregularities in the wall and to allow air to circulate. Then hang the mirror on to the screws.*

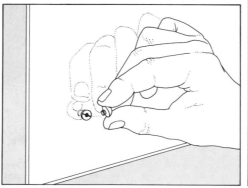

Fixing with sliding clips
A set of clips consists of two fixed clips, which support the bottom of the mirror, and two sliding clips, which secure the top. First drill holes for the bottom fixed clips. Insert wallplugs if *the wall is solid, and screw in the clips. Rest the mirror on these and pencil its outline on the wall. Drill holes 12mm from the top and side edges and insert the sliding clips which grip the mirror.*

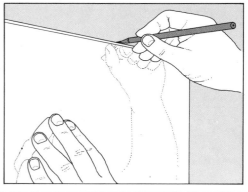

Arranging pictures and mirrors

For maximum impact and a harmonious effect, pictures and mirrors should be positioned with care. A special picture should stand on its own, provided it is not so small that it is lost in a large expanse of wall. Balance is as important as scale. It is not always a good idea to centralize a picture; it may look better offset but in harmony with a piece of furniture, for example. Smaller pictures often look best grouped together into a composite shape, but you can always try working out arrangements on the floor, before hanging them on the wall.

Mirrors can be both functional and decorative, but the positioning is crucial. A well-placed mirror can create the illusion of light and space, but it is usually wise to keep the bottom edge well above ground level.

Grouping pictures
Small pictures or photographs are often best assembled into a shape such as a pyramid or oval (right) or aligned with an imaginary line through the centre of the collection. For the best effects, the individual images should perhaps be linked by a common colour, style, shape or subject matter.

Creating space with mirrors
A dark, narrow corridor or a small, oppressive room will feel larger and lighter if a mirror is hung down the entire length of one wall (left). Full-length mirrored panels applied to cupboard doors, for example, can dramatically increase the sense of space.

Practical mirrors
Bedroom and bathroom mirrors, used as an aid to dressing and make-up, can in fact form an attractive focal point (above). Functional mirrors should be hung at a convenient height and can be positioned to link with a "back view" mirror on the back of a cupboard door.

Storage and shelving

Types of shelf material and support ◇ How to make a screw fixing ◇ Putting up shelves ◇ Types of storage

Well-placed storage and shelving units help to maximize the space in a home and will either conceal or display its contents. There are two basic types of shelving: a ready-made adjustable shelving system, to be assembled; and fixed shelves which you can build from raw materials. Fixed shelves can be attached to a wall or into an alcove. More complex home-made systems can be constructed with a wooden carcass. These systems may be free-standing or secured to the wall. Storage units may also be fixed or free-standing and can be built from raw materials, assembled from a kit, or bought ready-made.

Points to remember

◇ Shelf supports must be chosen for the load the shelf is intended to carry. Six average-sized paperbacks weigh 1kg, while six average-sized hardbacks weigh 2kg.
◇ Timber merchants will cut shelves to size if asked.
◇ Plan to fit built-in shelves after, not before decoration.
◇ If the carpet raises the back of a bookshelf, add a strip of wood under the front edge.
◇ The front edge of a shelf should not project more than 25mm beyond the end of its bracket support.
◇ Always fix shelves securely.

Tools and equipment

If you are buying an adjustable shelving system, you may need a hacksaw. If you have not bought your shelves ready-cut, or if you are building a timber framework, you will need a small hand- or power saw. For boring holes, use a hand-brace and drill bit, or a power drill with a masonry bit for solid walls, and a twist drill bit for wood. Use 50mm, 62mm 62mm or 75mm countersunk screws of the correct gauge and wallplugs for solid walls, and cavity dowels or toggles for hollow walls. You will also need a measuring tape, rule and spirit level.

Types of shelf material

Chipboard, blockboard and plywood are the most usual materials for indoor shelving. Chipboard is readily available, reasonably priced and supplied in varying thicknesses, from 12mm to 25mm. It is sold in standard widths, from 15cm upwards, to be cut to the required length. Veneered chipboard will provide extra strength. Plywood, blockboard or rough-sawn softwood is appropriate in a shed, garage or store room, while hardwood, when available, provides more expensive, high-quality shelving material. Metal is mainly restricted to ready-made systems, but it is useful for heavy loads. Glass can be used for ornamental, lightweight display. Glass merchants supply standard stock sizes and will cut sheets to size and polish exposed edges. A limited range of plastic shelving is also available.

Bearing weights
A shelf collapses because the material is inadequate for the load, or because the supports are not fixed securely to the wall. The shelving material must be the right type and thickness; the supports must be strong enough and spaced at reasonable intervals; and the screws should be long and thick enough to anchor the supports. The sizing is largely a matter of common sense, but the figures (below) give a guide to the maximum span between supports for medium loads.

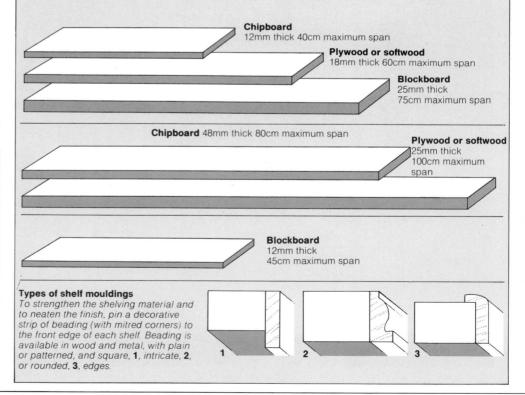

Chipboard 12mm thick 40cm maximum span

Plywood or softwood 18mm thick 60cm maximum span

Blockboard 25mm thick 75cm maximum span

Chipboard 48mm thick 80cm maximum span

Plywood or softwood 25mm thick 100cm maximum span

Blockboard 12mm thick 45cm maximum span

Types of shelf mouldings
To strengthen the shelving material and to neaten the finish, pin a decorative strip of beading (with mitred corners) to the front edge of each shelf. Beading is available in wood and metal, with plain or patterned, and square, 1, intricate, 2, or rounded, 3, edges.

1   2   3

Types of shelf support

A variety of shelf supports is available for home-made shelving. For strong, fixed shelving, brackets or wooden and metal battens can be fixed to the wall. Some are suitable for a flush wall, others fit into an alcove. For lightweight, more adjustable shelving, pegs, dowels, plastic studs, clips and wire can be inserted into holes in wooden uprights. Fixed supports can also be used to make a built-in shelf system, and adjustable supports are useful for a free-standing unit. Alternatively, adjustable systems can be bought ready-made, to be assembled at home. All these systems offer good support.

Wall-mounted fixed shelf supports

L-shaped brackets
These metal, steel or aluminium brackets come in 15 to 60cm sizes to fit standard shelf widths and are fixed to a flush wall. The front edges of the shelf should not project beyond 25mm of the bracket tip, so choose a suitable size and thickness.

Cantilever brackets
These metal rods are inserted into a hole in the wall and into the back edge of the shelf at each end. They are made of impact-resistant plastic and are moulded to a high-tensile steel pin for extra strength. They come in 12cm and 19cm sizes and fit at each end of the shelf.

Triangular brackets
These are only used for fitting a shelf in an alcove. The triangular section fits against the side wall and the shelf sits on the ledge.

Wooden battens
These lengths of wood are fixed to the walls to support the edges of the shelf and are also only suitable in a recess, since they have no supporting arm. The battens are usually 25mm × 25mm, 37mm × 25mm or 50mm × 25mm, according to the load the shelf will have to support, and are cut to the required length. For a standard shelf, spanning a small recess and supporting a light load, you will need only two side battens. For wider spans and heavier loads, fix an extra (narrower) batten to the back wall.

Angled metal strips
These strips are "L-shaped" in cross-section and are used in place of wooden battens. They are cut to length with a hacksaw and secured to the side walls through pre-drilled holes. The shelf sits within the "L", so it is important that it does not fit too tightly against the wall.

Panel-mounted adjustable shelf supports

Pegs
These metal or plastic "pegs" or studs, which come in various shapes and sizes, slot into a hole in a wooden upright. The holes are spaced at equal intervals up the length of the upright and four pegs are inserted at each level to sit under each corner of the shelf for an invisible fixing.

Pegs for glass
Metal slotted pegs are designed to grip a plate of glass and are plugged into pre-drilled holes. Other types have a soft, felt pad for the glass shelf to sit on.

Dowels
Wooden dowels can be cut to length and simply tapped into snug fitting holes, at each corner of the shelf.

Invisible wire support
Holes are drilled in the uprights to hold the ends of a shaped length of 3mm galvanized wire. The ends of the shelf are grooved and slide over the wire which supports the shelf horizontally at each side.

Two-part clips
These metal clips support heavier weights. The socket part fits into an 8mm diameter hole, drilled 10mm deep. The angled bracket then slots into the socket until it locks, and its other arm supports the shelf.

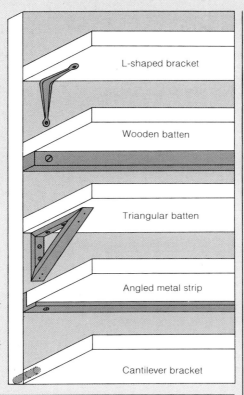

L-shaped bracket

Wooden batten

Triangular batten

Angled metal strip

Cantilever bracket

Plastic peg

Peg for glass

Dowel

Invisible wire

Two-part clip

Ready-made adjustable shelving

These systems consist of aluminium uprights and brackets, and may include shelf material. Most systems are made in a satin, white or coloured finish, and some come in anodized silver and gold, enamelled black, brass or bronze. A limited range of timber systems is also available.

Bookcase strips
An alternative adjustable metal system takes clips instead of brackets. The strips are usually available in 90cm lengths in bronze or zinc-plated steel. The strip is cut to size and four lengths are screwed to the sides of an alcove or to the side panels of a bookcase. For a neater finish, the strips can be rebated into side panels. Bookcase clips slot into the strip and come in a variety of shapes and sizes. Some are designed for heavy loads, some for glass shelves, and others for wooden shelves.

Uprights and brackets
*The uprights are available with regularly spaced square, oval, **2**, T-shaped, **3**, or double slots into which the brackets fit, allowing a wide choice of shelf heights. Alternatively, the upright may have a continuous channel, **1**, which allows the brackets to be fixed at any point. Both types are usually available in lengths ranging from 37cm to 2.4m, and can be trimmed to size with a hacksaw. Those with a continuous channel are easier to fit, since it is not so critical that the two uprights line up perfectly, provided they are vertical. Some systems come complete with screws and wall-plugs; others recommend the size of screw needed to secure the upright to the wall. The brackets vary from 15cm to 60cm deep and should be chosen to suit the depth of the shelf. Brackets for the slotted system have lugs which hook on to the slots. Continuous channel brackets are usually L-shaped and come with a clip, which is locked with an integral screw.*

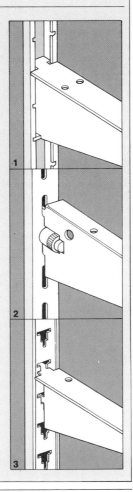

Basic technique

How to make a screw fixing

Most shelf supports need to be secured to a wall or panel by means of screws. The weight of the load will determine the size and strength of the screw, and the type of wall will determine the style of the fixing. For most shelves you will need 50mm, 62mm or 75mm-long screws, according to the size of shelf. Likewise, you should choose a screw gauge suitable for the maximum shelf weight. No. 6 screws are adequate only for light weights, while No. 10 screws will support a heavily laden shelf. Use these two extremes as a guide for choosing a suitable gauge. Screws will not grip on their own in masonry or plasterboard, so in most cases, you will have to use some sort of wallplug (see *The Home Tool kit, p. 225*).

Fixing screws in solid walls
*Choose a wallplug to match the screw size. Then, using a masonry drill bit the same diameter as the wallplug, drill a hole into the wall to the depth of the wallplug, **1**. To prevent the drill bit slipping before you begin, make a small indentation in the wall by turning the drill manually. Plaster is not strong so be sure to penetrate deeper into the masonry. To avoid drilling too far, however, wrap some adhesive tape around the drill bit, the length of the plug away from the tip. Insert the wallplug into the hole, **2**, and drive in the screw. The plug will then expand and the screw will be held securely in the wall. Take care, however, not to tighten the screw so hard that it breaks through the end of the plug. Do not drill holes near electrical switches or sockets or if you think pipes may run behind the wall; it could prove dangerous.*

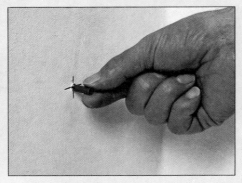
1 Drill a hole in the wall with a masonry drill bit

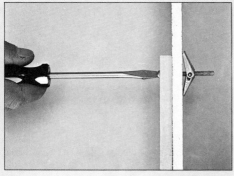
2 Push the wallplug into the hole

Fixing screws in cavity walls
*A partition wall is too thin to allow a screw to grip sufficiently. Special "toggles" and expanding wallplugs are available to hold the screw in place. They are inserted into the wall, like a closed umbrella, **1**, and when they no longer meet the resistance of the wall their "wings" open and anchor the fixing in position. Drill a small hole, just wide and deep enough to take the plug or toggle, and drive in the screw, **2**, while maintaining tension by pulling back the fitting. This pressure will cause the plug or toggle to expand or open and so gives the screw a surface to grip on. If you have a partition wall with a timber framework, it is best to drill and screw directly into the timber supports for a secure fixing. To locate the timber uprights, tap the wall and where it makes a dull sound, make your drill holes. If the studs are inconveniently positioned, screw on a batten to span two studs.*

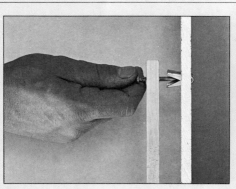
1 Push the toggle into a pre-drilled hole

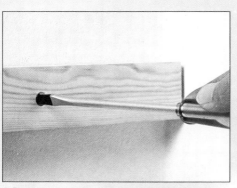
2 Drive the screw into the toggle with a screwdriver

Fixing screws in wooden surfaces
*If you are attaching wooden side panels to alcove walls or putting up a wooden batten, you will need to make screw holes through the wood and into the wall. To ensure straight fixing holes, try drilling right through the wood and into the wall in one go. Using a twist drill bit, drill a hole slightly smaller than the screw. This will ensure that it grips well. Alternatively drill a pilot hole, then countersink the hole, **1**. Insert a wallplug, tap it flush, then tap the screw into the end of the plug. When the end of the plug lies flush with the wall, drive in the screw with a screwdriver, until it lies just below the surface, **2**. The countersunk screw can be covered with a wooden plug for an invisible fixing. Simply glue the plug into place, ensuring that the grain direction matches the surrounding wood. For larger holes, use a handbrace and bit, or a power drill and flat bit.*

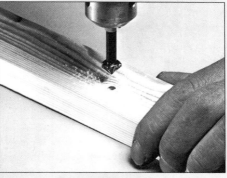
1 Use a countersink bit to widen the opening of the hole

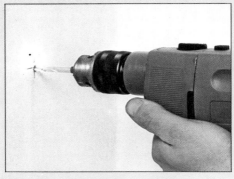
2 Drive the screw into the wood until it is countersunk

157

Putting up a fixed shelf

When you have decided how much weight the shelf is to bear, choose a suitable thickness and width of shelving and sufficiently sturdy brackets and screws. L-shaped brackets are the best for fixed shelves. For small shelves or if your wall is even, it is worth fixing the bracket to the shelf before screwing it to the wall. If your wall is uneven, or if the shelf is very long, it may prove easier to put the brackets on the wall first, then fix the shelf to the brackets. If the shelf is to bear a very heavy load, it is best to use cantilever brackets.

Fixing brackets to the wall
If you intend to add beading, pin a strip of wood or metal beading to the front edge of the shelf first. Then hold the shelf up to the wall with a spirit level on top, and when you have it at the correct height and level, mark the position of both brackets on the wall. Drill two holes in the wall for the first bracket, and when it is in position,

insert and tighten the screws, **1** (see Basic technique, p. 170). Then repeat for the second bracket. With the two brackets in position on the wall, put the shelf on top, centre it over the brackets and push it firmly against the wall. When it is in position, screw the first bracket to the underside of the shelf, **2**. Check that the shelf is straight, then screw the second bracket to the shelf.

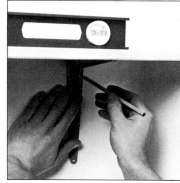

1 *Screw the second bracket to the wall in line with the first*

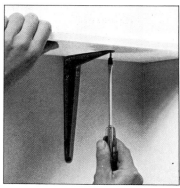

2 *Screw the bracket to the underside of the shelf*

Fixing cantilever brackets
Mark a horizontal line on the wall against a spirit level, to indicate the shelf height, then mark drill holes for the cantilever pins, taking care to position them the correct distance apart. Drill two 6.5mm diameter holes in the wall, 62mm deep and at a perfectly horizontal angle. Insert the cantilever pins into the holes, and mark a second set of drill holes through the fixing holes. Remove the bracket, drill the holes and insert a wallplug in each. Replace the bracket and fix a screw through the fixing hole into the wallplug.

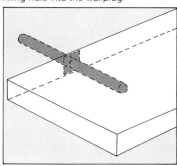

158

Fitting alcove shelving

Recessed shelving can be supported by wooden battens, angled metal strips or triangular brackets, which are fitted to the wall in the same way as L-shaped brackets. If, however, the walls are very uneven, it may be best to make two wooden side uprights to fit against the walls and fix the shelves to them.

Fixing battens
Cut three battens to length, one to span the back wall, and two for the side walls, each slightly shorter than the width of the shelf. Drill holes in the battens, every 45cm, then drill corresponding holes in the wall, along the horizontal line. Insert wallplugs and screw the battens into position. Place the shelf in the alcove and rest it on the battens. If the side walls are not perfectly straight, you will have to shape the side edges of the shelf to fit.

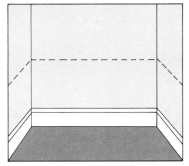

Marking out the alcove
Use a spirit level to mark position guides for the battens on each of the three walls at the height of each shelf. Measure the alcove width and cut the shelves to size.

159

Fixing adjustable shelving

Ready-made systems are easy to assemble. The uprights are fixed to the wall, the brackets are slotted or screwed into position at the appropriate level and the shelves slide into place. When assembling the shelving, remember that the uprights must be fixed at the same height if the shelves are to sit level. If you need to cut the uprights to length, use a small hacksaw.

Securing the uprights
*Fix the first left-hand upright to the wall with one screw at the top and let it hang. Then use a spirit level to bring it into vertical line and mark drilling holes down the wall, **1**. Swing the upright aside to drill and plug the holes, then screw it into place. Clip a bracket to the left-hand upright, and use a shelf and spirit level to bring the right-hand upright into line. Clip on a parallel bracket, **2**, and when the shelf is straight, mark a fixing hole for the right-hand upright. Remove the shelf and brackets and screw the right-hand upright to the wall at the top. To align it, fix three shelves at the top, centre and bottom, and mark drilling holes. Then drill, plug and screw as before.*

1 *Use a spirit level to align the left-hand upright*

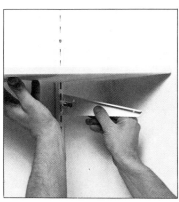

2 *Use a shelf to level the right-hand upright before fixing it*

Types of storage units

There are three basic types of storage system: fitted, free-standing and modular. Fitted cupboards have the advantage of maximizing storage space, while free-standing systems can be easily transferred to a different room or home and can be used as room dividers. Modular units may be free-standing or fixed, but those attached to the wall will support heavier weights than a free-standing unit. Many storage systems are available as a ready-cut kit to be assembled at home, but if you need to work to exact requirements, it may be best to build your own. Before you start work on assembling a kit, it is best to check that all the parts, screws, knock-down fittings and cam joints have been included, and to spend a little time working out the construction principles, and the purpose of each element. It will then prove easier to follow the instructions.

Modular units

Units built up from shelves, drawers and cupboards into complete storage systems offer flexibility and the choice of open storage for decoration and closed storage for protection. The system can be adapted or enlarged to suit your needs; some sophisticated designs even incorporate wardrobes with sliding or louvre doors, drop-flap desk tops and glass doors. Two modules can be spaced apart to allow a shelf or desk top to rest on top, and a conglomerate of shelves and drawers can be arranged to produce boxed-in storage areas within the system. Free-standing modular units are easier to assemble than fitted ones, since they do not depend on the angles of the walls and corners. They can also be used as room dividers, though tall units should be weighed down at the bottom, to prevent toppling.

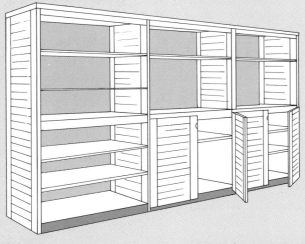

Built-in units

Fitted cupboards come in a variety of forms. They may be designed to fit into chimney-breast alcoves, to turn a corner, to span a bed or to bridge the gap between kitchen fixtures. It is vitally important to measure precisely before buying, since a few millimetres can make all the difference. If the cupboard is too big, you may have to call in a carpenter; if it is too small, you may be able to close the gap with a length of wood. Fitted cupboards must also be firmly attached to the wall, particularly if they are raised off the ground. Sliding, folding and up-and-over hinged doors and those with concealed hinges, help to increase the working or living space in a small area.

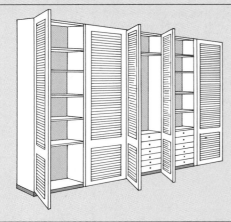

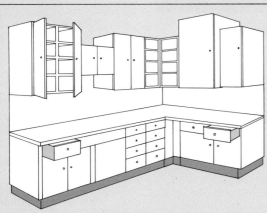

Free-standing drawer units

Drawers can be introduced into the house in one of three ways. They may be bought ready-made, incorporated into a piece of furniture, such as a chest of drawers, or a kitchen storage unit; they can be bought as a kit, or they can be built from raw materials. Drawer kits come with side and corner pieces, and, in some cases, 3mm thick white baseboard for the drawer bottom, and a front panel. You would use a three-sided kit if you wanted to supply your own front panel to match the rest of your furniture. Moulded drawers, made from high-impact polystyrene, are also available and moulded inserts can be added to create extra compartments.

Using storage space

Every room offers more storage space than meets the eye. Under beds, sofas and window seats, over doors, beds and staircases, in corners, lofts and cellars, and behind doors, there is usually space to be used. Storage units can be built around washbasin pedestals, to span alcoves and overhang beds; wardrobes can be fitted to the full height of the wall, and extra shelves to be added to cupboards. Fold-away and pull-out tables and beds help to keep the living area of the room clear. Practical storage ideas can also be decorative, and it is worth improvising for individual effects. Everyday items such as shoes can be openly displayed on hooks, for example; and old tins, paint cans, barrels and chimney pots make useful and attractive containers. Ideally, all storage and shelving systems should be versatile, so they can be moved to another room, extended, enlarged or adjusted to take different contents. Keep an eye open for the decorative possibilities of storage systems.

Using grids and hooks
Hanging racks and hooks provide convenient and easy-to-reach storage in a busy kitchen (below). They also make an inexpensive and attractive grid frame for clumps of herbs and cooking utensils (below). Wall hooks and rails likewise form an ideal storage system for tools.

Using loft space
The existing room shape will often suggest storage space. Alcoves, corners or the space created by the slope of an attic roof (right) can be transformed into attractive features, while housing books, ornaments or household items. Cellars and attics need to be warm and dry for storage.

Using window space
Light filtering through objects displayed on window shelves and sills adds interest to a simple
arrangement (above). Window shelves also help to disguise an ugly view, but the window must be sealed.

Appliance fault-finding

Detecting basic faults
Mending small electrical
appliances ◇ Mending large
electrical appliances

Most electrical appliances give
years of reliable, trouble-free
service. But when they receive hard
and regular use over the years,
some breakdown is to be expected.
Faults are always irritating, not
least because we take smooth
running for granted, yet many
problems can be solved quickly
and easily. Basic faults, such as
disconnected wires and blown
fuses can be corrected in a matter
of minutes and it is always worth
checking these as a matter of
course before consulting a specialist. Some internal faults can also be
easily put right when you know
how to do it.

Points to remember

◇ Switch off any electrical gadget
before examining and mending it.
◇ Switch off at the wall before
unplugging.
◇ Operate the appliance according to
the instructions given in the booklet
supplied with it.
◇ If the fault is not apparent, call in an
engineer and do not tamper with the
inner workings of the device unless you
know what you are doing.

**For more information on Electricity, see
pp. 180-3.**

Detecting basic faults

When an appliance stops working, the
most usual cause is loss of receiving
power. The plug and flex, which convey
the current to the appliance, may have
become disconnected, or the fuse may
have blown. It is worth making a few
basic checks before looking for more
specific faults.

Checking the wiring
Open the plug and check that the
colour-coded cores are securely connected to their correct terminals (brown
or red core to live, blue or black core to
neutral, and green-and-yellow or green
– if a third core is present – to earth).
Then check that the flex is firmly
anchored in the cord grip to prevent
the cores dislodging. It is always wise to
throw away an old cracked, chipped or
discoloured plug and replace it with a
new, modern one.

Checking the fuse
The fuse should blow if there is a fault
in the appliance, but it may also fail if it
needs replacing. Try fitting a new fuse
of the correct rating, reassemble the
plug and plug it in. If the appliance
works, the fuse needed replacing. If the
fuse blows again, isolate the appliance
for repairs. Another way of testing the
fuse is to unscrew a metal torch, hold
one end of the fuse against the metal
casing and the other against the bottom
of the battery. A sound fuse will light the
torch, a blown one will not. Use a 3 amp
fuse for appliances that use up to 700
watts, a 5 amp fuse for lighting circuits
up to 1kw and a 13 amp fuse for
appliances such as TVs, kettles, irons,
heaters and washing machines, which
use up to 3kw.

Checking the flex
First examine the flex for signs of
damage. If there are no obvious signs
of a break, check the flex connections
within the appliance. If you need to
open the appliance casing to do this,
unplug it first. If the flex is worn, do not
use insulating tape to repair it. Instead,
you should replace it, taking care to
buy the right type and rating. If the flex
is inconveniently short, take the opportunity to fit a longer length. Alternatively, use a flex connector to join two
flexes, or use an extension lead. Choose
bright-coloured leads for use outdoors.

Appliance	Symptom
Drip type coffee pot (gravity)	Coffee does not keep warm
	Ready light does not work
Electric iron	Iron will not heat/control lamp is not lighting
	Iron will not heat/control lamp glows
	Iron overheats or underheats
Upright vacuum cleaner	Vacuum overheats/loss of suction
Cylinder vacuum cleaner	Loss of suction power
	Intermittent power
Toaster	Toaster will not heat
	Toast does not brown

Correcting faults in small appliances

Cause	Cure	Where to look
Failed keep-warm element	**Replace keep-warm element** Remove the base screws and pull off the rubber feet and bottom plate. Unscrew the nut holding the element guard and remove the old keep-warm element. Then remove the screws from the top unit, pull the casing and remove the reservoirs. Use long-nosed pliers to disconnect the lead wires from the terminal board and slide out the main element. Remove the retaining rod and separate the element from its pan. In some models, the entire heating arrangement can be replaced as a single unit. In others, the main and keep-warm elements are fitted individually. Specify the model number when you order a replacement. Reverse the procedure to reassemble the coffee pot.	Top unit Main element
Failed light	**Replace light** Disconnect the leads from the terminals within the base. Push out the old light. Insert a new light and reconnect the terminals.	Keep-warm element
Damaged flex	**Replace flex** Fit a braided, non-kink flex of the correct rating for the iron.	
Failed element	**Replace element** Locate the cover fixing screws and lift the cover off to expose the element. Disconnect the flex connections from the element and remove the element from the sole plate. Find an exact replacement for the element, fit it into position, reconnect it to the flex connections and replace the cover and screw it back on.	Flex connections Thermostat contacts Element
Failed thermostat	**Replace thermostat** Thermostats are tricky to replace, so take it to a specialist.	Sole plate
Failed drive belt	**Replace drive belt** Remove the cover plate from the front, then turn the cleaner over and remove the metal cover. Prise out the roller, slip off the old belt and fit a new one of the same type and size around the roller. Replace the roller and metal shield, turn the cleaner right way up and hook the new belt over the drive pulley, following the diagram on the casing. If there is no diagram, hook it on one way and if the belt slips off, hook it on the other way.	
Punctured hose	**Replace the hose** For a temporary repair, bind the hose with plastic insulating tape. For a long-term repair, remove the hose from its slot and insert an identical hose.	Drive pulley Drive belt
Worn carbon brushes	**Replace carbon brushes** Take to a specialist.	Roller
Failed element	**Replace the element** You will have to work carefully and methodically or you will upset the pop-up mechanism. Open the toaster and have a look at the mechanism, and if you can see how it works, unscrew the old element and fit a new one. If the toast will not pop up, you will have to take the toaster to a specialist since the mechanism is very intricate.	Element
Faulty thermostat	**Replace the thermostat** Take it to a specialist or return to the manufacturer.	Pop-up mechanism

Correcting faults in large appliances

Appliance	Symptom	Cause	Cure	Where to look
Electric cooker	Ring will not heat	Faulty ring	**Replace ring** Disconnect the cooker, then lift the hob and undo the box-like cover to gain access to the ring terminal. Remove the screw on the element fixing plate, free it from the hob and disconnect the faulty ring from its terminals. Fit the new ring by reversing the operation. Call the service engineer for faulty controls or a failed grill.	Electric ring
Gas cooker	Automatic lighter fails	Blocked pilot jet	**Unblock the pilot jet** Use a long pin to clear debris in the jet.	
Dishwasher	Slow washing	Clogged waste filter or inlet holes	**Clear obstructions** Empty the perforated metal or plastic filter at the bottom of the cabinet. Then if the machine has a rotor arm that splays water into the cabinet, lift it off and clean it under a tap to prevent the hard water scale forming around the inlet holes. If inlet or outlet hoses have perished, replace as for a washing machine.	
	Dishes will not dry	Faulty blower or element	**Replace blower or element** Consult the service engineer.	Filter
Washing machine	Leaks	Perished inlet hose Perished internal hose Perished door seal	**Replace inlet hose** The inlet hose may perish if the stop taps are not turned off when the machine is not in use. Turn off the mains, remove the old hose and fit a new hose with new threaded couplers. Fit the couplers on to the supply pipe at one end of the hose and on to the machine inlet at the other. **Replace internal hose** To replace an internal hose, use a screwdriver to undo the worm drive or wire clips holding the hose in place, and smear a little petroleum jelly over the spigots before slipping the hose into place. **Replace door seal** The door seal usually fits in a channel around the door. Remove the old one and press the new one into place. If the seal links the cylinder of the machine with the casing, leave the repair to a service engineer.	Internal hose
Tumble dryer	Over-heating/ slow drying	Build-up of fluff in the filter	**Clear the filter** Fluff and fibres collect in the filter, so try to clean it out every time the machine is used, or once a week. Other faults, including problems with the heat setting control, door switch or motor should be dealt with by the service engineer.	
	No power	Loose connection	**Check the plug and flex** Reconnect any loose cores.	Door seal
Spin dryer	Drum will not revolve/pump will not work	Faulty drive belt	**Fit new drive belt** Turn the machine on its side, unscrew the bottom plate and examine the drive belt. If it has become dislodged from its groove, adjust it into its correct position. If the old belt has snapped or worn thin, replace it. Match the length and thickness of the old belt, and stretch the new belt over the pulleys and fit them into the grooves.	Drum drive belt
	Excessive vibration	Worn bearings	**Replace the bearings** Consult the service engineer.	Pump drive belt

Home maintenance

Electricity ◇ Plumbing ◇ Heating ◇ Insulation
Roofs and guttering ◇ External walls
Damp-proofing ◇ Rot and woodworm
Home safety ◇ Home security

It is tempting to leave home maintenance until things start to go wrong. But if you keep a regular check on the essential services of the house, and undertake necessary work at an early stage, you can hold down household and repair bills, increase the value of your house, and ensure comfort and safety in all weathers. This chapter maps out the electrical, plumbing and heating systems, details how they operate and gives instructions on simple upkeep and repair. It concentrates on the structure of the house, suggests how to solve problems such as damp, rot and woodworm explains the guttering system and gives advice on preventing fires, floods, accidents and burglaries. While major structural work and difficult installations are not included, the chapter covers all the important aspects of basic home upkeep – from fitting a light switch and clearing a blocked drain to insulating a roof and repointing masonry.

Electricity

The electrical system ◇ Types of cable, flex, and fitting ◇ Fitting a ceiling light ◇ Fitting a light switch ◇ Fitting a socket ◇ Fitting a plug Fitting a fuse

Electricity can kill. It is therefore essential to take great care in its everyday use, and to carry out all electrical work in the home to the highest possible standard. Never tackle any electrical job unless you know exactly how to go about it and understand fully what you are doing. If you are not sure about anything, employ a qualified electrician.

Before you start any electrical job, get to know the basic principles of how household electricity works. The diagrams on the opposite page show how electricity arrives in your home and how the wiring beneath the floorboards and behind the wallcoverings makes up the various different electrical circuits. These diagrams are important even if you do not want to replace the fixed wiring, because they show you why you should connect wires in sockets, switches and plugs, in a particular way. Once you know why the system works in the way it does, you will be much less likely to make dangerous mistakes.

Points to remember

◇ When working on the fixed wiring, turn off the house's mains switch first, remove the fuse that protects the circuit you are working on, and put it safely in your pocket.
◇ Double-check that the circuit is dead by plugging in an appliance or using a mains tester.
◇ Always unplug any portable appliance from the mains before attempting to repair it.
◇ Use good-quality materials that conform to British Standards specifications and are marked as such.
◇ Use cables, flexes, and plugs of the correct rating for the circuits and appliances they serve.
◇ For appliances up to 700 watts, use a 3 amp fuse; for others use a 13 amp fuse.

Colour coding for electric wires

In this section, the wires have been colour-coded as: pink for live; grey for neutral and black and white for earth. In a real flex, the live wire is brown, the neutral is blue and the earth is striped green and yellow.

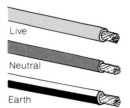

Live

Neutral

Earth

Tips for care of plugs and flexes

◇ Check all your plugs and flexes at least once a year to ensure that they are not worn or damaged.
◇ Remake loose connections and replace damaged flex – do not patch up worn flexes.
◇ Keep flexes as short as possible.
◇ Keep flexes away from heat sources such as electric cookers and fires.
◇ Make sure that each appliance has flex of the correct rating and that each plug is fitted with the correct fuse (see Power consumption, below).
◇ Use two-core flex only on double-insulated appliances and for light fittings with no metal parts.

A guide to electrical terms

Amp Unit measuring the amount of current flowing in a circuit.
Circuit Complete path round which an electric current flows.
Conductor Substance, such as the metal core in a flex or cable, that will carry an electric current.
Earth Pathway along which an electric current can flow safely to the ground if a fault develops.
Fuse Protective device that cuts off the current if the circuit is overloaded or a fault

develops in the system.
Live The core of a cable or flex carrying current to where it is needed, or any terminal to which the live core is connected.
Neutral The core of a cable or flex carrying current back to its source, or any terminal to which the neutral core is connected.
Volt Unit measuring the electrical "pressure" driving the current round a circuit.
Watt Unit measuring the amount of power consumed by an electrical appliance.

Power consumption

The amount of electricity you use is measured in kilowatt-hours, commonly called "units". The number of units used is calculated by multiplying the rating of the appliance in kilo-watts by the number of hours for which it is used. So a 2kW electric fire used for half an hour consumes one unit of electricity ($2 \times \frac{1}{2} = 1$).

Common power ratings

Oven	Spin dryer	Radio
4kW	750W	30W
Hob	Immersion heater	Black-and-white TV
4kW	3kW	150W
Refrigerator	Kettle	Colour TV
40W	2kW	350W
Freezer	Vacuum cleaner	Music centre
80W	500W	200W
Washing machine	Radiant heater	Light bulb
3kW	2-3kW	100W
Tumble dryer	Fan heater	Clock
1kW	2-3kW	0.5W

The electrical system

The fixed wiring of a household electrical circuit connects the sockets, ceiling lights, and switches to the mains supply. It should be made up of cable of the correct rating, and the switches and sockets should be mounted on proper backplates or mounting boxes. There are separate circuits for power, lighting, and powerful appliances such as cookers.

The power circuits
These are looped or "ring" circuits, with continuous cable running out from the fusebox, feeding a number of sockets around the loop, and returning to the fusebox. Most homes have at least two rings – often one serving the ground floor and one for the upstairs rooms. Spurs – single cables connected to the ring running to one socket – can also be added to give an increasing number of outlets.

Each ring is made up of 2.5mm² cable and is protected by a 30 amp circuit fuse. The socket outlets have rectangular holes to take the familiar 13 amp plug.

The service head
Electricity reaches the home through underground or overhead supply cables. After the cable enters the home it is connected to the service head, a sealed unit containing the main fuse that protects the whole system. From the service head single-core cables run to the meter.

The fusebox
From the meter, two single cables run to the main fusebox or "consumer unit". The job of this unit is to divide up and distribute the electric current to the various circuits in the home, and to allow you to turn off the whole installation, or any part of it, for repair or extension work. Each circuit in the home is also protected by passing through a circuit fuse. If there is a fault, or if the circuit is overloaded, the fuse "blows". This has the double effect of warning you that there is a fault, and of cutting off the power to the circuit, making it safe and allowing you to carry out repairs.

Bathroom wiring
The only type of socket outlet permitted in a bathroom is a special unit for electric shavers. You should never take an appliance into a bathroom using an extension lead from a socket elsewhere. Any switches that can be reached from the bath or shower should be cord-operated and all light fittings should be enclosed. For complete electrical safety, all exposed metalwork in the bathroom should be connected to earth.

Radial circuits
Radials start at the fusebox and feed one or more outlets along the line. The circuit terminates at the outlet furthest from the fusebox. Radial circuits are used mainly for high-powered appliances, such as cookers, electric showers, and immersion heaters. Sockets are not fed from radial circuits, with the exception of the socket incorporated in a cooker control unit.

For a floor area of less than 20m², a radial circuit is made up with 2.5mm² cable and protected by a 20 amp fuse. For areas of up to 50m², 4mm² cable is used and there is a 30 amp fuse.

The lighting circuits
These are always wired as radials, with the cable starting at a 5 amp fuse in the fusebox, running from one light to the next, and terminating at the most remote light.

Each light needs switching at a convenient point. This is achieved either by using junction boxes or "loop-in" roses. With junction boxes, the circuit cable runs from one junction box to the next. Each box contains four terminals, allowing two circuit cables to be connected, a third cable to pass to the light, and a fourth to feed the switch. With loop-in roses, savings on cable are made by using ceiling roses with extra terminals. The circuit cable runs from rose to rose, and a cable links each rose to its switch.

Lighting circuits are normally wired with 1.0mm² cable. In theory, each circuit can supply up to twelve 100 watt lamps, but in practice each circuit is normally restricted to eight lights.

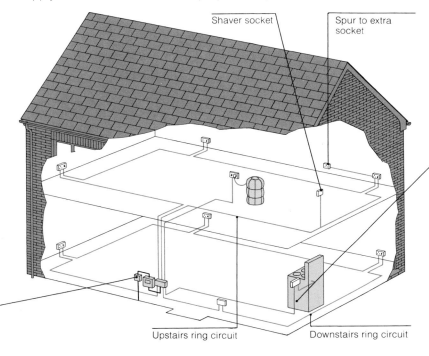

Shaver socket

Spur to extra socket

Upstairs ring circuit

Downstairs ring circuit

Junction box

Two-way switch

One-way switch

Loop-in ceiling rose

Types of cable and flex

Cable is used to wire all the fixed electrical circuits in the home, running between the fusebox or consumer unit to the power points and lighting outlets. Flex is the flexible cord used to link appliances to the fixed wiring. Both come in a range of thicknesses. You must use the right type for each circuit or appliance.

Cables
Cable usually contains three solid wires. Two are insulated with coloured pvc – red for the live core and black for the neutral. The third wire is not insulated and is used as the earth for the circuit. The three cores are wrapped in a thick outer pvc covering, usually grey or white. Cable is available in a range of different sizes for different current capacities. The sizes are measured by the cross-sectional area of the cores.

1mm² cable for 12 amp lighting circuits

1.5mm² cable for 15 amp lighting circuits

2.5mm² cable for 21 amp power circuits

4mm² cable for 27 amp power circuits

6mm² cable for 35 amp power circuits

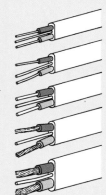

Flexes
Flex usually contains three wires, all of which have colour-coded insulation. Brown represents live, blue is neutral, and green-and-yellow stripes are used for earth. (Old flex uses red, black, and green for the three cores.) The cores are protected with an outer sheath, which may be made of rubber or pvc, and may be covered with braiding. Two-core flex (without an earth) is used to wire lights with no metal parts and for double-insulated appliances (marked with a double-square symbol) that do not require an earth. Different flex sizes are used for different current ratings.

0.5mm² flex 3 amp (lights)
0.75mm² flex 6 amp (small items)
1mm² flex 10 amp rating (to 2000 w)
1.25mm² flex 13 amp (to 3000 w)
1.5mm² flex 15 amp (to 3500 w)
2.5mm² flex 20 amp (to 4500 w)

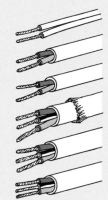

Types of electrical fitting

As well as lighting roses and single sockets, there are a number of fittings that can make your electrical installation more flexible. Multiple switches and sockets, dimmer switches, and pull-cord switches are all quite simple to install in an existing circuit. There are also special sockets for cookers, and fused connection units for freezers.

Ceiling rose
This is the basic lighting fitting. Modern slim-line designs protrude only slightly from the ceiling.

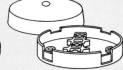

Junction box
Normally found in the loft, this fitting allows you to connect ceiling roses and switches together.

Batten lampholders
Bathroom ceiling lights should have batten lampholders, so that there is no need for a rose and flex.

Lampholders
These hold the bulb and also allow you to attach a shade. Metal types need an earth connection.

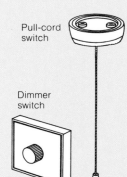

Pull-cord switch

Dimmer switch

Single switch

Double switch

Alternative light switches
Pull-cord switches are essential in bathrooms and useful in bedrooms. Dimmers are increasingly popular in living rooms.

Light switches
As well as single switches, two-, three-, and four-gang versions are available for controlling several lights.

Socket outlets.
Surface-mounted sockets protrude from the wall, so that you do not have to remove plaster to accommodate the fitting. With flush sockets, the connections are housed in a recessed box.

Cooker point
An electric cooker is a powerful appliance that should be wired directly into one of these units.

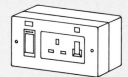

Fused connection unit
This type of unit is ideal for items such as freezers, which must not be disconnected.

Estimating time

These times assume that the fixed wiring is in position and all you have to do is connect the cable and fix the fitting in place.

Lighting

Fitting a ceiling light

$\frac{1}{4}$ – $\frac{1}{2}$ hour

Fitting a fluorescent light

1 hour

Fitting a light switch

$\frac{3}{4}$ – 1 hour

Power

Fitting a socket outlet

$\frac{3}{4}$ – $1\frac{1}{2}$ hours

Fitting a fused connection

$\frac{3}{4}$ – $1\frac{1}{2}$ hours

Connecting an immersion heater

$2\frac{1}{2}$ – 3 hours

Fitting a plug

$\frac{1}{4}$ hour

Mending a rewirable fuse

$\frac{1}{4}$ hour

Tools and equipment

For everyday electrical repairs and emergencies, there are several inexpensive items that you should keep together, perhaps near the fusebox. The most important items are: a torch, a pair of pliers (ideally with insulated handles), a knife or wire strippers, small and medium insulated screwdrivers, a roll of pvc insulating tape, fuse wire or cartridge fuses to replace circuit fuses, and spare 3 amp and 13 amp plug fuses. A screwdriver with a built-in bulb for circuit testing is useful.

For larger-scale repair or extension work, you will need additional equipment. The most useful items are: a floorboard saw for removing floorboards, a bolster chisel and club hammer for recessing cable in solid walls, and a measuring tape

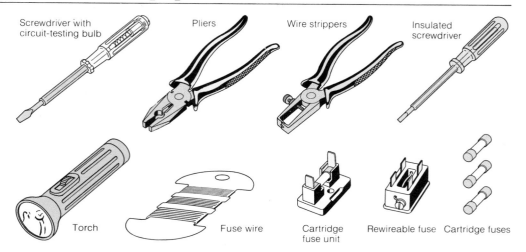

Screwdriver with circuit-testing bulb — Pliers — Wire strippers — Insulated screwdriver — Torch — Fuse wire — Cartridge fuse unit — Rewireable fuse — Cartridge fuses

---

160

Fitting a ceiling light

Roses should always be fixed securely to the ceiling, either to the underside of a joist or to a batten fixed between the joists, above the ceiling surface. The cables enter the rose through knock-out panels in

Fitting the rose
With a loop-in system, there should be three or four cables at the rose. The two circuit cables are the ones that connect two junction boxes or roses; the switch cable links the light to the switch; and there may be a branch cable, to which another rose is connected. After pulling the cables through the holes in the rose, 1, the live, neutral,

and earth cores are grouped together in the rose terminals, 2. The exception is the switch neutral, which is connected to the live flex core. The live flex core is connected to the switch return terminal of the rose, and the neutral flex core is connected to the neutral terminal of the rose. At the other end of the flex, 3, the two cores are connected to the lampholder.

its base before being connected up to the terminals. The connections differ according to whether the ceiling wiring is done with junction boxes or by the loop-in method. If there is a junction box for the light fitting, there will only be one cable at the rose itself – the switch cable should be connected to the junction box in the loft. With a loop-in rose, connect the wires to the terminals as marked.

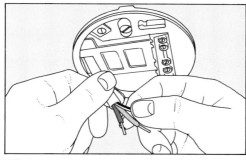

1 *Pull the cables through the back of the rose*

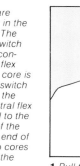

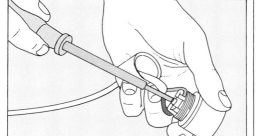

2 *Connect the cables to these terminals in the rose*

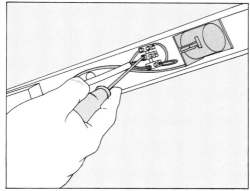

3 *Connect the other ends of the flex cores to the lampholder*

161

Fitting a fluorescent light

Fittings such as fluorescents, rise-and-fall units, and close-ceiling lights, require a method of connection that is slightly different from that used for pendant fittings. The flex from the fitting is connected to the circuit wiring via a multi-way connector block. This must be housed in a non-combustible enclosure, provided by recessing a metal or plastic box (called a BESA or terminal conduit box) into the ceiling or wall.

Connecting the fitting
The connections between the fitting's flex and the circuit cables are made with either three or four connectors, depending on whether the wiring uses a junction box or the loop-in method. The

fitting's backplate is then fixed to the BESA box. The box can be screwed into a recess chiselled into the underside of a joist, but it is easier to attach it to a batten securely fixed between two joists in the ceiling.

162

Fitting a light switch

To control the light from a single point you can use either a one-way or a two-way switch. In large rooms and on staircases it is often useful to be able to switch the light on and off at two places, for which you need a two-way switch.

A one-way switch has two terminals at the back, and the two separate switch cable cores are connected to these. A two-way switch has three terminals. These are marked C, L1, and L2. For two-way control, one of these switches is installed at each switching position. The light is linked to one switch in the usual way using two-core and earth cable. The two switches are then connected by three-core and earth cable. The red core links the two C terminals, the blue core links the two L1 terminals, and the yellow core links the two L2 terminals. Two-way switches can be used for one-way control, using terminal C and one of L terminals.

Wiring a switch for one-way control
*Before you start to connect up the cable to the terminals in the switch, make sure that they are trimmed to the right length, and bare a few millimetres of each core. Use a pair of cable strippers, **1**. Connect the earth core to the terminal inside the mounting box and mark the black core of the cable with red pvc tape to show that it is live, **2**. With a simple one-way switch, **3**, connect the red core to terminal L1 and the black core to terminal L2.*

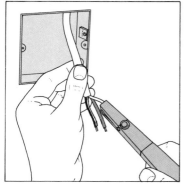

1 *Trim the cable cores to the correct length for the fitting*

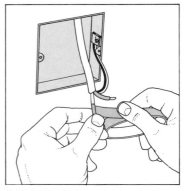

2 *Mark the black core with red tape and make the earth connection*

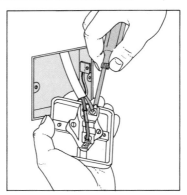

3 *Connect the switch cable to the two terminals*

163

Fitting a socket

Every socket on a power circuit has three connections with the circuit cable. The live core is linked to the socket's live terminal (marked L), the neutral core to the neutral terminal (marked N), and the bare earth to the earth terminal (marked E or ⏚). On a ring main, there will be two separate three-core cables to be connected to the socket – two cores should be connected to each terminal. On a spur there will only be one cable. Whether on a spur or a ring circuit, the connections must be made within a fireproof enclosure. This is normally provided by the metal or plastic box on which the socket is mounted.

Wiring a socket in a ring circuit
*First check that the core cables are the correct length and strip them with cable strippers if necessary. The earth core in power cable is uninsulated, and before connection you should cover the earth cores with green-and-yellow pvc tubing. It will then be insulated and clearly identifiable. Next connect the cables to the terminals on the back of the socket **1**, pairing up the two live cores, the two neutrals, and the two earths. Then fit the socket on to the mounting box with the two fixing screws, **2**.*

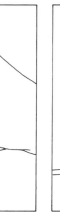

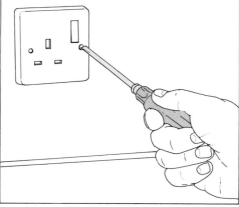

1 *Connect the cores to the terminal on the socket*

2 *Screw the socket to the mounting box*

164

Fitting a fused connection

This is a special type of outlet, to which the flex to the appliance is permanently connected. Fused connection units are especially useful for freezers and refrigerators, where you want to avoid accidental unplugging. They are also used to connect storage heaters. Most designs give easy access to the fuse through a flap on the front of the unit. The connections are the same as for conventional sockets, except that you also have to connect the flex.

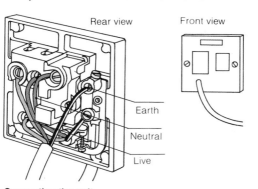

Rear view   Front view

Earth
Neutral
Live

Connecting the unit
There are six separate terminals which take the individual cores of the cable and the flex.

165

Connecting an immersion heater

Powerful appliances such as immersion heaters, showers, and cookers have their own radial circuits and are connected to individual fused connection units. But unlike less powerful appliances, they are connected via special double-pole switches that break both the live and the neutral side of the circuit. A warning light shows when the heater is on.

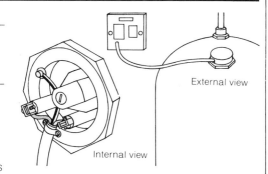

External view

Internal view

Connecting the flex
Connect the three cores to the relevant terminals in the heater and the switching unit.

166

Fitting a plug

Always replace a plug if its body is cracked or broken. With portable appliances fit a resilient rubber plug. A modern plug has three small, screw-down terminals, to which you connect the three cores of the flex. When wiring a plug, make sure that the core insulation reaches right up to the terminals, that there are no stray strands of metal conductor loose in the plug, and that the flex is anchored by the cord grip so that it does not pull out.

Connecting up a plug
Strip the outer casing from the flex, 1, and bare the metal conductor in each core using a knife or a pair of wire strippers, 2. Then make the connections, 3. The brown core goes to the live terminal, the blue to the neutral, and the green-and-yellow to the earth. Finally fit the fuse, 4, screw down the cord grip, and fit the outer casing.

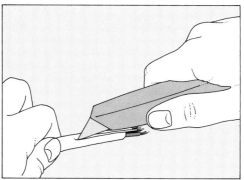

1 *Remove enough of the outer casing for the individual cores to reach the terminals.*

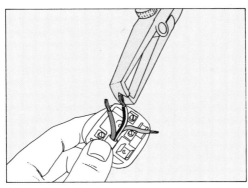

2 *Strip a few millimetres of casing from each of the cores*

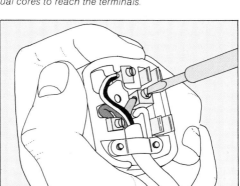

3 *Connect the three cores to the plug terminals*

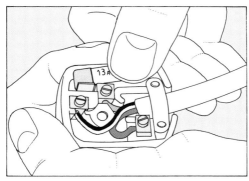

4 *Fit a fuse of the correct rating for the appliance*

167

Mending a fuse

If a fuse blows, there is a fault somewhere in the circuit. You must make sure that the fault has been put right before replacing or mending the fuse and switching on again. There are two basic types of fuse. Cartridge fuses are used in plugs and in many modern fuse boxes. To change this type, all you have to do is remove the old fuse and insert a new one of the correct rating. Older fuse boxes have traditional rewirable fuses. To repair this type, you remove the old wire and replace it with new wire of the correct rating, attaching this to the fuse's two terminals.

Replacing fuses
Rewirable fuses have a screw terminal at either end. A hole in the back of the body allows you to see whether the wire is broken. Remove the old fuse wire and thread the new wire through the fuse body and attach each end to a terminal. To change a cartridge fuse, remove the fuse carrier and take out the old fuse. A new cartridge simply clips into place.

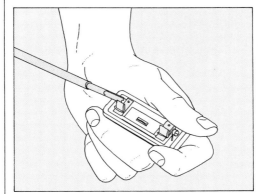

Rewirable fuse
Use enough wire to pass right through the fuse and wrap around both the terminals.

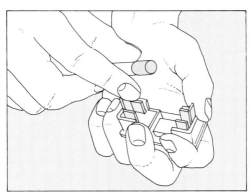

Cartridge fuse
Insert a new fuse between the two metal holders in the fuse carrier.

Plumbing

The plumbing system ◇ Types of pipe and tap Tools and equipment ◇ Clearing a blocked waste pipe ◇ Clearing a blocked drain Clearing a blocked WC ◇ Repairing ball and flap valves ◇ Installing a tap and replacing a washer ◇ Curing leaks ◇ Plumbing-in a washing machine

The plumbing system consists of a network of pipes carrying hot and cold water around the home and taking waste material away. These pipes, together with the sinks, basins, baths, and WCs they serve, usually need little maintenance. But when something does go wrong – whether it is a burst pipe or a blocked drain – a great deal of damage and inconvenience can result. With a basic knowledge of how household plumbing works, however, most of the necessary repairs are straightforward.

Modern pipes and fittings are easy to take apart and re-assemble, although repairs to old-fashioned lead pipes are more difficult and are best carried out by a professional. If you have old lead pipes, it is probably best to get them replaced – copper and plastic are much easier to maintain.

You can avoid some problems by taking care of the plumbing in your home. For example, lagging pipes will reduce the likelihood of freezes and bursts (for more information on insulation, see pp. 194-7).

The household plumbing system is divided into three distinct parts – the cold-water system, the hot-water system, and the drainage system. Although the actual layout will vary from home

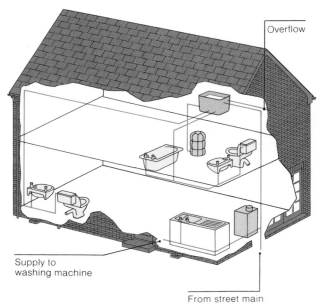

Overflow

Supply to washing machine

From street main

Cold-water system

The cold-water system
There are two basic types of cold-water system – direct fed and tank fed. With the direct system, the taps are fed from the water authority's main supply. With the tank system, the main supply is taken to a tank, called a storage cistern, in the loft, and the cold taps are fed from the cistern. With the direct system it is still necessary to have a small storage cistern, holding a reserve of water to feed the hot-water system.

The direct system has two draw-

backs. Because there is no storage tank, there is no back-up if the supply of cold water is interrupted. Also, the direct-fed cold taps work at a higher water pressure than the hot taps, making it impossible to install a conventional shower mixer valve. However, you can fit an instantaneous electric shower, which will run off the cold-water supply alone.

Most water authorities prefer a tank-fed system with the kitchen cold tap connected directly to the mains supply,

Points to remember

◇ Prepare yourself for emergencies by getting to know where the stopcocks and control valves are so that you can turn off the water quickly.
◇ Tell other members of the household where the stopcocks and control valves are so that they can act quickly if you are not there.
◇ Use a spring or pipe-bending machine to bend metal pipes, otherwise they will kink at the bend.
◇ After cutting metal pipes, rub the edges with a fine file to remove metal waste that may make joining the pipe difficult.
◇ If possible, replace old lead pipes with modern copper or plastic ones.
◇ When replacing lengths of pipe, check the size carefully – you may need an adaptor to join metric pipe to pipe measured in inches.

Emergency action

If you have a water leak or a burst pipe, first turn off the water supply to stop flooding and isolate the fault for repair. Remember these points.
◇ Turn off central heating boilers and water heaters.
◇ Turn off the whole cold-water supply at the stopcock where it enters the house.
◇ Drain the pipes by turning on all the taps with the supply turned off.
◇ The water in the hot-

water tank, the radiators, and the closed system between the boiler and the hot tank can only be drained by opening the appropriate drain cocks – ask a plumber if you do not know where these are.
◇ If water is pouring from an overflow pipe, check the ball valve in the tank or cistern (*see Job 171, p. 188*).
◇ For more information on repairing leaks, *see Job 175, p. 189*.

The plumbing system

to home, most domestic plumbing systems work in the same way and once you have a working knowledge of the basic principles involved, you will be able to carry out simple repairs and maintenance. Remember that large parts of the system are hidden from view – water storage tanks are usually in the loft, while the drainage system takes away waste below ground.

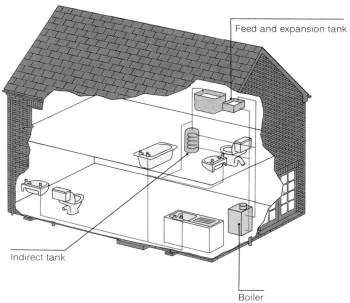

Hot-water system

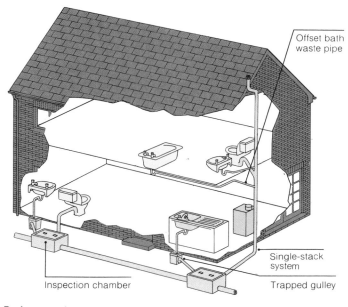

Drainage system

to provide a source of drinking water. The cistern, which has a capacity of at least 225 litres, feeds all the cold taps except the one in the kitchen, as well as the WC cisterns. It also has an outlet pipe to feed the hot-water system. The only drawback with tank-fed systems is that drinking water should be taken only from the kitchen tap. There is a slight danger that water from the other taps might be polluted by debris falling into the storage cistern, although in practice, most people drink water from tank-fed bathroom taps without coming to harm.

The hot-water system
The most common household hot-water system is the indirect type. This has two parts. The first part (the "primary circuit") consists of a boiler that heats water. This water passes through a pipe into a coil inside a tank and back again to the boiler. The second part carries the heated water from the tank to the hot taps throughout the home. With a boiler of the correct capacity, a hot-water radiator system can be run off the primary circuit. A small storage system in the loft, called a feed-and-expansion tank, makes good any small water loss by evaporation from the primary system. With a direct system, hot water from the boiler is stored in the tank.

The drainage system
Houses that are more than 30 years old usually have a "soil pipe" for the waste from the WCs and a separate "waste pipe" for the waste from the baths, basins, showers, and sinks. These often connect at an underground inspection chamber, from which the combined waste is taken by drains to the sewer under the road or to a septic tank.

In newer homes, "single-stack" drainage systems, with one soil pipe, are generally used. With this modern type of drainage system, separate branch pipes connect all the WCs, sinks, baths, and basins to the stack.

A guide to plumbing terms

Air lock Pocket of air preventing water circulating properly.
Ball valve Device that keeps a pre-set level of water in a tank or cistern.
Capillary joint Type of joint used with copper tubing. The fitting is slightly larger than the pipe, leaving a small space for solder.
Cistern Open-topped or lid-covered water-storage tank. Large cisterns are used for storing water, small cisterns store water for flushing WCs.
Compression joint Type of joint used with copper, and sometimes plastic, tubing. When the nuts are tightened they compress rings (known as "olives") to form a tight joint.
Drain cock Valve or tap used for draining water from the system.
Gulley Earthenware trap into which waste and rainwater pipes discharge before entering the drains.

Inspection chamber Underground chamber topped by a manhole cover, allowing access to the drains.
Jumper The part of a tap that carries the washer.
PTFE Thin plastic sealing tape that ensures watertight connections on screwed fittings.
Plumber's mastic Waterproof compound for sealing joints.
Push-fit joint Plumbing connections that simply push together.

Soil pipe Vertical pipe that takes sewage to the drains.
Stopcock Valve or tap on a water supply pipe that is used to cut off the water supply.
Trap Loop in a waste fitting that catches debris before it can enter waste pipes and drains.
Vent pipe Continuation of a soil pipe above roof level to ventilate the soil pipe.
Waste pipe Pipe that takes waste water to the drains.

Types of pipe

There are two basic types of pipe – supply and waste pipes. Supply pipes carry water to the taps and fittings in the home. Waste pipes carry water from waste outlets to the drains. In older homes both types were often made of lead, but copper is now the most popular material for supply pipes and plastic for waste pipes. Some modern cold water pipes are made of rigid plastic.

Supply pipes and fittings
Copper piping is easy to cut, it can be bent with a spring or bending machine, and a wide variety of fittings is available for it. Lengths of corrugated copper tubing can be bent easily by hand.

Copper pipe produced before 1971 had imperial measurements, and joining these to the more recent metric sizes can be difficult. With compression fittings, you need an adaptor to join 22mm tube to $\frac{3}{4}$in. tube, although 15mm can be joined to $\frac{1}{2}$in. and 28mm to 1in. without an adaptor. With capillary fittings, adaptors are needed for all sizes when joining metric to imperial.

Plastic supply pipes are semi-flexible, light, easy to handle, and very simple to join using push-fit connectors. Plastic has good thermal insulation properties (although it does need lagging in lofts), and special fittings are available for connecting plastic pipes to other types.

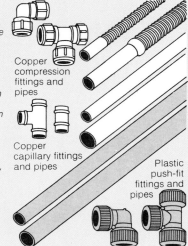

Copper compression fittings and pipes

Copper capillary fittings and pipes

Plastic push-fit fittings and pipes

Waste pipes and fittings
Some homes have lead waste pipes, but, because of the difficulty of joining and repairing them, it is best to replace them with pipes of another material. If possible, remove all the lead, but if you have to join lead pipes to plastic or copper, ask a plumber to make the join. Copper is highly effective, but, because of its high cost, plastic is almost exclusively used for modern waste systems. For basin and bidet wastes, the $1\frac{1}{4}$in. size is used, for bath, shower, and sink wastes, the $1\frac{1}{2}$in. size is used. Most systems have simple push-fitting joints with O-ring seals, although you should keep to one brand since they are rarely interchangeable.

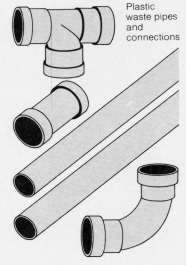

Plastic waste pipes and connections

Types of tap

The traditional tap is made of chromium-plated cast brass, and has a "capstan" head with four arms. There is a "rising head" mechanism, in which the head is directly connected to the washer that seals off the water supply. Modern taps often have shrouded heads, together with a non-rising head mechanism that prevents water leaks around the spindle. There are also mixers and shower heads.

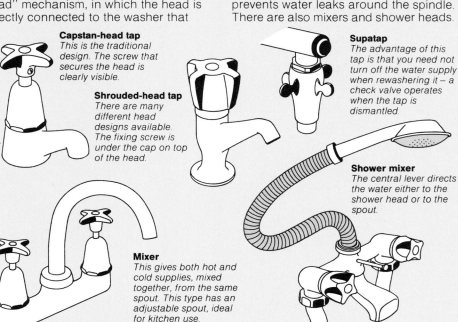

Capstan-head tap
This is the traditional design. The screw that secures the head is clearly visible.

Shrouded-head tap
There are many different head designs available. The fixing screw is under the cap on top of the head.

Supatap
The advantage of this tap is that you need not turn off the water supply when rewashering it – a check valve operates when the tap is dismantled.

Shower mixer
The central lever directs the water either to the shower head or to the spout.

Mixer
This gives both hot and cold supplies, mixed together, from the same spout. This type has an adjustable spout, ideal for kitchen use.

Estimating time

These times will vary according to your skill and experience, and, in the case of blockages, according to the seriousness of the problem.

Blockages

Clearing a blocked waste pipe

$\frac{1}{4}$ hour

Clearing a blocked drain

$\frac{1}{2}$ hour

Clearing a blocked WC

$\frac{1}{2}$ hour

Cisterns

Repairing a ball valve

$\frac{1}{2}$ hour

Repairing a flap valve

1 - $1\frac{1}{2}$ hours

Taps

Installing a tap

2 - 3 hours

Replacing a washer

$\frac{1}{4}$ hour

Pipework

Curing leaks

$\frac{1}{4}$ - $\frac{3}{4}$ hours

Plumbing-in a washing machine

$1\frac{1}{2}$ - 2 hours

Tools and equipment

Two fairly large adjustable spanners and a $\frac{1}{2}$in. or $\frac{3}{4}$in. wrench, for removing and repairing taps, will all be useful for plumbing work. A crowsfoot spanner is ideal for use in confined spaces. If you are working with copper pipes, a pipe cutter is better than a hacksaw for cutting the ends square. Use bending springs or hire a bending machine for larger sizes.

Fine steel wool and a strip of emery cloth are useful for cleaning the ends of copper tubing. Plumber's mastic should be used for bedding joints, and PTFE tape for wrapping around threaded joints to ensure watertight connections.

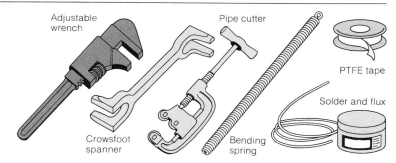

Adjustable wrench

Pipe cutter

PTFE tape

Crowsfoot spanner

Bending spring

Solder and flux

168

Clearing a blocked waste pipe

If working a rubber plunger over the outlet does not free the blockage, clear out the waste trap, as this is where the blockage is most likely to be. Place a basin or bucket under the trap ready to catch the contents.

Traps vary in design. Old-style traps have a drain plug, which you take off to remove debris. Newer traps unscrew completely. If cleaning the trap fails to cure the blockage, clear the pipes on either side with a length of wire. Pull out anything that is blocking the pipe, so that it is not pushed farther along.

Clearing a U-bend trap
Unscrew the drain plug, 1. It may have a square head for a spanner, or two protrusions so that you can turn it with a steel bar. Use hooked wire to pull out the debris. If this does not work, remove the trap, 2.

1 Using a piece of wood to hold the trap, undo the drain plug

2 Remove the whole trap if the blockage is difficult to dislodge

Clearing a plastic trap
More modern traps, especially those made of plastic, may not have a drain plug. There may be several sections which unscrew for cleaning, 1, or the whole base may unscrew. Use wire to clear the pipes on either side.

1 Unscrew the sections of the plastic trap, using a bucket to catch debris

2 Probe the pipes with a piece of wire if there is still a blockage

---

169

Clearing a blocked drain

Drain blockages are indicated by overflowing gulleys, water leaks from around inspection chambers, and WC pans that are either obviously blocked or fill higher than usual before the water level slowly drops back to normal.

Unblocking a gulley
Lift the cover grip to give access to the trap. The best method to clear it is to use the type of vacuum cleaner suitable for wet or dry cleaning. Otherwise, use a garden trowel. Break up any sediment in the trap with a stick or trowel, remove it by hand, 1, then use a small hose to flush the gulley clean, 2.

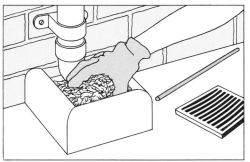

1 Break up the sediment in the gulley then remove it by hand

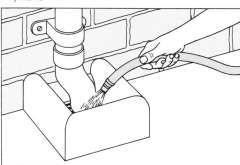

2 Remove the debris with a small hose pipe

170

Clearing a blocked WC

This job is easier with special equipment, and you may prefer to leave it to a specialist drain cleaner. If you do it yourself, start by finding the site of the blockage. Lift the drain inspection covers, beginning with the one closest to the pan. If the chamber is empty, this indicates that the blockage is between this chamber and the pan, probably at the pan itself. If the first chamber is full you will need to clear the drains using a set of special clearing rods.

Unblocking a WC pan
First try pushing flexible drain-clearing wire down the WC pan, or try plunging the pan using an old mop with a polythene bag tied around the head, 1. It is a good idea to get a helper to stand by the first inspection chamber while you do this, to retrieve anything that might have been lodged in the pan, causing the blockage. If it is not retrieved immediately, it may block the drains further down the pipe. Use drain-clearing rods, 2, to clear the pipes if this does not work.

1 *Plunge the pan with a mop protected by a polythene bag*

2 *To clear the pipes, insert rods at the inspection chamber*

171

Repairing a ball valve

If there are drips from the cistern overflow, examine the mechanism inside the cistern: the ball-valve washer or diaphragm probably needs replacing. The way you remove the washer or diaphragm depends on whether the valve is made of brass or whether it is a modern plastic valve.

It is most likely that you will have to replace a brass valve, which involves turning off the water, and taking apart the valve and piston assemblies.

Replacing a valve washer
With a brass valve, turn off the water supply and remove the split pin holding the float arm to the valve assembly. Unscrew the cap end of the valve case and ease the piston assembly out of the valve. The washer is at the end of the piston. Undo the end of the piston, or simply prise the washer out of place. Fit a new washer either by replacing the cap, or by easing the new washer carefully under the lip of the cap so that it rests flat in the recess. Rub the piston with wire wool, so that it slides easily in the valve case, and then replace the float arm and the split pin.

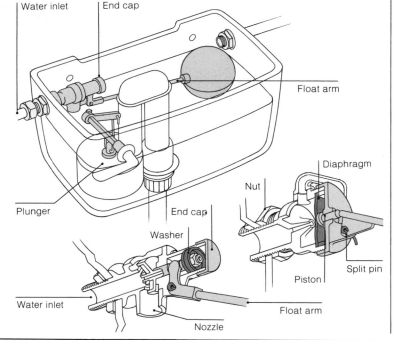

WC fault finding

◇ If the overflow is dripping, you probably need to replace the ball-valve washer (*see Job 171, left, bottom*).
◇ If the cistern will only flush with repeated pressing of the handle, replace the flap valve (*see Job 172, below*).
◇ If water is pouring from the overflow, the ball float is likely to be leaking and will need replacing.
◇ If your cistern is leaking, make a temporary repair by emptying the cistern, drying it out, and inserting a wad of epoxy putty; replace the cistern with a new one as soon as possible.

172

Replacing a flap valve

If the WC handle has to be depressed several times to make the cistern flush, the flap valve, which controls the amount of water that leaves the cistern, probably needs replacing.

Replacing a diaphragm
With a modern plastic ball valve with a small float, the water flow is controlled by a rubber diaphragm. After turning off the water supply, remove and replace the diaphragm by loosening the large knurled nut just behind the float-arm pivot.

Tie up the ball valve to stop the water flowing in, and empty the cistern by flushing. Mop up the last of the water with a rag. Disconnect the flush pipe and slacken the large nut that holds the siphon assembly in place. Remove the metal link that connects the flushing handle to the flap, lift the plate, and remove the siphon. The plate will fall out and a new plastic flap valve can be slipped in before you refit the assembly.

173

Replacing a washer

A tap that drips when you turn it off needs a new washer. Basin and sink taps have $\frac{1}{2}$in. washers, while bath taps require $\frac{3}{4}$in. washers. Start by turning off the water supply and opening the tap to drain the pipe. The method used to replace the washer depends on the type of tap. The two main types are the traditional capstan-head tap and the modern shrouded-head design.

Capstan-head tap
Remove the cover to reveal the hexagonal nut of the headgear. Unscrew the nut (turning it anti-clockwise) to reveal the jumper, which holds the washer. Fit a new washer or a complete washer and jumper unit, and replace the headgear.

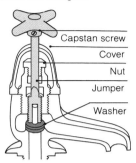

Capstan screw
Cover
Nut
Jumper
Washer

Shrouded-head tap
If the tap is a modern, shrouded-head type, either pull off the head shroud or remove the central fixing screw that holds it in place. Once you have done this the headgear unscrews like that on a conventional tap.

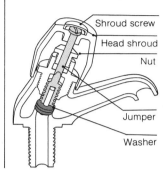

Shroud screw
Head shroud
Nut
Jumper
Washer

Tips for thawing pipes

◇ Do not use a blowtorch – it is very easy to start a fire, especially in a loft.
◇ An electric hot-air paint stripper is ideal for thawing pipes.
◇ If you do not have a paint stripper, try a hair dryer, although it will work more slowly.
◇ Thaw out first the areas that are most likely to be frozen – unlagged areas and bends.
◇ If the frozen pipe has obviously burst, turn off the water supply to the pipe before thawing it.
◇ If the pipe has only recently frozen, thaw it as soon as possible – if you leave it, a burst will almost certainly occur.

174

Installing a tap

First remove the old tap. Disconnect the water supply and turn the tap on to drain away the water in the pipe. Unscrew the tap connector, which is attached to the tail of the tap, and using a wrench undo the back nut, which holds the tap to the fitting. Then lift the tap out of place.

Attaching the tap
Apply a little non-setting mastic to the underside of the new tap before putting on the plastic bedding washer that fits between the tap and the top of the sink or basin. Put the tap in place, fit a fibre washer on the tail from beneath, and replace the back nut. If you are fitting the tap to a thin surface such as a steel sink surround, put a "top-hat" washer over the tail to act as a spacer before fitting the fibre washer. Wrap the lower part of the tap tail with three or four turns of PTFE tape. Finally, fit the tap connector and a new fibre washer.

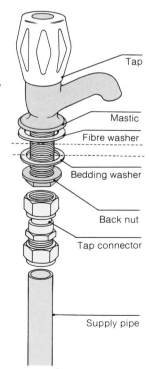

Tap
Mastic
Fibre washer
Bedding washer
Back nut
Tap connector
Supply pipe

175

Curing leaks

The most common cause of leaky pipes is frost damage. This can have the effect of pushing fittings apart or of causing a split in the pipes themselves. Pipes also leak because of corrosion.

Push-fit joints that have separated can be simply pushed together. For compression fittings that are parted by frost, slacken the cap nut, push the pipe back into place, and retighten the cap nut. If the problem is in the pipe itself, cut out the affected section and insert a new length, using straight connectors at each end. Plastic pipe is ideal for this.

Mending pipes
To make a temporary repair to a split or corroded pipe, drain it, dry it out, and then bind it with waterproof mastic repair tape. For a permanent solution to the problem, cut out the affected pipe and insert a length of plastic pipe using straight connectors. Plastic pipe is easy to use as it springs easily into place.

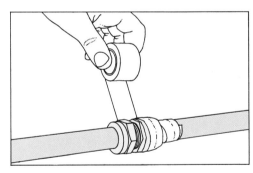

176

Plumbing-in a washing machine

Most washing machines must be connected to both hot and cold supply pipes. You also have to add control valves and make provision for the waste.

Connecting up
Take short lengths of 15mm pipe from the Tee-connectors in the supply pipes to the washing machine's control valves. The flexible supply pipes of the washing machine are connected to the outlets of these valves with hose union nuts. The waste can discharge directly through the wall into a gulley, can be connected to the kitchen waste by a "swept-Tee" fitting, or it can be connected directly to a modern single-stack drainage system.

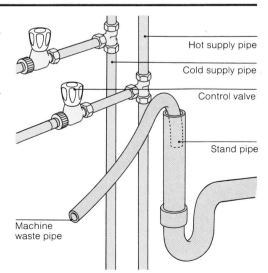

Hot supply pipe
Cold supply pipe
Control valve
Stand pipe
Machine waste pipe

Heating

Fuel costs ◇ Types of central heating
Bleeding a radiator ◇ Curing a leaking valve
Replacing a radiator ◇ Repairing leaking pipes
Replacing a pump ◇ Flushing out a central
heating system

Today most people opt for central heating. Once installed it is more efficient, more versatile, and usually cheaper to run than an assortment of portable heating appliances. If you are planning a new system, assess your requirements carefully. Before you consult a firm of heating engineers, work out which fuel you prefer, how many radiators you need, and what form of control you require. Do not skimp at this stage. It is easier to fit plenty of radiators when the system is installed than to extend the system later. And remember that extending a system may not be as simple as adding a new radiator. You may also have to change to a bigger-capacity boiler. Most systems need little maintenance, and jobs such as bleeding radiators and flushing out the system are quite straightforward.

When planning central heating, select a boiler that will give you sufficient capacity for your present and future needs. The other important factors when choosing a boiler are the type of fuel (see right, top) and where you are going to install the boiler. Some gas and oil boilers have a balanced flue, which both supplies air for combustion and removes exhaust gases. This type must be sited on an outside wall. Other types require a conventional flue, and in most cases a metal tube must be passed up the chimney to line the flue and prevent exhaust gases escaping into the room. Most modern home boilers are compact, and wall-mounted designs are available to fit in single kitchen cupboard units.

Points to remember

◇ Plan a new heating system carefully, taking the fuel costs and your own requirements into account.
◇ Repair small leaks quickly; they will worsen if left unattended.
◇ Insulate loft pipes and lag hot-water tanks to avoid bursts and save fuel.
◇ Flush out a wet central-heating system once a year to remove any rust that may have accumulated.

Choice of fuel

Central-heating systems can be powered by gas, oil, or solid fuel. Gas is generally the cheapest fuel and is very versatile. It can power a variety of boilers – including concealed back-boilers and compact wall-mounted models. Gas makes no mess, does not have to be stored, and is easy to control.

Solid-fuel is widely avail-able and competitively priced, but a lot of space is required for storage. The boilers also require a flue and need regular attention – you usually need to top up the fuel supply at least once a day. The flues also need to be cleaned frequently. Control is less flexible than with gas or oil. The price of oil can vary and it must be stored outside.

Types of control

The versatility of any central heating system is affected by the amount of control you are given over the heat. You should be able to control easily both the temperature and the time when the system is working.

Programmers and timers
These vary in sophistication, but most offer two separate on–off switchings every day and manual override.

Room thermostats
Every system has a room thermostat mounted on a wall to give overall temperature control.

Thermostatic valves
With these you can set the temperature of every radiator.

Estimating time

The times for bleeding and flushing are for all the radiators in the system. The other times are for repairing or replacing individual items of the system.

Radiator maintenance

Bleeding radiators
 $\frac{1}{2}$ hour

Curing a leaking valve
$\frac{3}{4}$ hour

Replacing a radiator
 1 - $1\frac{1}{2}$ hours

System maintenance

Repairing a leaking pipe joint
 $\frac{1}{2}$ - $1\frac{1}{2}$ hours

Replacing a pump
2 - 3 hours

Flushing out a central heating system
 1 - 2 hours

Types of central heating

A central heating system has a single heat source from which warmth is distributed to the places where it is needed around the home. The way in which the heat is circulated defines the type of system. Wet systems work by circulating hot water around a number of radiators, dry systems circulate warm air around the home through a network of ducts.

Wet systems
A central boiler heats water, which flows to the radiators. Here the water gives off its heat and returns to the boiler to be reheated. Most systems have a pump that sends the water around the circuit, but some older systems rely on the tendency of hot water to rise to create a flow.

To link the boiler and the radiators, small-bore pipes of 15mm diameter are usually used. Most installations have two pipes. The flow pipe takes hot water from the boiler to each radiator inlet in turn. A second pipe is connected to the outlets of all the radiators, and returns to the boiler.

Some older installations use a single pipe to feed and collect water from each radiator in turn. The draw-back with this system is that only the first radiator receives water that is fully hot, so the others have to be progressively larger to give the same heat.

Another type of central heating uses microbore piping. The main supply pipes run to and from a mani-fold, a section of larger-diameter pipe from which smaller pipes run to and from the radiators. Microbore pipes are easier to install and conceal than conventional pipes, but they require a more powerful pump and are more easily blocked and damaged.

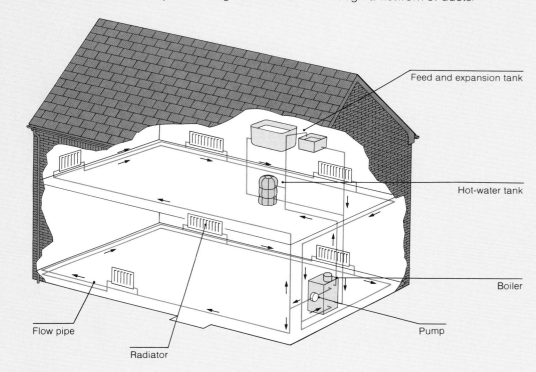

Feed and expansion tank

Hot-water tank

Boiler

Pump

Flow pipe

Radiator

Dry systems
These use air to carry the heat around the home. The most common type uses a central boiler and a fan to blow heated air through ducts under the floors to each room. Most systems of this type need to be installed when the house is built, although there is one type, called a stub-duct system, that can be put in later. This discharges warm air to several points close to a central shaft. The other type of dry system is electric underfloor heating. This is also built in when the house is con-structed. It consists of large heating elements laid in each solid floor slab and which heat the air above.

Warm-air grille

Return duct

Warm-air duct

Outlet duct

Boiler

177

Bleeding a radiator

One of the most common problems with a wet central heating system is a radiator that is not as warm at the top as it is elsewhere. This is usually caused by a build-up of air in the radiator. The reason for this is either air dissolved in the water or corrosion within the system which produces gas that collects in the radiators. The solution is to "bleed" the radiators by opening the bleed valve with a special key.

Bleeding a radiator
Opening the air-bleed valve at the top of the radiator will allow the air to escape. Use a special radiator key and be ready to catch any escaping water. Close the

valve as soon as water starts to escape. As you do this, the system will be topped up again from the feed-and-expansion tank. The radiator should now heat evenly.

178

Curing a leaking valve connection

If the leak is where the radiator is connected to a valve, try tightening the nuts linking the fitting to the pipe and the radiator. Use two spanners, one to tighten the nut, the other to brace the fitting as you work, so that you do not damage the pipework. If this does not cure the leak, isolate the radiator by closing the valves at either end, undo the connections and remake them. (For more information on dealing with pipe leaks in central-heating systems, *see Job 180, opposite.*)

Connecting a radiator valve
Close the valves at either end of the radiator, using a small spanner for the lock shield valve. Note how many turns are required to turn it off. Put a large, shallow container under the leaking valve to catch the contents of the radiator, and undo the

*coupling nut, **1**. As water flows out, open the bleed valve slightly using a radiator key. When all the water has run out, clean the ends of the connector with wire wool, **2**, and reassemble it. When opening the lockshield valve, use the same number of turns of the spanner as you used to close it.*

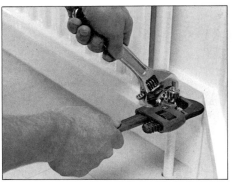

1 Unscrew the coupling nut of the leaking valve and catch the water

2 Use wire wool to clean out the ends of the connector before reassembly

179

Replacing an old radiator

Radiators sometimes leak along the bottom seam. If this is happening, corrosion has probably taken hold inside and you should replace the radiator. To remove the old

radiator, start by closing both the valves and disconnecting the radiator at both ends (*see Job 178, above*). Then lift the radiator off its brackets. You should also remove its fittings, which may also be corroded. Replace the radiator with one of the same capacity. Do not attempt to fit a larger-capacity radiator. Your boiler may not be powerful enough for this.

Fitting a new radiator
*Fit two new couplers, a bleed valve, and a blanking nut to the new radiator, lift it on to the wall brackets, **1**, and connect it to the pipework at each end, **2**. To fill the radiator, open the bleed valve and the two valves at the bottom, **3**.*

Use as many turns of the spanner to open the lockshield as it took to close it. If you do not do this, the radiators in the system may heat unevenly. As the radiator fills, air will escape from the bleed valve. Close this valve when water starts to escape from it.

1 Attach the radiator to the brackets on the wall

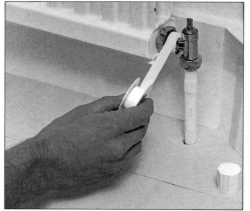

2 Connect the radiator to the lockshield and hand valves and seal, using PTFE tape

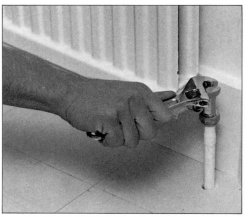

3 Open the valves so that the radiator fills up with water

180
Repairing leaking pipes

If there is a leak in the pipework or where the pipe enters the radiator valve, drain the system. First turn off the boiler and the pump, and stop water entering the system by tying up the ball valve in the feed-and-expansion tank, or by turning off the appropriate stopcock. Attach a length of garden hose to the system draincock (usually placed near the boiler or on the lowest run of pipework) and take the hose to an outside gulley. Open the draincock with a spanner. Then open the radiator bleed valves, starting from those on the upper floors, working downwards.

Replacing damaged piping
Cut out and replace damaged pipework as necessary. Insert a new piece of pipe, joining it to the old with compression or capillary joints. When you have finished, refill the system by closing the draincock and bleed valves, and restarting the water flow at the feed-and-expansion tank. When the system is full, bleed all the radiators (see Job 177, p. 192). You may also need to bleed the pump by turning the bleed screw located on the outer casing.

181
Replacing a pump

A central-heating pump may become blocked as a result of corrosion within the system. If it fails, replace it with one of identical specifications. Disconnect the old pump from its power supply and drain down the system (*see Job 180, left*) before unscrewing the couplings at each side and removing the old pump. Some pumps have isolating valves on either side. If you close these you do not have to drain the system.

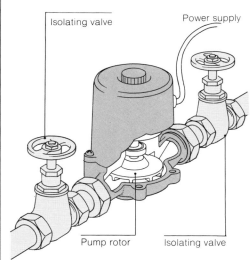

Isolating valve — Power supply — Pump rotor — Isolating valve

Installing a new pump
Fit the new pump in place, using new sealing washers. Reconnect the power supply and bleed air from the pump by turning its bleed screw.

182
Flushing out a central heating system

If it is often necessary to bleed the radiators, flush the system through to remove any rust or sludge that could damage the pump or cause cold spots in radiators. To do this, keep draining and refilling the system until the water coming out of the draincock is reasonably clear. You should also put anti-corrosion liquid into the water, to prolong the life of the radiators.

Adding anti-corrosion fluid
To introduce a corrosion inhibitor to the circulating water first tie up the ball valve in the feed tank. Drain off about 20 litres of water through the draincock to empty the expansion tank and part of the pipework. Pour the recommended amount of corrosion inhibitor into the tank, restore the water supply to top up the system, and start the pump so that the water circulates.

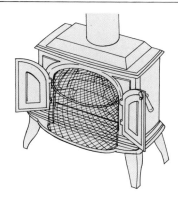

Other heating systems

There is a wide choice of appliances that offer alternatives to central heating. These include a wide range of portable electric heaters. They are efficient, easy to move, and not expensive to buy, though electricity itself is a costly fuel to use.

Radiant heaters are the cheapest. Convector heaters can take a long time to heat a whole room and are best used for providing background heat. Like convectors, electric oil-filled radiators are also slow-acting. Fan heaters are probably the quickest-acting type.

Electric storage heaters are a sophisticated form of convector heater linked to a timer. They are more economical than other forms of electric heating because they use cheap-rate electricity. But they suffer from the major disadvantage that their reserve of heat may be almost exhausted by the evening.

Modern gas fires provide a combination of radiant heating and convection. They must be connected to a suitable flue, to remove the by-products of combustion. Gas convector heaters can use a balanced flue, a short duct leading directly from the back of the heater through the outside wall. This means that gas convectors can be installed almost anywhere on an exterior wall.

Wood-burning stoves are worth considering if you have regular access to supplies of cheap or free wood. Paraffin and bottled-gas heaters are useful as stand-by appliances.

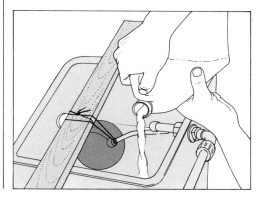

Wood-burning stove
Attractive and economical, this type of stove gives a good heat source if you have a plentiful wood supply. Old-fashioned and modern designs are available.

Insulation

Types of insulation material ◇ Reducing heating costs ◇ Lining and insulating a roof Insulating a loft ◇ Lagging pipes and tanks Types of draughtproofing ◇ Insulating floors and ceilings

Much of the warmth created by your heating system disappears through the walls, roof, windows, and doors of your home. Insulation offers a way of saving some of this warmth, which in turn saves you money on heating bills. If your home has no insulation, you may be wasting three-quarters of the money you spend on heating. With proper insulation, it is possible to cut down this loss by almost half.

You can insulate almost every part of the structure of your home. But some areas are responsible for a greater heat loss than others, and so are more important to insulate. Certain areas are also easier and cheaper to insulate than others. For example, it is simple, and relatively inexpensive, to insulate a loft, which might be responsible for up to one quarter of the entire heat loss. Windows lose less heat, and double glazing is an expensive form of insulation. Of course, your own insulation requirements will vary according to the type of home you live in. In general, the more outside walls you have, and the larger the area of the roof, the more insulation will be required.

Insulation can also save you money and trouble in the plumbing system. If you lag your pipes and water tanks, they will retain heat and will be unlikely to freeze and cause bursts, and if you insulate your hot-water cylinder you will save money on heating water.

Points to remember

◇ Whichever part of the home you are insulating, leave some ventilation – otherwise you run the risk of condensation.
◇ When insulating a loft, leave the area under the cold-water cistern uninsulated, so that a little warmth comes through from the room below.
◇ Cover water tanks with a lid and insulate this with the same material as the rest of the tank.
◇ Wear stout gloves and a protective face mask when working with glass-fibre insulation material.
◇ Make sure windows and doors are draughtproof, but maintain an adequate air supply for fuel-burning appliances.

Types of insulation material

A wide range of materials is used for insulation. Some of the most common materials are glass fibre and expanded polystyrene, which have excellent heat-saving properties and are made up in various forms for insulating different parts of the home. Aluminium foil, which reflects radiant heat, is also a useful material. The types illustrated below are all simple to install. But there are some types of insulation, such as foam cavity-wall fillings, which require special equipment and should be installed by a professional.

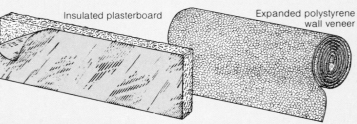

Insulated plasterboard

Expanded polystyrene wall veneer

Wall insulation materials
Builders use blown glass fibre or other mineral-fibre material for cavity-wall insulation. This is often inserted in slab form during new building work. Beads of expanded polystyrene are also sometimes used. Some types *of glass-fibre matting are backed with building paper, polythene, or foil. This enables them to be stapled between the framework of a timber stud wall. You can use expanded polystyrene wall veneer for insulating walls and reducing condensation.*

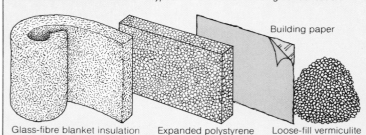

Building paper

Glass-fibre blanket insulation   Expanded polystyrene   Loose-fill vermiculite

Roof and loft insulation materials
The most popular method of insulating lofts to stop heat escaping through the ceiling is to lay glass-fibre matting. This consists of cotton-wool-like filaments and is supplied in rolls. It comes in several thicknesses, from 150mm and 100mm for new work to 80mm for adding extra material to areas that are already *insulated. It is also ideal for lagging water tanks and cisterns. Similar mineral-wool matting is also available. Other alternatives in the loft are beads or slabs of expanded polystyrene, and vermiculite, a material that expands to form spongy, lightweight granules. For lining the roof in a loft area, you can use either building paper or fibre boards.*

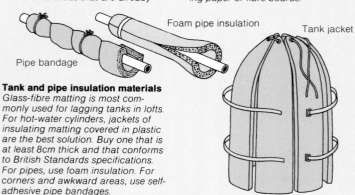

Foam pipe insulation

Tank jacket

Pipe bandage

Tank and pipe insulation materials
Glass-fibre matting is most commonly used for lagging tanks in lofts. For hot-water cylinders, jackets of insulating matting covered in plastic are the best solution. Buy one that is at least 8cm thick and that conforms to British Standards specifications. For pipes, use foam insulation. For corners and awkward areas, use self-adhesive pipe bandages.

Reducing heating costs

The diagram below shows the proportions of heat loss for which the parts of a typical house are responsible. The proportions vary for other types of building. A bungalow loses proportionally more heat through the roof and less through the walls, while in a ground-floor flat there is less heat loss through the ceiling than there is through the roof of a house.

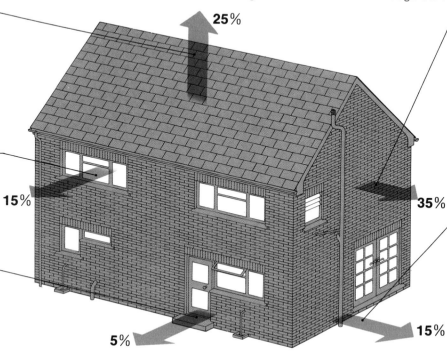

25%

15%

35%

5%

15%

Roof
As much as 25 per cent of the heat can escape from an uninsulated roof. This can be cut to 8 per cent by the simple method of insulating the loft with glass-fibre blanket material or loose-fill insulation. Loft insulation can have the further advantage of protecting the water pipes in the roof. If they are covered by glass fibre or loose-fill material, there is no need for them to be separately lagged.

Windows
Ordinary single-glazed windows can be responsible for losing 15 per cent of the heat. This can be reduced to 5 per cent by double glazing, but the cost of installation hardly justifies the saving on heat. But you can save some warmth cheaply by fitting draught excluders to windows that fit badly.

Doors
Draughts under and around doors can cause a heat loss which you can reduce by making sure the doors fit well and have the necessary draught excluders.

Walls
Potentially the greatest heat loss can occur through the walls. They can be responsible for losing as much as 35 per cent of the heat produced in the home. If you have cavity walls, the best method is to have the cavities filled with insulating foam by a specialist company. If this is not possible, you can dry-line the walls with sheets of insulated plasterboard.

Underfloor area
Up to 15 per cent of the heat can escape from under the floor. One of the simplest ways to cut this down is to fill under-skirting gaps by fitting strips of beading to the bottom of the skirting boards.

Estimating time

The times for insulating roofs and lofts are for a 10m² area. Work out your own roof or loft area and increase the times accordingly.

Lining a roof
 1 - **2** hours

Lining and insulating a roof
2 - **3** hours

Insulating a loft
 ½ - **1** hour

Lagging a tank or cistern
 ½ - **1** hour

Lagging a hot-water cylinder
 ¼ - **½** hour

Lagging pipes
 ¼ hour

183
Lining a roof

In an old house with an unlined roof, draughts and blown-in rain can create problems. Lining the rafters with water-proof or foil-backed building paper can provide a solution. It will both keep out the rain and help cut heating bills.

Putting up the lining
Foil-backed building paper is best. It provides much better standards of insulation than ordinary waterproof building paper. Staple the lining to the rafters in horizontal strips, starting at the apex of the roof and working down to the eaves. If you are using foil-backed paper, the foil should face inwards. To stop the paper from tearing at the fixing points, cut small squares of cardboard, place these over the paper, and staple through them, 1. Overlap adjacent strips of paper by about 5cm. Before fixing the last strip, tuck pieces of building paper into the eaves between the rafters, 2. This will ensure that any water that is blown under the tiles will run down the lining and into the eaves, where it will disperse. If you do not do this, water will build up and cause damage to the roof timbers. However, the whole roof space must not be sealed from the outside air. Make sure that there is a ventilation gap at the eaves. Poor ventilation will increase the risk of rot and structural damage.

1 Staple through small squares of cardboard so that the paper is not torn by the staples

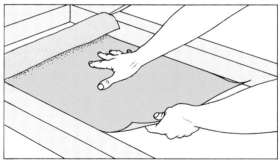
2 Tuck paper into the eaves to direct water away from the roof timbers

184

Lining and insulating a roof

When you want the entire loft space insulated – for example, if you use the loft as an occasional room – fit a more substantial insulating lining. This involves attaching strips of waterproof paper or polythene to the roof itself, then adding insulating material between the rafters, and finally, if a neat finish is required, putting up lining boards. Make sure that the roof is still adequately ventilated.

Fitting the insulation
First fix strips of waterproof material between the rafters running from the apex to the eaves, 1. The best material to use is roofing felt, attached with battens tacked to the sides of the rafters. Leave an air space between the felt and the underside of the battens to which the slates or tiles are fixed. Building paper and polythene can also be used for waterproofing.

Fit the insulating material under the lining. This can be slabs of expanded polystyrene, cut to fit between the rafters, and held in place by small nails driven into the rafter sides. Alternatively, you can use rolls of insulating matting tucked between the rafters and held in place with garden bamboo canes, 2. To give a neat finish, attach fibre insulating board, vapour-check plasterboard, or tempered hardboard to the rafters, 3. Doing this will also add to the insulating effect.

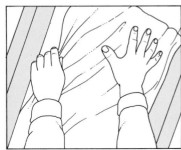

1 *Line the roof with waterproof felt*

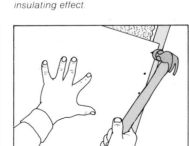

2 *Put the insulation between the rafters and fix it in place*

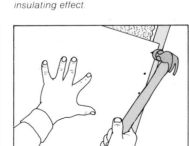

3 *Finish off with sheets of plasterboard nailed to the rafters*

185

Insulating a loft

Glass fibre and mineral wool in roll form are the most popular materials for loft insulation because they are very easy to lay. Loose-fill materials are also available, but they are not suitable for use under unlined roofs, since the granules can be blown around by winds. They can also be disturbed by draughts created when you open the loft hatch.

Before you start work, examine the roof timbers for signs of woodworm and dampness (*see pp. 204 and 208*) and take remedial action before fitting the insulation. Then vacuum the loft. Use an industrial vacuum cleaner if one is available, and take care with lath and plaster ceilings not to damage them.

When you are working in a loft, walk only on the tops of the ceiling joists. To avoid putting a foot through the ceiling, lay a few planks on the joists as temporary walkways. Protect your hands with plastic or rubber gloves when working with blanket insulation, and wear loose-fitting, long-sleeved clothing. A dust mask is also a worthwhile precaution.

Laying glass-fibre matting
To fit the matting, simply unroll it, butt-joining when you come to the end of a roll. If the roof itself is unlined, *tuck the insulation right into the eaves to cut out some of the draughts, 1. If the roof is lined, keep the matting clear of the eaves, to allow a little* *air to circulate, and prevent condensation. Take the matting over water pipes that run along the loft floor, 2, so that you do not have to insulate them separ-* *ately. But do not take the matting under the water tanks. A little rising warmth from the rooms below will help to prevent them from freezing.*

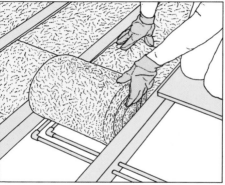

1 *With an unlined roof, tuck the matting into the eaves to stop draughts*

2 *Butt-join the edges and run the insulation over the water pipes*

186

Lagging tanks and cisterns

Insulate the sides and tops of the water-storage and feed-and-expansion tanks in the loft. Place the top insulation on a close-fitting lid, so that it does not fall into the tank. Leave the bases uninsulated, so that gentle warmth can rise from the rooms below. Cover the tank with a lid, which should also be insulated. When fitting a lid you may have a problem accommodating the expansion pipe that discharges over the tank. The most effective solution is to drill a hole in the lid beneath the point where the expansion pipe ends and fit a large funnel that will direct any water back into the tank.

Fitting glass fibre
Wrap the matting around the sides and hold it in place with loops of string. Make a wooden lid wrapped in polythene, and cover this in matting.

Fitting polystyrene
Slabs of polystyrene at least 25mm thick can also be used. Hold them in place with cocktail sticks or meat skewers pushed through the corners.

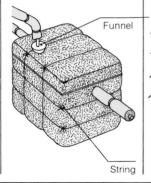

Funnel

String

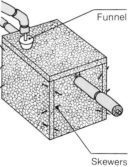

Funnel

Skewers

187
Lagging a hot-water cylinder

The heat losses from an uninsulated cylinder are very great, so lag an uninsulated cylinder with a purpose-made jacket at least 8cm thick. If your cylinder has an old jacket, measure its thickness – the filling disintegrates and drops down to the bottom of the jacket leaving the hottest part of the tank almost uninsulated.

Fitting a jacket
Drape the segments over the cylinder and loop them around the pipe at the top. Arrange them neatly around the pipes connected to the cylinder and leave the top of the immersion heater uncovered. Loop the fastening tapes around the cylinder to keep the jacket in place.

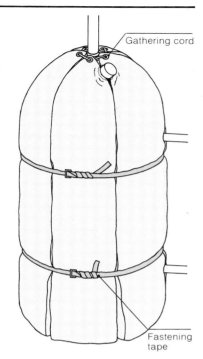

Gathering cord

Fastening tape

188
Lagging pipes

To help prevent freezing, insulate all exposed pipes in the loft space, including overflow and expansion pipes, even though these are normally empty. It is also worthwhile insulating long runs of hot-water pipes, especially if they are fitted under floors. This will keep the water hotter and will prevent the waste that occurs when hot water in the pipes cools down quickly even when you have only drawn off a small amount at the tap. The ideal material for lagging pipes is moulded foam, though you may also need to use blanket-type material at stopcocks, valves, and difficult corners.

Fitting the insulation
Some types of foam insulation have a press-to-close fastener which is very quick to use. Otherwise, hold the insulation in place with adhesive tape, 1. It can be bent around large bends, but at tight bends and elbows, cut the insulation and make a 45° mitre joint. At Tee-joints you should also cut the insulation to make a neat 45° angle. At valves and stopcocks it can be difficult to fit pre-formed foam. Use self-adhesive foam pipe insulation or traditional blanket-type material cut into strips, wound in a spiral around the pipe, 2, and secured with string.

1 Use adhesive tape to fix the tubing to straight pipe runs

2 Wrap insulation around the pipes at valves and stopcocks

Types of draughtproofing

Heat loss from draughts can account for up to 16 per cent of the fuel bill. Double glazing can stop draughts from windows. (For more information, see p. 101.) But it is best to fit draught excluders.

Hinged windows
For hinged and pivoting windows, fit self-adhesive foam tape. Fix it to the rebate of the frame so that the window closes against it. On the hinge side, fit the foam to the side face of the frame – the same side on which the hinge flaps are mounted.

For frequently used hinged windows, V-shaped strips of plastic, copper, or bronze are a good choice. They are either self-adhesive or designed to be pinned to the fixed frame. For windows that are not opened in winter, press tubular strip into the cracks and remove it in the spring. It is re-usable.

For frames with irregularly shaped gaps, use silicone rubber sealant. This comes in a cartridge, and you squeeze it into the gap around the frame. It sets to the exact shape of the gap. It is ideal for metal-framed windows.

Sash windows
Nylon-pile strip is best for sash windows. It is supplied in a plastic or metal holder and you tack it around the frame so that the brush strip presses against the sliding sash. For sealing the meeting rails where vertical sash windows overlap, use sprung V-shaped strips.

Doors
Draughts between doors and door frames can also be treated with draught excluder, provided that you use a durable type. Fit brush or tubular strips around the door frame. Position these so that the brush or soft tube touches the face of the door. For under-door draughts, treatments range from simple self-adhesive plastic strips to two-part excluders with one part fixed to the threshold under the door and the other to the door itself.

Window draught excluders

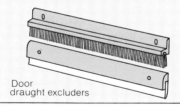

Door draught excluders

Tips for insulating floors and ceilings

◇ The simplest method is to lay aluminium foil, or foil-backed building paper, beneath underlay or foam-backed carpet.

◇ Insulate a cold solid floor by laying polythene sheeting and polystyrene slabs, covered by a floor of tongue-and-groove edged chipboard.

◇ Insulate a wooden floor with fibre insulation board covered by hardboard.

◇ If you do not want to raise the height of a wooden floor, insulate it by taking up the floorboards and inserting either glass-fibre matting or slabs of polystyrene cut to fit between the joists.

◇ Cover underskirting gaps with beading (*see Job 71, p. 70*).

◇ If there is no access to the floor above a ceiling, insulate with material fixed between battens screwed to the ceiling; cover the battens with panelling (*see Job 99, p. 87*).

◇ Use thermal board for a heat-saving ceiling.

Roofs and gutters

Equipment ◇ Types of roof covering ◇ Replacing a slate Replacing a tile ◇ The guttering system ◇ Clearing a blocked gutter ◇ Clearing a blocked downpipe Repairing a sagging gutter

The roof is one of the most important parts of any building. If you keep it in good condition, it will protect your home from wind and rain, preventing damp getting into the rooms below and rot establishing itself in the timbers. Because of their exposed position, roofs often need repair. Tiles and slates get damaged or dislodged and the covering of flat roofs starts to crack.

The gutters, important in keeping rainwater away from the walls and stopping penetrating damp, should also be kept in good repair.

Basic roofing repairs such as replacing slates and tiles are not difficult. But it is essential to pay attention to safety.

Points to remember

◇ Always take care when working at a height – never try to cut corners to save time.
◇ Wear soft, rubber-soled shoes that give a good grip.
◇ For work on a roof, use a roof ladder – never walk directly on a slate or tile roof surface.
◇ For major jobs, such as slate or tile replacement and fixing new gutters, work from a scaffolding tower fitted with safety rails and toe boards.
◇ Support ladders and scaffolding with strong, wide boards.

Equipment

To gain access to roofs and gutters you will need a ladder or scaffolding tower and, possibly, a roof ladder. Choose a double or triple extending ladder. A triple extending ladder is easier to store and to erect single-handed. Aluminium alloy ladders are lighter than timber ladders. The treads should be wide enough for comfort and positioned so that they form flat surfaces when the ladder is at the correct angle. At the top and bottom of each section there should be rubber safety grips so that the ladder cannot slip.

Scaffolding towers cost more than ladders, but they can be hired. They take longer to erect than a ladder and are more difficult to move, but they provide a working platform that is safe and secure. They are essential for extensive roof work and gutter replacement, and very useful for other work on roofs, gutters, external walls, and upper-floor windows.

Roof ladders are essential for work on all roofs except the flat, bitumen-felt type. They are usually made of lightweight aluminium alloy and have small wheels that enable the ladder to be pushed up the roof to the ridge. Roof ladders vary in length. Choose one that just fits the distance between the ridge and the eaves of your roof. They can be hired, or, if you have a spare sectional ladder, you can convert it to a roof ladder using a bolt-on wheel-and-hook set.

Building a scaffolding tower
Put the tower on firm ground or position the feet on thick, wide boards. When the tower is 1m high, check with a spirit level that it is vertical. If it has screw feet, you can adjust the tower's stability easily. If not, pack one or more of the corners with strong, wide boards. If the tower is over 5m tall, tie it to the building. Screw an eye-bolt into the brickwork just below the eaves and secure the tower to this using strong rope. Stabilizing outriggers provide good additional support for a tall tower. Fit safety rails and toe boards to the tower before you start to use it.

Using a roof ladder
Push the ladder's wheels up the roof towards the ridge. Then invert the ladder and check that the hook is secured firmly over the ridge of the roof.

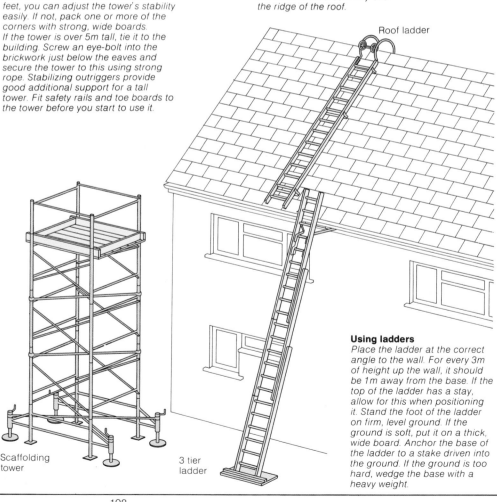

Roof ladder

Scaffolding tower

3 tier ladder

Using ladders
Place the ladder at the correct angle to the wall. For every 3m of height up the wall, it should be 1m away from the base. If the top of the ladder has a stay, allow for this when positioning it. Stand the foot of the ladder on firm, level ground. If the ground is soft, put it on a thick, wide board. Anchor the base of the ladder to a stake driven into the ground. If the ground is too hard, wedge the base with a heavy weight.

Types of roof covering

The main materials used for roofing are tiles and slates, which are used on pitched roofs, and bitumen felt, which is used on flat roofs.

Slates are often used for roofs on older houses, but they are usually too expensive to use on new roofs. A slate roof in good condition will give excellent service. New slates are still available for repairs, and secondhand slates in good condition form a cheaper alternative. Imitation asbestos-based slates are also suitable both for repairs and for replacing a complete slate roof, to keep it in the same style as the original. There are variations in slate sizes, so measure a slate from your roof before buying replacements.

Plain tiles are the most common tiles. They are rectangular, have a curved surface, and have two holes at the top for fixing nails. They usually also have two projections (known as nibs) at the top, which hook over the tiling battens to hold each tile in place. If the tiles have nibs, nails are only used for fixing in exposed places.

The usual size of plain tiles is 265mm × 165mm, but there are many types and colours, so take care when buying replacements. At the eaves and ridges special shorter tiles are used to maintain the correct overlap, and there are special wider tiles for use at the edges of the roof.

Interlocking tiles are also known as single-lap tiles. They are sometimes made of clay, and concrete versions are common on new homes and in replacement roofs. Sizes and styles vary.

Flat roofs, such as those often built on home extensions, are often covered with bitumen-felt. This material is also sometimes used on sloping roofs.

Slate roof construction
Each slate is fixed by two nails to a horizontal timber batten which is nailed to the rafters. To ensure that the covering is waterproof, alternate rows of slates are staggered, and each row overlaps by half the one below it. At any place on the roof there are therefore at least two thicknesses of slates. Old slate roofs are rarely lined with underfelt.

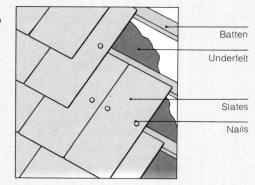

Plain-tile roof construction
Plain tiles are hung overlapping to give a double thickness. Their nibs hook over horizontal tiling battens which are nailed to the rafters. The tiles are attached to the battens with nails. Not every tile is nailed – every fourth row should be nailed, together with the tiles along the edges of the roof, at the eaves, and at the apex.

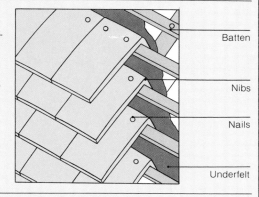

Interlocking-tile roof construction
These tiles are laid in a single layer and interlock at the edges. Like plain tiles, they have nibs that hook over the tiling battens and they are also attached to the battens with nails.

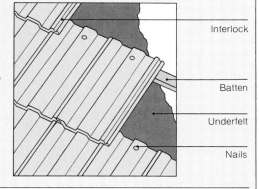

Bitumen-felt roof construction
On flat roofs the felt is usually fixed in three separate layers, bonded together with bitumen. The first layer is nailed to the roof boards and the subsequent layers are bonded to it. Flat bitumen-felt roofs are usually finished with light-coloured stone chippings that reflect the sun's heat.

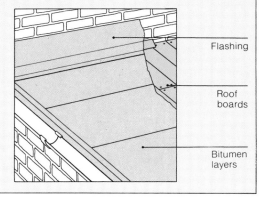

189

Replacing a slate

Remove any broken pieces of slate with a slater's rip. Slide it upwards under the broken slate and move it to one side until you can feel the fixing nail. When you pull the rip downwards, the barb on the end will hook around the nail, pulling it out of place or cutting through it. Repeat the process on the other nail, and then pull out the remaining broken pieces of slate.

To secure the new slate in position, a strip of lead about 20cm long and 25mm wide is nailed to the roof timbers and then bent back up over the lower edge of the slate.

Fixing the slate
After removing the old slate, 1, cut a strip of lead to the right length and nail it between the two slates in the row below using a 38mm aluminium or galvanized nail. The nail should pass into the timber batten to which the lower row of slates is fixed, 2. Then push the replacement slate into place and line it up with the others in its row. Secure it in place by bending the protruding end of the lead strip up and over the lower edge of the slate. Double over the end so that the lead strip is not easily flattened by melting snow sliding down the roof.

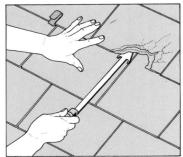

1 *Using a slater's rip, take out the old pieces of slate*

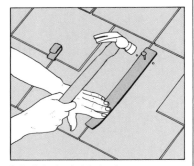

2 *Nail the lead strip in place*

Tips for repairing bitumen-felt roofs

◇ To recondition an old roof, scrape off the stone chippings, deal with any serious cracks or blisters, and re-coat the whole roof.
◇ Re-coat a roof by treating the entire area with a bitumen primer, adding a coat of roofing bitumen, pressing down an open-weave glass-fibre mesh, adding further coats of bitumen, and finally applying chippings.
◇ Prepare an area for repair by scraping away the chippings and drying out the area using a hot-air paint stripper.
◇ After preparing a cracked area, press down the crack with a wooden wallpaper roller; paint the area of the crack with flashing-strip primer and when this has dried, press metal-backed self-adhesive flashing strip over the crack.
◇ If the roof is covered with chippings, paint the repair with liquid bitumen and sprinkle chippings over the surface of the roof while it is still wet.
◇ If there are blisters and bubbles, make two cuts at right-angles across the centre of the blister, turn back the edges, and treat in the same way as a crack; the edges will overlap slightly, because the blister will have stretched the surface of the felt.
◇ Use patches of self-adhesive flashing strip to complete small bitumen-roof repairs.

190

Replacing a tile

To avoid leaks, you should inspect your roof regularly to check that there are no cracked or broken tiles. As well as looking at the roof from the outside, go into the loft while it is raining and check for leaks. Replace cracked, crumbling, or broken tiles with new ones as soon as possible.

The method is similar whichever type of tile you have, except that interlocking tiles require extra fixing – either with 32mm aluminium alloy nails, driven through the fixing holes, or with clips. With both types of tile, make sure you have removed all the broken pieces before fixing the new tile in position on the roof.

Fixing a plain tile
Lift the tiles in the row above the broken one using two wedges cut from scraps of wood. Then, with the point of a bricklayer's trowel, remove the broken pieces. Slip the trowel under the tile, so that you can lift it over the tiling batten. Push the new tile upwards until its nibs hook over the batten; then pull the wedges out of the way.

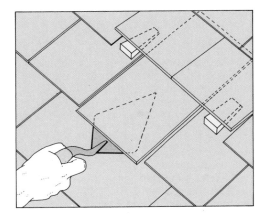

191

Repairing flashing

Flashings seal the joints where a roof meets a brick wall. Traditional flashings are made of sheet lead or zinc, and the top edge is usually tucked into the brickwork. If this pulls out, leaks can occur. Rake out the old mortar, tuck the flashing back into place, holding it firm with lead strip, dampen the joint, and press fresh mortar into place. If there are tears, cracks, or holes in the flashing, clean the areas with a wire brush, paint the surrounding areas with flashing-strip primer, and when this has dried fit self-adhesive flashing strip to cover up the holes and create a waterproof seal.

Badly corroded flashing is best replaced with a self-adhesive strip. This involves preparing and priming the surface carefully first.

Fitting self-adhesive flashing strip
Remove the old flashing and clean the brickwork with a wire brush. Repoint the brickwork if necessary (see Job 197, p. 203). Paint a band of flashing-strip primer where the new flashing strip is going to be fitted. The band of primer should be about 10cm wide on the roof and 15cm wide on the wall. When the primer has dried, press down the first band of flashing strip, so that it overlaps the roof by about 10cm, with a 5cm overlap on to the wall. Then apply a second strip, to cover the primer on the wall and overlap the turn-up of the first strip. Use a wallpaper seam roller to flatten bubbles and creases.

The guttering system

The basic system consists of gutter channelling fixed so that it falls slightly towards an outlet. This is connected, by means of a swan-neck fitting, to a downpipe that either discharges directly into a rainwater gulley or stops just short of a gulley and discharges its water through a shoe, which directs the water away from the wall. Sometimes another pipe is fed into a downpipe by means of an open-ended, funnel-shaped inlet called a hopper.

Half-round guttering, available in both metal and plastic, is fixed to the fascia board at the eaves by means of brackets. Ogee-shaped guttering, made of cast-iron or steel, is a more angular design with a flat back that allows the gutter to be screwed directly to the fascia board. Most modern guttering systems are made of plastic, because it does not rust and is easier to handle than cast iron. Sometimes, seamless aluminium gutters are used on new homes and in replacement work. Asbestos cement gutters were also once made, but are no longer available.

Gutter and downpipe sizes vary according to the area of roof they drain. It is important that gutters and downpipes are large enough to deal with heavy rainfall. A generally adequate size for half-round guttering is 10cm, with circular downpipes 68mm in diameter. Square-section guttering systems usually have a greater water-carrying capacity than half-round systems. If you are uncertain about which size to use, consult the manufacturer of the systems you are considering.

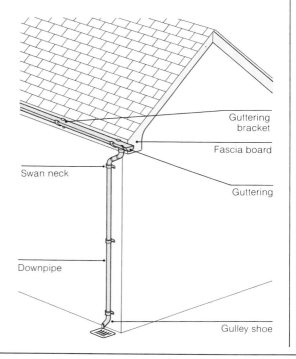

Guttering bracket

Fascia board

Swan neck

Guttering

Downpipe

Gulley shoe

192

Clearing a blocked gutter

If a gutter is overflowing or there is a severe water leak from a downpipe, there may be a blockage in the gutter, in a downpipe, or in the rainwater gulley. Start by clearing out the gutter. When you have done this, pour a bucket of water from the stop end and check that it drains quickly. This test may highlight other faults, such as leaking joints. After clearing a metal gutter, let it dry and apply two coats of black bitumen paint to the inside.

Scraping out the debris
When cleaning out a gutter, work from the downpipe outlet to the stop end, to prevent debris being pushed down the pipe. Use a garden trowel, or, to make the job easier, cut a scrap of hardboard or plywood to the shape of the gutter to act as a scraper.

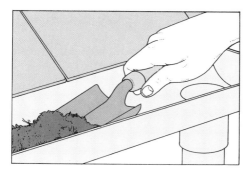

193

Clearing a blocked downpipe

Place a tray under the downpipe outlet to catch debris. Clean the swan-neck, either by removing it or with drain-cleaning wire. Probe upwards through the rainwater shoe. Clear the straight sections with bamboo canes.

Clearing a swan neck
Try clearing the swan neck by pushing flexible drain-clearing rods down from the top. This may force debris down, so put a container under the shoe.

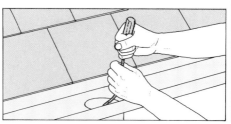

194

Repairing a sagging gutter

The most likely cause is that the fixing screws have corroded and worked loose. The solution is to put in new gutter fixing screws. With an ogee gutter, drill new fixing holes; with a half-round type, fit new brackets.

Refitting a half-round gutter
Put up new brackets with new fixing screws. Move the fixing positions along the fascia board slightly and drill new screw holes.

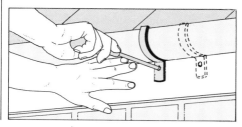

Tips for repairing leaking gutter joints

◇ Before repairing a leaking joint, clean out the gutter and allow it to dry.
◇ On a metal gutter, use non-setting mastic, injected into the joint from the inside and outside, or remake the joint with strips of thick mastic or metal window putty.
◇ Self-adhesive flashing strip can also be used to seal joints in metal guttering.
◇ With a leaking joint in a plastic gutter, unclip the affected section and replace the sealing gasket.
◇ Check for blockages below a leak.
◇ Clean a leaking downpipe joint during dry weather with non-setting mastic or a waterproof mastic bandage.

External walls

Repairing rendering ◇ Repairing pebbledash ◇ Pointing a wall Dealing with wall stains

Brick, stone, and concrete are the most common materials for external walls. They all vary greatly in their appearance, although they can be disguised by the addition of rendering or pebbledash. Most people prefer to leave large projects involving external walls to a professional, but there are a few smaller jobs that are quite straightforward. The most useful of these are pointing – repairing the mortar joints in brickwork – and patching up areas of rendering and pebbledash.

It is also possible to paint external walls. Brick and stone walls are usually attractive without painting, but painting can considerably improve the appearance of a rendered or pebbledash wall. It is important to prepare the wall carefully (by brushing off stains and loose material, filling holes, and applying primer) and to use a paint that is suitable for exterior masonry.

When treating stains on walls, remember that these are often caused by damp, which must also be treated.

Points to remember

◇ For a small area of pointing buy ready-mixed dry mortar.
◇ Before pointing or repairing rendering, scrape out all the loose material and dirt.
◇ Brush water into the joints before pointing – otherwise the moisture will be sucked out and the pointing will crumble.
◇ Keep the mortar mixture fairly dry – it should not run out of the joints.
◇ Never wash walls covered with efflorescence.

Estimating time

All these times are for working on a square metre of wall – multiply them to get a time for the repair you want to carry out. If the repair is high up, you will also need extra time to set up a ladder or scaffolding tower.

Repairing rendering
(1¼)-(2¼) hours

Repairing pebbledash
(1½)-(2½) hours

Repointing
(1)-(2) hours

195
Repairing rendering

Use a bolster chisel and a club hammer to cut away all the loose rendering. Mix some render using one part Portland cement, one part hydrated lime in powder form, six parts clean plastering sand, and water to make a butter-like consistency. Render mix sets quite quickly, so make no more than you can apply in about twenty minutes. The mix should be free from lumps. Before applying the render, dampen the wall well.

Applying the rendering
Take the first coat to within 6mm of the surrounding render surface. Use a trowel to spread it on to the wall and work upwards from the bottom of the patch, 1. Press the lower edge of the trowel hard against the wall and then sweep it up firmly. Before the first coat sets, scratch it with the point of the trowel, 2.

Apply the second coat on the following day. Work from left to right and from the top of the repair towards the bottom. To get a level finish, use a piece of straight-edged wood. Draw it upwards across the repair, keeping its ends resting firmly on the rendering on either side, 3. Finish off with a wood float.

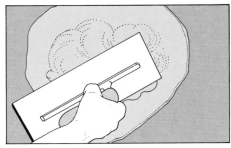
1 Put on the first coat with firm, upward movements of the trowel

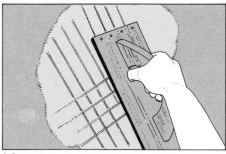
2 Score lines on the rendering to create a key for the next coat

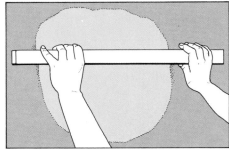
3 Smooth down the second coat with a straight piece of timber

---

196
Repairing pebbledash

Mix some rendering and apply it in two coats (*see Job 195, above*). While the second coat is still wet, throw on the stones using a small trowel. Most of them will stick, although you may have to press some of them into the rendering using a small piece of board. If you paint the wall when the pebbledash is dry, the repair will be disguised.

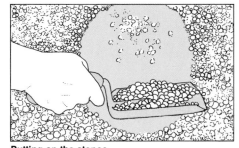
Putting on the stones
Using a trowel, throw the stones so that they stick to the rendering

197
Pointing a wall

Old mortar that is cracked and loose will let in rainwater and cause dampness on interior walls. If only a small area of your brickwork needs repointing, buy a small bag of dry mortar mix, to which you only need to add water. If the area to be pointed is larger, it is worth buying separate ingredients and mixing one part cement, one part lime, and six parts soft sand. Add a little water, but keep the mix on the dry side – if it is too runny it will be weak and may run down the wall causing stains.

1 *Clear out the old mortar, including all the crumbling material and debris*

2 *Brush the joints with water immediately before pointing*

Applying mortar
*First chip away the old mortar using a slim cold chisel and a club hammer, **1**. Avoid damaging the bricks. Brush all the flaking pieces of mortar and dust from the cracks. Just before pointing, brush out the joints with water, **2**. This will ensure that water is not sucked from the mortar by the dry bricks, causing it to crack or crumble again quickly. Using a hawk and pointing trowel, cut*

*off rounded slices of mortar, **3**, and press these into the vertical joints. Trim off excess mortar with the edge of the trowel, **4**. Match the finish with the original pointing. When you have completed the vertical joints, tackle the horizontal ones. In hot weather, keep the joints soft for a few days by sprinkling water on them. If you do not do this, the heat will make the joint start to crumble.*

3 *Start pointing the joints, using the trowel and hawk to get pieces of the right size*

4 *Remove excess mortar with the point of the trowel*

External wall fault-finding

Brickwork stains
Brickwork can be stained in a number of different ways. Stains are quite often caused by damp, which you should eradicate, both to get rid of the stains and to prevent structural damage. (For more information, see pp. 204-7.)

Algae, moss, and mould
These are caused by dampness, which you must cure to prevent them recurring. Moss can be lifted with a scraper, while algae and mould are best removed by scrubbing with a stiff-bristled brush. When the wall is clean, apply a coat of fungicide solution. You should wear rubber gloves while using this liquid. After 24 hours, remove the solution by washing and brushing the wall with clean water.

Water stains
First cure the cause of the dampness and leave the wall to dry out. To make sure that the stain is not visible through fresh paintwork, seal the wall with a coat of alkali-resistant primer.

Dust and dirt
With a dusty surface, treat the wall with a proprietary stabilizing solution. Brush on a generous coat and allow 24 hours before painting the wall. Remove ingrained dirt by scrubbing with a solution of sugar soap and water. Rinse off the solution and allow the wall to dry before painting. Small areas of loose dirt on a wall can be scrubbed off using clean water.

Efflorescence
This is a powdery deposit, sometimes spread over considerable areas, which is often found on new homes. It will disappear naturally as the wall dries out. The powder consists of salts from the brickwork or mortar which are drawn to the surface together with moisture. You can buy a chemical treatment to cure this problem, but it is sufficient to clear away the powder with a dry brush as it appears. Do not try to wash the salts away – this will only make the problem much worse.

A wall covered with algae and mould should be brushed clean and treated with fungicide

Efflorescence is caused by mineral deposits and can be brushed off with a dry brush

Damp-proofing

Defences against damp ◇ The causes of damp
Types of damp-proof course ◇ Estimating time
Damp-proofing with chemicals ◇ Types of
condensation control

Any home that is not well maintained is a potential
victim of damp. The roof, walls, windows, and doors
are battered by the elements; the floors and walls may
be attacked by rising damp from below the ground;
and inside the house the plumbing pipework represents another potential source of dampness. The
result can be anything from spoiled decorations to a
very damp environment, which can cause poor health
for the occupants of the home and major structural
damage as timbers start to rot. Another source of
dampness in the home is condensation, moisture that
gets trapped in a room and cannot escape. It is often
produced in a building that is well insulated and
heated, but poorly ventilated.

To protect your home from rising damp, a damp-
proof course – a water-proof barrier in the brickwork –
must be fitted in the walls. Although most people
prefer to leave the job of installing a damp-proof
course to a specialist company, there are a number of
other ways in which you can protect your home from
damp. Many of the potential sources of damp are in
parts of the home that are not normally noticed – for
example, the tops of chimney stacks and the guttering
system. It is essential to keep these areas in good
repair, and many of the jobs involved, such as keeping
the gutters unblocked, are quite simple. The difficulty
is being aware of the causes of damp, so that you can
make any repairs before too much damage is done.

Points to remember

◇ Make regular checks of outside walls at ground level to
ensure that the damp-proof course is not bridged.
◇ Keep gutters clear and in good repair to avoid leaks and
penetrating damp.
◇ Examine regularly the condition of chimney stacks, pots,
and flaunching.
◇ To avoid condensation, ensure that ventilation is adequate,
particularly if your home is well insulated.
◇ Check the condition of your roof by examining it from
inside the loft during heavy rain.
◇ Keep airbricks clear of all obstructions to ensure good
sub-floor ventilation.

Defences against damp

Most homes built in the last
fifty years have damp barriers
built into their masonry, and so
they are less likely to suffer
from damp than older buildings.

Modern homes have cavity
walls made up of two layers of
bricks with a space between
them. The two layers are joined
together at regular intervals by
metal wall ties. At the base of
each wall about three or four
courses of bricks above ground
the damp-proof course is fitted.
This prevents moisture rising up
the wall. The cavity stops
rainwater coming through.

Houses with timber ground
floors are usually less prone to
damp problems in the floor. If
damp does occur, it is usually
the result of a faulty damp-

proof course or because airbricks on the outside walls
have been blocked. The air.
bricks ensure that the floor
timbers are ventilated and dry.

If the roof, gutters, and damp-
proof course are kept in good
condition, your home should be
free from damp. But damp-
proof barriers can break down
and poor building practices
can also cause problems.
During bricklaying, mortar can
fall into the cavity, land on the
metal ties, and form a bridge
for damp to get to the inner
layer of the wall. Another
problem can be an imperfect
link between the damp-proof
membrane in a concrete floor
and the damp-proof course in
the walls.

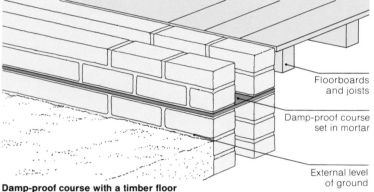

Floorboards
and joists

Damp-proof course
set in mortar

External level
of ground

Damp-proof course with a timber floor
*When there is a cavity wall and a
timber floor, the damp-proof course is
normally a thin strip of impervious
material such as slate or bituminous
felt. It is fixed in the mortar above
ground level but below floor level.*

Damp-proof course with a concrete floor
*Solid concrete floors incorporate a
sheet of waterproof material that
stretches right across the building and
links with the DPC in the walls.*

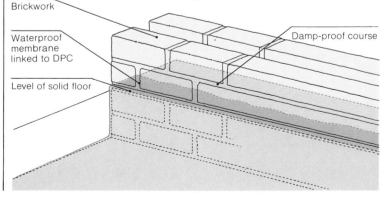

Brickwork

Waterproof
membrane
linked to DPC

Level of solid floor

Damp-proof course

The causes of damp

A damp patch in a room can usually be linked quickly with a nearby structural fault. For example, a wet patch at the top of a wall in an upstairs room may be caused by a leaking gutter or downpipe, while a stain on a wall near a window could be caused by rain being blown through a gap between the frame and the wall. But sometimes a damp patch inside the home is some distance from its cause on the outside of the building. For example, water leaking through a crack in a roof tile can drip on to the roof timbers and run along for several metres before dropping on to the ceiling below.

Cracked flaunching
This should be repaired to keep out damp and to keep the chimney pots securely fixed.

Crumbling mortar or rendering
Repoint mortar joints between the bricks of the stack that show signs of crumbling. Replace any missing patches of rendering or pebbledash.

Chimney stack
Damp patches on a chimney breast can often be traced to rainwater coming down the chimney. This is frequently a problem if the fireplace has been blocked up without allowing for ventilation – the flue must be ventilated to keep it dry.

Gutters and downpipes
Failures are caused by blockages in the gutter or downpipe, leaks caused by rusted metal or faulty joints, or a sagging gutter caused by loose brackets or fixing screws.

Walls
Look for cracked, loose, or missing patches of rendering or pebbledash. Defective mortar joints between bricks, and cracked or flaking brickwork, can also admit rainwater.

Loose flashing
Replace loose or defective flashing at the base of the stack. This seals the joint between the base of the stack and the roof. Flashing may be set into the mortar courses of the stack in a stepped formation, or it may be a straight band at the base of the stack. Use a self-adhesive metal flashing strip as a replacement.

Problems with chimneys

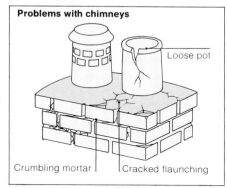

Loose pot

Crumbling mortar — Cracked flaunching

Loose chimney pots
Replace or refix loose or broken pots soundly into the flaunching that surrounds their bases. If the flue is no longer in use, insert a special capping pot that lets in air but keeps out rainwater.

Roof
Slipped, cracked, or missing tiles or slates are the likely problems on the roof. The best way to identify cracks is to climb into the loft on a rainy day and look and listen for any drips.

Plumbing
Damp patches on a ceiling may be caused by leaks, overflows, or bursts in the plumbing system. Keep pipes and tanks well insulated to help prevent them freezing in the winter.

Doors
Look for gaps between the frame and the wall that could admit water. If rainwater blows underneath a door, fit a weatherbar.

Windows
Check for gaps between the frame and the wall where rainwater can seep through. Clear out the groove in the underside of the sill – if it is blocked, rainwater can run across and soak through the wall.

Problems with airbricks

Debris blocking the airbrick

Airbricks
Keep these clear and make sure that earth is not piled against them to restrict the airflow. They provide essential ventilation for timber floors.

Damp-proof course
Make sure that there is a clear gap, preferably at least 15cm, between the ground level and the damp-proof course. The damp-proof course must not be bridged by a pile of earth or a rockery.

Types of damp-proof treatment

In most homes, especially modern houses, damp is prevented from rising more than a few inches up the wall by a built-in damp-proof course (see p. 204). Should this fail, or if one has not been installed, moisture will gradually rise several feet up the wall, causing considerable damage. A faulty damp-proof course cannot be repaired, but a new one can be installed. As well as the basic slate damp-proof strip (see p. 204) there are two other types – porous tubes and chemical injection. Slabs of bitumen are normally used instead of slates.

Chemical injection
A silicone-based liquid is fed into the wall, where it forms an impervious barrier across the brickwork. To do this, a series of 10mm diameter, down-ward-sloping holes are drilled into the wall and the chemical is intro-duced. It is either put in under pressure from special injection equip-ment or left to soak in from special bottles fixed in the holes. It is possible to carry out this method of damp protection yourself (see Job 198, right). You can hire equipment for pumping in the liquid.

Porous tubes
Earthenware tubes are fixed into the wall at an angle so that they slope downwards to the open air. Any moisture in the wall is absorbed by the tubes and cooled; this increases its density causing it to flow out-side and be replaced by fresh air drawn in. In other words, the tubes act like a series of small airbricks. A grille is fitted on the outside of each tube to repel rainwater.

Bitumen slabs
A special chainsaw that can cut masonry is used to make slots in the brickwork. Slabs of bitumen are inserted into the slot, making a damp-proof barrier similar to the tradi-tional slate damp-proof course.

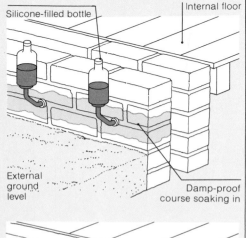

Silicone-filled bottle · Internal floor · External ground level · Damp-proof course soaking in

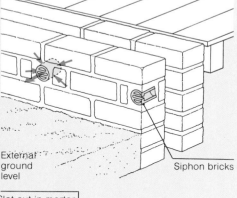

External ground level · Siphon bricks

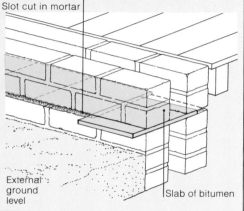

Slot cut in mortar · External ground level · Slab of bitumen

Estimating time

The time for putting in a chemical damp-proof course is for treating a 5 metre run of wall. When testing for condensation, wait up to two days for the result.

Putting in a chemical damp-proof course

 2-**3** hours

Testing for condensation

¼ hour

198

Damp-proofing with chemicals

The basic method depends on the thickness of your wall. If it is 112mm thick, drill holes 75mm deep in one side only. If the wall is 225mm thick, you should either drill from both sides or drill deep holes in two stages working from one side only. Start by drilling a 75mm hole, then insert some of the chemical solution. Next drill the hole to 190mm and insert more of the solution.

Putting in the chemical solution
If you are working on a solid wall from the inside, remove the first few floorboards nearest the wall (see Basic technique, pp. 68-9), and hack off any damp plaster, going right back to the brickwork (see Job 100, p. 89). Drill the holes about 150mm below floor level and about the same distance above the level of the ground outside. Angle the holes so that they slope downward towards the centre of the wall, 1. Put in the fluid, using the specially designed bottles, 2. As it soaks in, the bricks will become saturated and will sweat, showing that treatment at that point is complete. Finally, plug the holes with mortar, 3. Before replastering the wall on the inside, allow it to dry out completely – you should allow one month for each 25mm of wall thickness.

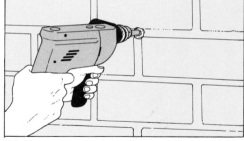

1 *Drill downward-sloping holes into the brickwork at 110mm intervals*

2 *Attach the bottles to the holes and leave the liquid to soak in*

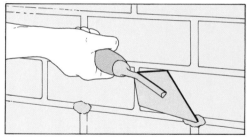

3 *After removing the bottles, fill the holes with mortar*

199

Testing for condensation

Condensation is caused when moisture builds up and gets trapped inside a room. The most common sources of moisture in the home are cooking, washing, and the breath of people in the room. But the presence of these factors alone does not cause condensation. It is when a home is so well insulated that moisture cannot escape that condensation

occurs. It is sometimes difficult to distinguish between condensation and structural damp. A steamed-up window is a sign of condensation, but a wet patch on a wall may be caused either by damp or condensation. If the wet patch appears after rain, the problem is likely to be penetrating damp. If it develops on a cold, dry day when the windows are steaming, condensation is probably the cause. If you are not certain of the cause of a damp patch, you can do a test with a piece of aluminium foil, sticking it over a dried-out patch of the affected wall.

Using foil to test for condensation
Dry out the damp patch with a heater and stick a piece of aluminium foil to the wall with adhesive tape. Ensure the edges are well sealed. If moisture reappears on the visible surface of the foil, it has obviously originated from within the atmosphere in the room, and the cause is condensation. If the moisture comes back on the face of the foil next to the wall, then it is caused by dampness coming through the wall.

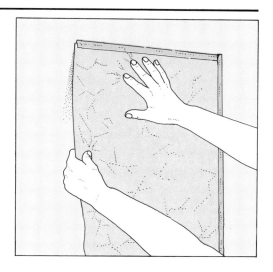

Types of condensation control

The key to curing condensation is to get the right balance between heat and ventilation in the home. But it is important to cut down the sources of condensation. Avoid paraffin heaters and unflued gas and oil heaters; reduce steam by covering saucepans and turning off the kettle as soon as it has boiled; and if possible avoid drying laundry inside the home.

Extractor fans
Portable fans simply recirculate the air in a room to keep it cool. An extractor fan will give you precise control over ventilation. Some simply suck air from the room; reversible types can be switched to remove air or blow air into the room from outside. Some have shutters that automatically close when the fan is switched off, to prevent draughts. An extractor fan will also help cut down condensation.

Choose a fan of the right size for the room. A huge fan in a small room creates a "wind-tunnel" effect, while a fan that is too small is almost useless. Before you buy a fan, calculate the cubic capacity of the room (length · width · height). Buy a fan that will give the right number of air changes per

hour in a room of that cubic capacity. Kitchens need about 15 air changes per hour; bathrooms need about six changes per hour. Fit the fan as high as possible and preferably opposite a door so that air is drawn right across the room. If there is a solid-fuel-burning appliance in the room, allow sufficient air replacement for the fire, so that air and fumes are not drawn back down the flue.

Dehumidifiers
When condensation is a serious problem, use a dehumidifier. This is a machine that works rather like a refrigerator. It draws warm, damp air over a cold coil so that the water condenses, and then passes the air over a warm coil so that it is warmed again as it passes back into the room.

Cooker hoods
These deal with cooking smells and steam very efficiently. There are two types. One extracts the steam directly to the outside air, the other filters the air and recirculates it into the room. Some models offer a choice between recirculation and extraction.

Ventilators
An open fire needs adjustable ventilators – ideally situated on either side of the hearth and fitted in the floor. With a solid floor, the ventilator should be fixed over the door leading to the hall.

A timber floor also requires ventilation. Airbricks are set in the walls for this purpose and they should be kept clear at all times. Blocked fireplaces should also be ventilated with an airbrick or a grille.

Thermal insulators
Lining cold walls and ceilings with sheets of expanded polystyrene before wallpapering will eliminate condensation. Thermal insulating plasterboard, cork tiles, or tongue-and-groove edged boards will have the same effect. Special anti-condensation emulsion paint is also available. This absorbs moisture when the humidity is high and releases it later when the air is drier.

Windows
Double-glazing with sealed units will solve the problem, although other types of double glazing may produce misting between the panes. (*For more information about curing condensation with double glazing, see p. 101.*) The best solution may be to increase the ventilation by fitting a fan or vent.

Extractor fan
Grille
Power source
Motor
Controls

Cooker hood
Wall-mounted fixing
Renewable filter
Vent to admit smells

Dehumidier
Heated coil
Air out
Air in
Cold coil
Power source

Rot and woodworm

Types of timber infestation ◇ Treatments for rot and woodworm ◇ Treating wet rot

Rot and woodworm are the enemies of timber. Both, if left unchecked, can destroy woodwork completely. Where structural timbers are concerned, the damage can be far reaching and very expensive to put right. So if there is any evidence of rot or woodworm in the timbers of your home, eradicate it immediately.

There are two types of wood rot – wet and dry. Both are caused by fungi that originate in wet timber. The signs of rot vary from rapidly growing fungal threads to timber that breaks up in a pattern of squares.

Woodworm is the general name for a number of wood-eating beetles, of which the furniture beetle is the most common. Other common beetles are the powder post beetle, which can reduce timber to powder, and the house longhorn beetle, which can spend as long as eight to ten years eating away a piece of wood. Evidence of an attack is provided by the holes from which the beetle larvae emerge, together with small piles of dust around the exit holes. However, this dust is often difficult to see.

Rot and woodworm need not be serious problems if they are diagnosed and treated in time. It is possible to deal with small, isolated attacks yourself, provided that you are sure to treat or replace all the affected timber. But if the infestation has taken hold and spread, it is difficult to eradicate without professional assistance. A specialist company should offer a long-term guarantee on its timber treatment.

Points to remember

◇ Keep lofts, sub-floors, and other parts of the home made of timber well ventilated, to prevent condensation and cut down the risk of rot.
◇ Make sure that tiles, slates, gutters, and downpipes are all in good repair, to keep out penetrating damp.
◇ Watch out for rot around leaking pipes.
◇ Treat small areas of wet rot yourself.
◇ Treat timber infestation quickly – if the damage is extensive, call in a specialist company.
◇ Treat all the timber that has been attacked, paying particular attention to the dry-rot fungus.

Types of timber infestation

Rot or woodworm may not be immediately apparent because they tend to start in places that cannot be seen – in concealed timbers beneath floorboards, in cellars, and in lofts. But once you examine timber, the signs of infestation are obvious.

Dry rot
Attacks of dry rot usually originate in areas that are damp and poorly ventilated – floor joists, cellars, and under sinks are common places. First, matted fungal strands appear, which develop a silver-grey skin possibly tinged with streaks of lilac or yellow. A texture like cotton wool forms, followed by a pale grey, corrugated fruiting body resembling a pancake and surrounded by rust-red spore dust.

Because the attack usually starts in a hidden place, the first sign you notice may be a musty smell or the sight of the cotton-wool-like material appearing from below floorboards, skirtings, or wall panelling. Once you have exposed the area, the dry-rot will be obvious. The timber that has been attacked will become dark brown and cracks will have developed, breaking up the surface into squares. If touched, the wood will crumble easily.

The danger with dry rot is that it will transfer from wet to dry timbers. It does so because it is able to produce water-carrying roots that can be up to 6mm in diameter. These roots can travel anywhere, even through brickwork, until they find dry timber which they can dampen to provide ideal conditions for growth.

Dry rot
Furred, corrugated and smooth fungal growths are the tell-tale signs.

Wet rot
The areas where dry rot can develop – wherever there are damp, unventilated timbers – may also be prone to wet rot. This form of rot has yellow-brown streaks or patches, accompanied by string-like strands that grow in a fern shape on timber or damp plaster. The wood becomes brownish-black and cracks along the grain, though criss-cross cracking is sometimes possible. In timbers such as window frames and doorsteps bubbling paintwork is sometimes the first clue to wet rot. Though equally serious, wet rot is easier to treat than dry rot, because it is always found in damp timber. But if you have wet rot, you must remember that a dry-rot attack may be developing nearby

Wet rot
Wood attacked by wet rot develops streaks, then darkens and cracks.

Woodworm
All beetles attack timber in the same way. A beetle lays its eggs in cracks or crevices in the wood. Larvae hatch out and spend several years tunnelling through the wood eating, on average, about 50mm of wood each year. Hundreds of tiny tunnels can be created in this way, making badly infested timber liable to collapse.

Woodworm
A spattering of pin-sized holes is the unmistakable sign of woodworm.

Treating rot and worm

The initial cause of rot is dampness somewhere in the house structure. The first thing to do is to cure the cause of the dampness (for more information, see pp. 204-7); there is no point in treating rot until the cause is removed. Once this is done, act quickly to treat the rot.

Using a wood-repair system

If only a limited area of wood has been damaged by wet rot, eradicate the rot and repair the timber using a commercially available wood-repair system. This should contain a wood hardener, a filler, and preservative tablets to prevent further decay. A small area takes only 1 to 3 hours to treat.

Treating dry rot
Dry rot can have a devastating effect on a building, and treatment should be carried out with the utmost care and efficiency. If structural timbers have been affected, it is usually safest to leave the job to a specialist company

Timber should be cut away at least 1m beyond the edge of the dry rot. If water-carrying roots have passed through the walls, plaster and mortar joints must be hacked out. If dry rot is discovered below the floorboards and in the joists about 10cm of soil may *have to be removed. As soon as the affected area is cleared the debris should be taken away and burned. If this is not done, red spore dust could recontaminate the property. Surface spores and strands can be destroyed using a blowtorch.*

The treatment itself involves spraying a fungicide over the affected areas and 2m beyond. Two coats of fungicide are required, the second applied after the first has dried. New timber should also be coated, and sawn ends dipped in timber preservative for a few minutes *before fixing.*

Roots in the walls are killed by drilling downward-angled holes, 1cm in diameter, on both sides of the brickwork. They should be 15cm deep and drilled at 60cm intervals. The holes should be filled with fluid, which eventually soaks into the brickwork.

Any replastering should be done in three coats. The middle coat should consist of zinc oxychloride plaster 6mm thick. If walls are not replastered, they should be covered with two coats of zinc oxychloride paint.

Eradicating wet rot
Begin by digging away the worst of the rotten wood and then brush quick-drying wood hardener over the entire area, 1. Rebuild the shape of the wood with filler, 2, and finally drill holes into the surrounding wood and insert the preservative tablets, 3.

1 *Apply wood-hardener over the affected area*

Window frames
Wooden window frames are susceptible to rot, especially at the joints between the uprights and the lower rails.

Sub-floors
Look out for rot when sub-floor ventilation is poor. Woodworm can also be a problem in joists and floorboards.

Roof timbers
If the roof has been leaking, rot may have taken hold here. Woodworm also attacks roof timbers.

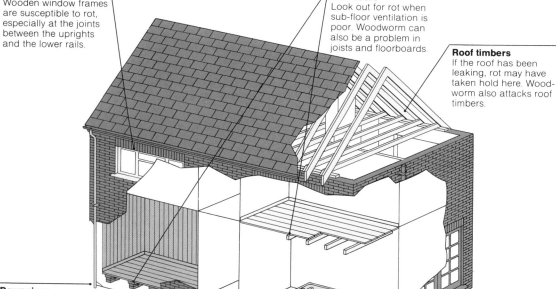

Downpipes
Leaking downpipes can cause penetrating damp, which creates conditions ideal for both wet and dry rot.

Door frames
Rot as a result of rising damp can occur here.

Kitchens
Rooms, such as kitchens and bathrooms, where condensation is a problem are often susceptible to rot.

2 *Fill the hole, putting on the filler with a filling knife*

Treating wet rot
Where there is a large amount of damage, it is best to leave treatment to a specialist company. First, any rotten timber should be cut out and the surrounding wood treated with two liberal coats of dry-rot fluid or wood preservative. New timber should also be treated with preservative (see Job 200, right). Small areas of damage can be repaired with wood filler. Where only a small amount of wood has been affected, you can make good the damage with a wood-repair system.

Treating woodworm
Woodworm attacks are most likely in rough-sawn, unplaned timber in lofts, understair cupboards, and cellars. You should also check floorboards by taking up every fourth or fifth board and inspecting the underside (for more information on taking up floorboards, see pp. 68-9). The most obvious sign of woodworm is small holes in the surface. It is often difficult to tell whether the attack has died out or whether the problem is current. A current attack can be identified by light-coloured dust *around the holes, but since structural timbers are often dirty anyway, this can be difficult to see. If you are in any doubt, treat the timber by cleaning it thoroughly and brushing or spraying it with woodworm fluid. Wear old clothes when you are applying the fluid. If you find woodworm in the loft, treat all the loft timbers. You need not treat the other timbers in your home, such as the floorboards, unless they too show signs of woodworm. If the damage is extensive, call in a specialist company to carry out the treatment.*

3 *Drill holes in the wood to take preservative tablets*

Household safety

Emergency action ◇ Types of fire-fighting equipment ◇ Danger areas in the home Children and home safety

Safety in the home is largely a matter of common sense. If you keep your electrical and gas installations in good repair, take steps to prevent fire, and make sure children are not able to reach any of the potentially dangerous items (from cans of bleach to boiling saucepans) in the home, you will avoid most accidents. But you should also be prepared for the unexpected. Find out how to turn off your electricity and gas supplies, and read the instructions on emergency action (see right) for gas and fire emergencies.

Points to remember

◇ Get to know the positions of your main gas and water supply taps and the main electricity switch, so that you can turn them off in an emergency.
◇ Keep heater air grilles clear.
◇ Never drape clothes over a heater, or leave them where they could fall on to the appliance.
◇ Always keep radiant fires at least 1m away from curtains and furniture.
◇ Make sure that flues and chimneys used for gas and other fuel-burning appliances are kept clear of soot and debris.
◇ Keep paraffin heaters where they cannot be knocked over by children or elderly people.
◇ Turn paraffin heaters off before refilling them.
Electricity
◇ Check your electrical equipment regularly, or have it checked by a qualified electrician.
◇ Make sure that plugs have the correct fuses (3 amp for up to 700 watts, 13 amp for 700 watts to 3kW).
◇ Ensure that all electrical equipment is correctly earthed.
◇ Use flex correctly, do not trail it across floors, run it under carpets, or staple it to walls or floors.
◇ Only buy new electrical equipment that bears the BEAB mark of safety.
◇ Have electric blankets serviced every two years by the manufacturer.
◇ Keep electric blankets uncreased.
Gas
◇ Take prompt action if you smell gas (see light, top).
◇ Have gas appliances serviced regularly.
◇ Always have gas appliances professionally repaired.
◇ Change old-style open-flue water heaters for modern, balanced-flue types.

Emergency action

If you suspect a gas leak
◇ Extinguish all flames including cigarettes.
◇ Open doors and windows.
◇ Turn off all gas taps.
◇ Check whether an unlit appliance has been left on.
◇ Check whether a pilot light has blown out.
◇ Do not operate electrical switches.
◇ If you suspect a leak, test for it using a fairly strong solution of concentrated washing-up liquid; this will bubble where the gas is leaking. Call the Gas Board.
◇ Have repairs carried out straight away by a gas fitter.
◇ If an obvious source of the leak cannot be found, turn off the entire supply at the gas meter and call the gas emergency service.

In case of fire
◇ Get everyone out.
◇ Close all the doors behind you.
◇ Call the fire brigade.
◇ If anyone is still in the building, tell the officer in the first fire engine.
If you are trapped in a room
◇ Check the temperature of the door handle – if it is hot, the fire is probably burning on the other side, so do not open the door.
◇ Use blankets or mats to prevent smoke from entering under the door.
◇ Even in a smoke-filled room, 50mm to 75mm immediately above the floor will be clear of smoke.
◇ Go to the window and shout for help – do not jump, wait for rescue.

Types of fire-fighting equipment

Small domestic fire extinguishers are useful, but they have a limited capacity, so they should be used promptly. For this reason it is worth installing a smoke alarm to warn you quickly of any fire. These alarms are battery-operated and can be mounted unobtrusively on a ceiling.

One of the most useful pieces of equipment is a fire blanket. Keep one in the kitchen, where it is ideal for putting out a fire of burning fat. Turn off the heat, cover the pan with the cloth, and allow the pan to cool before taking it outside. Never use water on a pan of burning fat or oil.

Fire extinguishers
Water extinguishers are coloured red. They are suitable for combustible materials such as wood and paper, but not for fires involving electricity, fat, or oil. Water comes out of a jet, which should be directed at the base of the fire and kept moving across the burning material. Damp down the embers to prevent re-ignition.

Coloured blue, dry-powder extinguishers can be used on all fires, particularly those involving oil, fat, and electricity. Choose one with at least 1kg of powder. Direct the jet of powder *at the nearest edge of the fire and drive the flames away from you with a quick, sweeping action. The material can be removed with a vacuum cleaner, although you should discard contaminated liquids and clean electrical equipment thoroughly before you attempt to use it.*

Vapourizing-liquid extinguishers are coloured green, and can be used on any small fires, particularly electrical fires. The extinguisher should weigh at least 680g. It is used in the same way as a dry-powder extinguisher.

Water extinguisher

Dry-powder extinguisher

Vaporising-liquid extinguisher

Danger areas in the home

Certain areas of the home are more prone than others to accidents. Most people know that the kitchen (see bottom of page) presents many potential dangers, but there are other parts of the home where accidents can easily happen if you allow them to do so. But by simply thinking in terms of safety and using items in the proper way, you can avoid most accidents. The important areas are electrical and gas equipment, which should be serviced regularly, and open fires.

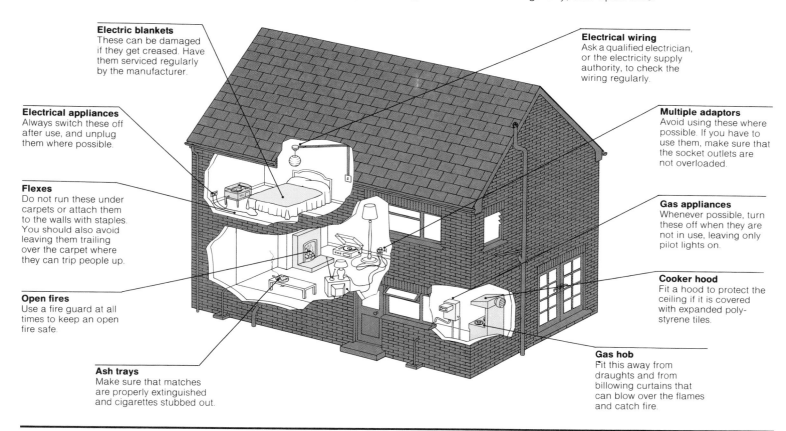

Electric blankets
These can be damaged if they get creased. Have them serviced regularly by the manufacturer.

Electrical appliances
Always switch these off after use, and unplug them where possible.

Flexes
Do not run these under carpets or attach them to the walls with staples. You should also avoid leaving them trailing over the carpet where they can trip people up.

Open fires
Use a fire guard at all times to keep an open fire safe.

Ash trays
Make sure that matches are properly extinguished and cigarettes stubbed out.

Electrical wiring
Ask a qualified electrician, or the electricity supply authority, to check the wiring regularly.

Multiple adaptors
Avoid using these where possible. If you have to use them, make sure that the socket outlets are not overloaded.

Gas appliances
Whenever possible, turn these off when they are not in use, leaving only pilot lights on.

Cooker hood
Fit a hood to protect the ceiling if it is covered with expanded poly-styrene tiles.

Gas hob
Fit this away from draughts and from billowing curtains that can blow over the flames and catch fire.

Safety in the kitchen

More accidents occur in the kitchen than in any other room in the home. This is mainly because kitchens are busy places that are full of potential hazards to children, such as hot fat, sharp knives, and jagged tins. So it is important to take special precautions in the kitchen, especially if you have young children. Design the kitchen so that hot fat and kettles of boiling water do not normally have to be carried across the room. Keep knives well out of reach of children, whether on a wall rack or in a drawer. If possible, keep young children out of the kitchen using a safety gate on the door, especially when you are preparing or cooking food. Teach children safety habits from the beginning.

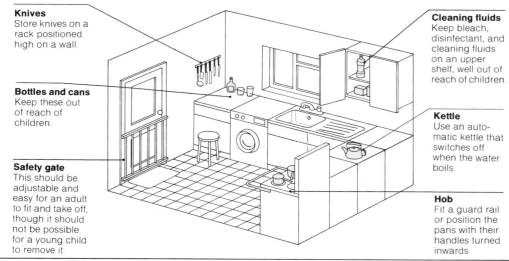

Knives
Store knives on a rack positioned high on a wall.

Bottles and cans
Keep these out of reach of children.

Safety gate
This should be adjustable and easy for an adult to fit and take off, though it should not be possible for a young child to remove it.

Cleaning fluids
Keep bleach, disinfectant, and cleaning fluids on an upper shelf, well out of reach of children.

Kettle
Use an auto-matic kettle that switches off when the water boils.

Hob
Fit a guard rail or position the pans with their handles turned inwards.

Security

Preventing burglary ◇ Types of window lock
Types of door lock ◇ Fitting a mortise
deadlock ◇ Types of alarm system

Being burgled is always a disturbing experience. It is disruptive enough to lose valuables which can be replaced with insurance money, worse to lose items of sentimental value. But the cruellest aspect of burglary is not necessarily that things are stolen. You may be the victim of vandals who smash ornaments, slash upholstery, empty food and drinks around your home, and daub the walls. The effect of this on even the most stable personality can be devastating.

You may think that you have nothing worth stealing. But a thief will not know this before breaking in and may vandalize your home in anger and frustration at discovering nothing worth removing.

There are two main ways in which you can protect your home from intruders. The first is simply a matter of thinking in terms of security and following a number of simple procedures – such as locking the door when you leave the home, cancelling deliveries if you go away, closing windows when the house is empty, and leaving on lights and a radio when you go out in the evening. The second way in which you can make your home more secure is by fitting extra equipment, such as window locks, better door locks, and even alarm systems and security grilles. If you do both of these things, you will greatly reduce the risk of your home being burgled.

Although it is impossible to make your home absolutely secure from the most determined thief, you can protect yourself and your possessions by following a few simple procedures. Mark valuable items with an ultra-violet pen, make a note of serial numbers, and take photographs of valuable items. Do not keep valuable papers such as house deeds in your home, and make sure that you are properly insured.

Security devices
There are several items that you can fit to your doors and windows to improve the security of your home. Mortise deadlocks should be fitted to the doors – the simple night latch found on most doors is not adequate as it can be forced very easily. On windows, locks should also be fitted. In addition, it may be worthwhile installing a burglar alarm or, in a high-risk area such as a basement window facing on to a street, a security grille or bars.

Care with keys
Do not leave any identification on your keys and avoid carrying keys in a purse or handbag that may contain some form of identification. Even if a lost key is returned, a copy may have been made. If you lose a key that is marked with your address, the only solution is to change the locks or lock mechanisms. Do not be lured from your home by a call, purporting to be from the police, telling you to collect your lost keys. As you go out the caller may let himself in.

Dealing with callers
Beware of confidence tricksters. Old people, in particular, should be on their guard against callers who say they are from organizations such as the local authority or the welfare department. Many such ploys are used to gain entry to homes, and even if nothing is removed on the first visit, thieves can call again to take specific items. You should leave a strong door chain in place while you establish callers' identity, if possible telephoning their office to check on them.

Another common trick is for one caller to keep you talking at the front of the house while someone else enters through the back door.

Points to remember

◇ Lock all doors and windows at night and when you leave your home unoccupied.
◇ Cancel deliveries to your home whenever you go away.
◇ Leave lights on when you go out in the evening.
◇ Fit secure locks to both doors and windows.
◇ Simple window catches and cylinder-rim night latches on doors do not give adequate protection against break-ins.
◇ Avoid louvre windows or glue the glass panes securely to the metal fittings.
◇ When buying an aluminium door, ensure that it has a good lock – it is almost impossible to fit a replacement.
◇ Make sure upstairs windows are secure – particularly if they are accessible by climbing up a tree, a drain pipe, or an extension to the house.

201

Fitting a mortise lock

A mortise deadlock is the most secure type of lock and it should be fixed to all outside doors. It fits in a slot cut in the door. When locked, the bolt shoots into another slot in the door post, and the mechanism locks the bolt in position so that it cannot be forced out. Narrow versions are available for glazed doors, and two-bolt types for back and side doors.

Fitting this type of lock involves cutting slots in both the door and the door post. If you are working on a door that is hanging in its frame, wedge it open or ask a helper to hold it steady. First mark the lock position carefully, using the lock itself as a guide. The best way to cut the slots is to remove the bulk of the wood with a hand brace containing a large-diameter bit. The slots can then be finished off with a chisel. Once the lock slot is the right size, a hole should be cut through the door to accept the key. Then the lock can be fitted and the hole for the striker plate cut. Fit the striker plate using long screws to ensure a secure fixing to the door post.

Preventing burglary

Glazed doors
There is a further security risk with any glazed door. It is worthwhile changing to a door made completely of wood, but if you want to keep the glass, replace it with strengthened glass (see p. 95) or fit a grille or bars.

Doors
A solid hardwood door fitted with a mortise deadlock is best in terms of security. Lock all doors at night and whenever you leave your home unoccupied. Do not leave door keys where they can easily be found. Avoid such places as on a string attached to the back of the letterbox, and under a paving stone, brick, flowerpot, or doormat. When moving into a new home, it is worth changing the locks.

Doorstep evidence
Items such as milk bottles, newspapers, and letters near the front door give a clear sign that a house is unoccupied. Notes left for tradesmen are also clues, so cancel all deliveries verbally whenever you go away.

Lights
You can also ask your neighbour to help by coming in each day to switch on and off lights and perhaps a radio or television set, to make the house look as if it is occupied. Alternatively, use a time switch to turn lights on and off. Light-sensitive switches, which turn on one light when it gets dark and turn it off again after a set time, are also available.

Windows
Fit window locks and keep all your windows locked at night and whenever there is no one at home. Lock even small windows – burglars will push a small child through an open window who can then open other windows or doors.

French windows
Because of their large area of glass and the way they fasten together in the middle, French windows are difficult to secure. Hinge bolts on both sides and mortise rack bolts in the middle will make them much more burglar-proof.

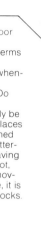

Cutting a mortise and fitting the lock and striker plate
Begin by marking the fitting position carefully, using the lock as a guide, 1. With the door held firmly in position, drill a series of holes with a hand brace using a 10mm bit. When you have drilled all the holes to the required depth, use a chisel to cut away the remaining wood, **2**, and insert the body of the lock to check that it fits. When it does, mark the size of the lock's face plate on the edge of the door and cut a rebate with the chisel. Next cut a hole for the key, **3**. You may need to use a pad saw to extend the hole into a slit of the right shape for the key. Once more, check that the lock fits and that the hole is in the correct position. Finally, mark the position of the striker plate on the door post, cut a slot in the same way that you did for the lock, and fit the plate, **4**. It is important to fit the striker plate as securely as possible.

1 Use the lock itself when marking its position on the door

2 Cut away the waste wood with a chisel

3 After drilling the key hole, check its position by inserting the lock

4 Fit the striker plate to the door post

Types of window lock

Windows provide a common route of entry and any that are accessible from the ground, via a tree, or by climbing on to a roof, should be well protected. Burglars do not normally climb in through broken glass. If they break glass it is usually in order to open a window or door through which they can then gain entry. To stop this happening, fit window locks. Alternatively, you can use immobilizers, which are attached to the existing catch and stop it being moved. The most useful types of lock and immobilizer are described in the table on the right.

You should always remove the keys from window locks, but it is advisable to leave them nearby. Put them where they cannot be reached or seen by a would-be intruder, but where they can be quickly found from the inside in an emergency such as a fire.

Immobilizers for casement windows are available for fitting both to the cockspur handle and to the casement stay. Locks for casement windows include locking bolts, and screws.

A range of devices is available for locking the two halves of a sash window together, or to prevent either half being moved. The types include acorn stops, sliding window locks, dual screws, and sash locks. When choosing from this range, make sure that you buy locks that fit the width and thickness of the window frames, and remember that some types allow you to leave the window locked slightly open, for ventilation.

French windows present other security risks that can be overcome with bolts. Mortise rack bolts should be fitted to the top and bottom of the part that opens first; hinge bolts should be fitted on both parts.

Type	Window	Fitting method	Security rating A = very good B = good C = fair	Notes
Automatic self lock	Timber casement	Screws to the surface of the frame. Some types have a wedge, for fitting to tapering frames.	B	Locks automatically when the window is closed. A simple key is used to open the lock.
Casement stay lock	Timber or metal casement	On wooden types, a mounting plate is screwed to the frame. On metal windows, the lock clamps over the stay.	C	Cheap and easy to fit, these locks can hold the window closed or partially open.
Cockspur handle lock	Metal casement	The lock screws to the frame below the handle.	B	A key-operated bolt immobilizes the handle. Some designs allow the window to be left slightly open.
Key-operated lock	Timber or metal casement	Screws to the surface of the opening frame. The securing screw heads should be plugged to prevent the lock from being removed.	B	Two should be fitted to each window – one to the top of the frame and one to the bottom. Can also be fitted to fanlights.
Mortise rack bolt	Timber casement	Fits into a hole drilled into the edge of the opening frame.	A	Operated by a special key, these bolts are excellent as secondary security devices.
Sliding wedge lock	Metal casement	Fits in the channel of the opening frame. One fixing hole needs to be drilled.	A	Because the lock is hidden and cannot be tampered with, this type is ideal for metal windows.
Stay screw	Metal casement	The locking screw passes through one of the holes in the stay and holds a bar under the stay retainer.	B	This type of lock is particularly useful for vulnerable metal fanlights.
Dual screws	Timber sash	A hole is drilled through the meeting rail of the top sash into the lower sash.	B	A bolt, secured by a special key, locks the two sashes together.
Sash lock	Timber sash	Screws on to the top edge of the lower sash.	B	Key-operated and quick-acting, this lock should be used in conjunction with conventional sash fasteners.
Screw stop	Timber sash	A hole is drilled in the side rail of the upper sash.	C	The locking stop screws into the metal plate with a special key. The window can be locked slightly open or fully closed.
Sliding window lock	Metal sliding	Screws to the edge of the inner frame.	B	A key-operated bolt locks the inner sliding window to the fixed outer frame.
Clamp-on sliding window lock	Metal sliding	Clamps on to the sliding window track.	C	A simple key clamps the lock on to the track.

Types of door lock

Outside doors provide a common route of entry for intruders and should be well protected with locks and bolts. On the front door two locks are needed – an automatic deadlocking latch to hold the door closed while you are at home, and a mortise deadlock to keep it secure when you are out. The most important feature of a deadlock is that when the key has been turned, the bolt is immobilized so that it cannot be forced back out of the door jamb. You can get either a single- or double-throw mortise deadlock. With the double-throw type, you can turn the key a second time to throw the bolt further into the staple, making it more secure. The deadlocking latch and the mortise deadlock will provide extra security if they are placed some distance apart on the door. The best positions are one-third of the way from the top and one-third of the way from the bottom of the door. Do not rely on a simple night latch to protect an outside door. It is very easy to force from the outside.

Back-door protection
Burglars are more likely to attack a rear door than the front door, so this too should be well protected. Fit a mortise deadlock with a handle.

For extra security, the back door should also be fitted with bolts. The simplest to fit are tower and barrel bolts. These are useless if they are fixed with weak screws into thin wood. In addition they can be opened easily if they are installed near glass that can be broken. Mortise rack bolts are more secure. Fit one near the top and another near the bottom of the door frame.

Outward opening doors pose another security problem. The hinges are exposed, so that it is easy to knock out the hinge pins and force the door open. You can solve this problem by fitting two hinge bolts on the hinge side of the door, one a third of the way from the top, the other a third from the bottom. With this type of fastening, a fixed bolt engages in a hole cut in the door frame, so that the door cannot be lifted off its hinges.

Type		Door	Fitting method	Security rating A = very good B = good C = fair	Notes
Cylinder rim night latch		Timber front door	Screws to the back face of the door. A box to take the fastened bolt is screwed to the door post.	C	This type of fastener can easily be opened by an intruder; it should only be used as a latch in conjunction with a deadlock.
Deadlocking rim latch		Timber front door	Screws to the back face of the door A box to take the fastened bolt is screwed to the door post.	A	Turning the key from the inside or outside deadlocks the bolt and the internal handle. The latch should conform to British Standards specifications.
Hinge bolt		Timber door that opens outwards	Fits in a hole drilled in the edge of the door on the hinge side. Should be fitted in pairs.	B	Prevents doors from being forced open on the hinge side when the hinge pins are exposed.
Mortise deadlock		Timber front door	Fits into a slot chiselled in the door edge. A slot for the bolt must also be made in the door post.	A	This type of key-operated lock can give excellent security, especially if a five-lever type is fitted.
Narrow-stile mortise deadlock		Glazed timber front door	Fits into a slot chiselled in the door edge. A slot for the bolt must also be made in the door post.	A	Provides the same high level of security as a standard mortise deadlock.
Mortise rack bolt		Timber door that can be bolted from inside; French windows	Fits into holes drilled into the head and foot of the door, so that the bolt shoots into the head of the frame and the sill.	B	This is a neat-looking bolt, operated by a special key.
Sliding door lock		Sliding aluminium alloy patio doors	Screws to top and bottom of the fixed frame.	B	A key-operated bolt prevents the door from sliding or from being lifted off its track.
Two-bolt mortise sash lock		Timber back and side entrance doors	Fits into a slot chiselled into door edge	A	In addition to a key-operated lock, this type has a springbolt operated by a handle. It gives the same level of protection as a conventional mortise deadlock.

Other security equipment

There are several items that you can fit in addition to window and door locks to improve the security of your home. Door viewers and door chains can protect you when answering the door to unknown callers. The various security grilles and bars that are available offer protection from all but the most determined thief and are particularly useful in areas where the risk of criminal activity is high. Viewers and chains are easy to fit. Bars are best fitted by a professional.

Door chains
A simple chain may deter some burglars, but since it is only as strong as its securing screws, it is not difficult to force most chains by kicking the door. But door chains do have some value and if you are going to fit one, use long screws rather than the small ones that are often supplied. Chains should also be fitted in a way that makes it impossible for someone on the outside to reach through the gap and take the chain off. Some chains are lockable and some models also incorporate an alarm.

Door viewers
A simple barrel tube containing a one-way lens giving a panoramic view allows you to identify callers before you open the door. Buy a viewer that is the right length for the thickness of the door. Fitting is simple. A hole is drilled through the door and the two halves of the viewer are slipped through and screwed together.

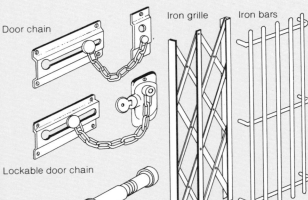

Door chain

Lockable door chain

Door viewer

Iron grille   Iron bars

Grilles and bars
Mild steel bars can be fixed externally or internally. If they are used externally, the ends of the bars should be embedded 50mm to 75mm deep in the brickwork. Inside, bars should be attached to a flat metal frame which can be bolted to the brickwork around the window. The bars themselves need to be strong enough to withstand forcing. A locksmith will be able to advise you on your own particular requirements, but you will usually need bars at least 15mm square or 15mm in diameter, spaced at intervals of 125mm.
Most security grilles are made to measure by a locksmith. They are made from expanded metal mesh welded to a steel frame which is bolted to the inside wall. Scrolled grilles, fixed in the same way, are more attractive but less secure.

Types of alarm system

Further protection for your home can be provided by a burglar alarm system. You should fit an alarm in addition to window and door locks. It will not stop someone from breaking in, but it may make them go away quickly or alert you to the fact that your home is being broken into.

An alarm system operates from a central control panel and works from the electrical supply or from a battery. Usually, you set the system to operate as you leave home. There is a delay of about a minute to allow you to set the alarm and leave, and there is a similar delay to let you switch it off when you return. Many systems also incorporate a second switch, located in a hidden position inside the house, from which the alarm can also be operated.

A common problem with alarms is that they often sound by accident – because they have been set incorrectly, because they have been activated by children or animals, or because the wind has blown open windows or doors. An alarm will only be effective if you and your neighbours always take it seriously.

Magnetic alarm systems
With the most elaborate alarm systems, the wiring connects to a series of magnetic contacts attached to doors and openable windows. One half of the contact is fixed to the window and the other half to the frame. If the window is opened the two parts separate, the electrical contact is broken, and the alarm bell on the outside of the building is instantly activated.
As a second line of defence against an intruder who manages to get in without sounding the alarm, magnetic contacts can also be fitted to internal doors. In addition, alarm-activating pressure pads can be installed under the carpet at points where a burglar is likely to walk.
There are many magnetic alarm systems available, some of which you can fit yourself. They are not difficult to put in but care must be taken to conceal all the wiring, pressure pads, and magnetic contacts.

Infra-red alarm systems
Another type of alarm system, which you can fit instead of, or as well as, a magnetic type, uses infra-red rays to throw an unseen barrier over a wide area. Similar alarms are available that use ultra-sonic waves and microwaves. The bell sounds when the barrier is broken. Some of these alarms can be triggered by draughts and normal air movements, although the best models are far more dependable.

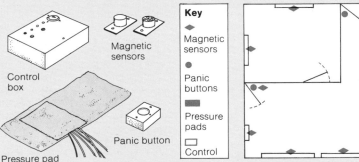

Control box

Magnetic sensors

Pressure pad

Panic button

Key
- ◆ Magnetic sensors
- ● Panic buttons
- ▬ Pressure pads
- ▢ Control

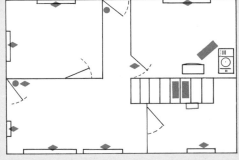

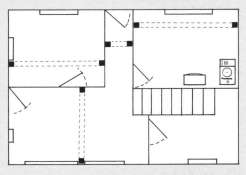

The home tool kit

Workshop equipment ◇ Measuring and marking tools
Cutting tools ◇ Hammers, nails, tacks and pins
Screws, screwdrivers and wallplugs ◇ Drills, chisels
and planes ◇ Scrapers, sanders, filling knives
and trowels ◇ Brushes, rollers and paint pads
Pliers, pincers, spanners and wrenches

A comprehensive, all-purpose DIY tool kit is essential if you
plan to tackle your own home improvements. This chapter
specifies the recommended tools for a basic home tool kit
and catalogues them according to function. Together with
identification photographs, you will find information on how
to use individual tools, the range of sizes and designs available, and advice on caring, storage and safety. You may
need to supplement this basic kit with more specialist tools
as you progress to more complicated jobs.

Workshop equipment

A workshop or working area – whether a shed in the garden, a corner of the garage, or simply part of a room in the home – is the ideal place to store the tools needed for home maintenance and improvement. The basic essentials for a work area are good light night and day, plenty of storage space, a work bench, and a vice or clamps to hold the work steady. The area should also be free of damp. A number of socket outlets just above bench height will be needed for power tools, and in the winter, heating will be needed. A fire extinguisher positioned near the door is a worthwhile safety precaution in the workshop.

A fixed worktop bench with cupboards or shelf space below is ideal for one end of the workshop. Bench-mounted tools, such as a drill stand or a small grinder, can then be permanently mounted. It is useful to fix a vice to one end of the bench. If you do not have the space for a permanent workbench, a free-standing, folding bench is very useful and easily stored.

Benches

Folding bench
The portable bench incorporates full-width jaws that act as a vice. The bench can also be used as a simple table, trestle, or saw horse. The folded size is 800mm × 725mm × 190mm.

Workbench
This sturdy bench is fitted with a vice and includes storage for tools. A useful size is 1.5m × 600mm × 810mm.

Vices and clamps

Woodworker's vice
Timber and other materials need to be held still when they are being sawn, drilled, or otherwise prepared. A bench-mounted vice is ideal for this. The best type for general purpose is the woodworker's vice. Some types are permanently mounted to the bench ; others can be clamped on and removed when necessary. The jaws are usually 175mm or 200mm wide, with an opening capacity of about 200mm.

Clamps (or Cramps)
These are used to secure objects to the bench when you are working on them. The most common are G-clamps, very versatile clamps with a large adjustable screw. The strongest types have ribbed malleable iron or dropped forged-steel frames. The fully open sizes range from 20mm to 300mm.

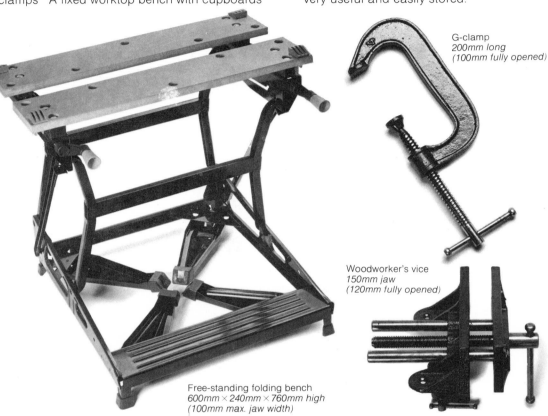

G-clamp
*200mm long
(100mm fully opened)*

Woodworker's vice
*150mm jaw
(120mm fully opened)*

Free-standing folding bench
*600mm × 240mm × 760mm high
(100mm max. jaw width)*

Workshop storage

Hand tools
Store in accessible racks. Use plastic or wire tool-hanging clips fixed on to sheets of perforated hardboard, or make your own wooden racks.

Saws, hammers, and pincers
Hang on simple racks made by driving nails or dowels into battens fixed above the bench. Most will hang over one peg, but hammers have to span two pegs.

Chisels, files and screwdrivers
Store in a simple rack. Nail a strip of plywood, about 75mm wide, to the top edge of a timber batten that can be fixed horizontally to the wall. Drill holes in the plywood so that the blades of the tools pass through, and the handles are supported.

Power tools
Cover bench-mounted tools with cloths. Store portable tools in lockable cupboards or on shelves. Keep the cables wrapped around the tools when they are not in use.

Cutters, blades, and tool attachments
Drill and auger bits are best stored upright in wood blocks drilled with holes of suitable sizes. If you have a large number of twist drill bits, store them in a cabinet with small drawers made of clear plastic, to allow the contents to be seen.

Hardware
Store nails, screws, nuts, and bolts in jars or labelled tins. One method is to fix the lids of screw-top jars under shelves, allowing the glass jars to hang down with the contents clearly visible. Cutlery-type wooden trays or plastic drawer units can also be used. Adjustable shelving is useful for storing larger materials and paint cans. Various size plastic trays, some with covers, which hang in slots on a wall-mounted board are also available.

Measuring and marking tools

Accurate measuring and marking up is essential. It is particularly important in woodwork, but is also vital in decorating and other work. The most useful measuring and marking tools are: a good retractable measuring tape, a steel rule, a try square for marking right angles, and a good quality spirit level. Treat these tools very carefully – if they are damaged they will become inaccurate. Check them regularly for accuracy, and store them in a dry place. Buy the best quality measuring and marking tools you can afford. Make sure that wooden and metal parts are firmly attached.

Tapes and rules

Flexible steel tape
Probably the most useful measuring tool, this can be used for sizing many different materials. Tapes are available with both metric and imperial markings, or with metric units only. Buy one with a thumb lock. A top sight is also useful. This is a plastic window in the case which allows an internal measurement to be read off directly, without it being necessary to add the width to the dimension shown on the tape. The most useful all-round length is 3m.

Steel rule
This is a very precise rule for measuring and laying out work. It is marked with exact metric measurements, usually down to 0.5mm. Although unmarked steel straight edges are available, you can use a steel rule as a straight edge for cutting and marking. Lengths range from 150mm to 2m.

Folding rule
This can be used in confined spaces where it is difficult to use a one-piece rule. Traditional folding rules are made of boxwood, but modern folding rules are often made of engineering plastic. The most common type is a four-section rule, although there are also steel rules with a single fold. Lengths range from 300mm to 2m.

Levelling tools

Spirit level
This tool is used to determine whether or not a surface is level. It should be as long as possible. When the surface is horizontal, the bubble in the vial should fall between the two lines. There should also be vials for checking verticals, and some method of adjusting the vials. It is useful if the body of the level is cut away, so that you can read the vial either above or below eye level. The best modern levels have aluminium or plastic bodies. Sizes range from 75mm to 2m.

Plumb bob
This is a useful aid for marking vertical lines. It is a torpedo-shaped brass or steel weight used with a chalked line to mark verticals on a wall, particularly when hanging wallpaper. Weights available range from about 43g.

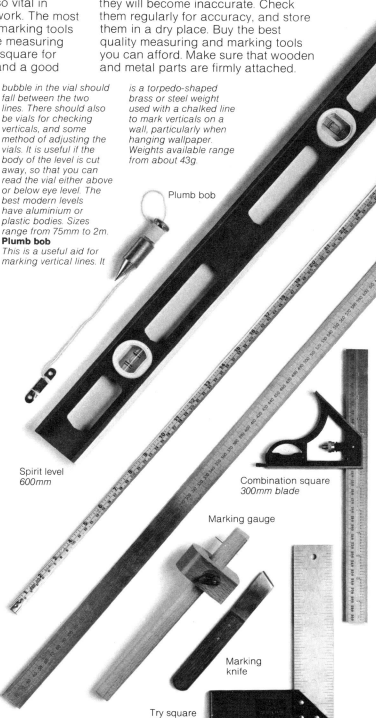

Plumb bob

Spirit level
600mm

Marking gauge

Marking knife

Try square
200mm

Retractable
steel ruler

1m steel rule

1m Folding wooden rule

Combination square
300mm blade

Squares

Try square
Essential for marking square ends across a length of timber, there are both traditional try squares with a rosewood stock at right-angles to a tempered steel blade, and modern designs with a plastic stock. On the best try squares, the blade extends into the stock and is firmly riveted to it on both sides. This makes it less likely that the square will go out of true. Both inside and outside edges form a 90-degree angle. Sizes range from 150mm to 300mm.

Combination square
This is a very versatile measuring and marking tool, which can be used as a steel rule, try square, mitre square, and level. It consists of a steel rule, clamped in a square head, which is often fitted with a level vial. It can check levels, the depths of mortises, and angles. The usual blade length is 300mm.

Marking tools

Marking knife
For precise marking, use this knife instead of a pencil. It has an angled steel blade, which is ground and sharpened on one side only, like a chisel. A trimming knife can be used when a marking knife is not available. The flat side of the blade can run against a try square or a rule. The usual size is 150mm.

Marking gauge
Use this gauge for marking lines parallel to the edge or end of a piece of timber or board. The line is marked by a steel point fixed close to the end of a stem, on which an adjustable stock can be locked at the required distance from the point. The stock is locked in place by a metal screw on the side. On some models, there is a graduated scale on the stem. This shows the distance from the stock to the point. Sizes range from 160mm to 240mm.

Saws and other

Saws are the most versatile cutting tools, particularly for cutting wood. They come in a variety of types and sizes. Items such as scissors and trimming knives also perform many useful functions.

Saws have very sharp teeth. The size of these affects the fineness and speed of cut – more teeth give a finer but slower cut. Saws are sold in point sizes. There is always one tooth less per 25mm than the point-size number, so a 10-point saw has nine teeth every 25mm.

When using a saw, grip it firmly. Support the wood and start the cut by drawing the blade backwards in an upright position. Saw steadily and rhythmically, using the full length of the blade, and only apply pressure on the down stroke. Keep your shoulder in line with the blade and support the waste end to prevent splitting.

General-purpose saws

Panel saw
This all-round handsaw is used to cut large planks, boards, or panels to size. It has cross-cut teeth, and the most useful size has a 550mm blade and 10-point teeth. Lengths range from 500mm to 550mm.

Cross-cut saw
With a larger blade than the panel saw this tool is ideal for cutting timber across the grain. The usual length is 600mm, and 7- and 8-point teeth are available.

Rip saw
The chisel-shaped teeth have their edges almost at right-angles to the length of the saw. This enables the teeth to cut quickly along the grain of the timber. The usual length is 650mm, with 5-point teeth.

Tenon saw
This saw has a straight, rectangular blade with a stiffened back. It is used for cutting wood accurately, especially when making joints. Lengths range from 200mm to 300mm, with teeth from 11 to 20 point.

Saws for intricate cutting

Coping saw
The coping saw can make curved cuts in wood and plastic. The blade is narrow and has very fine 14-point teeth. The rectangular frame keeps the blade taut, and the tension is regulated by turning the handle. It can be adjusted to cut in any direction by turning the blade pins. The usual length is 160mm.

Fret saw
For cutting tight curves in wood, plastic and glass fibre, the fret saw is ideal. The blade is under tension in the 290mm-deep frame. It is 125mm long and is set to cut on the down stroke. Teeth sizes range from 16 to 32 point.

Pad saw
This saw can cut small holes in places such as keyholes, where the saw frame makes using a coping saw impossible. Its simple handle clamps on to the narrow, tapering blade. Blade lengths range from 125mm to 375mm, teeth sizes from 8 to 10 point.

Saws for cutting metal

Hacksaw
For cutting metals and plastics, use a hacksaw. Modern types have a pistol-grip handle and an adjustable bow frame to accept different blades. These are fitted with the teeth facing forwards. The latest blades have

Coping saw
150mm

Tenon saw
230mm

Panel saw
560mm

Pad saw
200mm blade

Rip saw
710mm

Cross-cut saw
685mm

cutting tools

hard teeth, but have none of the brittleness of old-style hacksaw blades. Hacksaws are available with 200mm, 250mm, and 300mm blades with 14-18-, 24-, and 32-point teeth.

Junior hacksaw
This saw is ideal for cutting metal and plastic in confined spaces. The traditional type is made from a one-piece spring-tension frame. To fit a blade, insert one end into the frame slot, then press this against the edge of a bench to fit the other end. The usual length is 150mm, with 32-point teeth.

Power saws

Jigsaw
A versatile power saw, the jigsaw will make straight, curved, or scroll cuts in timber, man-made boards, metals, plastics, and many other materials. Jigsaw attachments are available for some power drills, but self-powered jigsaws are better balanced and more powerful. The straight, narrow blade is about 100mm long and moves up and down at about 3,000 strokes per minute. Some saws are single speed, while others offer a slower speed of 2,400 strokes per minute, which is ideal for cutting plastics and metals. There are also continuously variable speed models which will cut as slowly as 500 strokes a minute. Some models have a pendulum blade action, which increases the speed of cut and also allows the saw to cut thicker metals. Different blades are needed for cutting different materials.

Circular saw
This power saw is useful for fast, straight cutting of timber, man-made boards, plastics and laminated boards, sheet metals, thicker soft metals, masonry and ceramic tiles. Special blades are required for some materials. The circular blade revolves at between 3,000 and 5,000 rpm. Upper and lower blade guards should be fitted for safety. Circular-saw attachments are available for power drills, but some drills are not really powerful enough to drive them adequately. Common blade diameters are 125mm, 155mm, and 185mm. Maximum cutting depths range from 35mm for the smallest blade size, to 62mm for the 185mm blade. As a safety precaution, all circular saws should be fitted with upper and lower blade guards before connecting to the electricity supply.

Other cutting tools

Scissors
General-purpose scissors are particularly suitable for work with fabrics and for decorating. Paper-hanger's scissors for wallpapering are available in 255mm, 280mm, and 305mm blade lengths.

Trimming knife
One of the most useful general-purpose tools, the trimming knife can be used for many tasks, including cutting soft floor tiles, trimming wallpaper, and scoring lines on most materials. Replaceable, razor-sharp blades are held in an easy-grip handle. The handle is often in two halves, which should be separated to change a blade. This also provides a place for storing the blades. Some models have retractable blades. A range of straight and curved blade shapes is available.

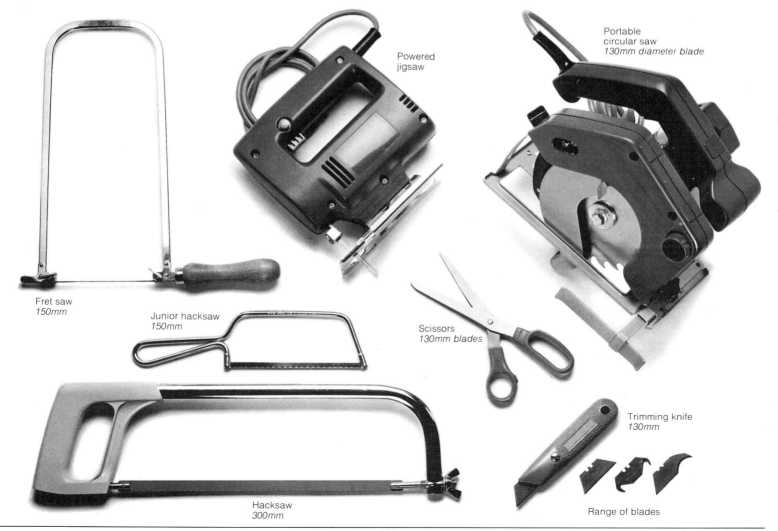

Fret saw
150mm

Junior hacksaw
150mm

Hacksaw
300mm

Powered jigsaw

Portable circular saw
130mm diameter blade

Scissors
130mm blades

Trimming knife
130mm

Range of blades

Hammers

There are several types of hammer that can be used for a number of different jobs, from tapping in a tiny panel pin to breaking up concrete. They are generally sold by the weight of their metal heads. The heavier the head, the more pressure you will get. A 280g hammer is a useful, easily handled average weight for the majority of jobs. A claw hammer is the most useful general-purpose hammer, while a cross-pein hammer is good for tapping in panel pins. Sledge-hammers are necessary for work on masonry, and wooden mallets are often useful in carpentry.

When using a hammer, hold it firmly at the shaft, watching the nail carefully. Regularly sand down the hammer's face to ensure that the head does not slip. Be careful when selecting hammers; inexpensive tools may seem attractive, but often they will not stand repeated use.

General-purpose hammers

Claw hammer
This is ideal for inserting and pulling out nails. The "straight-claw" hammer can be used to lever up floorboards. Claw hammers are available with shafts of wood, glass fibre, or steel, in weights up to 570g. They often have easy-grip, shock-absorbing rubber sleeves. The claw should taper to a fine "V" so that small panel pins, as well as large nails, can be extracted.

Cross-pein hammer
This type of hammer is used for general carpentry work. The tapered head (the pein) is useful to get into awkward corners to tap nails home or for starting small panel pins. The hammer has a wooden shaft and head weights up to 450g are available.

Pin hammer
A lightweight version of the cross-pein hammer, the pin hammer is used for delicate work such as knocking panel pins into picture frames. It is available in head weights of up to 110g.

Specialized hammers and mallets

Club hammer
Used for heavy-duty work, this hammer is ideal for demolishing walls or for driving bolster chisels. Wear gloves and goggles when doing this type of work. The sledge-hammer is a larger version of the club hammer and can be used two-handed.

Upholsterer's hammer
This is used mainly to drive in upholstery tacks, although some types also have claws for extraction. The head is usually magnetized so that tacks can be held and accurately positioned. The hammer is available in weights up to approximately 200g.

Mallet
There are several types, but a carpenter's mallet is the most useful, especially for driving chisels. Carpenter's mallets come in head widths up to 175mm.

Punches

Nail punch
Punches are used with a hammer to drive nail heads below the surface. They are available with tip diameters from 0.5mm to 4.5mm.

Pin push
A pin push is used for driving thin pins without a hammer. The pin is placed in the magnetized barrel and is driven home by pumping the spring-loaded handle.

Nail punch
2.5mm diameter

Pin push
No 14-16 pin gauge

Claw hammer
560gms

Cross-pein hammer *283gms*

Pin hammer *115gms*

Upholsterer's hammer *170gms*

Club hammer *1.5kgs*

Wooden mallet *130mm head*

Nails, tacks, and pins

Nails provide permanent fixings which join together materials such as wood. An extremely strong joint can be made if the right type of nail is used correctly.

A wide range of nails is available, suitable for many different tasks, ranging from woodwork and roofing to upholstery. Nails are specified by their name and their length in millimetres; as the length increases, so normally does the thickness. Nails can be bought loose, in 500g or 1kg bags, or in smaller plastic packs.

Nails are usually driven straight in. But if they are hammered in at an angle, they will be less likely to be pushed out, giving extra strength.

As nails can split wood, drill small pilot holes in delicate work, or nip off the nail points to blunt them. Nailing near the end of a piece of wood can cause a split. It is best to cut the wood oversize and trim it after nailing to the exact size you require.

Round wire nail
This is the most common nail of all. It is used in rough work, where strength, rather than appearance, is important. Most types are made of plain steel, which can rust, although galvanized versions are available. Lengths range from 20mm to 150mm.

Oval wire nail
This type is useful where appearance matters. The head can be driven below the surface, and the nail is unlikely to split the wood if inserted with the larger side parallel with the grain. Lengths range from 20mm to 150mm.

Cut-clasp nail
Rectangular in section, these nails are used where strength is impor-
tant. They are driven into pre-drilled holes in wood or brick. Lengths range from 50mm to 100mm.

Cut floor brads
These nails secure floorboards. They have L-shaped heads which are difficult to strike correctly, but they are unlikely to split the wood. They are made of steel and are available in 50mm, 60mm, and 65mm lengths.

Masonry nails
These can be driven directly into brick or block walls. Smaller, hardened-steel pins are available for tasks such as hanging pictures. Masonry nails are available in a range of lengths from 20mm to 100mm.

Clout nails
Used for fixing roofing felt and for some types
of fencing, clout nails are galvanized and are available in aluminium, copper, silicon bronze, or zinc. They are distinguished by the noticeably large heads and small shanks.

Wiggle nails
Sometimes called corrugated fasteners, these are used for frame construction, and can also be used to make butt joints in wooden panels.

Tacks
Several different types of tack are available. Those used for upholstery work have a bright, domed head, while those intended for securing carpets have a smaller steel head.

Staples
Wire staples can fix wire
to wood and are particularly useful for fence construction. Electrician's staples can be used with either flex or cable.

Glazing sprigs
These small sprigs are used with putty to secure glass in wooden frames.

Hardboard nails
Made both with a copper finish and in steel, these nails have diamond-shaped heads and come in 20mm and 25mm lengths.

Panel pins
These very useful pins can fix mouldings and thin sheets of plywood to battens. They are also ideal for making picture frames. They are available in plain and non-rusting steel and in lengths ranging from 12mm to 50mm.

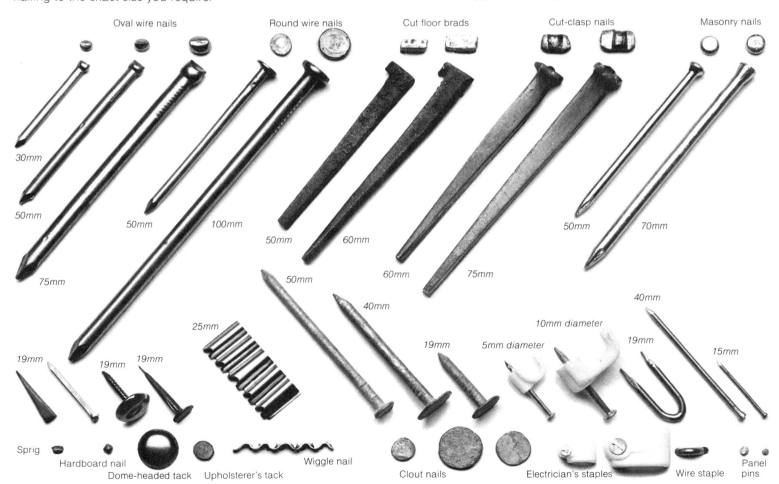

Oval wire nails — 30mm, 50mm, 75mm, 50mm, 100mm

Round wire nails — 50mm, 60mm

Cut floor brads — 60mm, 75mm

Cut-clasp nails — 50mm, 70mm

Masonry nails — 50mm, 40mm, 19mm

25mm — 19mm — 19mm — 19mm — 40mm — 10mm diameter — 5mm diameter — 19mm — 15mm

Sprig

Hardboard nail

Dome-headed tack

Upholsterer's tack

Wiggle nail

Clout nails

Electrician's staples

Wire staple

Panel pins

Screwdrivers

Screwdrivers are essential for everyday maintenance and construction tasks around the home. Three or four different sizes will probably fit most of the screws used, but there are two types of screw head – single-slot and cross-head – so you will need six to eight screwdrivers in your home tool kit.

When using a screwdriver, make sure that the blade fits well in the screw head and keep the tool vertical. A ratchet, or pump-action, screwdriver is easier and faster to use, but you need to keep one hand on the shank to stop it slipping. The traditional bulbous screwdriver handles in wood or plastic are comfortable to grip and less likely to cause blisters than other designs. Sets of screwdriver bits can be bought with a single handle, often with a ratchet mechanism. Store screwdrivers in a drawer or hanging in a rack, and sharpen single-slot screwdrivers on an oilstone.

General-purpose screwdrivers

Single-slot screwdrivers
There are several different designs for ordinary single-slot screws. The tips are flared and may be ground on the sides, while the handles may be rounded, fluted, or rubber-covered. Blades vary in length, but generally, the larger the tip, the longer the blade. A range of tip widths will be required to fit the usual screw gauges. Use a 5mm tip for No. 4 and No. 6 screws, a 6mm tip for No. 8, an 8mm tip for No. 10, and a 9mm tip for No. 12 and No. 14.

Cross-head screwdrivers
Various patterns of screws are available and it is important that the tips fit well to give a good grip. Otherwise the screws will get damaged and be difficult to remove. Of the different patterns, the Supadriv screwdriver (which will also drive Pozidriv screws) is the most useful. Like the older Phillips type, they are available in three sizes, 1, 2, and 3 point.

Stubby screwdrivers
With their short blades, these are ideal for use in confined spaces. They are available in a range of tip sizes in both single-slot and cross-head styles. You can also get them with a T-bar for extra leverage. The usual blade lengths are 25mm and 38mm.

Ratchet and impact screwdrivers

Ratchet screwdrivers
The advantage of these tools is that they allow you to drive in a screw without altering your grip. They are available in single-slot and cross-head styles. A thumb slider control changes the action to drive clockwise or anti-clockwise as well as to remain fixed in one direction. Ratchet screwdrivers are available in blade sizes from 75mm to 150mm.

Spiral-ratchet screwdrivers
These pump-action screwdrivers are designed to work by pressure on the handle, giving a very fast action to the spiral grooves along the length of the blade. For final tightening the screwdriver can be locked to give a standard screwdriver action. The spiral can also be locked closed, to give a simple ratchet action. This type of screwdriver has a chuck, allowing different bits to be fitted. Blade lengths range from 240mm to 711mm.

Offset screwdrivers
These give more leverage to drive screws in inaccessible places. The blades are made of steel and cranked in shape, with the ends forming the screwdriver tips. They are double-ended, and suitable for cross-head or single-slot screws.

Blade sizes range from 75mm to 150mm.

Impact drivers
Use these for freeing seized screws and nuts. You strike the handle with a hammer and the mechanism creates pressure to free a tight fitting. The most common size is 140mm.

Electrical screwdrivers

Electrician's screwdrivers
These have thin blades with parallel tips, so that they can turn a screw at the bottom of a hole. The handles are well insulated in heavy-duty plastic and some blades are insulated in a plastic sleeve. Blade sizes range from 75mm to 250mm.

Mains tester
This is used to test electrical currents. It has an insulated blade and handle, and features a neon bulb which lights up if the blade touches a live terminal.

Screwdriver bits

Power screwdriver bits
These are used to drive screws with electric drills featuring variable-speed controls. Single-slot and cross-head bits are available and they have hexagonal shanks to give a non-twist grip in the chuck. Some single-slot bits can slip, so it is best to choose bits with a sliding sleeve to hold the screw in the slot.

Screwdriver bits
These bits are used in a hand brace to tighten or free large screws. They are often reversible, with different-sized blades on each end. Single-slot and cross-head types are available.

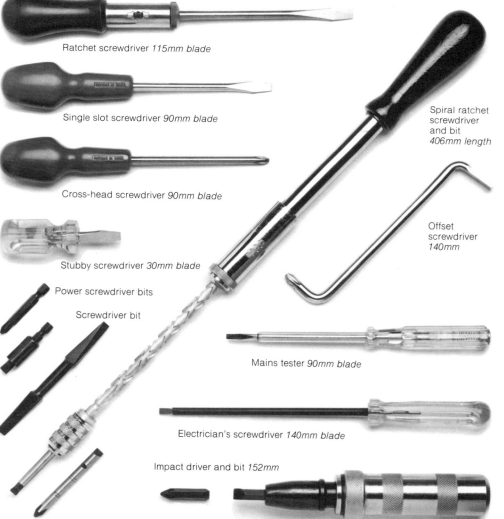

Ratchet screwdriver 115mm blade

Single slot screwdriver 90mm blade

Cross-head screwdriver 90mm blade

Stubby screwdriver 30mm blade

Power screwdriver bits

Screwdriver bit

Spiral ratchet screwdriver and bit 406mm length

Offset screwdriver 140mm

Mains tester 90mm blade

Electrician's screwdriver 140mm blade

Impact driver and bit 152mm

Screws and wall plugs

Screws produce really firm, strong joints between pieces of timber. They are used in high quality woodwork, and are the best choice when components may have to be dismantled. Joints are stronger with screws than nails because the turning action draws the pieces together. They are also essential for fixing metal items, such as hinges and brackets, to wood.

It is important to choose screws of the right length. If possible, use a screw that is three times as long as the thickness of the wood being attached. But make sure that the screw is not so long that it will pierce the reverse side of the work. A screw that is too thick may split the wood. As a general rule, a screw should not exceed 1/10th of the width of the wood. If you are fitting a hinge, the screw size will be limited by the size of the holes in the fitting.

When using screws, keep them a distance of five times their diameter from the side edge of the wood and ten times their diameter apart. To minimize the risk of the wood splitting, drill pilot holes for the threads and clearance holes for the shanks.

Screws

Countersunk-head screws
The heads lie flush with the surface after fixing. These screws are used to join pieces of wood and for fittings such as hinges. They are available in both single-slot and cross-head designs. Lengths available range from 6mm to 150mm, gauges from 0 to 20 in single slot; the range in cross-head is more restricted. The usual materials are plain steel, plated steel, and various corrosion-free metals.

Round-head screws
The heads remain above the surface. These screws are used mainly for attaching metal fittings to wood. Lengths range from 6mm to 75mm; gauges from 0 to 14. The usual materials are steel and brass.

Raised countersunk-head screws
These attractive screws can be used either alone or with screw cups. Lengths range from 9.5mm to 50mm; gauges from 4 to 10. They are usually steel or brass.

Chipboard screws
The thread is deeper and wider than usual, and runs the whole length of the screw. This makes it ideal for man-made boards and soft wood. Lengths range from 13mm to 45mm; gauges from 4 to 10.

Wood-thread dowel screws
These double-ended screws are used to attach two wooden items invisibly. Lengths range from 25mm to 50mm; gauges from 6 to 12.

Mirror screws
These brass wood screws have a screw-on decorative chromium or satin-finish dome head.

Self-tapping screws
These cut a thread in metal when driven into a pilot hole. Lengths are from 6mm to 50mm; gauges from 4 to 10.

Plugs and toggles

Fibre wallplugs
These plugs can be used in brick, concrete, and masonry. The length of the plug should suit the threaded part of the screw; the thickness should suit the screw gauge.

Plastic wallplugs
These are suitable for the same materials, but are able to accept a wider range of screw sizes than fibre plugs. Different types are available for solid and cavity walls. The plug should suit the screw length.

Aluminium wallplugs
Suitable for masonry or wood, these are available in strips that you cut to length.

Rivet anchor
This can be used with ordinary screws. As the screw is tightened, the anchor flattens in the cavity.

Rubber-sleeved anchor
Useful in thin cavity walls and hollow doors, this anchor can only be used with the screw supplied. The rubber plug expands as the screw is tightened.

Spring toggle
This makes fixings into lath and plaster, into low-strength plaster-board and panelling. It can be used only with the screw supplied. The arms are pushed through a pre-drilled hole and spring apart in the cavity.

Gravity toggle
This can be used only for fixing to vertical surfaces. When passed through a pre-drilled hole, a bar swings down to form a right-angled fixing.

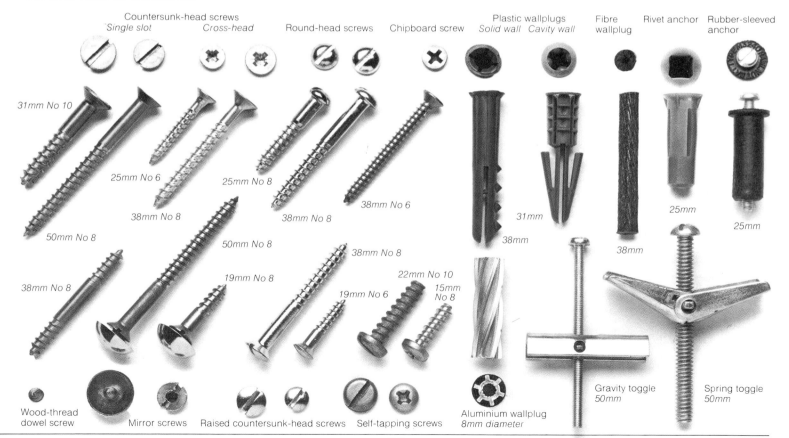

Countersunk-head screws
Single slot — Cross-head
Round-head screws
Chipboard screw
Plastic wallplugs — Solid wall — Cavity wall
Fibre wallplug
Rivet anchor
Rubber-sleeved anchor

31mm No 10
25mm No 6
38mm No 8
50mm No 8
38mm No 8

25mm No 8
50mm No 8
19mm No 8
38mm No 8

38mm No 6
38mm No 8

38mm No 8
19mm No 6
22mm No 10
15mm No 8

31mm
38mm

25mm
38mm
25mm

Wood-thread dowel screw
Mirror screws
Raised countersunk-head screws
Self-tapping screws
Aluminium wallplug 8mm diameter
Gravity toggle 50mm
Spring toggle 50mm

Drills

Drills can be used to make holes in a variety of materials, such as wood, masonry, and plastic. The simple hand drill is slow, but it is easy to control and is essential when no electric power is available. It is easy to use and can make holes in both wood and metal. But for masonry work you will need either a breast drill or a power drill, while a push drill is required for plastics. Hand drills are not expensive, but only a limited range of bits is available for them, mostly for drilling into wood.

Power drills are more expensive, but are quicker and much more versatile. With the correct bits, they can make holes in almost any material, and a variety of attachments, such as sanding discs, can also be fitted for specific jobs.

Both hand and power drills need even, steady pressure, otherwise you will get jagged-edged holes. It is worth the extra expense of buying good quality bits, as these will stay sharper and be less likely to break during use.

Drills and braces

Hand drill
Used to drill holes in wood and metal, this drill is operated by a drive handle and a gear wheel, which gives variable speeds for different materials. More modern designs have enclosed gears, so that they do not get dusty. Some models have a detachable side handle which can be used when extra grip is needed. The chuck takes twist drill bits up to 8mm in diameter.

Hand brace
To drill large-diameter holes in wood, use a hand brace. This turns by means of a rotating frame that applies sustained power to the drill bit. With the appropriate bit it can also drive and withdraw screws. Different sizes of brace are available, and the best types have a ratchet action so that the brace can be used in confined spaces.

Breast drill
This is a larger version of the hand drill and it can make holes in wood, metal, and masonry. It has a curved, saddle-shaped plate, which you can lean on for extra pressure.

Push drill
This is a pump-action drill for making small-diameter holes – usually pilot holes for screws in wood. It takes bits, called drill points, which range in size from 2mm to 4.4mm.

Electric drill
An electric drill can be used on a variety of materials. For general hand-held use, choose a drill that offers 350-500 watts power with at least two speed settings. The most common chuck capacities are 10mm or 13mm, and the latter is also the largest hole that this type of drill can make in steel. Additional features available on electric drills include a high-speed hammer action that is very useful for drilling hard materials. A reversing switch is also available on some models. Attachments, such as sanders and wire brushes, are made.

Drill bits

The part of a drill that actually makes the holes is called the bit. A limited range of bits is available for hand drills and there is a much more varied range for use with power drills. The range includes twist drill bits for drilling wood and metal; dowel bits for wood; masonry bits; countersink bits; auger and spade bits for making large holes; and screwdriver bits.

Hole borers

Bradawl
This tool is used to make starting holes for screws.

Gimlet
With its spiral shaft, this can also be used to make starting holes.

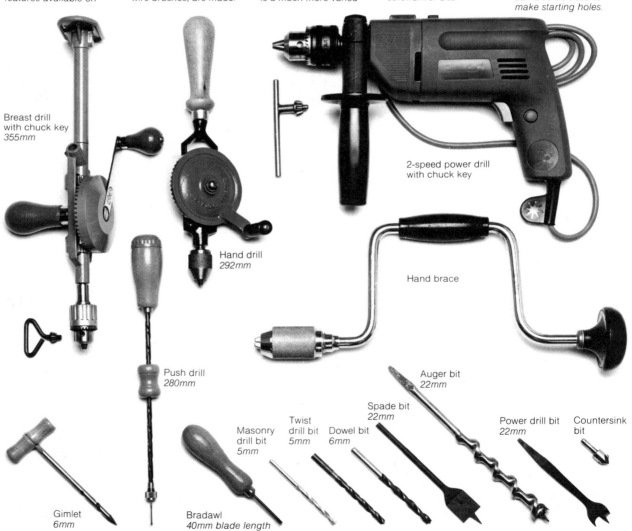

Breast drill with chuck key
355mm

Hand drill
292mm

2-speed power drill with chuck key

Hand brace

Push drill
280mm

Auger bit
22mm

Spade bit
22mm

Power drill bit
22mm

Countersink bit

Masonry drill bit
5mm

Twist drill bit
5mm

Dowel bit
6mm

Gimlet
6mm

Bradawl
40mm blade length

Chisels and planes

Chisels are wood-shaping tools, useful for paring and chopping out areas of wood to take hinges and other fittings. All new chisels need honing on an oilstone to sharpen them for easy use.

For the best finish, chisel either with, or at right-angles to, the grain of the wood. Use a wooden mallet to tap chisels with wooden handles; with hard plastic handles, an ordinary hammer can be used.

Planes are used for slicing off unwanted pieces of wood, shaping and reducing wood to size, and also for smoothing wood. The longer the piece of wood you are planing, the longer the plane you should use. Before planing, check that the blade is sharp and that its edge is parallel with, and just protruding from, the sole plate. Work with the wood grain.

Plane blades can be sharpened, but this is a skilled job, best left to a professional. For this reason, rasp planes, with replaceable disposable blades, are increasingly popular.

Chisels

Bevel-edge chisels
This is the most versatile type of chisel. Blade widths of 6mm, 12mm, 19mm, and 25mm are the ones most commonly used. The blades' tapering edges enable the chisel to cut in confined spaces, such as the undercuts in dovetail joints and in shallow hinge recesses. Since this type of chisel is designed for lightweight work, if a mallet is used, tap it only lightly.

Firmer chisels
Available in widths from 3mm to 50mm, these chisels feature stout blades with straight sides. They are much stronger than bevel-edge chisels and can be hit harder with a mallet. Their uses are limited, but they are good for chopping out mortises and making frames for partitions.

Cold chisel
This strong steel chisel is ideal for removing mortar from brickwork before pointing. It can be hit with a hammer and lengths from 125mm to 205mm are available.

Bolster chisel
This chisel can be used for a variety of levering tasks, such as taking up floorboards, and for cutting masonry. Lengths from 175mm to 190mm are produced.

Honing equipment

Oilstone
This is used for honing chisel and plane blades. It is available in coarse, medium, and fine grades and also as a combination stone; fine on one side and medium on the other. Oilstones should be kept in a box and oiled before use. Hold the blade at 30 degrees to the stone and work it back and forth.

Honing guide
A very useful wheeled gadget, the honing guide helps to keep the chisel or plane blade at the correct angle when it is being honed. The blade is clamped in the guide, which is then moved to and fro on the oilstone.

Planes

Smoothing plane
This is used for smoothing wood on smaller jobs. The sole plate is usually 245mm long. It should be used with care on long pieces of timber.

Jack plane
The sole plate of the jack plane is 355mm long, making it easier to plane a flat surface. It is a useful all-round tool

Block plane
This small plane, with a sole plate 140mm to 180mm long, can be used with one hand. The blade is set at a shallow angle with the bevel uppermost for smoothing end grain.

Bench rebate plane
The broad cutting blade of this plane allows it to be used for smoothing open-sided rebates and the shoulders of large joints. The sole plate is 235mm to 330mm long.

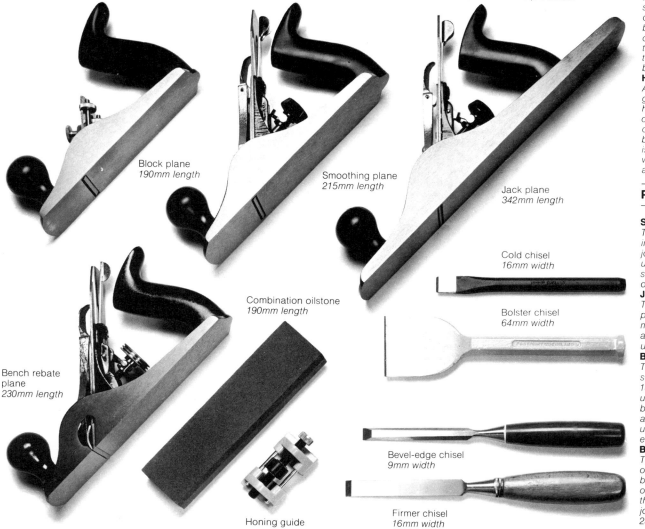

Block plane
190mm length

Smoothing plane
215mm length

Jack plane
342mm length

Cold chisel
16mm width

Bolster chisel
64mm width

Combination oilstone
190mm length

Bench rebate
plane
230mm length

Bevel-edge chisel
9mm width

Honing guide

Firmer chisel
16mm width

Scrapers and sanders

Paint scrapers are useful for removing old paint, in conjunction with paint-stripping solution. Old wallpaper can also be stripped after it has been liberally soaked in warm water or stripping solution. A simple upward motion is all that is needed. Shavehooks can remove flaking and softened paint from wooden mouldings. Gas blowlamps can strip off layers of paint but should be used with care because of the fire risk. Hot-air strippers are far safer.

Sanders are invaluable for smoothing surfaces. But some surfaces clog the abrasive, so wet-and-dry types are produced, which can be used wet and wiped down. Whenever using abrasives on wood, work in line with the grain. Abrasive papers are available in grades from coarse to fine and are graded according to the grit size – 40 is very coarse, 100 is medium, 200

Scrapers

Paint and wallpaper scraper
This is the most versatile scraper. Use it to remove old, softened paint and dampened wallpaper. Scrapers with wide blades are suitable for large areas; narrow blades are useful for window frames. Blade widths range from 25mm to 125mm.

Shavehook
For removing softened paint from wooden mouldings around doors and windows a shavehook is best. A drawing action should be used. Shavehooks are available with a choice of three different blades: triangular, pear-shaped, and a combination blade with straight, convex, and concave edges.

Window scraper
Use this to trim excess, dried paint from window panes. It has a standard trimming knife blade fixed in a plastic handle. When using a window scraper, start flush with the frame and scrape downwards.

Hook scraper
Also known as a Skarsten scraper, this tool can be used for fine cabinet finishing or heavy-duty scraping. A range of interchangeable blades (straight, convex, concave, serrated, and double-ended) are produced, together with two handles allowing you to use the tool with either one or two hands. You work by pulling the tool towards you. Blades are available in 40mm to 65mm widths.

Sanding papers

Glasspaper
This is used to finish timber roughly. It wears quickly but is inexpensive. It is often called "sandpaper", because of its yellow colour.

Garnet
A hard, sharp abrasive, garnet is made from the semi-precious red stone. It is ideal for wood finishing. It is fairly long-lasting and is available in finer grades than glasspaper.

Silicon carbide
This is often called "wet-and-dry paper". It can be used wet to prevent clogging when rubbing down painted surfaces. It can also be used to clean metals.

Emery
This black abrasive is available with paper or cloth backing. It has a slow-cutting action and is used mainly to clean and polish metal. The cloth-backed type is long-lasting and ideal for cleaning pipes.

Tungsten carbide
This very sharp, hard abrasive is expensive but long-lasting.

Sanding block
This is a cork or wooden block around which you wrap a sheet of abrasive paper. You can buy a sanding block or make one from a piece of wood.

Other sanding equipment

Sanding attachments
These can be fitted to an electric drill. Sanding discs are the most common type. Attached to a flexible rubber backing pad, and mounted in the drill chuck, the disc is used to sand wood, metal, and plastic. The main problem with this type is that it produces swirl marks. Flap-wheel sanders have a gentler action and do not produce swirl marks. Foam-drum sanders consist of an abrasive belt, wrapped around a foam drum mounted in the drill chuck. They are used on flat and curved surfaces.

Power sanders
Finishing or orbital sanders are the most widely used type. A strip of abrasive, moving at high speed in a series of tiny orbits, gives a fine finish on wood and painted surfaces. Belt sanders are powerful machines that can be used to sand wood and metal quickly. They are more expensive than orbital sanders, but sand in a straight line.

Rasps and files

Files
These are used to smooth metal and wood, to remove burrs and other irregularities, to enlarge and finish holes, and to sharpen some cutting tools. There are two basic types of teeth – precision single-cut and fast-cutting double-cut. Each is available in three degrees of coarseness – bastard, which has a very coarse face; second cut, which is medium-smooth; and smooth, which is used for finishing. Flat, round, half-round, and needle files are available.

Rasps
Used mainly on wood, rasps are also effective on plastics, aluminium, and lead. They are available in bastard and smooth cuts, and in flat, round, and half-round shapes. Rasp teeth are coarser than file teeth, so they slice off slivers of wood easily.

Surform tools
These are hollow rasps with handles. They have steel blades with sharp-edged holes which can cut wood away rapidly. The blades can be replaced very easily.

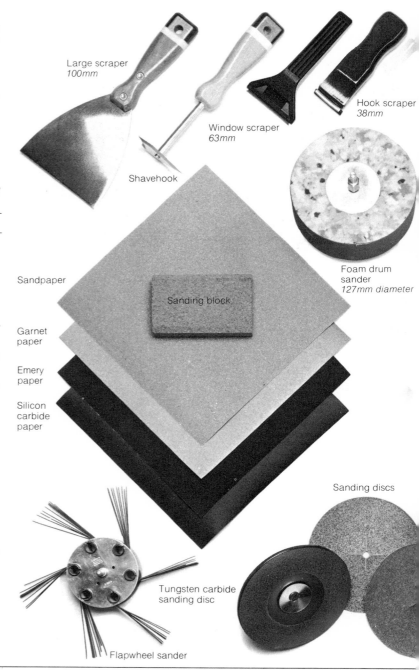

Large scraper
100mm

Window scraper
63mm

Hook scraper
38mm

Shavehook

Sandpaper

Garnet
paper

Emery
paper

Silicon
carbide
paper

Sanding block

Foam drum
sander
127mm diameter

Sanding discs

Tungsten carbide
sanding disc

Flapwheel sander

is very fine, for finishing.

Files and rasps can be used to shape metal and wood. Round files can enlarge holes in metal, while triangular files can sharpen saw blades. The file cuts on the forward stroke, so apply even pressure. Chalk the file's teeth before use, to prevent clogging, or brush the file with wire wool during use. Most files are sold without handles, so you should buy these separately.

Filling and plastering tools

Filling knives are useful for general repair work. The most common type has a wide, flexible blade to spread filler into holes in wood or masonry.

Trowels are essential for mixing, shaping and applying mortar. Different types are available for different functions – a rectangular trowel for applying plaster; a pointed trowel for brickwork. Keep all metal trowels lightly oiled to prevent them from rusting.

Fillers

Filling knife
Used to spread fillers in wood or plaster, this has a flexible blade, so that filler can be pushed into holes. Blade widths range from 25mm to 100mm.

Putty knife
Designed for applying and smoothing putty when glazing windows, putty knives are available with straight, spearpoint, or clipped-point blades. Blade widths range from 40mm to 50mm.

Plastering and bricklaying tools

Brick trowel
The traditional trowel for applying mortar is available in blade lengths of 160mm to 300mm.

Pointing trowel
This slightly smaller trowel is used for applying mortar and repairing joints between bricks. Blade lengths range from 75mm to 200mm.

Brick jointer
Jointers give the right finish to mortar joints between bricks. Blade lengths range from 125mm to 300mm.

Plasterer's trowel
This is used to apply and smooth plaster on walls and ceilings. Sizes range from 100mm · 250mm to 120mm · 275mm.

Wooden float
For a fine, matt finish on the surface of skim plaster, cement mortar, or concrete. The usual size is 125mm · 275mm.

Hawk
A hawk is used to hold small amounts of plaster or mortar when working. Sizes range from 250mm square to 350mm square.

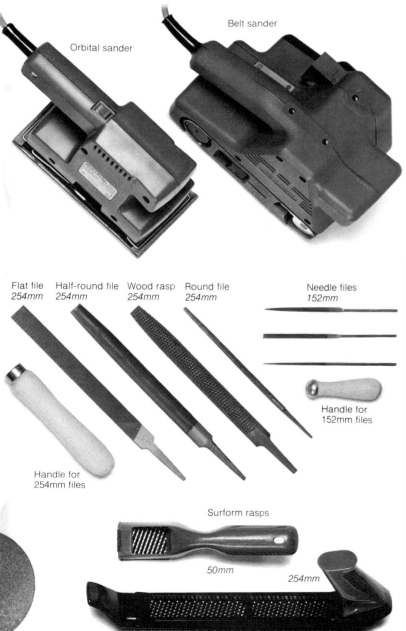

Orbital sander

Belt sander

Flat file
254mm

Half-round file
254mm

Wood rasp
254mm

Round file
254mm

Needle files
152mm

Handle for
152mm files

Handle for
254mm files

Surform rasps

50mm

254mm

Aluminium plasterer's hawk
330mm square

Pointing trowel
152mm blade length

Brick trowel
280mm blade length

Filling knife
50mm

Wooden float
330mm · 120mm

Putty knife

Plasterer's steel trowel
280mm · 115mm

Brick jointer
254mm

Brushes

For top-quality results it is vital to use good brushes. The best are made with pure hog's bristle. When choosing a brush, a good guide to quality is price – the more you pay, the better it should be. A top quality brush will also be less likely to shed bristles. Look for a good length of bristle and a bulky filling. The bristles should flex without spreading too much and spring quickly back into place when bent back.

Artificial fibre bristles tend to be smooth and not as springy as true bristles, so they do not hold paint as well as those made with natural bristles, and tend to leave brush marks on the surface. But good quality nylon brushes are very hard wearing and, if their bristles are tapered and textured, can hold emulsion paint very well.

Paint brushes

Flat brushes
Use these to apply gloss or semi-matt paint or varnish to woodwork. When working, do not overload the brush; apply the pain in even strokes. Sizes range from 12mm to 100mm. Use 12mm and 25mm brushes for small areas and intricate work, and 50mm and 75mm brushes for larger areas, windows and doors. For walls and ceilings, if you do not want to use a roller, a 100mm or 125mm brush will give quick coverage. To prevent new brushes shedding hairs and spoiling new paint, flick the brush and rub it along a rough surface, until all the loose bristles have come free.

Cutting-in brush
The slanting angle of the bristles enables you to take the paint neatly right up to an edge, such as the glass in a window frame, a skirting board or a door panel. The usual width is 18mm.

Crevice brush
The brush is set at an angle, and the long wire handle can be bent if necessary so that the brush can be used in awkward and confined areas, such as behind radiators and pipes. For painting behind panel radiators, however, it is often more convenient to use a crevice roller. Sizes range from 25mm to 50mm.

Wall brushes
Large versions of flat brushes, these are used mainly for painting walls and other large areas instead of a roller. They are available in a wide range of sizes, particularly between 100mm and 300mm. The larger sizes can be heavy and tiring to use for long periods so it is best not to overload these. Some wall brushes have a wide stock into which the bristles are set in two or three rows of round bunches. This type of brush is particularly suitable for stippling paint on to pebbledash walls. A cheap wall brush is suitable for applying wallpaper paste.

Wallpaper brushes

Smoothing brush
This is used for smoothing down wallpaper when it is being pasted to a wall. The brush should be used from the centre of each strip of wallpaper outwards to remove air bubbles and creases. The brushes are available in sizes between 187mm and 250mm.

Wallpaper paste brush
A special brush, with synthetic bristles, is available for applying wallpaper paste. An ordinary wide wall brush is quite adequate for this job. To remove traces of paste before it dries and hardens, soak the brush in warm, soapy water.

Other brushes

Wire brushes
These brushes are used for cleaning metal and masonry surfaces before decorating them. They may also be used for scoring the surface of washable wallpapers prior to soaking them. Some types have a metal scraper attached to one end to aid the removal of loose flakes. Power-tool attachments are also available that perform the same function. Several shapes are made, including small brushes for confined spaces.

Wallpaper pasting brush *127mm*

Crevice brush *25mm*

Wallpaper smoothing brush *177mm*

Cutting-in brush *19mm*

Paint brush *25mm*

Paint brush *50mm*

Wire brush *280mm*

Wall brush *100mm*

Rollers and paint pads

With a roller you can apply paint quickly to large areas of wall and ceiling. Rollers are used in conjunction with a paint tray – you fill the tray with paint and load the roller from it. Apply the paint carefully, taking care to avoid spattering. When buying a roller, make sure the roller sleeve can be removed from the handle assembly for cleaning. Clean the roller well after use.

Paint pads are easy to use, and will cover large, flat surfaces quickly. They apply paint smoothly, do not spatter very much, but are not very versatile. With the larger pads, it is often possible to insert a broom handle into the pad handle, for easy painting above arm's reach. It is difficult to clean pads after using oil-based paints, so it is best to confine their use to emulsion paints and the type of easy-clean oil-based paints that can be removed with hot water and detergent.

Rollers

Paint rollers

Ideal for painting large areas quickly, rollers tend to give a slightly more stippled finish than either brushes or pads, but, unlike pads, are not confined to use on flat surfaces. Short-pile rollers are best for smooth surfaces, while those with longer pile can be used for textured surfaces. Many rollers spatter paint during use, but this is less of a problem with lambswool and nylon pile types than with foam rollers. Most rollers are about 18cm wide. When using rollers, a paint tray is also required to enable you to load the paint evenly. Foam rollers are the cheapest and they are best used with water-based paints.
Mohair rollers have short, fine pile, suited to applying oil-based paint to give a gloss finish.
Lambswool and nylon pile rollers are ideal for applying emulsion paints. The longer the pile, the deeper the texture of the paint surface.
Textured foam rollers give attractive finishes with self-texturing paint. A range of patterns is available.

Seam roller

This small hardwood roller is used to press down the edges of wallpaper before they dry out. It should be used firmly, but without pressing so hard that all the paste is forced out to give a weak seam. After use, you should wipe the roller and wallpaper to remove surplus paste. Seam rollers are available in hardwood and plastic, in sizes ranging from 25mm to 50mm.

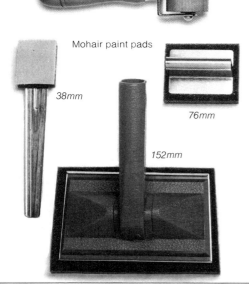

Wooden seam roller
38mm roller width

Mohair paint pads

38mm

76mm

152mm

Textured rollers *177mm*

Bark pattern

Diamond pattern

Paint roller handle
230mm

Foam roller
230mm

Lambswool roller
230mm

Mohair roller
230mm

Paint pads

Lighter than brushes and rollers, these are ideal for applying water-based paints to large, flat surfaces such as ceilings and walls. Before use, the mohair pile should be cleaned with a clothes brush to remove any surplus hairs. Small pads can be dipped directly into a paint tin, but larger pads require the use of a tray. Sizes range from 50mm × 25mm to 200mm × 90mm.

Pliers and pincers

As well as cutting and shaping wire, pliers can be used for a wide variety of holding and gripping tasks. When using pliers, hold them firmly, keeping your palm away from the pivot, which can pinch your skin as the jaws close. Pliers can also bend sheet metal. The sides of the jaws should align with the bending line to produce a neat bend. The side cutters on many pairs of pliers will cut soft wire.

Use pincers to pull out tacks and nails. Grip the shank of the nail as closely as possible to the surface of the wood and protect it with a small piece of hardboard next to the nail. Lever the handles to one side so that the jaws roll over the hardboard, and the nail emerges. Grip the nail again lower down the shank and repeat.

General-purpose pliers

Engineer's pliers
Suitable for general-purpose work, these pliers have serrated jaws for gripping flat objects, and curved jaws for gripping rods. There is a side cutter for cropping soft wire and usually one or two hard wire croppers near the pivot. The handles sometimes have plastic insulation. Sizes range from 125mm to 250mm.

Flat-nosed pliers
For the long reach needed to grip thin sheet metal and small objects, use these lightweight, flat-nosed pliers. Sizes available range from 100mm to 190mm.

Specialized pliers

Electrician's pliers
These are used to grip, bend, and cut electrical cable and flex. They are the same design as engineer's pliers, but always have insulated handles. Sizes range from 150mm to 200mm.

Snipe-nosed pliers
Also known as long-nosed pliers, these are used for handling small objects and cutting small wires, especially in confined spaces. They are lightweight and have narrow, tapering jaws with fine serrations for a good grip. A range of different jaw shapes is available. Sizes range from 115mm to 200mm.

Slip-joint pliers
These are particularly useful for holding pipes. They combine the functions of pliers and spanner and are invaluable when an adjustable, long-handled tool is required. Multiple slip-joint pliers have four or six adjustments that allow the jaws to grip

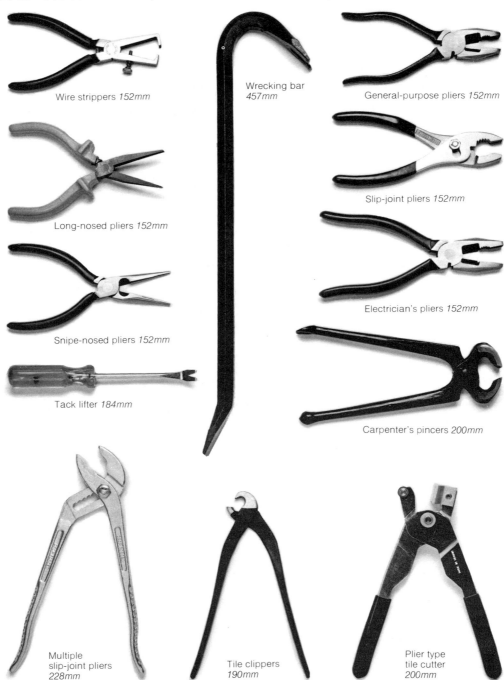

Wire strippers 152mm

Long-nosed pliers 152mm

Snipe-nosed pliers 152mm

Tack lifter 184mm

Wrecking bar 457mm

Multiple slip-joint pliers 228mm

Tile clippers 190mm

General-purpose pliers 152mm

Slip-joint pliers 152mm

Electrician's pliers 152mm

Carpenter's pincers 200mm

Plier type tile cutter 200mm

tightly to suit the size of the object. Slip-joint pliers are also available with bent or narrow jaws. Sizes range from 125mm to 250mm.

Other equipment

Carpenter's pincers
These are gripping tools for pulling out nails and tacks. The heads are rounded and polished, so that they will roll easily on the surface as the nail is being extracted. Sizes range from 150mm to 250mm.

Tack lifter
For quick extraction of tacks and small nails, use this screwdriver-like tool. It has a curved, V-notched blade which slips under the head of the tack. The handle is pressed down to lift the tack. Sizes range from 160mm to 200mm.

Wrecking bar
The large claw at one end of the bar allows you to lift large nails, such as those securing floorboards. The flattened end of the bar can be used to prise up boards. The length of the bar gives good leverage.

Wire strippers
These remove insulation from the ends of electrical flexes and cables. Various styles are available, but they are all adjustable for different thicknesses of wire. The traditional type has spring-return handles and V-notched, high-tensile blades, adjusted by a side-locking screw. Sizes range from 150mm to 200mm.

Tile cutters
Plier-type tile cutters have an angled face, so that the tile breaks evenly on either side of a scored line. Tile snips allow you to remove small pieces of waste material from the edge of a tile.

Spanners and wrenches

Spanners and wrenches are tools for loosening and tightening nuts and bolts. Fixed open-ended spanners are easy and fast to use. Enclosed ring spanners are stronger, but less versatile. Both types are available in a variety of sizes and can be used for many jobs, from working on electrical and plumbing fittings to servicing domestic appliances.

Adjustable spanners will fit a wide range of nut and bolt sizes. They are normally open-ended with one movable jaw, set at an angle to the shaft, operated by a screw, although there is also a limited range of adjustable ring spanners. Adjustable spanners are particularly useful for making plumbing joints with compression fittings and for fitting taps.

General-purpose spanners

Open-ended spanners
These are the most common and versatile spanners. They will slide on to a nut or bolt from the side, and they are faster to use than ring spanners, although not as strong. They can also be used on pipe joints where it is impossible to use a ring spanner. They are available in many different sizes, which vary according to manufacturer.

Ring spanners
Slower to use but safer and stronger than open-ended spanners, these grip more tightly. The ring of the spanner has either 6 or 12 points which link with the sides of the nut or bolt. A 12-point spanner can be used on both hex-agonal and square bolt heads. Ring spanners are available in many different sizes, varying according to maker.

Combination spanners
These versatile spanners have a ring at one end and an open-ended jaw at the other.

Multiple spanners

Multiple ring spanners
Intended only for light-weight work, the ends contain a selection of five different-sized rings.

Adjustable spanners and wrenches
These are particularly useful in plumbing work. Several different designs are available but most are bulkier than the same-sized open-ended or ring spanners. But they are weaker and should be used care-fully. They fit a wide range of nut sizes.

Front-rack wrenches have a fixed jaw and a rack. Sizes range from 150mm to 450mm.

Crescent spanners are adjusted by a worm screw in the handle. Sizes up to 600mm are available.

Adjustable ring spanners are also available. They feature a metal shaft with two pivoting heads, which tighten against the shaft as you turn the spanner. With this design, you do not have to remove the spanner between turns. Sizes up to 215mm are produced.

Wrenches

Pipe wrenches
Similar in design to adjustable spanners, these are used for grip-ping pipes and rods.

Footprint wrenches have an adjustable pivot and grip the pipe when the handles are squeezed. Lengths up to 525mm are available.

Stilson wrenches are very strong, have spring-loaded jaws, but may damage the pipe. Sizes range from 15mm to 200mm.

Self-grip wrench
Often known as a Mole grip, this wrench has a locking device that allows it to grip flat or circular metal objects very firmly. The jaws are controlled by an adjust-ing screw, and extreme force is applied when the handles are closed. Designs with straight and curved jaws are avail-able in sizes ranging from 125mm to 300mm.

Basin wrench
This is used on nuts, such as those under a sink, that a conventional wrench will not reach. It has a moving-jaw head which turns by means of a tommy bar. Sizes are available for fittings up to 50mm wide.

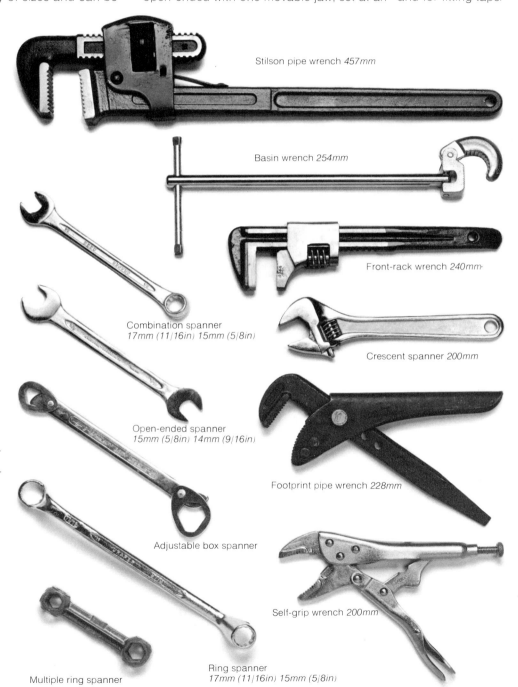

Stilson pipe wrench 457mm

Basin wrench 254mm

Front-rack wrench 240mm

Combination spanner 17mm (11/16in) 15mm (5/8in)

Crescent spanner 200mm

Open-ended spanner 15mm (5/8in) 14mm (9/16in)

Adjustable box spanner

Footprint pipe wrench 228mm

Self-grip wrench 200mm

Multiple ring spanner

Ring spanner 17mm (11/16in) 15mm (5/8in)

Index

A

Abrasives 14, 72, 228
Acrylic primer/undercoat 13
Adhesives (and uses)
  carpet 62, 65
  china 143
  contact 143
  coving 49
  epoxy 143, 145
  expanded polystyrene 37
  fibre insulation board 75
  flexible 45, 52, 124
  frost-proof 124
  furniture 152-3
  glass 143
  heat-resistant 124
  household goods, repairing 142-3
  picture frames 164-5
  plastic 145
  PVA 70, 148, 152
  spreaders 45
  stains, removing 147
  tape, double-sided 60, 62, 78
  textured wallcoverings 42-3, 121
  thixotropic 143
  tiles 45, 48, 124
  vinyl floors 78
  wallpaper 29, 30, 35, 121
  waterproof 45, 124
  wooden panelling 83, 86
Adjustable shelving 169, 171
Adjustable spanner 233
Aerosol paint 114
Airbricks 204, 205
Air lock 185
Alarm systems 216
Alcoves, shelves in 171
Algae 203
Alkali-resistant primer 13
Aluminium
  doors 109
  -oxide paper 14
  paint 13
  primer/sealer 13, 114
  windows, anodized 12
Anti-condensation paint 24, 114
Appliances, electrical 174-6
Arches, papering around 41
Architraves
  carpeting around 62
  laying woodblock floors around 76-7
  out-of-true 38
  painting 116
  tiling around 54
Asbestos 78
Axminster carpet 56, 132

B

Ball valve 185, 188
Bamboo furniture 155
Banisters, carpeting under 56
Basins
  blockages 187
  gap with wall, sealing 52
  splashback 124
  taps 189
Basin wrench 233
Bathrooms
  accessories, ceramic 52
  condensation, avoiding 207

curtain materials 136
floor coverings 133, 140
floor insulation 75
hardwood floors 66, 72
lighting 162, 179, 180
mirrors 166
panelled ceilings 87
tiles 47, 125, 140
vinyl floors 78-81, 140
wallpaper 29, 121, 140
wiring 179
Baths
  blockages 187
  gap with wall, sealing 52
  plumbing 186
  taps 189
Battens
  for fixing brackets 105
  for fabric wallcoverings 43
  for panelling 83-4, 86, 87
  for plastering 89-90
  for tiles 50
  as shelf support 169
Beading
  cane furniture 151
  glazing 97
  around panelling 85, 86
  to reduce heat loss 195
  on shelves 168, 171
Bedrooms
  carpets 57, 133, 140
  children's 116, 121
  lighting 162
  wallpaper 121, 140
Benches 218
Bench rebate plane 227
BESA box 181
Bevel-edge chisel 227
Bi-folding doors 109, 110
Binder bars 62, 78, 81
Bits, drill 224, 226
Bitumen
  damp-proofing 206
  impregnated insulation board 75
  roofing felt 199, 200
  underlay 76, 127
Blinds
  festoon 102, 107, 136
  measuring for 102
  roller 102, 106, 136
  Roman 107
  Venetian 102, 107, 136
Blisters, paint 25, 41
Blockages, clearing
  gutters and downpipes 201
  pipes 186-8
Blockboard 168
Block plane 227
Blowtorch 14, 19, 228
Body carpet 56
Boilers, central-heating 190-1
Bolster chisel 46, 89, 227
Bolts, door 215
Bonded carpet 132
Bonding plaster 88, 89
Borders
  tiles 48, 50, 52
  wallpaper 34, 118
Boring tools 226
Brace 226
Brackets
  fixing to wall 105, 170, 171
  shelving 168-9
Bradawl 226
Brads 68, 70, 223
Breast drill 226
Brick
  cutting for tiles 53
  dry rot 208-9

jointer 229
pointing 202, 229
stains 203
tiles 44, 53, 122-3, 124, 125
trowel 229
Brighton catch 99
Broadloom carpet 56
Browning plaster 88, 89
Brushes
  paint 14, 230
  wallpaper 30, 230
Brushmarks, avoiding 25
Building paper 194-5
Bullions 95
Burglar alarms 216
Burst pipes 184, 189

C

Cable, electrical 178, 180
Cane furniture 148, 150-1
Cantilever brackets 169, 171
Capillary joint 185
Capstan-head tap 186, 189
Carpenter's pincers 232
Carpets
  Axminster 56, 132
  bedroom 57, 140
  berber 130
  binder bars 62
  body 56
  bonded 132
  broadloom 56
  cleaning 146
  designs 58-9
  foam-backed 56, 57, 64, 130
  grippers 57, 60-1, 63, 64-5
  hair and woolcord 130
  hall 57, 140
  hessian-backed 57, 61, 132
  joining 62
  laying 56, 57, 61-5
  living-room 57, 140
  loop pile 130
  non-woven 56
  oriental 58
  patching 65
  preparing floor 59
  quantity required, assessing 56
  sculptured pile 130
  shag 130
  short pile 130
  stair 56-7, 58, 63-5
  stretching 57, 61
  tacks 61, 62, 63, 223
  tape 60, 62
  tiles 56, 57, 62, 130
  tools, laying 57
  trimming 61
  tufted 56, 132
  twist 130
  underlay 56, 60, 63, 130, 132
  velvet 130
  wearing qualities 57
  widths 56
  Wilton 56, 132
  woven 56, 132
Casement windows
  bays and bows 94
  fastenings 99
  frames 95
  locks 214
  painting 23
  rattling 99
  sticking 99
Castors 153
Catches, door 136-8
Cavity walls
  insulation 194, 195

screw fixings in 170
Ceilings
  border tiles 48
  coving 44, 49
  cracks, filling 16, 17, 26
  curtain rails 105
  damp patches 205
  disguising high/low ceilings 14
  distemper, removing 16
  friezes 34
  guidelines, marking 38
  insulation 197
  lights 160, 181
  lining paper 36
  painting 13, 14, 16, 116, 140
  panelling 87, 140
  papering 16, 32, 34, 140
  rose 180, 181
  tiles 44, 45, 46, 48-9, 122, 140
  wallpaper, removing 16
  washing down 16
Cellulose fillers 17
Cellulose lacquer 115
Cement-based plaster 89
Cement floors, carpeting 59
Central heating
  air locks 192
  bleeding radiators 192
  boilers 190-1
  as cause of cracks 12
  control systems 190
  cost 190, 193, 194
  dry systems 191
  flushing out 193
  fuel 190
  insulation 194-7
  leaks 192-3
  pumps, replacing 193
  radiators, fitting 192
  radiators, painting 25
  underfloor 56, 75, 191
  wet systems 191
Ceramic tiles
  adhesives 124
  applications 125
  bathroom accessories 52
  cutting and laying tools 45
  floor 55, 123, 140
  laying 50-1
  wall 44, 122, 140
Chairs
  cane 150-1
  construction 156
  recovering 159
  repairs 152-3
  rush 154-5
  springs 157
  upholstery 134-6, 146-7, 156-9
Chemical damp-proofing 206
Chemical paint stripper 14, 18-19
Children's rooms 21, 116, 121
Chimneys, repairs to 205
Chimney breasts
  damp patches 205
  papering 38, 40
Chinaware 142-3
Chipboard
  cutting 68
  floors 74
  repairing damage to 17, 74
  screws 225
  shelving 168
  sub-floors 126-7, 129
Chisels 227
Circular saws 68, 74, 110, 221
Cisterns
  lagging 196
  water supply 184-5, 188
Cladded ceilings 87

Clamps 218
Claw hammer 222
Cleaning
  aluminium 144
  brass 144
  bronze 144
  ceilings 16
  china 142
  chrome 144
  copper 144
  cutlery 144
  dry-cleaning 146
  external walls 203
  equipment 142
  fluids 142
  glass 142
  gold 144
  ornaments 142
  leather 145
  paint brushes 14
  paintwork 18
  pewter 144
  scissors and shears 36
  scrapers 14
  silver 144
  sugar soap 16
  upholstery 146-7
  vinyl floors 78
  wallpapering tools 30
  walls 16, 32
Clips
  glazing 96, 97
  mirror 166
  panelling 84
  picture 164
Clout nails 223
Club hammer 46, 98, 222
Cockspur handle 99, 214
Cold chisel 227
Cold-water system 184
Colour
  carpets 58-9
  charts, unreliability of 116
  choosing 14
  effects 14
  fastness 146
  intensity 15
  and mood 15
  and pattern 30-1
  variations 28
  wooden floors 67
Cooker 176
Combination spanner 233
Combination square 219
Compression joint 185
Concealed lighting 161
Concertina doors 109, 110
Concrete floors 59, 116
Condensation
  with double glazing 101
  preventing 59, 207
  -resistant wallpaper 29
Consumer unit 179
Contact adhesives 143, 145
Convector heaters 193
Cookers
  hoods 207 211
  power point 180, 183
Coping saw 68, 220
Copper piping 186
Cork
  adhesive 124
  applications 125
  floor tiles 45, 54, 140
  veneer 118, 124
  wall tiles 44, 53, 122, 140
Corners
  carpeting 61
  coving 49

lining material 37
out-of-true 29, 31, 38
panelling 85, 87
papering 40
plaster repairs 93
sanding floors 73
vinyl floors 80
Corrugated fasteners 223
Cotton-fibre coving 49
Countersinking 98, 170, 225
Covering rates, paint 13
Covers, chair 159
Coving 44, 45, 49
Cracks
  in ceiling 16
  concealing, with textured paint 26
  filling 17
Crescent spanner 233
Crevice brush 230
Cross-cut saw 83, 220
Cross-head screwdriver 224
Cross-pein hammer 222
Crowbar 98
Cupboards 172
Curtains
  cleaning 146
  effects 103
  fabrics 134-6
  heading tape 102
  matching fittings 103
  measuring for 102
  net 103
  pelmets 104
  poles 104
  pull cords 104
  rails 102, 104-5
  single 103
Cushions 136
Cut-clasp nails 223
Cut floor brads 223
Cutting-in brush 14, 23, 230
Cutting tools 220-1
Cylinder hinge 138

◆ D ◆

Damp
  courses 204, 205
  in older houses 12
  patches 83, 203-5
  -proofing treatments 206-7
  rising 59, 204-7
  through cracks in mortar 204, 205
Deadlocks 212, 215
Dehumidifiers 207
Dented metal, repairing 144
Desk lamps 160
Devilling 89, 91
Dimmer switch 160
Dining rooms
  floor covering 133, 140
  wallpaper 121, 140
Disc sander 14
Dishwashers 142, 176
Distemper, removing 16, 18
Doors
  aluminium 109
  bi-folding 109, 110
  bolts 215
  carpeting around 62
  catches 136-8
  chains 216
  concertina 109, 110
  cutting out 109
  draught exclusion 195, 197
  escutcheons 139
  handles 111, 137
  hanging 109, 110
  hinges 110, 112, 137-8

KD fittings 138
keyholes plates 139
knobs 137, 139
knockers 139
laying woodblock floors around 76-7
locks 212-13, 215
loose frames 112
measuring 110
out-of-true 38
painting 13, 21, 116
panelled 109
panelling around 85
papering around 40
sagging 112
sliding 109, 111, 215
stable 109
standard sizes 110
tiling around 54
squeaking 112
sticking 112
viewers 216
warped 112
water seeping in 205
Dormer windows 41
Double glazing 94, 100-1, 195
Downlighters 161
Downpipes 201, 205
Dragging 26
Drains 185, 187-8
Drain cock 185, 193
Draped pelmets 104
Draught excluders 99, 197
Drawers 172
Drills
  bits 224, 226
  countersinking 98
  electric 226
  hand 226
  storage 218
D-rings 165
Drum sanding machines 72-3
Dry-cleaning 146
Dry heating systems 191
Dry rot 208-9
Ducts, warm-air 191

◆ E ◆

Efflorescence 203
Eggshell paint 13, 114
Electrical system
  appliances 174-6
  bathroom wiring 179
  cable 178, 180
  ceiling lights 181
  cooker points 180, 183
  current capacities 180
  flex 174, 178, 180, 211
  fusebox 179
  fused connections 182-3
  fuses 174, 178, 181, 183
  household circuit 179
  junction box 179
  lighting circuits 179, 180
  light switches 180, 182
  loop-in roses 179, 181
  overloading 179
  plugs 174, 178, 183
  power circuit 179
  power consumption 178
  radial circuit 179
  ring circuit 179, 182
  safety precautions 174, 178, 210-11
  service head 179
  sockets 180, 182
  spurs 79, 182
  tools 181, 224, 232
  wall sockets 180. 182
Electrician's pliers 181, 232

Electrician's screwdriver 181, 224
Embossed wallpaper 118, 120
Emery paper 228
Emergencies, plumbing 184
Emulsion paint
  anti-condensation 24
  application 117
  brushing-on 20-1
  covering rates 13
  finishes 114
  roller applications 14, 21
  solid 14
Enamel paint 114
Engineer's pliers 232
Epoxy adhesives 143, 145
Escutcheons 139
Espagnolette bolt 99, 139
Ethnic rugs 131
Expanded polystyrene
  anti-condensation protection 29
  insulation material 194
  wall lining 37, 118, 140
Exterior preservatives 115
Extractor fans 207

◆ F ◆

Fabrics, furnishing 134-6, 146-7
Fabric wallcoverings 42-3, 118, 120, 140
Fan heaters 193
Fastenings, window 99
Faults
  paint 25
  wallpaper 41
Felt paper underlay 56, 60, 130
Fibre insulation board 75
Fibreboard tiles 45, 48, 122
Files 228
Fillers
  applying 14, 17
  grain filler 149
  plaster 93
  resin-based 114
  wood 17, 114
Filling knife 14, 17, 228
Finishes, wood
  applying 149
  choosing 115, 117
  natural 18
  restoring 66
Fire blanket 210
Fire extinguisher 210
Fireplaces
  carpeting around 62
  cork tiles around 53
  papering around 40
  soot deposits above 16
  wood-burning stoves 193
Firmer chisel 227
Fitch fastener 99
Flap valve 188
Flaking paint 25
Flashing 200, 205
Flat-nosed pliers 232
Flex, electrical 174, 178, 180, 211
Flexible tile adhesive/sealer 45, 52
Float, plasterer's 89-91, 229
Float glass 95
Flock wallpaper 118, 120, 140
Flokati rugs 131
Floorboards
  chipboard 74
  filling gaps 70
  fitting new 68-9
  lifting 68-9
  loose, securing 70
  relaying 69
  sanding 72-3
  sawing 68-9

sealing 73
Flooring, sheet 78-81, 131, 133, 140
Floors
    brads 68, 70, 223
    carpeting 56-65, 140
    chipboard 74, 126-7
    hardboard 72, 127, 140
    heat loss 195
    insulating 197
    paint 114
    parquet 75-7, 140
    plywood 127
    sub-floors 72, 126-7, 140
    tiled 44-7, 54-5, 122-5, 140
    vinyl 78-81, 140
    wooden 66-77, 126-7, 140
Fluorescent lighting 161, 181
Flush doors
    construction 109
    cutting to size 110
    painting 22
Foam-backed carpet
    laying 56, 57, 62
    on stairs 64
    underlay 132
    wearing qualities 130
Foam
    insulation 195, 197
    padding 158
    -rubber underlay 130
Foamed polyethylene wallcovering 118, 120
Foamed vinyl wallcovering 118
Foil wallcovering 43, 120, 121
Folding shutters 108
Folding rule 219
Footprint wrench 233
Frames, picture 164
French polishing 149
French windows
    catches 99, 138
    construction 95
    locks 213, 214
Friezes 34, 118
Fret saw 220
Frozen pipes 189
Fuel costs 190, 194-5
Furnishing fabrics 134-6, 146-7
Furniture
    chairs 150-1, 154-9
    children's 116
    handles 139
    hinges 138
    natural materials 155
    recovering 159
    repairs 152-3
    tables 152-3
    upholstery, cleaning and repairs 145-6, 156-9
Fusebox 179
Fused connections 182-3
Fuses 178, 181, 183

G

Garnet paper 228
Gas
    central heating 190
    fires 193
    hob 211, 176
    leaks 210
Gimlet 226
Glass
    broken, removing 96
    cleaning 142
    cutting 96
    fixing methods 96
    keeping paint off 23
    picture frames 164

putty 96-7
replacing window panes 97
shelves 168, 169
window glass 95-7
Glass fibre insulation material 194, 196
Glass paper 14, 228
Glassware 142-3
Glazes 26-7
Glazing
    beading 97
    clips 96
    cutting glass 96
    doors 97
    double-glazing 94, 100-1
    glass types 95
    putty 96
    sprigs 96, 97, 164, 167, 223
    tools 96
    See also Windows
Glossary 8-9
Gloss paint
    application 117
    brushing-on 20
    covering rate 13
    liquid 13, 114
    loss of gloss 25
    non-drip 13, 114
    painting over 13
Glue size 33
Grain filler 149
Grasscloth 43, 118, 120
Gravity toggle 225
Grippers, carpet 57, 60-1, 63-5
Grout 45, 51
Guidelines, marking 38, 46, 54
Gulley 185
Guttering 201, 205

H

Hacksaws 220-1
Hallways
    carpeting 57, 133, 140
    floor coverings 133, 140
    lighting 160, 162
    tiled 47, 125, 140
    wallpaper 29, 121, 140
Hammers 46, 222
Hand drills 226
Hand-printed wallpaper 118, 126
Hand-sanding machines 72-3
Handles, door 111
Hardboard
    conditioning 72
    nails 223
    sub-floors 72, 127, 129
Hardwood
    floors 66-77, 127-9
    shelving 168
Hawk, plasterer's 89-91, 229
Heading tape 102
Heating systems 190-3
Hessian
    carpet backing 57, 61, 132
    carpet underlay 56
    scrim 89
    upholstery 158
    wallcovering 42, 118, 120
High-relief wallpaper 118, 120
Hinges, door 110, 112, 137-8
Holes
    filling 17, 93
    drilling 170
Honing tools 145, 227
Hooks, picture 165
Hook scraper 228
Hopper 201
Hot-air gun 14, 18-19
Hot-water system, 185, 197

I

Immersion heaters 183
Immobilizers 214
Impact driver 224
Insulated screwdriver 224
Inspection chamber 185, 187
Insulation
    cavity-wall 194, 195
    carpeting as 60
    and condensation 207
    double glazing 100-1
    floors 75
    lagging 196-7
    lofts 194, 196
    materials 194, 197
    pipes and tanks 194, 196-7
    roof 194, 196-7
    wall lining 29, 37
Iron, electric 174-5

J

Jack plane 227
Jig saw 68, 83, 221
Joints, repairing 152
Joists 69, 70
Joist hanger 70
Jumper 185
Junction box 179, 180
Junior hacksaw 221

K

Kettle, electric 174-5
Keyhole plates 139
Kitchens
    appliances 174-6
    condensation, avoiding 207
    cooker hoods 207, 211
    cookers, wiring 180, 183
    curtain material 136
    floor coverings 133, 140
    floor insulation 75
    hardwood floors 66, 72
    lighting 162
    panelled ceilings 87
    tiles 125, 140
    vinyl floors 78-81, 140
    wallpaper 29, 121, 140
Knee kicker 57, 61
Knives
    marking 219
    sharpening 145
Knob set 111, 137
Knockers, door 139
Knots, sealing 18, 114
Knotty cedar 128
Knotty pine 128

L

Lacquers 115
Ladders 24, 32, 198-9
Lagging
    hot-water cylinder 197
    pipes 194, 197
    tanks and cisterns 194, 196
Laminated glass 95
Lampholders 180
Lampshades 146, 160
Landings
    carpet 65, 140
    wallpaper 29, 121, 140
Latches, door 215
Lath and plaster 12, 93
Lay-flat vinyl 78
Laying-off 20
Lead piping 186

Leaded lights, replacing 96-7
Leaks
    central heaing system 193
    gutters and downpipes 201
    water pipes 184, 189
Leather, care of 145
Light bulbs 160
Light fittings
    bathroom 179, 180
    electrical circuit 179
    lampholders 180
    panelling around 85
    papering around 41
    types of 160-1
Lighting
    bathroom 162, 179, 180
    bedroom 162
    concealed 161
    controlling with blinds 107
    controlling with shutters 108
    diffused 160-1
    directional 160-1
    hall 160, 162
    kitchen 162
    living room 162
Lights, window 94
Lining fabrics 136
Lining paper
    on ceilings 36
    grades 29
    heavy-duty 118
    painting over 118
    patch lining 37
    sizes 28
    for textured wallcoverings 42-3
    on walls 37
    weights 118
Lining, roofs and lofts 195-6
Linoleum 131
Linseed oil 115
Living rooms
    carpet 57, 133, 140
    lighting 162
    wallpaper 121, 140
Locks
    door 212-13, 215
    window 214
Lofts
    insulation 194, 196
    lining 196
    storage space 173
Long-nosed pliers 232
Loop-in rose 179, 181
Loose covers 136
Lost-head nails 68, 70
Louvres
    doors 109
    shutters 108
    windows 95, 96

M

Magnetic catches 138
Mains tester 224
Mallet 222
Marble tiles 123, 125
Marking-out 38, 46, 50, 54, 90
Marking tools 219
Masonry discs 53
Masonry drill 52, 170
Masonry nails 223
Masonry paint 114
Mastic gun 83, 86
Matt emulsion 13
Matting 131, 133
Measuring rules 30, 219
Metalwork
    cleaning 144
    painting 116

priming 13
repairs 144
rust protection 16
Metallic materials
  foil wallcovering 43, 120, 121, 125
  paints 24
  tiles 123
Mildew 147
Mirrors
  hanging 166
  screws 166, 225
  visual effects 167
Mirror tiles
  fixing 44, 45, 53
  visual effects 122, 125
Mitre block 164, 165
Mitre clamp 164, 165
Mixer tap 186
Mole grip 233
Mortar 203, 205
Mortise locks 111, 212-13, 215
Mosaics
  floor 76, 127
  tiled 46-7, 52, 122, 125
Moss 203
Mould 203
Mouldings 49, 86, 168
Murals
  painted 21
  tiled 46-7, 52

N

Nail punch 222
Nails 68, 70, 75, 223
Needles, upholstery 156
Non-drip gloss 13, 117
Non-woven carpet 56
Nosings 56

O

Offset screwdriver 224
Oil-fired central heating 190
Oil-stain preservative 115
Oilstone 145, 227
Open-ended spanners 233
Orbital sander 14
Ornaments, cleaning and repairing 142-3
Oval wire nails 223
Overflow. dripping 188

P

Pads. paint 14, 21, 231
Pad saw 68, 83, 220
Padded plate 57
Padding, furniture 158
Paint
  aerosol 114
  anti-condensation 24, 114
  brushes 14, 230
  cleaning down 18
  chipped, repainting 17
  colour intensity 15
  covering rates 13
  discolouration 16
  estimating quantities 12-13
  faults 25
  finishes 26-7
  flaking 25, 33
  metallic 24
  pads 14, 21, 231
  rollers 14, 21, 231
  sanding down 20
  scrapers 14, 18-19, 228
  softening 14
  stains, removing 147

stripping 14, 18-19
surfaces, suitability for 116, 140
textured 17, 26-7, 114
  for tiles 48
types 13, 114
washing down 18
See also Emulsion, Gloss. Undercoat
Paint brushes 14, 230
Painting
  avoiding brushmarks 25
  bathrooms 24
  brushing-on 20-1
  ceilings 13, 15
  coats required 13
  covering rates of paint 13
  doors, 13, 22
  dustmarks, avoiding 21, 24
  faults 25
  kitchens 24
  metal surfaces, preparing 16
  murals 21
  pipework 24
  preparatory work 16-19
  radiators 25
  skirtings 13, 22
  stairs and stairwells 24
  techniques 20-1
  walls, preparing 13, 16-17
  windows 13, 23
  wood, preparing 18
Panel pins, 83, 86, 223
Panel saw 220
Panelled doors 22, 109
Panelling
  boards 82, 84, 126, 128
  ceilings 87
  around corners 85
  conditioning timber 84
  near electrical fittings 85
  fixing battens 83-4
  fixing boards 84-5
  fixing clips 84
  joining boards 85
  laying time 82
  materials 126, 128
  panel pins 83, 84, 85, 223
  preparatory work 83
  quantities required, estimating 82
  sheet 86-7, 126, 128
  shiplap 82, 84, 126, 128
  tools 83
  tongue-and-groove board 82, 84, 126, 128
  wallboard 126. 128
  wood types 129
Paper-hanging brush 30
Parquet floors 75-7, 107, 140
Paste brush 230
Paste table 30, 35
Paste, wallpaper
  applying 35
  buying 121
  consistency 121
  for expanded polystyrene 37
  for lining paper 36
  matching to paper 30
  as size 33
  for textured wallcoverings 42-3
  for vinyl papers 121
Patch lining 37
Patching carpets 65
Pattern
  cane furniture 151
  carpets 58-9
  fabric 136
  tiles 46-7
  glass 95
  tiles 122
  vinyl floors 78

wallpaper 29-31, 34, 38
wooden floors 71, 76
Pebbledash 202
Pegs, shelving 169
Pelmets 104
Pendant lights 160
Philips screwdriver 224
Picture frames 164-7
Picture rails 34, 83
Pile, carpet 130
Pin hammer 222
Pin push 222
Pincers 232
Pipe wrench 233
Pipes, water
  bending 184, 187
  burst 184, 189
  central heating 191
  copper 186
  cutting 187
  frozen 189
  lagging 194, 197
  lead 186
  leaking 184, 187, 189, 193
  plastic 186
Pipework
  carpeting around 62
  painting 24
  tiling around 51, 54
  laying woodblocks around 76
Pivoting windows 94, 95
Plaster
  absorbency 13, 89
  consistency 90, 91
  damage to 32
  coving 45
  deterioration 13
  finishing coat 91
  floating coat 91
  holes, filling 93
  mixing 90
  painting 16
  plastering tools 89, 229
  quantities required, estimating 88
  removing old plaster 89
  setting times 89
  types 88-9
Plasterboard
  applying 92
  cutting 92
  finishes 88, 92
  fixing 92
  painting 16
  patching 93
  primer/sealer for 16
  walls 88
Plastic
  cleaning 145
  matting 131, 133
  piping 86
  repairing 145
  tiles 54, 123, 125
  wall coverings 118, 120
Pliers 181, 232
Plugs, electrical 178, 183
Plugs, wall 105, 170, 225
Plumb-bob 30, 37
Plumber's mastic 185
Plumbing
  ball valve, replacing 188
  blockages, clearing 186-8
  burst pipes 184
  central heating 191-3
  cisterns 184-5, 188
  cold-water system 184
  copper piping 186
  drainage system 185, 187
  emergencies 184
  expansion pipe 196

flap valve, replacing 188
hot water system 185
joints, 185
leaks 184, 189, 192-3
lead pipes 186
main supply 184
overflow 188
plastic piping 186
radiators 191-3
tank-fed system 184-5
taps 186
terms 185
tools 187, 232-3
traps 185, 187
waste pipes 186-7
washers, replacing 188-9
washing machine, plumbing-in 189
water tanks 184-5, 194
WC 187-8
Plywood 127, 129, 168
Pointing 53, 202, 229
Polystyrene
  coving 49
  expanded, anti-condensation 29
  expanded, wall lining 37
  tiles 44, 45, 48, 122
Polyurethane varnish 115, 117
Porous tube damp-proofing 206
Pozidriv screw 224
Power circuits 179
Power tools
  drills 226
  sanding attachments 228
  saws 221
  screwdriver 224
  storage 218
Preservatives, exterior 115
Primers
  acrylic 13
  alkali-resistant 13
  aluminium 13
  metal 13, 16
  plasterboard 16
  primer/sealer 13, 16
  red lead 16
  rust-inhibiting 16
  stabilizing 13, 16
  universal 13, 18
  wood 18, 114
  zinc chromate 16
  zinc phosphate 16
PTFE tape 185, 187
Pullcords 104
Pump, central-heating 193
Push drill 226
Putty 97-7
Putty knife 229
Pva adhesive 70, 148, 152
Pva bonding 59

Q

Quadrant tiles 124
Quarry tiles 123, 125

R

Radial circuits 179
Radiant heaters 193
Radiators
  bleeding 192
  leaks 192
  painting 25
  papering around 42
  replacing 192
  supply system 191
Ragging 27
Rasps 228
Ratchet screwdriver 224

Ready-pasted wallpaper 29, 39, 40, 118
Rebates, cutting 110
Relief vinyl wallcovering 118, 120
Rendering 202
Resin-based filler 17
Ring circuits 179, 182
Ring-shank nails 75
Ring spanner 233
Rip saw 220
Rising damp 59, 204-7
Rivet anchor 225
Rollers
  paint 14, 21, 231
  wallpaper 30, 231
Roofs
  coverings 199
  flashing 200, 205
  guttering 201
  heat loss 195
  insulation 194, 195-6
  ladders 198-9
  leaky 205
  slates 199, 200
  tiles 199, 200
  working on 198
Roofing felt 196, 199, 200
Rounded-head screws 225
Round wire nails 223
Rubber
  flooring 131, 133
  -sleeved anchor 225
  tiles 123
  underlay 56, 60-1, 130
Rugs 131, 133
Runs, paint 25
Rush furniture 148, 154-5
Rust
  protection 16
  removing 144

S

Safety precautions 162, 210-11
Saddle soap 145
Sags, paint 25
Sanding
  attachments 228
  block 14, 228
  drum sanders 72
  floors 72-3
  paintwork 20
  woodwork 18
Sash windows
  counterbalancing 95, 100
  draughtproofing 197
  fasteners 99
  locks 214
  painting 23
  rattling 99
  sash cord, replacing 100
Saws
  circular saw 68, 74, 110, 221
  coping saw 68, 220
  cross-cut saw 83, 220
  cutting brick 53
  cutting chipboard 74
  cutting floorboards 68
  cutting tiles 45, 51
  cutting wooden panelling 83
  fret saw 220
  hacksaws 220-1
  jig saw 68, 83, 221
  pad saw 68, 83, 221
  panel saw 220
  power saws 221
  rip saw 220
  tenon saw 220
Scaffolding tower 198
Scissors

cleaning 36
sharpening 144
types 221
Scrapers
  hook 228
  paint 14, 18-19, 228
  shavehook 14, 19, 228
  Skarsten 228
  wallpaper 30, 33, 228
  window 228
Scratches, removing
  metal 144
  woodwork 149
Screwdrivers
  bits 224
  cross-head 224
  electrician's 181, 224
  impact 224
  insulated 181
  mains tester 224
  offset 224
  power bits 224
  ratchet 224
  single-slot 224
  spiral-ratchet 224
  stubby 224
Screw-nails 75
Screws
  ceramic tiles 52
  mirror 225
  wall mountings 170
  wood 225
Scrim, hessian 89, 92
Seagrass 154
Sealers
  aluminium primer/sealer 13, 114
  combined with wood stain 115
  for cork tiles 53, 54
  on distempered ceilings 16
  on walls 33
  waterproof 124
  for wooden floors 73
  for wooden furniture 149
Seam roller 30, 231
Secondary glazing 100-1
Security equipment 212-6
Self-grip wrench 233
Self-tapping screws 225
Service head 179
Shampoo, carpet 146
Sharpening tools 145
Shavehook 14, 19, 228
Shaver socket 119
Shears, wallpaper 30, 36
Sheet flooring 78-81, 131, 133
Sheet panelling 86-7
Shelving
  adjustable 171, 218
  alcove 171
  brackets 168-9
  materials 168
  screw fixings 170, 225
  supports 168-9, 171
  systems 169
Shiplap panelling 82, 84
Showers
  plumbing 184, 186
  tiled 124, 125
Shrouded-head tap 186, 189
Shutters 108
Silicon-carbide paper 14, 228
Silicone rubber sealant 52
Silicone water repellant 83
Silk wallcovering 42, 118, 120
Sills, window 52
Single-slot screwdriver 224
Single-stack drainage 185
Sinks
  blockages 187

gap with wall, sealing 52
splashbacks 114
taps 189
Size, glue 33
Skarsten scraper 228
Skirting boards
  fixings 70
  heat-loss under 195
  painting 13, 22, 116
  removing 83
  replacing 70
Slater's rip 200
Slates 199, 200
Slip-joint pliers 232
Smoke alarms 210
Smoothing brush 230
Smoothing plane 227
Snipe-nosed pliers 232
Sockets, electrical 180, 182
Soft furnishings
  cleaning 146
  repairs 146
  stain removal 147
Soil pipe 185
Solar-control glass 95, 96
Solid-fuel central heating 190
Spanish windlass 165
Spanners 187, 233
Spin dryer 176
Spiral balance 100
Spiral-ratchet screwdriver 224
Spirit level 219
Splashbacks 124
Sponging 26
Spotlights 160, 161
Sprigs, glazing 96-7, 164, 167, 223
Springs, chair 157
Spring hinge 137
Spring toggle 225
Spurs, electrical 179, 192
Stains, removing
  on brickwork 203
  on carpets 147
  on ceilings 16
  on china 142
  cleaning fluids 142, 147
  dry-cleaning 146
  from furnishings 147
  on glass 142
  from leather 145
  from metals 144
  from plastics 145
  sealing off 114
  solvent-soluble 146
  on walls 203
  water-soluble 146
  on wood 148
Stains, wood
  applying 149
  choosing 115, 117
  natural finish 18
  restoring finish 66
Stairwells
  painting 24
  papering 32, 40
Standard clips 84
Staples 223
Starter clips 84
Steam stripper 30, 33
Steel rule 30, 219
Stencilling 27
Stilson wrench 233
Stone tiles 123
Stopper 17, 114
Storage
  shelving 168-71
  of tools 218
  units 172
  using space 173

Storage heaters 193
Straight-edge 30
Stringline 30, 33, 38, 46
Stripping
  paint 14, 18-19
  tiles 46
  wallpaper 32-3
Stubby screwdriver 224
Stub-duct heating systems 191
Stud spacings 92, 111
Sub-floors 72, 126-7
Sugar soap 16, 18
Supadriv screwdriver 224
Supatap 186
Surform 228
Synthetic fabrics 134

T

Table lamps 160
Tables
  warped tops 153
  wobbly legs 152
Tacks
  carpet 61-4, 224
  upholstery 156-9, 233
Tack lifter 156, 157, 232
Tape
  adhesive, for carpets 60, 62
  adhesive, for vinyl flooring 78
  PTFE 187
Tape measures 30, 219
Taps
  installing 189
  replacing washers 189
  supply system 184-5
  types 186
Teak oil 115, 149
Templates
  for cutting tiles 51, 54
  for laying vinyl floors 79
  for patching carpets 65
Tenon saw 220
Terminal conduit box 181
Textured paints
  decorative finish 26-7, 114
  filler for ceiling cracks 17, 26
Textured wallcoverings 42-3
Thermal insulators 207
Thermoplastic tiles, carpeting over 60
Thermostats 190
Thixotropic adhesives 143
Tiles
  adhesives 45, 48, 124
  bathroom accessories, ceramic 52
  battens, using 50
  brick 44, 53, 122-3, 124, 125
  carpet 56, 57, 62, 130, 140
  ceiling 44, 45, 46, 48, 122, 140
  ceiling cove 44
  ceramic 44, 45, 50, 51, 55, 122-3, 124, 125, 140
  clippers 45, 51, 232
  cork 44, 45, 53, 54, 122, 124, 125, 140
  cost 122-3
  cutter 232
  cutting 45, 48, 50, 51, 54
  decorative effects 46-7
  drilling 52
  durability 122-3
  fibreboard 45, 122
  floor 44, 45, 46-7, 54-5, 123, 140
  grouting 45, 51
  laying 44-55
  marble 123, 125, 140
  metallic 123, 125, 140
  mirror 44, 45, 53, 122, 124, 125, 140
  mosaic 45, 52, 122, 125, 140
  number required, estimating 44-5

painting 48
plastic 54, 123, 125
polystyrene 44, 45, 48, 122
preparing surfaces 46
quadrant 124
quarry 123, 125
roof 199-200
rubber 123, 140
saw 45, 51
self-adhesive 54
shapes 124
shaping 51, 54
sizes 45
spacers 50
stone 123
stripping 46
thermoplastic, carpeting over 60
vinyl 45, 54, 123, 125
wall 44, 45, 50-3, 122-3, 140
Tinted glass 95, 96
Toaster, electric 174-5
Toggle screws 170, 225
Tongue-and-groove board 82, 84, 128
Tools
brushes 230
carpeting 57
chisels 227
cutting 220-1
drills 226
electrical work 181, 232
files 228
glazing 96
hammers 222
honing 227
painting 14, 230-1
panelling 83
picture-framing 164
pincers 232
planes 227
plastering 89, 229
pliers 232
plumbing 187, 232-3
sanding 72, 228
saws 220-1
scrapers 228
screwdrivers 224
sharpening 145, 227
spanners 233
storage 218
tiling 45-6, 232
upholstering 156
vinyl floors, laying 78
wallpapering 30, 230
wooden floors, laying 67
wooden furniture, repairing 148
wrenches 233
Toughened glass 95
Tower and barrel bolts 215
Trap, drainage 185, 187
Trowels 229
Try square 219
Tufted carpet 56
Tumble dryer 176
Tungsten-carbide paper 228
Tungsten-carbide rod saw 53
Turnbuckle clips 164, 167
Two-part cold cure lacquer 115

U

Undercoat 13, 114
Underfloor heating
carpet underlay 56
heat loss 195
installation 191
with woodstrip floors 75
Underlay
carpet 56, 60, 63, 130, 132

woodblock floors 76
Universal primer 13, 18
Upholstery
cleaning 146-7
fabrics 134-6
hammer 222
repairs 146, 156-9
tacks 156, 157-9, 223
tools 156
Uplighters 161
Uprights, shelving 169, 171

V

Vacuum cleaner, 174-5
Varnish
applying 149
choosing 18, 115
removing stains 147
sealing cork tiles 53
Veneers 128, 153
Ventlight 94
Vent pipe 185
Vice 218
Vinyl flooring
applications 133, 140
joining sheets 81
patching 81
preparatory work 79
quantity required, estimating 79
tools for laying 78
trimming 79-80
types 78, 131
Vinyl tiles
adhesive 45
applications 125
durability 123
laying 54
Vinyl wallpaper
adhesive for 30, 121
stripping 33
wearing qualities 29

W

Wallboard 126, 128
Wallcoverings, textured 42-3
Wallpaper
adhesives 29, 30, 35, 121
applications 121, 140
batch numbers 28
borders 34, 118
brushes 230
carrying, when wet 38
cleaning 120
cost 120
cutting 34
embossed 118
floral designs 30
flock 118
folding 35
friezes 34
hanging 30, 38-43, 120
hand-printed 118
marking guidelines 38
matching patterns 29
measuring 34
paste 29, 30, 35, 121
patterns 29-31
ready-pasted 29, 39, 40, 118, 121
relief 118
roller 30, 231
rolls required, estimating 28-9
shade variations 28
sizing 33
soaking 32, 33, 35
storage 30
stripping 32-3
textured 42-3, 118

vinyl 29, 30, 33, 118
washable 29, 118
woodchip 118
Wallplugs 105, 170, 225
Walls
area, measuring 13
cavity insulation 194-5
damp 12, 83, 203, 205
dry rot 208-9
exterior, painting 116
external walls 202-3
growths on 203
heat loss 195
holes, filling 17, 93
lining paper 37
painting 13, 16, 21, 116
panelling 82-7
papering 28-43
pebbledash 202
plastering 88-93
plasterboard 88
screw fixings in 170
stud spacings 92, 111
tiles 44, 45, 50-3, 122-3
washing down 18, 32, 203
Wall sockets 180, 182
Warm-air heating systems 191
Washable wallpaper 29, 118
Washers, replacing 188-9
Washing machines 176, 189
Waste pipe 185
Water pipes see pipes
Waterproof materials
adhesive 45
paper 196
sealer 124
Water tanks
lagging 194, 196
supply 184-5
Wax finishes 66, 149
WC 187-8
Weather bar 205
Wet-and-dry paper 228
Wet heating systems 191
Wet rot 208-9
Wicker furniture 155
Wiggle nails 223
Wilton carpet 56, 132
Windows
anodized aluminium 12
bars 216
blinds 102, 106-7
broken glass, removing 96
casement 23, 94, 95, 99
condensation 101, 207
curtains 102-8
dormer 41
double-glazing 94, 100-1, 195
draughts 99, 197
fastenings 99
gaps in frames, filling 17
frames 38, 98
French 94, 95, 99
glass 95-6
grilles 216
heat loss 195, 197
leaded-light 96-7
locks 214
metal-framed 96
paint scraper 228
painting 13, 23, 116
panes, replacing 97
papering around 85
pivoting 94, 95
rattling 99
replacement 94
sash 23, 94, 95, 99, 100, 197
sash cord 100
shelves 173

shutters 108
sizes 13
sliding 94, 95
spiral balance 100
sticking frames, loosening 99
tiling around 52
water seeping in 205
Wire brush 230
Wire strippers 181, 232
Wired glass 95
Wiring see electrical systems
Wood
buying 128
conditioning 75
cost 128-9
dents, treating 149
dry rot 208-9
fillers 17, 114
finishes 18, 66, 115, 117, 149
infestations 208-9
knots, sealing 18, 114
natural finish 18
panelling 82-5
primer 18, 114
rubbing down 18
saws 68, 220-1
scratches, treating 149
screws 170, 225
sealing 18
shelving 168
stain 18, 66, 115, 117, 149
stains, removing 148
stopping 17
veneers 128, 153
woodworm 208-9
Woodblock floors 71, 75-7, 127, 129
Wood-burning stoves 193
Woodchip wallpaper 118, 120
Wooden floors
chipboard 74, 126-7
cost 129
durability 129
floorboards, fitting 68-9
floorboards, lifting 68-9
gaps, filling 70
insulating 197
mosaic 76, 127, 140
parquet 75-7, 140
plywood 127
quantities required, estimating 66
sanding 72-3
sawing to size 68-9
sealing 73
stain 115, 117
strip construction 71
sub-floors 72, 126-7, 140
and underfloor heating 75
varnishing 115, 117
woodblock 71, 75-7, 127, 129, 140
woodstrip 71, 75, 127, 129, 140
Wooden furniture
applying wood finish 149
caning 148, 150-1
repairs 152-3
re-rushing 154-5
treating blemishes and stains 148-9
Woodstrip floors 71, 75, 127, 129
Woodworm 208-9
Workbench 218
Woven carpets 56, 132
Wrecking bar 232
Wrenches 233
Wrinkles, paint 25
Wrought ironwork, painting 116

Z

Zinc chromate primer 16
Zinc phosphate sealer 16

Acknowledgments

Authors acknowledgments
The authors would like to thank the
following for their contributions to the
book:
David Holloway, Mike Lawrence,
Christine Parsons, Yvonne Rees,
Tony Wilkins.

Dorling Kindersley would like to
thank the following for their invaluable
help in producing this book:
Vic Chambers, Cathy and Fred Gill,
Jon Bouchier, Dominic Neville, Giles
Neville, Jackie Giles, Elizabeth Whiting,
Tony Wallace, Denise Weaver, Mike
Trier, Tim Shackleton, Corinne Ashby,
Judy Berman.

Photography
All photographs by Jon Bouchier except:

Key t = top, b = bottom, l = left,
r = right

Elizabeth Whiting Associates
15tl, tr and b, 21br, 30, 31, 34tl and tr,
46t, 47b, 58b, 67, 71b, 103, 107
163, 167bl and br, 173t and br

Camera Press
46b, 47t, 58t and c, 59, 71t, 87, 108,
155, 167t, 173b

"Coverplus" (Woolworths)
15rc

Demonstrators
All demonstrations by Dominic Neville
except:
Giles Neville pp. 48-55
Jackie Giles pp. 26-7, 42-3

Illustrators
Les Smith
Kevin Maddison
David Ashby
Kuo Kang Chen

Suppliers
The following kindly loaned or supplied
tools and materials for use in the book:
Ajax Flooring Co Ltd.,
London SE4

Black and Decker Ltd.,
Maidenhead,
Berks.

Buck and Ryan Ltd.,
London WC1.

Amtico,
London W1.

Artex Ltd.,
Newhaven,
Sussex.

Copydex Products Ltd.,
London WC2.

David Douglas (Carpets) Ltd.,
London SW8.

L. G. Harris & Co Ltd.,
Bromsgrove,
Worcester,
Worcs.

ICI Dulux Paints Ltd.,
Slough,
Berks.

Knobs and Knockers,
London W1.

On the tiles,
London SW6.

Arthur J. Sanderson & Sons Ltd.,
London W1.

Sphinx Tiles Ltd.,
Newbury,
Berks.

Uniroyal Ltd.,
London SW1.

Vigers and Blackmur Ltd.,
Barking,
Essex.

Welpac Hardware Ltd.,
Barking,
Essex.

Wicanders (GB) Ltd.,
Crawley,
W. Sussex.

Wimbledon Woodcraft,
London SW19.